The Structure of Modern Standard French

The Structure of Modern Standard French

A Student Grammar

Maj-Britt Mosegaard Hansen

OXFORD

UNIVERSITY PRESS

Great Clarendon Street, Oxford, OX2 6DP,
United Kingdom

Oxford University Press is a department of the University of Oxford.
It furthers the University's objective of excellence in research, scholarship,
and education by publishing worldwide. Oxford is a registered trade mark of
Oxford University Press in the UK and in certain other countries

First Edition published in 2016

Impression: 1

Published in the United States of America by Oxford University Press
198 Madison Avenue, New York, NY 10016, United States of America

British Library Cataloguing in Publication Data
Data available

Library of Congress Control Number: 2015948886

ISBN 978–0–19–872373–8 (Hbk)
978–0–19–872374–5 (Pbk)

Printed in Great Britain by
Clays Ltd, St Ives plc

Contents

Part II: The Grammar of French Verbs

Part IV: The Grammar of French Particles

Preface and acknowledgements

Nature and scope of the book

This book is intended as an advanced student's grammar of French which integrates traditional grammar with knowledge and insights from modern linguistics. Its target readership is English-speaking undergraduate students of French aiming to reach Level C1 or above in the Common European Framework of Reference to Languages (CEFRL). Ideally, students should have prior knowledge of French grammar corresponding to A-level study in the UK, but the book does not presuppose any knowledge of sentence parsing, nor of linguistics.

The approach to French grammar taken in this book can be characterized as structural, functional, and contrastive in nature.

The approach is structural because an underlying assumption is that grammatical rules can in many cases be stated more simply and more precisely if explicit reference is made to syntactic structure, rather than to collocations of particular words and expressions or to intuitions about meaning alone. This in no way implies, however, that no appeals to meaning differences and/or to collocations will be made in this book, nor does it imply an assumption that every aspect of French grammar can be reduced to productive rule. Like the grammars of most, perhaps all, languages, French grammar mixes productive rules with exceptions that must be learned in a list-like fashion.

The approach of this book is functional because it assumes that language is principally a tool for communication and that grammatical structures are to some extent shaped by the uses to which they are put in discourse.

Finally, the approach is contrastive in as much as there is descriptive emphasis on those grammatical structures of French which differ from those that would be used in corresponding contexts in English.

Considerations of space have meant that choices about which aspects of French grammar should be included in the book and which could be left out have had to be made. Saliently, apart from the forms of pronouns and adverbs, and degree marking of adjectives, the book does not include morphology. Knowledge of verb conjugation and the number/gender marking of nouns and adjectives is thus taken for granted. In practice, the book should therefore be complemented by a volume such as *Bescherelle: La conjugaison pour tous* or similar, and by a standard monolingual dictionary such as *Le Petit Robert*, which provides information about the plural and/or feminine forms of nouns and adjectives. This is deemed to be justifiable, in as much as degree students will require those tools in any case.

Structure and use of the book

Part I, comprising chapters 1–4, forms the basis for the rest of the book. In Part I, parsing-related notions are introduced that will be appealed to in later chapters. Parts II–V, in which the central aspects of French grammar are treated in a systematic way, are thus likely to prove challenging to students unless they have first familiarized themselves with the concepts and terminology introduced in Part I. Once the relevant concepts and terminology have been acquired, however, Parts II–V can be used like any other reference grammar, and do not need to be read sequentially from beginning to end.

The above remarks do not imply that Part I needs to be studied in its entirety before any of the more specific grammatical topics can be broached. While the treatment of mood, for instance, presupposes an understanding of the typology of subordinate clauses (which is the object of chapter 4), other topics, such as personal and reflexive pronouns, for instance, can potentially be discussed on the basis of the parsing notions introduced in chapter 1 alone.

Parts II–IV are structured around word classes, verbs being treated in Part II, nominals in Part III, and particles in Part IV. Part V, finally, deals with grammatical topics of broader scope, which are less straightforwardly related to a particular part of speech. This structure is intended to reflect the centrality of the different parts of speech and topics to the structure of clauses and sentences. Importantly, however, it does not reflect a perceived progression from less to more complex grammatical topics. Indeed, from a pedagogical point of view, it is probably advisable to teach a number of specific grammatical topics in a different order from the one in which they appear in the book.

Added value

The material covered in this book will sharpen students' analytical skills and their attention to detail. It will also strengthen their problem solving abilities and their capacity for abstract thinking.

Further, the material covered will improve students' ability to understand written French texts of a literary or otherwise more formal nature. In sensitizing students to the structure of the French language, it will also, indirectly, sensitize them to that of English, improving, in particular, their written communication skills in both languages.

Finally, the material covered will leave students who are interested in the linguistic aspects of French Studies well prepared to undertake further, more advanced study in that area.

Acknowledgements

The following colleagues and current/former undergraduate students deserve thanks for having read and commented on drafts of (parts of) this book: Peter Cooke, Martin Durrell, Claire Fitzgerald, Catherine Franc, Danica Gamble, Jonathan Hensher, Vladimir Kapor, Catherine Knight, James Murphy, Stephen Parker, and two anonymous OUP referees. Needless to say, they are not responsible for any remaining shortcomings.

Maj-Britt Mosegaard Hansen
Manchester, May 2015

List of abbreviations

Symbols

*	The following clause or sentence is ungrammatical
?	The following clause or sentence is borderline ungrammatical
#	The following clause or sentence appears odd out of context
Ø	An empty grammatical slot

Grammatical functions

Adv'al	Adverbial
Ant	Antecedent
AnticipSubj	Anticipatory Subject
Appos	Apposition
ApposPostmod	Appositional postmodifier
Aux	Auxiliary
CentrDet	Central determiner
Compl	Complement
Coord	Coordinator
DatObj	Dative object
Det	Determiner
DirObj	Direct object
FIA	Free indirect attribute
GrammDatObj	Grammatical dative object
GrammDirObj	Grammatical direct object
GrammSubj	Grammatical subject
H	Head
LocObj	Locative object
LogDatObj	Logical dative object

LogDirObj	Logical direct object
LogSubj	Logical subject
MainV	Main verb
NPI	Negative polarity item
ObjAttr	Object attribute
PostDet	Postdeterminer
Postmod	Postmodifier
PostponedSubj	Postponed subject
PreDet	Predeterminer
Pred	Predicator
Premod	Premodifier
PrepObj	Prepositional object
Subj	Subject
SubjAttr	Subject attribute
Subord	Subordinator

Linguistic forms

1.p.sg.	First person singular
1.p.pl.	First person plural
2.p.sg.	Second person singular
2.p.pl.	Second person plural
3.p.sg	Third person singular
3.p.pl.	Third person plural
Adj	Adjective
AdjP	Adjective phrase
Adv	Adverb
AdvP	Adverb phrase
Art	Article
CardNum	Cardinal numeral
Cl	Clause
CompCl	Comparison clause
ComplCl	Complement clause

ComplexDet	Complex determiner
ComplexPrep	Complex preposition
CompV	Compound verb
CoordConj	Coordinating conjunction
DefArt	Definite article
DemArt	Demonstrative article
DemPr	Demonstrative pronoun
Fem.sg.	Feminine singular
FinV	Finite verb
FreeRelCl	Free relative clause
FreeRelPron	Free relative pronoun
Ger	*Gérondif*
GerCl	*Gérondif* clause
IndefArt	Indefinite article
IndefPron	Indefinite pronoun
IndirInterrogCl	Indirect interrogative clause
Inf	Infinitive
InfMarker	Infinitive marker
InfCl	Infinitival clause
InterrogAdv	Interrogative adverb
InterrogArt	Interrogative article
InterrogPron	Interrogative pronoun
Masc.sg.	Masculine singular
N	Noun
NeutPron	Neutral pronoun
Non-finV	Non-finite verb
NP	Noun phrase
Num	Numeral
OrdNum	Ordinal numeral
PartArt	Partitive article
PastPart	Past participle
PastPartCl	Past participle clause
PersPron	Personal pronoun
PhrV	Phrasal verb

PossArt	Possessive article
PossPron	Possessive pronoun
PP	Prepositional phrase
Prep	Preposition
PresPart	Present participle
PresPartCl	Present participle clause
Pron	Pronoun
PronAdv	Pronominal adverb
PronP	Pronominal phrase
PropN	Proper noun
ReflPron	Reflexive pronoun
RelCl	Relative clause
RelPron	Relative pronoun
SubordConj	Subordinating conjunction
SubordCl	Subordinate clause

Semantic concepts

E	Event time
R	Reference time
S	Speech time

PART I

Understanding French Sentence Structure

1

Simple sentences and their basic constituents

Learning objectives

- To gain a basic understanding of how simple sentences are structured grammatically.
- To be able to define the most central *grammatical constituents* of simple sentences (ten in all).
- To be able to recognize those central constituents in a given sentence, using *standard tests*.
- To understand the relations among different types of central constituent.

1.1 The notion of grammatical structure

It is a simple, but fundamental, fact about languages that they are structured grammatically. The grammatical structure of any given language helps the users of that language to convey and comprehend messages more rapidly and effectively, and to convey and comprehend far more complex messages, than they could do if no grammatical structure were present.

At the most basic level, there are two aspects to grammatical structure, namely:

- **Morphology**: the study of the forms that the words of the language can take, and the rules that underlie those forms. Thus, when studying the morphology of French, we would look, for instance, at the rules governing the formation of plural *vs* singular nouns, as in (1); the formation of different verb tenses and moods, as in (2); the formation of manner adverbs from corresponding adjectives, as in (3), etc.

(1)   Un travail—des travaux

(2)   Je finis—je finissais—que je finisse

(3)   Lent—lentement

- **Syntax**: the study of the ways in which the words of the language can be combined in order to produce clauses and sentences that are deemed acceptable by native speakers. Syntax, in other words, has to do with

---

BOX 1.1   Important Definitions

For the purposes of this book, a **finite clause**, or clause for short, is defined as any grammatical structure that contains a finite verb,[1] i.e. (in the case of French) a verb form that is marked for **person**.[2] Finite verbs will also be marked for **tense**[3] and/or **mood**,[4] but in French, person marking is the simplest criterion for identifying them.

Thus, verb forms like *(nous) chantons, (vous) marchez !, (qu') (il) donne*, etc. are **finite verbs** because their endings show that they are in the 1st, 2nd, and 3rd person, respectively. Infinitives and participles/gerunds,

---

[1] As we will see in section 3.2.2, French also has a type of structure known as 'non-finite clauses'. These will be referred to as such throughout this book.

[2] See section 15.1, for a definition of the different grammatical persons.

[3] See chapter 6 for details on the use of tense in French.

[4] See chapter 5 for details on the use of mood in French.

i.e. verb forms like *marcher*, *chanté*, or *(en) donnant*, on the other hand, are **non-finite**, because their forms give no indication of person.

A **sentence** may consist of one or more clauses. A **simple sentence** will consist of a single, grammatically independent, clause, i.e. a clause that can constitute a complete message even in the absence of a context. In other words, (i)–(ii) below are **independent clauses**, and also simple sentences:

(i)   Pierre aime Marie.
(ii)   Marie préfère Jacques.

A **compound sentence** will consist of two or more clauses, which are in a relation of grammatical **coordination** (cf. (iii), where the finite verbs allowing us to recognize the individual clauses are underlined):

(iii)   Pierre aime Marie, mais Marie préfère Jacques.

A **complex sentence** consists in two or more clauses between which there is a relation of grammatical **subordination** (cf. (iv)–(v)):

(iv)   Pierre aime Marie parce qu'il la trouve gentille.
(v)   Marie préfère Jacques, qui est plus beau que Pierre.

Compound/complex sentences and coordination *vs* subordination will be dealt with further in chapters 3–4.

rules governing word order and the kinds of words (or groups of words) that can appear together in a given clause or sentence.

The division of labour between morphology and syntax is not the same from one language to another, or even within different varieties of the same language. If we compare Modern Standard French to Modern Standard English, for instance, we find that morphology plays a considerably more important role in French (particularly in writing) than it does in English when it comes to signalling meaning and grammatical relationships between the different parts of a clause or sentence. Whatever their respective roles in a given language, morphological and syntactic accuracy are, however, both crucial to successful communication in all but the simplest face-to-face situations, in as much as both will reinforce and very frequently even determine the meanings that speakers/writers are trying to communicate.

Indeed, the specific grammatical structure of a given language or language variety creates expectations on the part of its native speakers with respect to the kinds of information that can/should/must be grammatically expressed, as well as whether and how that information should/must be expressed morphologically or syntactically. In consequence, native users of a given language will orient—at a largely subconscious level—to the presence or absence of certain grammatical (morphological and/or syntactic) features both when they speak or write and when they listen or read. If their expectations are met, communication will proceed relatively smoothly. When they are not met, however, then important aspects of the intended message will be lost, and communication may even fail altogether.

1.2 Central grammatical constituents of simple sentences

Different languages may be structured in somewhat different—or even widely different—ways. Nevertheless, we do find some very basic, but abstract, structural entities and principles that are largely similar across languages. These are the entities and principles that belong to **sentence analysis**, or **parsing**. These entities and principles are the subject of Part I of this book, including the present chapter.

To a very significant extent, the specific grammatical rules of a given language can be explained with reference to the relations among the basic structural entities that are or may be present in a sentence or clause. In other words, the formulation of adequate grammatical rules makes reference to, and presupposes, an understanding of the principles of parsing.

To take a very simple example, this can be demonstrated with reference to what is sometimes described as a rule of French grammar, namely that in that language the indefinite article *un(e)* is not used with professions. Such a 'rule' is intended to account for the fact that the English sentence in (4) below will normally translate into French as (5):

(4) John is a teacher.

(5) John est [Ø] instituteur.[5]

---

[5] In mathematics, the sign Ø conventionally stands for the empty set. When it is used in examples in grammar texts, it thus means that a particular grammatical slot is empty. See the List of Abbreviations for the symbols and abbreviations used in this book.

However, as (6)–(7) show, the 'rule' as formulated above is incorrect, in so far as *instituteur* appears with a preceding indefinite article in these sentences:

(6) Un instituteur, c'est quelqu'un qui enseigne à l'école primaire.

(7) J'ai parlé avec un instituteur à la soirée d'Yvan.

We can improve our formulation of the rule by specifying that the name for the profession must follow the verb *être*. If we do that, however, we are no longer making reference merely to the meaning of words, but we are starting to take clause structure (or syntax) into account. And our rule is still imperfect, as (8)–(10) show:

(8) J'ai été chez un instituteur hier.

(9) Pierre deviendra sans doute [Ø] instituteur.

(10) Corinne est [Ø] fille unique.

In (8), we have the word *instituteur* following a form of *être*, but the sentence structure is different from that of (5), and so *instituteur* does take an indefinite article. Our proposed rule cannot account for this difference between the two sentences, but predicts that there should be no indefinite article in (8).[6]

In (9), we do not have a form of *être*, but of the verb *devenir*, and yet *instituteur* does not take an indefinite article. Our proposed rule cannot predict this, because it only makes reference to one particular verb.

In (10), *fille unique* does follow a form of *être* and it does not take an indefinite article, but this is in fact not predicted by our proposed rule, either, given that being an only child is not a profession.

To make the correct predictions (and thus allow non-native learners to 'get it right' not just some of the time, but ideally all the time), our rule needs to make reference, not to the meanings of specific words (such as the verb *être* or names for professions), but to the grammatical structure of the clauses in which those words appear. We will see in section 1.2.3.1 below that what the expressions *instituteur* in (5) and (9) and *fille unique* in

---

[6] Note that it will not do to stipulate that the name for the profession must follow *être* directly: as (i) shows, it is perfectly possible to separate the two and yet have no indefinite article:

(i) J'ai été pendant de longues années [Ø] instituteur en province.

(10) have in common is the fact that they all function grammatically as subject attributes in sentences whose subject (see section 1.2.2 below) is a so-called noun phrase (NP)[7] or a personal pronoun referring to a human being.

The rule that we want is therefore not that 'names for professions do not take an indefinite article in French', but the much more precise statement that 'normally, noun phrases that function as subject attributes in clauses where the subject referent is a human being do not take an indefinite article in French'[8]. This rule is simultaneously more specific, in as much as it does not (incorrectly) predict an absence of the indefinite article in (6)–(8), and more general, in as much as it does (correctly) predict such an absence in the case of (5), (9), and (10).

Now, let us look more systematically at the types of syntactic entity that we find in simple sentences. One very important principle of sentence analysis is that some parts of sentences (i.e. constituents) are more important than others in terms of both structure and meaning.

Thus, we find the following **hierarchy** among types of constituent, the type in 1 being the most important or indispensable, and that in 4 being the least important, hence most dispensable:

1. The predicator
2. The subject
3. The complement(s)
4. The adverbial(s)

We will now look at these types of clause/sentence constituents in turn.

1.2.1 The predicator

The predicator is the central constituent of any sentence or clause. Without a predicator, we have no sentence/clause, but at best a sentence/clause fragment.

In French, the predicator is characterized by the following properties:

- It consists of a **simple verb form** (cf. (11) below) or a **compound verb form** (cf. (12)). The predicator is or contains a finite verb (see the box in section 1.1 above for the definition of a finite verb):

---

[7] For further details on noun phrases, see section 2.3.2.
[8] See further section 12.3.2.1.

(11)   Jean <u>dort</u>.

(12)   Le gâteau <u>a été mangé</u>.

- It describes an event, an activity or a state.
- It agrees with the subject in person and number.
- It may be the only constituent of a sentence. In Standard French, this is the case only if the verb is in the **imperative** mood, in which case the person and number of the implied subject can be inferred from the verb ending (as in (13) below):

(13)   Entrez !

- It may consist of a fixed combination of a verb and one or more other elements which belong to other word classes, as with *avoir peur* in (14) below or *faire mention* in (15). For the purposes of this book, such combinations are called **phrasal verbs**:[9]

(14)   Elle <u>a peur</u> des araignées.

(15)   Marc <u>a fait mention</u> de votre rencontre.

1.2.1.1 Valency

A centrally important property of predicators is that they have **valency**.[10] With respect to language, the notion of valency refers to the fact that any

---

[9] The decision to analyse *avoir peur* as a phrasal verb, rather than as the verb *avoir* followed by a direct object, *peur*, is determined by observable patterns of pronominalization. As will be seen in section 1.2.3.2 below, direct objects can normally be represented by a direct object pronoun. However, *peur* in (14) cannot be pronominalized in this way. The construction in (14) only allows pronominalization of the prepositional object (cf. section 1.2.3.4 below) *des araignées*. Thus, only (i) below is possible with the same meaning as (14), whereas (ii)–(v) are not possible paraphrases of that sentence.

(i)   Elle en a peur.
(ii)   *Elle l'a des araignées.
(iii) *Elle l'en a.
(iv)   *Elle l'a.
(v)   *Elle en a.

[10] The notion of 'valency' has been borrowed from the field of chemistry, where it refers to the number of other atoms any given atom can unite with chemically, as measured by the number of electrons the atom will add, take, or share in order to form a chemical compound.

given predicator will require one or more other constituents to be present in the sentence in order for a complete meaning to be expressed. These required constituents are called **valency elements**.

If we take the English verb *give*, we find that it takes a total of three valency elements: an entity that performs the giving, an entity that is given, and an entity to whom/which something is given. In (16) below, all of these valency elements are expressed in the sentence, *John* referring to the giver, *a bouquet of flowers* to the thing given, and *Mary* to the person it is given to. (16) is thus a well-formed, or **grammatical**, sentence of English:

(16)   John gave Mary a bouquet of flowers.

The sentences in (17)–(19) below are less well formed, however, as they each leave one of the valency elements of *give* unexpressed. (17) is **ungrammatical** on an interpretation where Mary is the recipient (as opposed to the thing given), while (18)–(19) are acceptable only in very limited types of context:

(17)   *John gave Mary.

(18)   #Gave Mary a bouquet of flowers. (OK only as a diary entry or the like)

(19)   #John gave a bouquet of flowers. (OK only if the context is one of donating something to a charity or the like)

In French, we find a total of eight types of valency element, all of which will be discussed below. Only one of these types—the **subject**—is always present

---

BOX 1.2   Important symbols

In linguistics, an **asterisk**, or *, in front of an example conventionally indicates that the example is ungrammatical. A **question mark**, or ?, indicates that the grammaticality of the example is dubious.

A **cross-hatch**, or #, conventionally indicates that the example following it appears odd out of context, without, however, being downright ungrammatical.

See further List of Abbreviations for symbols and abbreviations used in this book.

Table 1.1. Types of valency element in French.

Independent of the specific predicator	Dependent on the specific predicator
Subject	Subject Attribute
	Direct Object
	Measure Complement
	Prepositional Object
	Dative Object
	Locative Object
	Object Attribute

(at least implicitly), and is therefore independent of the specific predicator. The presence of one or more of the remaining seven types of valency element (known collectively as **complements**) depends on the specific predicator used in the sentence or clause (Table 1.1).

1.2.2 The subject

The subject has a special status among the valency elements, as it is the relation between a predicator and a subject that creates a sentence. We might say that the subject 'actualizes' the predicator. No matter what other valency elements are present, a verb without a subject can only denote an abstract situation, as in (20):[11]

(20)   donner un bouquet de fleurs à Céline

Once we add a subject, the situation becomes concrete, and we can discuss whether it conforms to reality (i.e. whether the sentence is true at the moment of utterance) or not. Thus, if someone utters (21), the hearer can

---

[11] As suggested by the absence of capitalization and punctuation, the infinitive *donner* in (20) is not intended to be interpreted as a variant of the imperative form, but should be understood as a regular infinitive, yielding an incomplete sentence.

in principle reply either 'Yes, that's correct' or 'No, you're wrong', either of which responses would be meaningless in the case of (20):

(21)   Luc a donné un bouquet de fleurs à Céline.

In French the subject of a clause or sentence has the following properties:

- It can be identified by answering the question obtained by inserting the predicator of the clause into the [verb] slot in the following structure *Who or what* [verb]*s?* Thus, with respect to (21), for instance, we can find the subject by asking, 'Who or what gave (a bouquet of flowers to Céline)?' The answer to the question is *Luc*, who is therefore the subject of the sentence.

- Except in the case of imperative sentences, we can recognize the subject in the following way: it either takes the form of an unstressed pronoun in the so-called nominative case[12] (or 'subject case'), i.e. one of the forms *je, tu, il, elle, ce, on, nous, vous, ils, elles,* or (if it refers to the third person) it can be replaced by such a pronoun. Thus, with respect to (22) below, we can tell that the noun phrase *ma sœur* is the subject because we can replace it by *elle*, as in (23), without changing the meaning of the sentence, or rendering it ungrammatical:

(22)   Ma sœur a gagné une médaille d'or aux Jeux Olympiques de Beijing.

(23)   Elle a gagné une médaille d'or aux Jeux Olympiques de Beijing.

This second property is a very important one, for it turns out (as we will see in several instances below, and in this book more generally) that not just the subject, but most valency elements in French can be identified through pronominalization, i.e. by substituting a particular type of pronoun for the valency element in question.

Sentences in the **imperative** mood differ from other types of sentences with respect to the expression of the subject. As shown in (24)–(26) below, there is no separate element expressing the subject in such sentences in French. Instead, the nature of the subject is implicitly expressed by the form of the

---

[12] Case is a morphological feature which essentially signals the grammatical role played by the item carrying it. In some languages, for instance German, Russian, or Latin, all nouns must be case marked. That was true of Old French, as well, but in Modern French only certain kinds of pronoun (personal, relative, and interrogative pronouns) are marked for case. See chapters 15 and 19 for details.

predicator. Thus, (24) has a second-person singular subject (i.e. a single addressee), (25) a second-person plural subject (i.e. either more than one addressee or a single addressee with whom the speaker/writer is on formal terms), and (26) a first-person plural subject (i.e. a group consisting of the speaker/writer + one or more addressees).

(24)   Dors !

(25)   Dormez !

(26)   Dormons ! ('Let's sleep!')

Verbs that take a subject as their only valency element are known as **intransitive verbs**. The basic valency structure of such verbs is therefore as in (27) below. A concrete example of an intransitive French verb is given in (28):

(27)   Subject + Predicator + Ø = Intransitive verb

(28)   Andrée dort.

No predicator can take more than one subject. Thus, in sentences like (29) below, we do not have two subjects, but rather one subject consisting of a coordination (by the conjunction *et*) of two so-called noun phrases (or NPs), as indicated by the square brackets. (The internal grammatical structure of syntactic constituents such as noun phrases is introduced in chapter 2 below.) Thus, as shown by the contrast between (30) and the ungrammatical (31) below, the subject cannot be pronominalized more than once:

(29)   [[La petite fille]$_{NP}$ et [sa mère]$_{NP}$]$_{Subj}$ se promènent au Luxembourg.

(30)   <u>Elles</u> se promènent au Luxembourg.

(31)   *[Elle et elle] se promènent au Luxembourg.

1.2.3 The complements

Any constituent other than the subject that is required by the predicator is called a complement. Complements come in different types, and there can be more than one type of complement in a given sentence. However, in French, a predicator can only take a single complement of any given type.

1.2.3.1 The subject attribute

A small group of verbs take a complement, called the subject attribute, which either identifies the subject or ascribes a property to the subject. These verbs are known as **intensive (intransitive) verbs**. They have the basic valency structure in (32):

(32)   Subject + Predicator + Subject Attribute = Intensive verb

We can identify a subject attribute in any given French sentence or clause by the following criteria:

- It will be governed by one of the verbs *être*, *devenir*, *apparaître*, *paraître*, *sembler*, *demeurer*, or *rester*.
- It describes the subject, either by indicating an alternative way of referring to it, as in (33) below, or by ascribing a particular property to the subject, as in (34):

(33)   Julie et Jeanne sont <u>mes sœurs</u>.

(34)   Caroline reste <u>jolie</u>.

- It will (wherever possible) agree with the subject in gender and number, as in (33)–(34).
- It can usually be represented by the invariable neutral pronoun *le* (cf. (35)–(36) below). Notice that although *sœurs* in (35) is a feminine plural noun, the subject attribute pronoun nonetheless takes the masculine singular form *le*.

(35)   <u>Mes sœurs</u> ? Oui, Julie et Jeanne <u>le</u> sont.

(36)   <u>Jolie</u> ? Oui, Caroline <u>le</u> reste.

- It cannot be made the subject of a passive sentence (cf. the ungrammaticality of (37)–(38) below):

(37)   *<u>Joli(e)</u> est resté(e) par Caroline.

(38)   *<u>Mes sœurs</u> sont étées par Julie et Jeanne.

1.2.3.2 The direct object

A large group of verbs take a complement which typically describes an entity that somehow undergoes the activity or action described by the verb.

This complement is linked directly to the verb without an intervening preposition, and is called the direct object, cf. (39)–(40):

(39)   Le garçon taquine <u>la petite fille</u>.

(40)   Marie récitait <u>un poème</u>.

Verbs which govern a direct object are called **(directly) transitive verbs**, and they have the basic valency structure in (41):

(41)   Subject + Predicator + Direct Object = (Directly) transitive verb

In French, the direct object can be identified using the following criteria:

• It will be the answer to a question of the form *Who or what is/was being* [verb]*ed?* Thus, with respect to (39) above, we can ask 'Who or what is being teased?' and the response will be 'the little girl', which indicates that *la petite fille* is the direct object in that sentence.
• A direct object that is definite either takes the form of an unstressed pronoun in the accusative (or 'direct-object') case (i.e. *me, te, le, la, se, nous, vous, les*), or it can be replaced by such a pronoun, cf. (42)–(43) below. Notice that in contrast to the subject attribute pronoun exemplified in (35) above, the third-person singular direct object pronouns are not morphologically invariable, but are marked for gender:

(42)   Le garçon <u>la</u> taquine.

(43)   Marie <u>le</u> récitait.

• The direct object can normally be made the subject of a passive sentence, cf. (44)–(45):

(44)   <u>La petite fille</u> est taquinée par le garçon.

(45)   <u>Le poème</u> était récité par Marie.

1.2.3.3 The measure complement

Measure complements are a rather marginal type of valency element, which are only found with verbs that express measuring, weighing, pricing, and the like. With predicators of this type, the measure complement will express the dimension, weight, or cost of the subject, as in (46)–(47):

(46)   Caroline mesure <u>un mètre soixante-treize</u>.

(47)   Ce choufleur coûte <u>deux euros</u>.

Like subject attributes and direct objects, which they superficially resemble, measure complements are linked directly to the predicator without the use of a preposition, but unlike the former types of complements, measure complements cannot be pronominalized. Thus, (48)–(49) below are not possible paraphrases of (46)–(47):[13]

(48) *Caroline le mesure.

(49) *Ce choufleur les coûte.

The valency structure of measure verbs is this:

(50) Subject + Predicator + Measure Complement = Measure verb

1.2.3.4 The prepositional object

Another large group of verbs are **indirectly transitive**, which means that they take an object, but that object is linked to the verb by a preposition. This preposition is, in most cases, either *de* or *à*, but other prepositions may also be used. The object in this case is therefore not a direct object, but a prepositional object. The basic valency structure of indirectly transitive verbs is given in (51):

(51) Subject + Predicator + Prepositional Object = Indirectly transitive verb

As we will see below, prepositional objects are not the only grammatical constituents in French that can be introduced by a preposition. One criterion for recognizing a prepositional object is that:

• The preposition is determined by the verb, and not by the noun phrase that follows the preposition.

Thus, in (52) below, any game that the children are playing will be introduced by the preposition *à*, which means that we are dealing with prepositional objects of *jouer* in these cases. In (53), on the other hand, the places where the children are playing are not prepositional objects of *jouer* because, in those cases, the preposition to be used is determined by the noun that follows it:

(52) Les enfants jouent au foot/au tennis/aux échecs . . . (= PrepObj)

---

[13] (48) is of course grammatical on an interpretation where Caroline is taking the measure of an object or another person.

(53) Les enfants jouent <u>dans leur chambre/au parc/avec leurs poupées/pour le plaisir</u> ... (≠ PrepObj)

An additional criterion is that:

• A prepositional object can usually be replaced by one of the pronominal adverbs *en* or *y*, cf. (54)–(55) and (56)–(57):[14]

(54) Je m'attendais <u>à cela</u>.

(55) Je m'<u>y</u> attendais.

(56) Vous vous souvenez <u>de cela</u> ?

(57) Vous vous <u>en</u> souvenez ?

1.2.3.5 The dative object

Dative-transitive verbs also take an object which is linked to the verb by a preposition. Dative objects are, however, distinct from prepositional objects in a number of ways. First, the preposition in question is almost always *à*, or in a very few cases, *pour*, cf. (58)–(59):

(58) Cette voiture appartient <u>à Marie-Cécile</u>.

(59) J'ai réservé une place <u>pour Cadoual</u>.

  Secondly, unlike prepositional objects, dative objects cannot be replaced by *en* or *y*. Instead:

• The dative object either takes the form of an unstressed pronoun in the dative case (*me, te, lui, se, nous, vous, leur*), or it can be replaced by such a pronoun, cf. (60)–(61):

(60) Cette voiture <u>lui</u> appartient.

(61) Je <u>lui</u> ai réservé une place.

Note that it is only in the third person (singular or plural) than the pronominal forms distinguish between direct objects and dative objects. This means that, in order to determine whether a first or second person pronoun represents a direct object or a dative object, we may have to replace it with a third person pronoun. Thus, if we have to parse the sentences in (62) and (63) below, both of which contain first-person singular pronominal

---

[14] For more details on the uses of pronominal adverbs, see chapter 17.

complements, we can try to replace those complements by third-person pronouns, as in (64) and (65). This substitution clearly shows that *me* in (62) must be a direct object, because the corresponding third person form, seen in (64), is *le*. In (63), on the other hand, *me* must be a dative object, as the corresponding third person form in (65) is *lui*:

(62)   Marie <u>me</u> connaît.

(63)   Marie <u>me</u> téléphone.

(64)   Marie <u>le</u> connaît.

(65)   Marie <u>lui</u> telephone.

The basic valency structure of a dative-transitive verb is seen in (66):

(66)   Subject + Predicator + Dative Object = Dative transitive verb

1.2.3.6 Prepositional objects *vs* dative objects

In many languages, English among them, the grammar does not warrant a distinction between prepositional objects and dative objects. Hence, in grammars of French, the two are often conflated into one category called indirect objects.

Examples (67)–(72) below show, however, why it makes sense to distinguish the two in the case of French. Thus, it is not possible to replace the complement *aux arbres* by a pronoun in the dative case in (67). The pronominal adverb y, on the other hand, is perfectly grammatical. The complement *aux arbres* must therefore be a prepositional object in this sentence:

(67)   Jacques pense <u>aux arbres</u>. > Il $y_{PrepObj}$ pense. / *Il leur$_{DatObj}$ pense.

Similarly, it is not possible to replace the complement *à ses parents* by the dative pronoun *leur* in (68). In this case, y does not work very well, either (at least in more formal registers), because we are talking about human beings, so we must resort to *à* followed by the stressed pronoun *eux*:

(68)   Jacques pense <u>à ses parents</u>. > Il pense à eux$_{PrepObj}$ / ?Il $y_{PrepObj}$ pense. (OK only in a colloquial register) / *Il leur$_{DatObj}$ pense.

Conversely, in (69)–(70) below, neither *aux arbres* nor *à ses parents* can be replaced by y, nor does *à eux* work very well in (70). Both can, however, be unproblematically replaced by the dative pronoun *leur*. In these two sentences, we are therefore dealing with dative objects:

(69) Jacques parle <u>aux arbres</u>. > Il leur$_{DatObj}$ parle. / *Il y$_{PrepObj}$ parle.

(70) Jacques parle <u>à ses parents</u>. > Il leur$_{DatObj}$ parle. / *Il y parle$_{PrepObj}$ / #Il parle à eux. (only used contrastively)

Finally, (71)–(72) show that it is possible to have both a prepositional and a dative object in the same clause. This would be very odd if there were no syntactic distinction between them, as no other type of valency element can occur twice in a French sentence. (For further discussion of verbs that take more than one complement, see section 1.2.3.9 below.)

(71) J'ai parlé [du problème]$_{PrepObj}$ [à Florence.]$_{DatObj}$

(72) Je lui$_{DatObj}$ en$_{PrepObj}$ ai parlé.

For these reasons, the term 'indirect object' is not used in this book.[15]

1.2.3.7 The locative object
Locative-transitive verbs are verbs that must take a complement referring to a place (or location, hence the name). The basic valency structure of such verbs is shown in (73):

(73) Subject + Predicator + Locative Object = Locative-transitive verb

It must not be assumed that all linguistic expressions that refer to places are locative objects; in many cases, such expressions will fulfil the grammatical function of adverbial (see section 1.2.4 below). We speak of a locative object only if the clause would be incomplete (hence, ungrammatical) if the constituent expressing place were left out, cf. (74)–(75) below:

(74) Félicien habite <u>à Londres</u> depuis 20 ans.

(75) *Félicien habite [Ø] depuis 20 ans.

---

[15] Unfortunately, no general rule can be given that allows one to predict which verbs will take a dative object and which will take a prepositional object. This must be learned on a case-by-case basis. Quality monolingual dictionaries will, however, provide examples of the appropriate patterns of pronominalization.

That said, if a verb is capable of taking either a dative or a prepositional object without changing its basic meaning, then the dative object will be used to denote animate referents, and the prepositional object to denote non-animate referents, as shown by the contrast between (i) and (ii):

(i) Jean obéit <u>à sa mère</u>. > Jean <u>lui</u> obéit.

(ii) Jean obéit <u>à la loi</u>. > Jean <u>y</u> obéit.

The criteria for identifying a locative object are as follows :

- It will refer to a location.
- It will be governed by a verb like *être*, *habiter*, *demeurer*, *aller*, etc.
- It can frequently be replaced by *y* or, sometimes, *en*, cf. (76):

(76)   Félicien y habite depuis 20 ans.

1.2.3.8 The object attribute

The final type of valency element is the object attribute. The object attribute identifies, or ascribes a property to, the direct object in much the same way as the subject attribute identifies, or ascribes a property to, the subject (cf. section 1.2.3.1 above). Thus, any verb that takes an object attribute must necessarily also take a direct object, as in (77):

(77)   L'opposition trouve [cette politique]$_{DirObj}$ désastreuse.$_{ObjAttr}$

The general term for verbs that take more than one complement is **ditransitive verbs**. Verbs that take a direct object and an object attribute are just one type of ditransitive verb (see further section 1.2.3.9 below), and their basic valency structure is shown in (78):

(78)   Subject + Predicator + Direct Object + Object Attribute

Because the object attribute stands in a similar sort of relation to the direct object as the subject attribute does to the subject, the direct object and the object attribute can often (but not always) be paraphrased by a subordinate clause[16] containing a subject and a subject attribute, as in (79):

(79)   L'opposition trouve [que [cette politique]$_{Subj}$ est [désastreuse.]$_{SubjAttr}$]$_{SubordCl}$

The object attribute can thus be identified using the following criteria:

- It is governed by a verb such as *avoir*, *appeler*, *laisser*, *nommer*, *rendre*, *élire*, *trouver*, etc.
- It characterizes and/or identifies the direct object.
- It agrees with the direct object in gender and number wherever possible, as in (77) above.
- It may, in some cases, be introduced by *comme*, as in (80) below:

(80)   Je considère Henri comme mon meilleur ami.

---

[16] See chapters 3–4 for details on subordinate clauses.

• The relation between the object attribute and the direct object may sometimes be paraphrased by a subordinate clause with a subject and a subject attribute, as in (79) above.

1.2.3.9 Structures with two complements

As we saw above in connection with the distinction between prepositional objects and dative objects (cf. section 1.2.3.6 above) and with object attributes, it is possible for some French verbs to take two complements.

It appears that no French verb is capable of taking more than two complements, so the maximum number of valency elements we can find in any simple French sentence is therefore three (including the subject).

Table 1.2 lists and exemplifies the possible combinations of three valency elements in French. The second column first gives examples in which all valency elements are spelled out as full noun phrases or full prepositional phrases.[17] The second example in each row shows the pronominalization patterns that apply to the combination of valency elements in question.

Table 1.2. Possible combinations of three valency elements (i.e. a subject + two complements) in French.

Structure	Examples
Subj + Pred + DirObj + ObjAttr	Jeanne a rendu Max heureux./Elle l'a rendu heureux.
Subj + Pred + DirObj + PrepObj	J'ai remercié Paul de son cadeau./Je l'en ai remercié.
Subj + Pred + DirObj + DatObj	Marie-Cécile a vendu sa voiture à Loïc./Elle la lui a vendue.
Subj + Pred + DirObj + LocObj	J'ai laissé mes lunettes sur mon bureau./Je les y ai laissées.
Subj + Pred + PrepObj + DatObj	J'ai parlé de l'affaire à Max./Je lui en ai parlé.
Subj + Pred + SubjAttr + DatObj	Cette idée semble intéressante à Marc./Elle lui semble intéressante./Elle le lui semble.[18]

---

[17] A prepositional phrase is a group of words introduced by a preposition. They will be dealt with further in section 2.4.1 below.

[18] Although grammatically possible, neither the first nor the last of these three structures is particularly common. The more idiomatic pattern is to pronominalize only the dative object, but use the full form of the subject attribute, as in the second example.

1.2.3.10 One verb—more than one valency pattern

Some of the examples given above show that one and the same verb may occur with different types, and different numbers, of complements. Thus, we have seen that the verb *être*, for instance, can be an intensive verb, taking a subject attribute, as in (81) below. However, *être* was also mentioned in section 1.2.3.7 as a possible locative-transitive verb, as in (82):

(81)   Julie et Jeanne <u>sont</u> mes sœurs.

(82)   Franck <u>est</u> à Rome.

Indeed, *être* can even function as an intransitive verb, meaning 'to exist', as in the Biblical (83):

(83)   Et la lumière <u>fut</u>. ('And there was light.')

Être is far from the only French verb to have a choice of valency patterns. Another example of a common verb with as many as five different valency patterns is *parler*, which can be intransitive, taking no complements at all (cf. (84) below), directly transitive, as in (85); indirectly transitive, as in (86); dative-transitive, as in (87); and ditransitive, as in (88):

(84)   Marc parle [Ø] beaucoup.

(85)   Est-ce que John parle <u>français</u> ? Oui, il <u>le</u> parle couramment.

(86)   J'ai parlé <u>de la grammaire française</u>. / J'<u>en</u> ai parlé.

(87)   Jacques parle <u>à ses parents</u>. / Jacques <u>leur</u> parle.

(88)   J'ai parlé <u>du problème</u> <u>à Florence</u>. / Je <u>lui</u> <u>en</u> ai parlé.

Very frequently, different valency patterns will result in subtle or not-so-subtle differences in meaning, such that the verb may not translate into English in exactly the same way across contexts. To take a few simple examples, intransitive *être* can be appropriately translated as 'to exist', whereas intensive and locative-transitive *être* cannot. Similarly, intransitive, indirectly-transitive, and dative-transitive *parler* can be appropriately translated as either 'to talk' or 'to speak', but 'to speak' is generally preferable as the translation of directly-transitive *parler* (cf. *John <u>speaks</u> French* and *?John talks French*).

1.2.4 Adverbials

There is one final type of basic sentence/clause constituent, namely adverbials.[19] Adverbials express various **attending circumstances** of the basic state, activity, or event described by the predicator + valency elements, for instance such notions as time, place, manner, instrument, cause, condition, and a number of others.

Adverbials are not valency elements, and are thus characterized by the following properties:

- They can be left out without affecting grammaticality or changing the basic meaning of the sentence, cf. (89)–(90):

(89)   Tous les jours, il va au bureau.

(90)   Il va au bureau.

- In principle, there is no limit to the number of adverbials that can be contained in a sentence, cf. (91) below. As that example shows, adverbials moreover vary greatly in form:

(91)   Cependant, tous les jours, à huit heures du matin, il va au bureau, à pied et sans manteau, à ce que je sache.

- Typically, adverbials have much greater freedom of position within the clause or sentence than valency elements, cf. (89) above and (92)–(96) below:[20]

---

[19] The term 'adverbial' is somewhat misleading, in so far as it suggests that adverbials specifically modify the verb. While some adverbials, such as the manner adverbial in (i) below, do indeed modify the verb, many others do not do so in any meaningful sense. Thus, both *tous les jours* in (89) and *heureusement* in (94) modify their host clauses in their entirety (although in different ways).

(i)   Stéphanie parle très lentement.

In principle, pretty much any type of grammatical constituent can be modified by an adverbial. In (ii) below, for instance, *même* modifies the subject:

(ii)   Même Max est venu à la réunion.

[20] For further details on the position of different types of adverbial, see section 24.7.

(92)   Il va <u>tous les jours</u> au bureau.

(93)   Il va au bureau <u>tous les jours</u>.

(94)   Sophie s'est <u>heureusement</u> fait embaucher ailleurs.

(95)   <u>Heureusement</u>, Sophie s'est fait embaucher ailleurs.

(96)   Sophie s'est fait embaucher ailleurs, <u>heureusement</u>.

1.3 Conclusion

This concludes the overview of the central clause constituents. In addition, French clauses can contain a few other constituent types, which are less basic, and which will be introduced in chapter 3.

In this chapter, we have looked mainly at simple sentences where the valency elements and adverbials were realized as pronouns, noun phrases, prepositional phrases, or adverbs. However, one or more clause constituents will frequently be realized as non-finite clauses or subordinate clauses. An initial discussion of this is found in chapter 3. Chapter 4 treats the different subtypes of subordinate clauses, and chapters 9–11 the different subtypes of non-finite clauses, in greater depth. Appendix A contains a full list of clause-level grammatical functions in French.

As we have seen in several instances in the present chapter, even the central clause constituents very frequently consist of a group of two or more words. In the next chapter, we therefore look at the internal structure of such groups of words that together form a constituent, and we introduce the important distinction between grammatical function and linguistic form.

2

The internal structure of clause constituents

Learning objectives

- To understand the difference between *grammatical function* and *linguistic form*.

- To understand the nature of the different word classes in French (12 in all).

- To be able to identify and delimit different types of basic syntactic phrases in French (six in all).

- To understand and be able to analyse the internal structure of different types of syntactic phrases and of compound verb forms in French.

The Structure of Modern Standard French. First edition. Maj-Britt Mosegaard Hansen.
© Maj-Britt Mosegaard Hansen 2016. First Published 2016 by Oxford University Press

2.1 The distinction between function and form in language

Chapter 1 was concerned mainly with sentence- and clause-level **grammatical functions**, such as subject, direct object, etc. All of these are roles that **linguistic forms** (i.e. morphemes, words, phrases, and constructions) can play in sentences and clauses.

In (1) below, both the subject and the direct object take the form of a group of words that together form a meaningful unit, namely *le petit garcon blond* and *la grande fille brune*. Each of these two groups of words has a noun (*garçon* and *fille*, respectively) at its center. This type of syntactic unit is called a noun phrase (or NP, for short):

(1)   [Le petit garçon blond]$_{Subj/NP}$ embrasse [la grande fille brune]$_{DirObj/NP}$.

In this example, we thus see the same type of linguistic form (in this case a noun phrase) playing different grammatical roles.

Conversely, a given grammatical role can often be played by different types of form. As we saw in chapter 1, both of the noun phrases in (1) can, for instance, be replaced by unstressed, so-called 'clitic',[1] pronouns, as in (2), where *le petit garçon blond* has been replaced by the subject pronoun *il*, and *la grande fille brune* by the direct object pronoun *l'*:

(2)   [Il]$_{Subj/PersPron}$ [l']$_{DirObj/PersPron}$ embrasse.

We can attempt to make clearer the distinction between function and form by thinking of sentences as mini-plays, with the speaker/writer as director. We can then conceive of the grammatical functions in a sentence (predicator, subject, direct object, etc.) as roles in the play, and of the forms (noun phrases, pronouns, verbs, etc.) used to express those functions as the actors cast in those roles.

Now, Hamlet, for instance, has in the past been played by a great many different actors (Laurence Olivier, John Gielgud, Derek Jacobi, and Kenneth Branagh, just to mention a few), and all of these actors have played other roles besides Hamlet (Kenneth Branagh, for instance, has also played Henry V, Gilderoy Lockhart in *Harry Potter and the Chamber of Secrets*, Kurt Wallander, and many others). Just as we keep the actor and the role

---

[1] For the notion of clitics, see section 14.2.

distinct in our minds when watching plays or films, so we must keep grammatical functions and linguistic forms distinct in our minds when analysing sentences.

Example (3) below has been analysed into its immediate functional constituents, according to the principles discussed in chapter 1:

(3) [Victor]$_{Subject}$ [pense]$_{Predicator}$ [très souvent]$_{Adverbial}$ [à Claire.]$_{PrepositionalObject}$

If we then proceed to look at the linguistic forms that express the grammatical roles thus identified, we get the result in (4), where we see that this sentence contains three different types of phrase, as well as a simple finite verb form:

(4) [Victor]$_{Subj/NounPhrase}$ [pense]$_{Pred/SimpleFiniteVerb}$ [très souvent]$_{Adv'al/AdverbPhrase}$ [à Claire.]$_{PrepObj/PrepositionalPhrase}$

As already implied above, a phrase can be defined as a word or a group of words that together form a unit of meaning.

Sometimes, a phrase can consist of just one word, such as the noun phrase *Victor* in (4), which consists only of a proper noun. But very often, phrases consist of several words, as is the case with the adverb phrase (or AdvP, see further section 2.3.4 below) *très souvent* or the prepositional phrase (or PP, see further section 2.4.1) *à Claire*. What distinguishes multi-word phrases from just any sequence of words is that phrases are structured internally, and can be broken down into their immediate constituents, much as clauses can.

Thus, our analytical work is not yet complete when we have said that *très souvent* is an adverbial phrase, for we now want to know what the individual function and form of both *très* and *souvent* is. As a matter of fact, this adverbial phrase can be further analysed as in (5), where the terms **premodifier** and **head**[2] refer to grammatical functions, and the term **adverb** to a linguistic form class.

(5) [très]$_{Premodifier/Adverb}$ [souvent]$_{Head/Adverb}$

Note that, in both (4) and (5), we started by identifying grammatical functions, and only subsequently proceeded to look at linguistic forms. We must always proceed in this way when parsing sentences, going from function to form, and then, if necessary, to lower-level functions, and from

---

[2] These terms will be explained more fully in section 2.3 below.

there to lower-level forms. In other words, we must keep functions and forms strictly separate at all levels.

The reason that, for instance, *très souvent* in (4) is called an adverb phrase, while *le petit garçon blond* in (1) is called a noun phrase is that phrases are named after the word class of the element within them that is perceived to be most important in terms of the meaning of the whole.[3]

For this reason, we will start by taking a closer look at word classes (or 'parts-of-speech', as they are also called) before considering in detail the individual types of phrase found in French.

2.2 Word classes in French

Word classes[4] are defined by their morphological properties (i.e. the kinds of features they can be formally marked for, e.g. number, tense, degree, etc.), and to some extent, also by their syntactic properties (i.e. the kinds of grammatical relationships they can enter into with other words). There are three basic word classes in French, two of which can be further subdivided, such that we end up with a total of twelve classes, as follows.

2.2.1 Verbs

Verbs can be morphologically marked for **person**, **number**, **tense**, **aspect**,[5] and/or **mood**. Verbs describe events, activities, or states. Examples of verbs are given in (6):

(6) *être, marcher, aimer, lire, mourir*

---

[3] When in doubt, we have at our disposal certain tests that can help us identify the most important element of a given phrase. These tests are explained in section 2.6 below.

[4] A more detailed list of word classes in French, with examples of each class, can be found in Appendix B.

[5] Where tense has to do with 'external' time, i.e. with the location in time of the event, activity, or state described by a sentence or clause, aspect has to do with 'internal' time, for instance whether a given situation is seen as completed or on-going, habitual or one-off, etc. In French, the difference between the *imparfait* and the *passé simple/passé composé* is notably an aspectual difference. See further chapter 7.

2.2.2 Nominals

Nominals are or can be morphologically marked for **gender** and/or **number**, and in some instances, **case**, **person**, and/or **degree**. They are subdivided into the six categories seen in (7)–(12):

(7)   Nouns: e.g. *garçon, gâteau, amour, lecture*

(8)   Proper nouns: e.g. *Robert, Sarkozy, Le Figaro*

(9)   Pronouns: e.g. *je, la sienne, cela, quelqu'un*

(10)   Adjectives: e.g. *beau, simple, intéressant, vert*

(11)   Articles: e.g. *le, son, ce*

(12)   Numerals: e.g. *deux, cinquième*

Pronouns are further subdivided according to criteria which largely have to do with their meaning. Chapters 15–20 treat the different types of pronoun found in French in greater detail. A list with illustrative examples can be found in Appendix B.

Articles introduce noun phrases and convey instructions to the addressee on how to identify the referent of the noun phrase. Articles can be subdivided according to the nature of those instructions. The different types of article found in French are treated in greater depth in chapters 12, 18, and 19, and a list with illustrative examples can be found in Appendix B.

Numerals are subdivided into **cardinals**, i.e. numerals like *un, deux, trois*, etc., and **ordinals**, which express an ordering relation between different items, i.e. *première, deuxième, troisième*, etc.

2.2.3 Particles

Particles cannot normally be morphologically marked for anything. The only exceptions to this are the adverbs *bien, mal, beaucoup*, and *peu*, which can be morphologically marked for degree (i.e. *(le) mieux/pis/plus/moins*). In other words, particles are invariable in form. They come in the five subtypes shown in (13)–(17):

(13)   Adverbs: e.g. *vite, hier, plus, lentement*[6]

(14)   Prepositions: e.g. *de, sur, par rapport à*

(15)   Conjunctions: e.g. *et, si, parce que, si bien que*

(16)   Infinitive markers: *de, à*

(17)   Interjections: e.g. *oui, aïe, ouf*

Conjunctions are subdivided into coordinating and subordinating conjunctions, according to whether they connect two clauses of equal status or rather mark one clause as subordinate to the other. See further chapters 3–4, and section 22.3.

Note that the forms *de* and *à* may function as either prepositions or infinitive markers. Section 9.2.2.1 explains the difference between the two functions in some detail.

The different types of syntactic phrase are formed around words from a specific subset of these word classes, while words from the remaining word classes may play ancillary roles within phrases.

2.3 Hierarchically structured phrase types

Most phrases have a hierarchical internal structure. Such phrases have a single element, called a **head**, which must be present, whereas all other elements are optional. Optional elements that precede the head are typically known as **premodifying** elements, whereas elements that follow the head are called **postmodifying** elements.

2.3.1 Compound verbs

Any given French verb may be either:

• **finite** (i.e. inflected for person, and also typically for features like number, tense, aspect, and/or mood), or

---

[6] Some items listed contain a combination of elements that may function independently. They are, however, invariable in form. See further section 22.1.

- **non-finite** (i.e. an infinitive, a past participle, a present participle, or a *gérondif*).

A French clause will normally contain one and only one finite verb. In addition, it may or may not contain several non-finite ones, as seen in (18)–(20):

(18)   Aurélie [pense]$_{FiniteVerb}$ à Patrick.

(19)   Max [a]$_{FinV}$ [été]$_{Non-finiteVerb(PastParticiple)}$ [surpris]$_{Non-finV(PastPart)}$ par la pluie.

(20)   Il [va]$_{FinV}$ [pleuvoir.]$_{Non-finV(Infinitive)}$

If a finite verb on its own functions as the predicator of a clause, that predicator consists of a **simple verb** form, as in (18) above. As the name suggests, **compound verbs** consist of two or more verb forms which together constitute a meaningful unit. One of these verb forms will thus be finite, and the rest non-finite, as in (19)–(20).

The head of a compound verb form is either a **lexical verb** (= a verb that has independent meaning) or a **copula** (= *être*, when it serves as a link between the subject and a subject attribute). In the case of compound verbs, the head is usually referred to as the **main verb**. In French, the main verb of a compound form will always be non-finite.

The head or main verb may be premodified by one or more **auxiliaries**, principally *avoir*, *être*, *aller*, and *faire*, and more rarely *venir*.[7] Auxiliaries are 'helping' verbs, whose function is to express purely grammatical features of the compound verb such as tense, aspect or voice,[8] as in (21)–(24):

(21)   Il [[va]$_{Auxiliary}$ [pleuvoir.]$_{Head}$]

(22)   Catherine [[aurait]$_{Aux}$ [été]$_{H}$] malade.

(23)   Max [[a été]$_{Aux}$ [surpris]$_{H}$] par la pluie.

(24)   Sylvie s'[[est fait]$_{Aux}$ [teindre]$_{H}$] les cheveux.

---

[7] Unlike what is the case in English, this book does not consider modal verbs like *devoir* and *pouvoir* to be auxiliaries in French, but rather full verbs that may or may not take an infinitival clause as their direct object. See section 9.2.2.2 for further details.

[8] In this book, 'voice' is defined in terms of regular alternations in the valency structure of the main verb. The different types of voice alternation found in French are discussed in chapter 25.

As (23) and (24) above show, the auxiliary may itself consist of more than one verb, in which case it can be analysed into a head and an auxiliary at the next level of analysis. Thus, in the case of (23), we get a three-level complete analysis as in (25), while (24) yields (26):

(25) [a   été   surpris]_{CompoundVerb}
        [a   été]_{Aux/CompV}   [surpris]_{H/PastPart}
        [a]_{Aux/FiniteVerb} [été]_{H/PastPart}

(26) [est   fait   teindre]_{CompV}
        [est   fait]_{Aux/CompV}   [teindre]_{H/Inf}
        [est]_{Aux/FinV} [fait]_{H/PastPart}

2.3.2 Noun phrases

In a noun phrase, the **head** is a noun or a proper noun, hence the name.

Apart from the head, a French noun phrase will in the vast majority of cases also contain a **determiner**. The determiner instructs the addressee about the proper procedure for identifying the referent of the noun phrase, and it most frequently (but not always) takes the form of an article.

A definite article, for instance, tells the addressee that the speaker/writer is assuming that the referent will be uniquely identifiable in the context. Thus, if speaker and hearer are together in a room with just one door, the use of the definite article in (27) below is appropriate and will signal to the hearer that it is the door of that room that is creaking. If, on the other hand, they find themselves in a room with five doors, (27) would be confusing to the hearer, who would have no way of knowing which particular door was being referred to:

(27) La porte grince.

The different types of articles used in French will be discussed in greater detail in chapters 12, 18, and 19.

In Modern French, the relationship between the noun and the determiner is thus strictly speaking not hierarchical, but **solidary**. That is to say that both elements normally need to be present in order for the phrase to be grammatical, as shown by the contrast between (28) and (29):

(28) [Ma collègue] est arrivée.

(29) *[[Ø] Collègue] est arrivée.

However, there are a few grammatical environments, such as that in (30) below, where determiner-less noun phrases occur felicitously in French. For this reason, we can feel justified in considering the noun as the more important element of the two.

(30)   Nous sommes [[Ø] collègues].

Apart from the determiner, a noun phrase may contain one or more pre- and/or postmodifying phrases of various types, as shown in (31)–(32) below:

(31)   Ils ont loué [une très grande maison de campagne] >> [une]_{Determiner/} _{IndefiniteArticle} [très grande]_{Premodifier/AdjectivalPhrase} [maison]_{H/Noun} [de campagne] _{Postmodifier/PrepositionalPhrase}

(32)   [Ma belle collègue de Paris tellement élégante] est arrivée. >> [Ma]_{Det/PossArt} [belle]_{Premod/Adjective} [collègue]_{H/N} [de Paris]_{Postmod/PP}, [tellement élégante] _{Postmod/AdjP}

If pre- and postmodifiers consist of more than one word, they can normally be analysed into their own immediate constituents, with both a functional and a formal level of analysis. In (31) above, for instance, the premodifier *très grande* is an adjective phrase, while the postmodifier *de campagne* is a prepositional phrase. In other words, we can have phrases inside other phrases. Sections 2.3.3 and 2.4.1 below will explain how adjective phrases and prepositional phrases are structured.

Unlike the determiner, the pre- and postmodifiers of a noun phrase can always be left out without making the sentence or clause ungrammatical, cf. (32) above and (33) below:[9]

(33)   [Ma collègue] est arrivée.

---

[9] Occasionally, a noun phrase may consist in a non-hierarchical relation between two elements each of which would in itself have the status of a noun phrase, as in (i) below. As (ii)–(iii) show, we can leave either of these noun phrases out and still have a grammatical sentence, and in so far as they can meaningfully be said to modify one another at all, it is not clear which is the head and which is the modifier. This is normally only the case with combinations of title + proper name. We will refer to noun phrases of this type as **juxtapositions**:

(i)   [[Le Président]_{NP} [Obama]_{NP}]_{NP} a fait un discours hier à la télé.
(ii)   [Le Président] a fait un discours hier à la télé.
(iii)   [Obama] a fait un discours hier à la télé.

2.3.3 Adjective phrases

The head of an adjective phrase (AdjP) is an adjective. Apart from the head, an adjective phrase may contain **adverbial premodification** and/or one or more **postmodifiers** of various types, as shown in (34) below:

(34)   L'enfant était [si content de son nounours qu'il ne pouvait pas dormir sans lui.] >> [si]$_{Premod/Adverb}$ [content]$_{H/Adj}$ [de son nounours]$_{Postmod/PP}$ [qu'il ne pouvait pas dormir sans lui]$_{Postmod/Subordinate\ clause}$

As was the case with noun phrases, pre- and postmodifiers of adjective phrases can always be left out without making the sentence ungrammatical, cf. (35):

(35)   L'enfant était [content].

Adjective phrases can be used on their own, predicatively (i.e. as subject/object/free indirect attributes[10]) as in (36) below, or as pre- or postmodifiers inside a noun phrase, as in (37):

(36)   Il était [très content de son nounours]$_{SubjAttr/AdjP}$

(37)   [Un petit garçon très content de son nounours]$_{Subj/NP}$ me sourit. >> [Un]$_{Det/IndefArt}$ [petit]$_{Premod/AdjP}$ [garçon]$_{H/Noun}$ [très content de son nounours]$_{Postmod/AdjP}$

2.3.4 Adverb phrases

The head of an adverb phrase (AdvP) is an adverb. In addition, adverb phrases may optionally contain adverbial premodification and/or a post-modifier, as in (38) below, where *si* premodifies the head adverb, while the subordinate clause *que les autres ne pouvaient la suivre* postmodifies it.[11] Pre- and postmodifiers can always be left out, as (39) shows:

---

[10] On subject attributes and object attributes, see sections 1.2.3.1 and 1.2.3.8. On free indirect attributes, see section 3.2.4.1.

[11] For more details on subordinate clauses, see chapter 3 and, especially, chapter 4.

(38) Jeanne courait [[si]~Premod/Adv~ [vite]~H/Adv~ [que les autres ne pouvaient la suivre.]~Postmod/Subordinate clause~]

(39) Jeanne courait [vite].

2.3.5 Pronominal phrases

The final type of hierarchically structured phrase in French is pronominal phrases, where the head is a pronoun.

Pronouns are not normally premodified,[12] except in some cases by the indefinite *tout* (cf. section 20.3.1), but may sometimes constitute pronominal phrases in combination with a postmodifier, which may be of various kinds, as exemplified in (40)–(41):

(40) [Celui avec qui tu m'as vu(e)]~Subj/PronP~ vient du Togo. >> [Celui]~H/DemPronoun~ [avec qui tu m'as vu(e)]~Postmod/SubordCl~

(41) [Plusieurs de mes collègues]~Subj/PronP~ pensent que ce film est bon. >> [Plusieurs]~H/IndefPron~ [de mes collègues]~Postmod/PP~

2.4 Non-hierarchically structured phrases

A different type of phrase, of which we find only one kind in French, consists in a solidary relation between two elements, such that both elements must be present.

2.4.1 Prepositional phrases

Prepositional phrases consist in a (simple or complex) preposition, functioning as the head of the phrase followed by a **complement**. In (42) below, we see an example of a simple preposition, while in (43), we have a complex preposition as head of the phrase:

---

[12] The possessive pronouns, however, consist of a fixed combination of a definite determiner and an element indicating person, thus taking the form *le mien, la mienne* etc., cf. section 18.1.2.

(42)   Il l'a fait [pour son frère.]$_{Adv'al/PP}$ >> [pour]$_{H/SimplePreposition}$ [son frère]
       Complement/NP

(43)   Je suis venu [à cause de ta lettre.]$_{Adv'al/PP}$ >> [à cause de]$_{H/ComplexPrep}$ [ta
       lettre]$_{Compl}$

Unlike hierarchically structured phrases, which can function with only a head, neither the complement nor the head of a prepositional phrase can be left out, as shown by the contrasts in (44)–(46):

(44)   Je vais [[à]$_H$ [Paris.]$_{Compl}$]$_{PP}$

(45)   *Je vais à [Ø].

(46)   *Je vais [Ø] Paris.

2.5 Relations of coordination

Sometimes we find a single grammatical function fulfilled by a **coordination** of two phrases, as in (47) below, where the direct object takes the form of two coordinated noun phrases. Coordination links two different phrases, describing different things, each of which could on its own have fulfilled the syntactic function in question, as in (48)–(49). Note that we do not consider (47) to contain two direct objects: at the level of grammatical function, there is only one direct object in the sentence, as shown by the fact that it can only be pronominalized once (cf. (50) *vs* the ungrammatical (51)). However, at the level of linguistic form, that direct object consists of two coordinated noun phrases.

(47)   Il a acheté [des pommes et des poires.]$_{DirObj/CoordinatedNPs}$

(48)   Il a acheté [des pommes.]$_{DirObj/NP}$

(49)   Il a acheté [des poires.]$_{DirObj/NP}$

(50)   Il <u>en</u> a acheté.[13]

(51)   *Il [en et en] a acheté.

---

[13] Note that indefinite direct objects are normally pronominalized by *en*. See further section 17.2.2.

Elements can be coordinated with a coordinator, which takes the form of a **coordinating conjunction** (in French, *et, mais, car, ou (bien), soit,* or *ni,* cf. section 22.3, and section 23.2.2),[14] in which case we speak of **syndetic** coordination. This is what we find in (47) above. Elements can also be coordinated simply by being listed, however, without the use of a conjunction, as in (52) below. In that case, we are dealing with **asyndetic** coordination.

(52)   Il a acheté [des pommes, des poires, des oranges . . .]$_{\text{DirObj/CoordNPs}}$

2.6 Tests for determining the nature and extension of a given phrase and its syntactic function

When parsing sentences, we may sometimes find ourselves unsure about the exact extension of a given phrase and/or of its grammatical function. As we saw in chapter 1, there are various tests that can be used when trying to solve parsing problems of this kind. The two most central tests are the substitution test and the elimination test, but a few others are occasionally useful in addition to these two.

2.6.1 Substitution

The substitution test is the most important test we have at our disposal. It was applied a number of times in chapter 1, when explaining how various types of central sentence constituents can normally be replaced by pronominal elements of a specific kind.

Essentially, when using the substitution test, we replace the phrase whose extension and/or function we cannot immediately determine with an element that has a single function or a restricted range of functions.

Suppose we are trying to analyse the sentence in (53):

(53)   Ma cousine de Paris tellement élégante est arrivée.

---

[14] Some grammars consider *donc, or,* and *puis* to be coordinating conjunctions, as well. In this book, these items are considered to be (connective) adverbs.

Suppose further that we have determined that *est arrivée* is the predicator; we have a hunch that *ma cousine* is probably a unit of meaning, and that it probably functions as the subject of the sentence, but we are not sure if any other elements in the sentence belong to the same phrase as *ma cousine*. What we can do is to try and replace the phrase by the unstressed nominative (=subject) pronoun *elle*. What we observe is then that it is not only *ma cousine* that disappears, but also the elements *de Paris* and *tellement élégante*, such that we get the resulting sentence in (54):

(54) [Elle]$_{Subj}$ est arrivée.

A version of the sentence that replaces only *ma cousine*, but leaves *de Paris tellement élégante* behind, as in (55), is evidently ungrammatical, on the other hand, as shown in (55):

(55) *Elle de Paris tellement élégante est arrivée.

The substitution test thus shows that the entire string of words *ma cousine de Paris tellement élégante* is one single phrase, which functions as the subject of the sentence.

2.6.2 Elimination

The second very important test is the elimination test. Sometimes, we may be unsure about which element of a given phrase is the head of that phrase. In such cases, we can try and eliminate elements from the phrase, to see which ones can be dispensed with. If a given element can be eliminated from a phrase without causing ungrammaticality, then that element is non-central to the phrase, and hence cannot be its head.

If we go back to our previous example in (53) above, we determined, using the substitution test, that *ma cousine de Paris tellement élégante* is one single phrase, as indicated by the brackets in (56) below. Suppose, however, that we are still unsure of the exact nature of that phrase. What we find using the elimination test is that the elements *de Paris tellement élégante* can be eliminated without making the sentence ungrammatical, as shown in (57) below. Of the remaining two elements, *ma cousine*, *cousine* is the one that is more important in terms of the meaning of the phrase. *Cousine* being a noun, we therefore infer that we are dealing with a noun phrase in this case.

(56) [Ma cousine de Paris tellement élégante] est arrivée.

(57) [Ma cousine] est arrivée.

2.6.3 Coordination

If we are unsure of the grammatical function of a particular phrase, an alternative to the substitution test is the coordination test, whereby we add a coordinated element, of whose function we are certain, to the phrase we are unsure of. Suppose that we are parsing (58):

(58) Pierre est [de gauche.]

Suppose further that we determine that *de gauche* must be a (prepositional) phrase; we suspect it may be a subject attribute, but we are not sure whether prepositional phrases are possible subject attributes. On the other hand, we do know for sure that adjectives, such as *communiste*, can function as subject attributes, as in (59):

(59) Pierre est [communiste.]$_{\text{SubjAttr}}$

What we can try now is to coordinate *de gauche* and *communiste* as in (60) below. If that results in a grammatical sentence (as it does in this case), then we can infer that the two coordinated elements must have the same grammatical function. In other words, *de gauche* in (58) is, indeed, a subject attribute.

(60) Pierre est [de gauche, et même communiste.]$_{\text{SubjAttr}}$

2.6.4 Insertion and movement

If we find ourselves uncertain about the exact extension of a given phrase, and whether a fairly long sequence of words constitutes one single phrase or rather two or more individual phrases, we can use the insertion and movement tests.

In French, the constituents of a single phrase will typically be kept together, and the possibility of inserting extraneous elements will therefore be limited.

If, for instance, we want to find out whether *à la soirée de Claude* in (61) below is all one phrase, we can insert an adverbial such as *hier* into the sentence. What we find is that *hier* has to go either before the whole sequence *à la soirée de Claude* (as in (62)) or after it (as in (63)). It cannot go in the middle, as in (64). This allows us to conclude that *à la soirée de Claude* functions as one grammatical unit.

(61) Je t'ai vu(e) à la soirée de Claude.

(62) Je t'ai vu(e) <u>hier</u> [à la soirée de Claude].

(63) Je t'ai vu(e) [à la soirée de Claude] <u>hier</u>.

(64) *Je t'ai vu(e) [à la soirée] <u>hier</u> [de Claude].

Because the constituents of a single phrase will normally be kept together in French sentences, a phrase will typically move as a unit (to the extent that it can be moved at all). Thus, if we want to know whether *à la femme de mon frère* is a single phrase in (65) below, we can try moving (parts of) it to a different position within the sentence, and see if that makes the sentence ungrammatical (or radically changes its meaning). What we find is that only (68) is a grammatical paraphrase of (65). From that we can infer that *à la femme de mon frère* constitutes a single phrase here.

(65) J'ai offert un pull [à la femme de mon frère].

(66) *[A la femme] j'ai offert un pull [de mon frère].

(67) *[De mon frère] j'ai offert un pull [à la femme].

(68) [A la femme de mon frère] j'ai offert un pull.

2.6.5 Blocking

The blocking test consists in inserting a phrase whose syntactic function is not in doubt. If insertion fails, that function is already fulfilled elsewhere in the sentence (or cannot be fulfilled at all given the nature of the predicator).

Suppose that we are uncertain of the grammatical function of *à qui* in (69) below: we think it looks a bit like a dative object, and we know that the verb *parler* can take a complement of that type. If we insert a dative pronoun, as in (70), we find that this makes the sentence ungrammatical. We may therefore conclude that *à qui* must, indeed, be the dative object:

(69)   [A qui] viens-tu de parler ?

(70)   *[A qui] viens-tu de [lui]$_{DatObj}$ parler ?

2.6.6 Agreement

Finally, the agreement test may be used to discover whether specific elements in a sentence or clause are syntactically linked, for instance by being part of one and the same phrase, or—like subjects and subject attributes or direct objects and object attributes—by virtue of describing the same referent.

What we do is to change the gender, number and/or person marking on one of the elements of the sentence that we suspect are linked. If one or more other elements must then also change their morphological marking accordingly, they are syntactically linked to the first element.

Suppose we are wondering about the function of *très désagréable* in (71):

(71)   Je trouve votre histoire [très désagréable].

Because *désagréable* is an adjective, hence subject to gender/number agreement, we can try putting it in the plural form to see if any other element in the sentence likewise has to change its number in order for the sentence to remain grammatical. What we find is that *votre histoire* must now also take the plural, as shown in (72) below. This shows us that there is a syntactic link between those two phrases.

(72)   Je trouve vos histoires [très désagréables.]$_{ObjAttr}$

It does not, however, show us the exact nature of that syntactic link: as it happens, *très désagréable* is an object attribute here, but the agreement pattern would not in and of itself preclude its being a postmodifier inside the noun phrase headed by *histoire*. In this case, the possible valency patterns of the verb also need to be taken into account. (Readers may try to work out for themselves how the substitution test may be used to this end.)

2.7 Conclusion

In this chapter, we have reviewed the different types of phrases found in simple clauses. As already mentioned at various points, Appendix B contains a full list of word classes in French, with examples. A full list of sentence-, clause-, and phrase-level grammatical functions can be found in Appendix A.

In chapter 3, we turn to more complex sentence structures.

3

Complex sentence structures

Learning objectives

- To understand the difference between grammatical and *logical constituents* of clauses.

- To understand the difference between simple, complex, and compound sentences.

- To understand the notion of *reduced clauses*, and to be able to distinguish between different types of reduced clause (seven in all).

- To understand the difference between restrictive and non-restrictive modification.

3.1 Grammatical and 'logical' elements

When considering certain types of grammatical construction, including—but not limited to—the distinction between active and passive clauses, it is useful to make a distinction between grammatical and 'logical' constituents.

The Structure of Modern Standard French. First edition. Maj-Britt Mosegaard Hansen.
© Maj-Britt Mosegaard Hansen 2016. First Published 2016 by Oxford University Press

If we take a simple active sentence as our point of departure, we may say that a directly transitive[1] verb like *construire*, for instance, has the person who builds something as its 'logical' subject, and the thing built as its 'logical' direct object. This is because, in a simple active clause using *construire* as the predicator, the builder would be the grammatical subject, while the thing built would be the grammatical direct object, as in (1) below. Similarly, the ditransitive verb *envoyer*, for instance, will have the person who sends something as its logical subject, the thing sent as its logical direct object, and the person the thing is sent to as its logical dative object, as in (2):[2]

(1)   [Le maçon]$_{Subj}$ a construit [le pavillon.]$_{DirObj}$

(2)   [Frédérique]$_{Subj}$ a envoyé [un cadeau]$_{DirObj}$ [à Marine.]$_{DatObj}$

While the logical subject of a given verb will thus typically be coded as the grammatical subject of the clause, and the logical object of that verb as a grammatical direct object, there is not necessarily a direct relation between the logical level and the grammatical level. In other words, the logical subject is not always the grammatical subject, nor is the logical direct object always the grammatical direct object, as shown by the so-called causative *faire* + infinitive construction in (3) and the passive construction in (4) below:[3]

(3)   [Cédric]$_{Subj}$ a fait construire [son pavillon]$_{DirObj}$ [par un maçon du village.]$_{Adv'al}$

(4)   [Le cadeau]$_{Subj}$ a été envoyé à Marine [par Frédérique.]$_{Adv'al}$

As suggested by the examples above, the logical role played by a particular grammatical constituent is identified by paraphrasing the meaning of the syntactic structure in which that grammatical constituent appears as a simple active clause. Thus, the causative construction in (3) above implies (1), while the passive clause in (4) implies (2).

In finite clauses, the grammatical coding of logical roles will typically depend on what the topic of the discourse is, and on what the speaker thinks is already known to the hearer *vs* what will be new to the hearer. Speakers will typically prefer to start off their clauses with known information,

---

[1] For the notion of transitivity, see sections 1.2.3.2ff.

[2] In this book, no use will be made of the notion of semantic roles such as Patient, Theme, Recipient, Goal, etc.

[3] For further details on causatives and passives in French, see chapter 25.

adding new information later (see further chapters 25–26). Thus, in both French and English, we would usually prefer the reports in (5)–(6) below to those in (7)–(8), even though it is in each case the exact same event that is described:

(5)   Your brother has been shot by an unknown individual!

(6)   Ton frère a été descendu par un inconnu !/Ton frère s'est fait descendre par un inconnu !

(7)   An unknown individual has shot your brother!

(8)   Un inconnu a descendu ton frère !

The point here is that (5)–(6) are passive sentences (see section 3.1.1 below), in which the logical direct object, i.e. the person who suffers the shooting, is realized as the grammatical subject of the sentence. The logical subject, on the other hand (i.e. the person doing the shooting), plays the grammatical role of adverbial, and takes the form of a prepositional phrase headed by *by/par*. The rather less natural examples in (7)–(8), on the other hand, are straightforward active sentences, where logical and grammatical roles are in harmony.

So-called non-finite clauses (see section 3.2.2 below), on the other hand, usually do not or cannot take a grammatical subject at all, and their logical subject must therefore be expressed in other ways. In (9) below, for instance, the constituent enclosed in square brackets is such a non-finite clause, more specifically a present participle clause,[4] and it contains no subject. The hearer must therefore infer from the contents of the rest of the sentence who was responsible for the shooting:

(9)   [Ayant descendu ton frère,]$_{PresentParticipleClause}$ l'inconnu a fui la scène du crime dans une voiture verte.

3.1.1 Passive clauses

In a passive clause, the logical direct object of a transitive verb is promoted to grammatical subject position, while the logical subject is demoted to an

---

[4] See chapter 11 for details on the use of present participle clauses.

adverbial role, and may therefore be left out. In other words, the grammatical valency of a given verb is reduced when it is put in the passive voice.

Take a verb like *offrir*: its logical valency is as shown in (10) below, where the person doing the giving is the logical subject, the thing given is the logical direct object, and the person receiving the gift is the logical dative object:

(10)   Offrir (Samantha$_{Giver=LogSubj}$, ce livre$_{ThingGiven=LogDirObj}$, Walter$_{Recipient}$ $_{=LogDatObj}$)

In an active sentence like (11), the distribution of grammatical functions will correspond to those logical relations:

(11)   [Samantha]$_{Subj}$ a offert [ce livre]$_{DirObj}$ [à Walter.]$_{DatObj}$

In the corresponding passive sentence in (12), however, the logical direct object will be coded as the grammatical subject, while the logical subject is now coded as an adverbial taking the form of a prepositional phrase headed by the preposition *par*. Because the logical subject is coded as an adverbial, it can be left out without making the sentence ungrammatical, as shown in (13):

(12)   [Ce livre]$_{Subj}$ a été offert [à Walter]$_{DatObj}$ [par Samantha.]$_{Adv\ (LogSubj)}$

(13)   [Ce livre]$_{Subj}$ a été offert [à Walter.]$_{DatObj}$

Uses of the passive and other voice alternations in French are treated in greater depth in chapter 25.

3.1.2 Anticipatory and postponed subjects

Passive clauses are not the only way to avoid placing a logical subject that is new to the addressee or to the discourse in grammatical subject position. In some cases, a clause or sentence may contain two different types of subject, of different status.

In such constructions, the **grammatical subject**, i.e. the subject with which the predicator agrees in person and number, is filled by a **neutral pronoun** (*it* in English, *ce*, *il*, or *cela* in French), which does not refer to anything and is essentially empty of meaning.[5] At the same time, a phrase or clause that represents the meaning content of the subject (and which in that sense is the

---

[5] For a more detailed treatment of the uses of neutral pronouns, and the choice between them, see chapter 16.

logical subject of the clause) is placed later in the sentence, after the predicator. The contrasting English examples in (14)–(15) below illustrate the principle at work:

(14)   [To do this]$_{\text{LogSubj+GramSubj}}$ would be a grave error.

(15)   [It]$_{\text{GramSubj}}$ would be a grave error [to do this.]$_{\text{LogSubj}}$

In such cases, the empty grammatical subject is called an **anticipatory subject** (because it anticipates the logical subject expressed later on in the clause), and the logical subject is called a **postponed subject**. This is what we find in (16)–(17) below. Notice how in (17) the predicator *s'est produit* agrees in number with the third person singular anticipatory (grammatical) subject *il*, and not with the logical, postponed third person plural subject *deux faits que je tiens à signaler*:[6]

(16)   [Cela]$_{\text{AnticipSubj}}$ n'arrange pas les choses [de pleurer.]$_{\text{PostponedSubj}}$

(17)   [Il]$_{\text{AnticipSubj}}$ s'est produit ce matin même [deux faits que je tiens à signaler.]$_{\text{PostponedSubj}}$

We can recognize constructions with anticipatory and postponed subjects by the fact that, as (18)–(19) show, we can always put the postponed subject in the place of the anticipatory subject without changing the meaning of the sentence:[7]

(18)   [Pleurer]$_{\text{Subj}}$ n'arrange pas les choses.

(19)   [Deux faits que je tiens à signaler]$_{\text{Subj}}$ se sont produits ce matin même.

Constructions with an anticipatory and a postponed subject are typically used when the logical subject is indefinite, as in (18), where *pleurer* does not refer to a specific incident, and (19), where the two events in question are not assumed to be known to the hearer. In spoken French, in particular, the avoidance of indefinite grammatical subjects such as those in (8), (18), or (19) is very strong, indeed. Alternative constructions like (6), (16), or (17) are therefore preferred in usage (see further chapters 25–26).

---

[6] As this example shows, postponed subjects are found with a wider range of verbs in French than in English, where a word-for-word translation equivalent of (17) would not be grammatical.

[7] We may, however, have to change, add, or delete certain formal markers, such as the number marking on the predicator, as in (19), or the infinitive marker *de*, as in (18).

3.2 Subordinate clauses and reduced clauses

3.2.1 Subordination in grammar

One of the most important properties of natural languages[8] is the property known as **recursion**, or rank-shifting, i.e. the fact that languages allow the embedding of grammatical constituents within constituents of a similar, or even lower-ranking type. For instance, we saw in section 2.3.2, that a prepositional phrase can be embedded as a postmodifier within a noun phrase, and that such a prepositional phrase might itself contain a noun phrase as its complement, cf. (20) below:

(20)   C'est [le fils du voisin.]$_{NP}$
   >> [le]$_{Det/DefArt}$ [fils]$_{H/N}$ [du voisin]$_{Postmod/PP}$
   >> [de]$_{H/Prep}$ [le voisin]$_{Compl/NP}$
   >> [le]$_{Det/DefArt}$ [voisin]$_{H/N}$

Noun phrases and prepositional phrases are both clause-level constituents, and hence grammatically of similar rank, but of lower rank than clauses.

In a similar way, **subordinate clauses** or **non-finite clauses** (which—as we will see below—are essentially reduced finite clauses) can be embedded within other clauses as valency elements.[9] For instance, if we look at (21) below, we see that the noun phrase *une glace* plays the grammatical role of direct object, i.e. the thing that the speaker wants:

(21)   Je voudrais [une glace.]$_{DirObj/NP}$

Now, we can replace this noun phrase with a subordinate clause as in (22) below, and that subordinate clause will still play the role of direct object with respect to the predicator *voudrais*. The only difference between (21) and (22) is that rather than desiring a thing (*une glace*), the speaker of (22) desires that a particular situation should come about, namely that the hearer should leave:

---

[8] A 'natural' language is simply a language that has developed naturally within a given community. In other words, natural languages stand in opposition to consciously constructed languages, such as Esperanto or computer-programming languages. (The term thus has nothing to do with the perceived 'naturalness' with which someone might express him- or herself in a given context.)

[9] See section 1.2.1.1 for the notion of valency.

(22)   Je voudrais [que tu partes.]$_{DirObj/SubordinateClause}$

Finally, (23) shows that the direct object of the predicator *voudrais* may also be a non-finite clause, where what the speaker wants is for him-/herself to do something, namely to learn Japanese:

(23)   Je voudrais [apprendre le japonais.]$_{DirObj/InfinitivalClause}$

(22) and (23) are then **complex sentences**, because they contain more than one clause.

There are two clauses in (22) because there are two finite verbs in the sentence, namely *voudrais* and *partes*. There are various ways of ascertaining that it is the clause containing *partes*, and not the one containing *voudrais*, that is subordinate. For one thing, we have already seen that the subordinate clause *que tu partes* is dependent on the main clause *je voudrais* in the sense of being a valency element in that main clause. In other words, the meaning of *que tu partes* is dependent on the meaning of *je voudrais*. Secondly, *que tu partes* cannot function on its own as a complete message. Thirdly, (unlike what is the case in English) subordinate clauses in Standard French are always introduced by a subordinator, i.e. an element which explicitly marks the clause as subordinate. In this case, the subordinator is the subordinating conjunction *que*.[10]

We can tell that there are two clauses in (23) because the finite clause consisting of *je voudrais* + direct object and the infinitival clause *apprendre le japonais* describe two situations that are distinct in the real world: the speaker wants something at the time of speaking; whether or not s/he actually learns Japanese we cannot know at that point, as this is merely a potential future occurrence.

A subordinate clause or a non-finite clause can also be subordinated to another clause as an **adverbial**. In (24)–(27) below, the constituents in square brackets all provide information about the circumstances surrounding the speaker's departure. Thus, both (24) and (25) give information about the time of departure, the difference being that, in (24), that information is given in the form of an adverb, *demain*, whereas in (25), a subordinate clause describes a future event which coincides with the speaker's departure:

---

[10] See section 4.2.1.1, for a more detailed treatment of this conjunction. Note that, for the purposes of this book, no distinction is made between subordinators and complementizers.

(24)   Je partirai [demain.]$_{\text{Adv'al/Adv}}$

(25)   Je partirai [quand Hélène sera de retour.]$_{\text{Adv'al/SubordCl}}$

In both (26) and (27) below, the adverbial tells us about the motive for the departure, and in both examples, that adverbial takes the form of a prepositional phrase. The difference is that in (26), the complement of that prepositional phrase is a simple noun phrase, whereas in (27), it takes the form of a non-finite clause, more specifically an infinitival clause:[11]

(26)   Je partirai [pour une bonne raison.]$_{\text{Adv'al/PP}}$ >> [pour]$_{\text{H/Prep}}$ [une bonne raison]$_{\text{Compl/NP}}$

(27)   Je partirai [pour ne pas avoir à rencontrer Hélène.]$_{\text{Adv'al/PP}}$ >> [pour]$_{\text{H/Prep}}$ [ne pas avoir à rencontrer Hélène]$_{\text{Compl/InfCl}}$

Finally, a subordinate clause or a non-finite clause can be embedded as a postmodifier in a noun phrase. In (28)–(30) below, the direct object takes the form of a noun phrase with the noun *document* as its head. In (28), the head is postmodified by an adjective, *important*:

(28)   Il a rédigé [un document important.]$_{\text{DirObj/NP}}$ >> [un]$_{\text{Det/IndefArt}}$ [document]$_{\text{H/N}}$ [important]$_{\text{Postmod/Adj}}$

In (29), on the other hand, the postmodifier is a subordinate clause describing the contents of the document:

(29)   Il a rédigé [un document qui les condamnait à la détention perpétuelle.]$_{\text{DirObj/NP}}$ >> [un]$_{\text{Det/IndefArt}}$ [document]$_{\text{H/N}}$ [qui les condamnait à la détention perpétuelle]$_{\text{Postmod/SubordCl}}$

And in (30), the meaning of that subordinate clause has been paraphrased as a non-finite clause:

(30)   Il a rédigé [un document les condamnant à la détention perpétuelle.] $_{\text{DirObj/NP}}$ >> [un]$_{\text{Det/IndefArt}}$ [document]$_{\text{H/N}}$ [les condamnant à la détention perpétuelle]$_{\text{Postmod/PresentParticipleClause}}$

In these cases, we thus have (subordinate or reduced) clauses embedded within a phrase, i.e. a constituent being embedded within a constituent of lower rank than itself.

---

[11] For more details on the form and uses of infinitival clauses in French, see chapter 9.

This sort of embedding of clauses within clauses and of clauses within phrases can recur a potentially unlimited number of times in a sentence.[12] Thus, (31) below contains a total of seven subordinate clauses, several of which are embedded inside one or more other subordinate clauses, and many French writers have produced sentences of vastly greater complexity:[13]

(31) [Pendant qu'il faisait le ménage, [qu'il aurait d'ailleurs dû faire depuis des jours]], il se *disait* [que, [vu que cela faisait longtemps [qu'il n'avait pas parlé à l'ami italien [avec qui il était parti en Chine l'année dernière]]], il fallait absolument [qu'il passe un coup de téléphone à celui-ci]].

At the beginning of this section, recursion was said to be one of the most important properties of natural languages. It is partly thanks to the property of recursion that although human languages all have a finite number of words, they can nevertheless be used to create an infinite number of sentences, and can hence express an infinite number of meanings.

3.2.1.1 Subordinate clauses *vs* coordinated clauses

Some sentences contain more than one clause without there being a relation of grammatical subordination between those clauses. In the case of (32) below, for instance, either of the two clauses *Delphine est partie* and *Fabien a pleuré* could occur on its own as a grammatically complete message, as shown in (33)–(34):

(32) [Delphine est partie]$_{\text{Clause1}}$ et [Fabien a pleuré.]$_{\text{Clause2}}$.

(33) Delphine est partie.

(34) Fabien a pleuré.

In such cases, we speak of a **compound sentence** consisting of two or more **coordinated clauses**. Clauses can be coordinated using one of the

---

[12] Practical limits on recursion are set, not by the grammar as such, but by the capacity of both speakers/writers and addressees to keep track of what is being expressed.

[13] The main clause predicator being italicized and the square brackets indicating the limits of the individual clauses in (31), readers may attempt to work out for themselves exactly what is the grammatical role played by each of those seven subordinate clauses, and at what level of structure.

coordinating conjunctions *et, mais, ou (bien), soit, ni*, or *car*, or they can simply be separated by commas as in (35):[14]

(35)   [Delphine est partie], [Fabien a pleuré], [Corinne a essayé de le consoler].

Note that, unlike a subordinating conjunction, a coordinating conjunction does not belong to either of the clauses it coordinates, but plays the grammatical role of **coordinator** at the level of the sentence as a whole. Thus, if we change the order of the coordinated clauses in (32), the coordinator *et* stays in place, as shown in (36)–(37):

(36)   Fabien a pleuré et_{Coord} Delphine est partie.

(37)   *Et Fabien a pleuré, Delphine est partie.

Subordinating conjunctions, on the other hand, which introduce subordinate clauses, belong within the subordinate clause and will therefore move with it if the order of the clauses is changed, cf. (38)–(39):

(38)   [Je partirai]_{MainCl} [quand Hélène sera de retour.]_{SubordCl}

(39)   [Quand Hélène sera de retour,]_{SubordCl} [je partirai.]_{MainCl}

3.2.2 Non-finite clauses

Non-finite clauses have a non-finite verb form (i.e. either an infinitive, a past participle, a present participle, or a *gérondif*; see further chapters 9–11) as their head. They can thus be considered to represent reduced forms of finite clauses.

Non-finite verbs have valency just like finite verbs do, and their valency elements can be represented inside the non-finite verb phrase. In most circumstances, the subject will, however, remain implicit and its identity must be inferred from the context.

In some cases, the implied logical subject of a non-finite verb will be the grammatical subject of the main clause. Thus, in both (40) and (42) below, the logical subject of the infinitival clause is identical to the grammatical subject of the sentence as a whole, i.e. *je* representing the speaker. So from (40), we can infer (41), and from (42), we can infer (43). Notice that in both

[14] In addition, some grammarians consider *donc, puis*, and *or* to be coordinating conjunctions. In this book, they are considered to be instances of what is known as connective adverbs.

(40) and (42), the infinitival clauses contain grammatical valency elements, namely direct objects and in the case of (42), also a dative object:

(40)   J'aime [étudier la grammaire.]$_{\text{DirObj/InfCl}}$ >> [étudier]$_{\text{H/Inf}}$ [la grammaire]$_{\text{DirObj/}}$
$_{\text{NP}}$

(41)   J'étudie la grammaire.

(42)   J'ai promis [d'offrir à Dominique un livre sur la grammaire française.]$_{\text{DirObj/}}$
$_{\text{InfCl}}$ >> [d']$_{\text{Premod/InfinitiveMarker}}$[15] [offrir]$_{\text{H/Inf}}$ [à Dominique]$_{\text{DatObj/PP}}$ [un livre
sur la grammaire française]$_{\text{DirObj/NP}}$

(43)   J'offrirai à Dominique un livre sur la grammaire française.

In other cases, such as (44), it is the main clause direct object that is the implied logical subject of the non-finite verb. Thus, from (44), we can infer (45):

(44)   J'ai invité [Gabriel]$_{\text{DirObj/NP}}$ [à participer à la réunion.]$_{\text{PrepObj/PP}}$ >> [à]$_{\text{H/Prep}}$
[participer à la réunion]$_{\text{Compl of Prep/InfCl}}$

(45)   Gabriel participera peut-être à la réunion.

3.2.3 Absolute constructions

An absolute construction is a kind of reduced clause consisting of two elements, a 'base' and a 'predicate', between which there is a non-hierarchical relation (cf. section 2.4). In other words, neither the base nor the predicate can be left out of an absolute construction. These constructions are called absolute, because they are not introduced by a conjunction or a preposition.

In French, two types of absolute construction are found. In the first type, the base corresponds to the grammatical subject of a subordinate clause, while the predicate is equivalent to the predicator of such a clause. This type of absolute construction typically functions as an **adverbial** (but see section 9.2.1.1).

In (46) below, we have an absolute construction between square brackets. As shown in (47), it can be paraphrased as a subordinate clause:

---

[15] This *de* is analysed as an infinitive marker rather than as a preposition because the verb *promettre* takes the thing promised as a direct object (*promettre quelque chose*), not a prepositional object (**promettre de quelque chose*). For the distinction between prepositions and infinitive markers, see further chapter 9.

(46)   [Pierre$_{Base}$ parti$_{Pred}$]$_{AbsConstr}$, on parla de lui.

(47)   [Quand Pierre$_{Subj}$ fut parti$_{Pred}$], on parla de lui.

In the second type of absolute construction, exemplified in (48) and (50) below, the base corresponds to the direct object of an independent clause, while the predicate corresponds to an object attribute or a locative object, as shown in (49) and (51):

(48)   Laure se promenait <u>pieds nus</u>.

(49)   Laure se promenait. Elle avait [les pieds]$_{DirObj}$ [nus.]$_{ObjAttr}$

(50)   Pierre s'en alla, <u>les mains dans les poches</u>.

(51)   Pierre s'en alla. Il avait [les mains]$_{DirObj}$ [dans les poches.]$_{LocObj}$

Depending on its position, this type of absolute construction functions either as an **apposition** to a noun phrase or as a **free indirect attribute** (see section 2.2.4 below).

3.2.4 *Free indirect attributes and appositions*

Up until now, we have analysed as adverbials all clause constituents which could be left out without causing ungrammaticality. French does, however, possess a type of clause-level constituent which is not a valency element, but which is not really an adverbial either, as demonstrated by the fact that it will—wherever possible—agree in gender and number with some other constituent of the clause. This type of constituent is known as a **free indirect attribute**.

At the level of noun phrases, we also find a type of non-restrictive postmodifier, called **appositions**, which are rather like free indirect attributes in meaning. The two types of constituent differ only in their syntax. For one thing, they take up different positions inside a clause. Secondly, they do not have the same status: free indirect attributes are clause-level constituents, whereas appositions are normally phrase-level constituents. Both can be considered to be reduced clauses.

3.2.4.1 Free indirect attributes
Free indirect attributes (FIAs) are loosely connected to another constituent (normally either the subject or the direct object), which they describe in much the same way as a subject attribute describes the subject, or an object

attribute describes the direct object. They agree with that constituent in number and gender where possible, but are syntactically optional.

Free indirect attributes may occur before the constituent that they describe, as in (52) below. In that case, they can be paraphrased by a subordinate clause functioning as an adverbial, as in (53):

(52)   [Divorcée depuis dix ans]_{FIAtoSubj}, [j]_{Subj}'utilise encore le nom de mon ex-mari.

(53)   <u>Bien que je sois divorcée depuis dix ans</u>, j'utilise encore le nom de mon ex-mari.

Free indirect attributes may also follow the constituent they describe, in which case they will be separated from that constituent by one or more other constituents. This is what we see in (54) below, where the predicator *s'en est allé* intervenes between the free indirect attribute *très découragé*, and the subject *il*. In such cases, the attribute can usually be paraphrased by an independent clause, as in (55):

(54)   [Il]_{Subj} s'en est allé, [très découragé.]_{FIAtoSubj}

(55)   Il s'en est allé. <u>Il était très découragé.</u>

Unlike subject and object attributes, which express central new information and which are valency elements that cannot be left out of the clause (see sections 1.2.3.1 and 1.2.3.8), free indirect attributes express information that is backgrounded with respect to other parts of the clause, and like adverbials, they can therefore be left out without causing ungrammaticality, as (56)–(57) show:[16]

(56)   J'utilise encore le nom de mon ex-mari.

(57)   Il s'en est allé.

3.2.4.2 Appositions

Appositions occur as postmodifiers within noun phrases. In order to understand the concept of an apposition, we have to make a distinction between restrictive and non-restrictive modifiers. Appositions are of the non-restrictive type.

A restrictive postmodifier is necessary in order for the hearer to be able to identify the referent of the noun phrase.

---

[16] Because English does not have gender/number agreement in adjectives, nouns, and participles, English equivalents of French free indirect attributes are typically analysed as adverbials.

In both (58) and (59) below, we have subject noun phrases which, if spoken, would constitute only a single intonation unit. That is, no part of that noun phrase, other than the last syllable of *fatigués*, would receive stress, and we would not mark a pause between the head and the postmodifier, because the latter is in both cases a restrictive postmodifier. Both these postmodifiers allow us to identify a subset of the total number of students, namely those students, and only those students, who were tired. In other words, we can infer that some students were not tired and therefore did not go home.

(58)   Les étudiants fatigués sont rentrés. >> [[Les]$_{Det}$ [étudiants]$_H$ [fatigués] $_{RestrictivePostmod}$]$_{Subj/NP}$ (= only some of the students, namely those who were tired)

(59)   Les étudiants qui étaient fatigués sont rentrés. >> [[Les]$_{Det}$ [étudiants]$_H$ [qui étaient fatigués]$_{RestrictivePostmod}$]$_{Subj/NP}$

A **non-restrictive postmodifier**, i.e. an apposition, merely gives additional information about the referent, but is not necessary for its identification.

Thus, in (60)–(61) below, the determiner *mes* is sufficient to allow the addressee to identify the students in question, and the appositions just give additional information. Because we are not talking about merely a subset of the students in these sentences, we can add the quantifier *tous*. If spoken, an apposition normally constitutes a separate intonation unit from that formed by the rest of the noun phrase; in other words, it will be surrounded by pauses, and the last syllable of both the head noun and the apposition will receive stress. In written French, appositions are therefore usually (although not invariably) separated from the rest of the noun phrase by a comma, as shown in (60)–(61):

(60)   Mes étudiants, (tous) fatigués, sont rentrés. >> [[Mes]$_{Det}$ [étudiants]$_H$, [(tous) fatigués]$_{AppositionalPostmod}$]$_{Subj/NP}$ (= all the students, who just happened to be tired)

(61)   Mes étudiants, qui étaient (tous) fatigués, sont rentrés. >> [[Mes]$_{Det}$ [étudiants]$_H$, [qui étaient (tous) fatigués]$_{AppositionalPostmod}$]$_{Subj/NP}$

In contrast to restrictive modifiers, appositions are backgrounded information, as shown by the fact that we can add the adverbial *d'ailleurs* ('by the way') to an apposition, as in (62)–(63):

(62)   Mes étudiants, d'ailleurs (tous) fatigués, sont rentrés.

(63)   Mes étudiants, qui étaient d'ailleurs (tous) fatigués, sont rentrés.

In this way, appositions resemble free indirect attributes. Thus, (60) is very similar in meaning to (64)–(65), both of which contain free indirect attributes:

(64) [(Tous) fatigués]$_{\text{FIAtoSubj}}$, mes étudiants sont rentrés.

(65) Mes étudiants sont rentrés, [(tous) fatigués]$_{\text{FIAtoSubj}}$.

Unlike free indirect attributes, however, appositions are placed immediately after the noun phrase they modify, and if that noun phrase is replaced by a pronoun, the apposition cannot remain, but will disappear with the rest of the noun phrase, as shown in (66)–(67):

(66) Ils sont rentrés.

(67) *Ils, (qui étaient)(tous)fatigués, sont rentrés.

Normally, appositions can be paraphrased by an independent parenthetical clause, as shown in (68):

(68) Mes étudiants—ils étaient (tous) fatigués—sont rentrés.

3.3 Conclusion

All the major kinds of sentence constituent have now been introduced, along with the notions of subordination and coordination of constituents. Appendix A contains a full list of sentence-, clause-, and phrase-level grammatical functions in French.

French, however, possesses a wide range of different types of subordinate clauses, which are dissimilar in form, and have correspondingly different functions with respect to their main clause. Chapter 4 presents a typology of subordinate clauses in French.

As subsequent chapters will show, what specific type a given subordinate clause belongs to will often determine the grammatical form, meaning, and behaviour of some of the elements inside that subordinate clause. It is therefore important to be able to distinguish the different types of subordinate clause.

4

Subordinate clauses

Learning objectives

- To be able to identify different types of subordinate clauses in French at the most general level (three in total).
- To be able to identify different sub-types of the general types of subordinate clauses (14 in total).
- To be able to identify the grammatical role played by any given subordinate clause within the main clause.
- To be able to analyse the internal grammatical structure of subordinate clauses.

4.1 Introduction

As we saw in section 3.2, subordinate clauses function as (parts of) constituents within other clauses. Thus, in (1) below, the subordinate clause functions as the direct object of the main clause predicator *crois*, while in (2), the subordinate clause functions as a postmodifier inside the main clause subject noun phrase:

(1)   Je crois [que tu as raison.]_{DirObj/SubordCl}

The Structure of Modern Standard French. First edition. Maj-Britt Mosegaard Hansen.
© Maj-Britt Mosegaard Hansen 2016. First Published 2016 by Oxford University Press

(2) [L'homme [qui est venu]$_{Postmod/SubordCl}$]$_{Subj/NP}$ s'appelle Benoît Miellet.

Unlike English, subordinate clauses in standard French must always be introduced by a subordinator. Thus, while both (3) and (4) below are grammatical sentences of English, only (5) is possible in standard French. The construction in (6), on the other hand, is not:

(3) I think [that you're right.]

(4) I think [Ø[1] you're right.]

(5) Je crois [que tu as raison.]

(6) *Je crois [Ø tu as raison.]

Subordinators take the form of **subordinating conjunctions**, such as *que*[2] in (1) above, **relative pronouns/adverbs**, such as *qui* in (2), or (indirect) **interrogative pronouns/adverbs**, such as *quoi* in (7) below.[3]

(7) Je ne sais absolument pas [de quoi tu parles.]

4.2 Types of subordinate clauses

At the highest level, we can distribute subordinate clauses into three classes according to their most typical grammatical functions:

• **Nominal clauses**, which usually fulfil grammatical functions that are typical of noun phrases, i.e. subject, direct object, complement of a preposition, etc.
• **Adjectival clauses**, which usually fulfil grammatical functions that are typical of adjectives, i.e. postmodifier, object attribute, or free indirect attribute.
• **Adverbial clauses**, which usually fulfil the grammatical function typical of adverbs, i.e. adverbial.

---

[1] Recall that the symbol Ø represents an empty grammatical slot.
[2] No distinction will be made in this book between complementizers and subordinators.
[3] For further details on interrogative and relative pronouns and adverbs, see chapter 19.

4.2.1 Nominal clauses

Nominal clauses divide further into three different subtypes: complement clauses, indirect interrogative clauses, and free relative clauses. Each of these will be treated in turn below.

4.2.1.1 Complement clauses

Complement clauses in French are normally introduced by the subordinating conjunction *que* (= 'that'). This conjunction can only ever function as a subordinator;[4] that is, it does not have any additional grammatical function within the subordinate clause.

Complement clauses principally function as subjects (as in (8) below), direct objects (cf. (9)), or complements of prepositions (see (11)–(15) below). All of these are so-called **nominal functions**, because they are typically fulfilled by noun phrases:

(8) [Que_Subordinator/SubordinatingConjunction Juliette Binoche ait gagné le prix de l'interprétation féminine]_Subj/ComplementClause ne m'étonne pas.

(9) Je veux absolument [que_Subord/SubordConj tu viennes !]_DirObj/ComplCl

More rarely, complement clauses can function as subject attributes (cf. (10) below). This is a so-called adjectival function, because it is typically fulfilled by adjectives:

(10) L'essentiel, c'est [que_Subord/SubordConj tu signes.]_SubjAttr/ComplCl

As mentioned above, complement clauses can function as complements of prepositions. It is, however, impossible in French to have a complement clause introduced by *que* directly following a preposition. There are three possible solutions to this dilemma:

• In some cases, one can simply leave the preposition implicit, as shown in (11) below. This is the preferred solution if the preposition is *de*:

(11) Je m'étonne Ø [qu'il ait pu se tromper sur ce point.]_PrepObj/PP
      >> [Ø]_H/Prep [qu'il ait pu se tromper sur ce point]_Compl/ComplCl

---

[4] Note, however, that French has different types of function word taking the form *que*: besides the subordinating conjunction, we also find the form *que* as a relative pronoun and as an interrogative pronoun.

In such cases, pronominalization (i.e. application of the substitution test, cf. section 2.6.1) will show that the complement clause does nevertheless function as a prepositional complement, cf. (12)–(13):

(12)   Je m'étonne de cela.

(13)   Je m'en étonne.

- In other cases, *ce* can be inserted before *que*, to form a complex subordinating conjunction *ce que*, as shown in (14) below. This is the preferred solution if the preposition is *à*:

(14)   La secrétaire n'est pas habituée [à ce qu'on lui parle sur ce ton.]$_{PrepObj/PP}$
    >> [à]$_{H/Prep}$ [ce qu'on lui parle sur ce ton]$_{Compl/ComplCl}$
    >> [ce qu']$_{Subord/SubordConj}$ [on]$_{Subj/PersPr}$ [lui]$_{DatObj/PersPr}$ [parle]$_{Pred/FinV}$ [sur ce ton]$_{Adv'al/PP}$

- Finally, one can use the complex conjunction *le fait/l'idée que* instead of *que* alone, as shown in (15) below. This is the preferred solution after all prepositions other than *de* and *à*:

(15)   Nous attirons votre attention [sur le fait que le délai de réclamation est expiré.]$_{PrepObj/PP}$
    >> [sur]$_{H/Prep}$ [le fait que le délai de réclamation est expiré]$_{Compl/ComplCl}$
    >> [le fait que]$_{Subord/SubordConj}$ [le délai de réclamation]$_{Subj/NP}$ [est]$_{Pred/FinV}$ [expiré]$_{SubjAttr/PastPart}$

In contrast, (16)–(18) below are all ungrammatical, because in each case the complement clause directly follows the preposition:

(16)   *Je m'étonne [de [qu'il ait pu se tromper sur ce point.]$_{Compl\ of\ Prep/ComplCl}$] $_{PrepObj/PP}$

(17)   *La secrétaire n'est pas habitué(e) [à [qu'on lui parle sur ce ton.]$_{Compl\ of\ Prep/ComplCl}$]$_{PrepObj/PP}$

(18)   *Nous attirons votre attention [sur [que le délai de réclamation est expiré.]$_{Compl\ of\ Prep/ComplCl}$]$_{PrepObj/PP}$

4.2.1.2 Indirect interrogative clauses

Indirect interrogative clauses are derived from direct interrogative clauses. Direct interrogatives are a type of independent clause which is used to ask a question. Subordinate clauses of the indirectly interrogative type thus imply a question, typically presented as a form of reported speech or thought.

There are two subtypes of indirect interrogatives, depending on the type of direct interrogative they are derived from.

Yes/no interrogatives

Direct yes/no interrogatives ask whether the information presented in the clause is true or false. In other words, they can be answered by either *yes* or *no*. In French, direct yes/no-interrogatives can be constructed in three different ways: With verb-subject clitic inversion, as in (19) below:[5]

(19)   As-tu déjà été à Berlin ?

With *est-ce que*, as in (20):

(20)   Est-ce que tu as déjà été à Berlin ?

With rising intonation, as in (21)(where ↑ indicates sharply rising intonation on the following syllable):

(21)   Tu as déjà été à Ber↑lin ?

All of these are converted into indirect interrogatives in the same way, using the subordinating conjunction *si*,[6] as shown in (22) below. The conjunction *si* functions exclusively as a subordinator (i.e. it plays no additional grammatical role in the subordinate clause).

(22)   Marie-France te demande [si$_{\text{Subord/SubordConj}}$ tu as déjà été à Berlin.]$_{\text{DirObj/}}$
IndirInterrogCl

WH-interrogatives

Direct WH-interrogatives inquire about the identity of a specific constituent of the sentence, represented by a so-called WH-word, i.e. items like *who*, *what*, *when*, etc. in English and *qui*, *que*, *quoi*, etc. in French (where they are known as QU-words).

---

[5] Inversion is when you have the 'inverted' word order verb-subject rather than subject-verb. In formal French, direct interrogatives feature inversion when a WH-word is not the subject of the clause (cf. (25) and (29) below). For further details, see section 24.4.

[6] Note that this interrogative *si* is different from the *si* used to introduce conditional clauses (cf. section 4.2.3.2 below), and of course also from the response word *si* (cf. section 22.2).

WH-words in French take the form of interrogative pronouns, as in (23)–(27) below, adverbs, as in (29)–(30), or articles, as in (31) (see section 19.2 for details about the uses of these items):

(23) [Qui]$_{\text{Subj/InterrogPron}}$ a fermé la porte ?

(24) [Qui est-ce qui]$_{\text{Subj/InterrogPron}}$ a fermé la porte ?

(25) [Qu']$_{\text{DirObj/InterrogPron}}$ as-tu fermé ?

(26) [Qu'est-ce que]$_{\text{DirObj/InterrogPron}}$ tu as fermé ?

(27) Tu as fermé [quoi ?]$_{\text{DirObj/InterrogPr}}$

(28) J'ai fermé [la porte.]$_{\text{DirObj}}$

(29) [Pourquoi]$_{\text{Adv'al/InterrogAdv}}$ as-tu fermé la porte ?

(30) [Pourquoi est-ce que]$_{\text{Adv'al/InterrogAdv}}$ tu as fermé la porte ?

(31) Tu as fermé la porte [pour quelle raison ?]$_{\text{Adv'al/PP}}$
    >> [pour]$_{\text{H/Prep}}$ [quelle raison]$_{\text{Compl/NP}}$
    >> [quelle]$_{\text{Det/InterrogArt}}$ [raison]$_{\text{H/N}}$

(32) J'ai fermé la porte [parce qu'il y avait un courant d'air.]$_{\text{Adv'al/AdverbialClause}}$

Normally, the WH-word is placed at the beginning of the clause. However, as we see if we compare (27) above with (28), and (31) with (32), the WH-word may also occur in the same position where we would find the constituent answering the question in a declarative clause.

In many, although far from all, cases, direct WH-interrogatives can be converted into indirect interrogatives using the same interrogative pronoun/adverb, but without using inversion or *est-ce que/qui*, as shown in (33)–(34) below. When the referent of an interrogative pronoun is an inanimate entity, a *ce* must usually be inserted before the QU-form, as shown in (35). Further details can be found in section 19.2.2.

(33) J'aimerais savoir [qui$_{\text{Subord+Subj/InterrogPron}}$ a fermé la porte.]$_{\text{DirObj/IndirInterrogCl}}$

(34) Dis-moi [pourquoi$_{\text{Subord+Adv'al/InterrogAdv}}$ tu as fermé la porte !]$_{\text{DirObj/IndirInterrogCl}}$

(35) Max ne se souvenait pas [de ce qu'il avait dit.]$_{\text{PrepObj/PP}}$
    >> [de]$_{\text{H/Prep}}$ [ce qu'$_{\text{Subord+DirObj/InterrogPron}}$ il avait dit]$_{\text{Compl/IndirInterrogCl}}$

In indirect WH-interrogatives, the interrogative pronoun/adverb functions as a subordinator, but simultaneously fulfils another grammatical function inside the indirect interrogative clause, as illustrated in (33)

above, where the subordinator *qui* is also the subject of the indirect interrogative, and in (34), where *pourquoi* functions simultaneously as a subordinator and as an adverbial. Thus, from (33) we can infer (36) below, while
(34) allows us to infer (37), and (35) licenses the inference to (38):

(36)   [Quelqu'un]$_{Subj}$ avait fermé la porte.

(37)   Tu as fermé la porte [pour une raison.]$_{Adv'al}$

(38)   Max a dit [quelque chose.]$_{DirObj}$

Indirect interrogative clauses typically function as direct objects of the
main clause predicator, as (22) and (33)–(34) above show. This is true of
both *yes/no*-interrogatives and WH-interrogatives. Other possibilities do
exist, however, such as the structure in (35) above, where the indirect
interrogative is the complement of a preposition.

4.2.1.3 Free relative clauses

Free relative clauses[7] are introduced by *ce* followed by a relative pronoun or
adverb. We will refer to such combinations as free relative pronouns.[8]

Thus, free relative clauses frequently look like, and can therefore easily be
confused with, indirect WH-interrogatives of the type seen in (35) above.
Unlike indirect WH-interrogatives, however, free relative clauses do not
have interrogative meaning, i.e. they do not imply a question.

If we compare (39) and (40) below, we see that in both cases, the direct
object of the main predicator is a subordinate clause, and that in both cases,
this subordinate clause, superficially at least, has the exact same form:

(39)   Je ne sais pas [ce qu'$_{Subord+DirObj/InterrogPron}$ il a fait.]$_{DirObj/IndirInterrogCl}$
       ($\rightarrow$ I'm unsure about what he did.)
       'I don't know what he did.'

(40)   Je n'approuve pas [ce qu'$_{Subord+DirObj/FreeRelativePronoun}$ il a fait.]$_{DirObj/}$
       $_{FreeRelativeClause}$
       ($\rightarrow$ I know what he did.)
       'I disapprove of what/that which he did.'

---

[7] Free relative clauses differ from adjectival relative clauses (cf. section 4.2.2
below) by not being dependent on a preceding noun phrase, a so-called 'antecedent'.

[8] For further details on the use of (free) relative pronouns, see section 19.3.

However, in (39), we are dealing with an indirect interrogative because the meaning of the main clause *je ne sais pas* implies uncertainty, hence a question, about what it was that 'he' did. In (40), on the other hand, there is no such implied question; indeed, the main clause *je n'approuve pas* would not be meaningful unless the speaker already knew what 'he' did (because you cannot disapprove of something unless you know what that something is). In this case, we are therefore dealing with a free relative clause.

Notice that in (40), it is possible (although unidiomatic) to translate *ce que* into English as 'that which', whereas in (39), *ce que* can only be translated as 'what'.

Most free relative clauses are introduced by *ce qui, ce que, ce* + preposition + *quoi*, or *ce dont*. Free relative clauses can function as subjects, as in (41) below, as direct objects, as in (42), as complements of prepositions, as in (43), and as subject attributes, as in (44):

(41) [Ce que~Subord+DirObj/FreeRelPr~ tu penses]~Subj/FreeRelCl~ ne m'intéresse pas.

(42) Fais [ce que~Subord+DirObj/FreeRelPr~ tu veux.]~DirObj/FreeRelCl~

(43) Je pense souvent [à ce que Pierre m'a dit.]~PrepObj/PP~
      >> [à]~H/Prep~ [ce que~Subord+DirObj/FreeRelPron~ Pierre m'a dit.]~Compl of Prep/FreeRelCl~

(44) Pour lui, l'argent est [ce qui~Subord+Subj/FreeRelPron~ compte le plus.]~SubjAttr/~
      ~FreeRelCl~

In all cases, the free relative pronoun/adverb functions as a **subordinator** within the free relative clause, but it simultaneously fulfils an additional grammatical function within that clause, as shown by the subscripts in (41)–(44).

Sometimes a free relative clause may be introduced by *qui*. Free relative clauses of this type are used only about human beings. It is usually only in proverbs such as (45) below that these clauses can function as the subject of the main clause, conveying the non-specific sense of English *whoever*:

(45) [Rira]~Pred/FinV~ [bien]~Adv'al/Adv~ [qui~Subord+Subj/FreeRelPron~ rira le dernier.]~Subj/~
      ~FreeRelCl~
      'He who laughs last laughs longest.', literally 'Laughs well who(ever) laughs last.'

In less formal registers, free relative clauses of this type can function as either direct objects (as in (46) below) or complements of prepositions, as in

(47). In the latter example, the pronoun moreover refers – albeit obliquely –
to a specific individual:

(46)   Géraldine embrasse [qui_{Subord+Subj/FreeRelPron} en a envie.]_{DirObj/FreeRelCl}
'Géraldine will kiss whoever wants her to.'

(47)   J'ai parlé [à qui tu sais.]_{DatObj/PP}
>> [à]_{H/Prep} [qui_{Subord+DirObj/FreeRelPron} tu sais]_{Compl of Prep/FreeRelCl}
'I've spoken to you know who.'

4.2.2 Adjectival clauses

The second major type of subordinate clause in French is adjectival clauses.
Adjectival clauses are more commonly known as **relative clauses** (of the
non-free kind, as opposed to the free relative clauses discussed in section
4.2.1.3 above). They are called adjectival because they usually fulfil the same
grammatical functions as adjectives. Principally, relative clauses function as
postmodifiers within noun phrases. However, as we will see, some subtypes
of relative clauses have other grammatical functions.

In French, adjectival relative clauses must always be introduced by a
relative pronoun or a relative adverb referring back to a constituent of the
main clause, as shown in (48) below. This constituent is called the **antecedent**
of the relative pronoun.

(48)   Anne a parlé *du film*_{Antecedent} [qu'_{Subord+DirObj/RelativePronoun} elle avait vu la
veille.]_{RelativeClause}

In contrast, English relative clauses sometimes dispense with the relative
pronoun/adverb, as seen in (49), where *which/that* is optional in the slot
marked by Ø:

(49)   Anne talked about *the movie*_{Ant} [Ø she'd seen the night before.]_{RelCl}.

As shown in (50), a relative clause can, in principle, be paraphrased as an
independent clause in which the antecedent is simply repeated:

(50)   Anne a parlé *d'un film*. Elle avait vu [ce film]_{DirObj/NP} la veille.

Just like indirect interrogative pronouns/adverbs and free relative pronouns/
adverbs, 'regular' relative pronouns/adverbs function as subordinators, but
simultaneously fulfil an additional grammatical function inside the relative
clause (cf. (48) above).

French has three types of adjectival relative clauses, as described below. Only the first two of these have equivalents in English.

4.2.2.1 Restrictive relative clauses

Restrictive relative clauses follow directly after their antecedent, with no comma or intonation break, and they are necessary for the hearer to identify the referent of the antecedent (cf. section 3.2.4.2) Thus, when hearing or reading (51) below, we will understand that it is only some of the students who cheated in the exam:

(51)   [*Les étudiants*$_{Ant}$ qui ont triché à l'examen]$_{Subj/NP}$ seront punis.
>> [les]$_{Det/DefArt}$ [étudiants]$_{H/N}$ [qui ont triché à l'examen]$_{Postmod/RelCl}$

Restrictive relative clauses always function as **postmodifiers** within noun phrases (or more rarely, within pronominal phrases).

4.2.2.2 Non-restrictive relative clauses

Non-restrictive, also known as 'parenthetical' or 'appositional' (cf. section 3.2.4.2), relative clauses express information that is not considered necessary for the identification of the antecedent. This is why they are known as parenthetical relative clauses: they simply express additional information about the referent in question. When hearing or reading (52) below, we will therefore understand that all the students cheated and are going to be punished.

(52)   [Les étudiants, qui ont (tous) triché à l'examen,]$_{Subj/NP}$ seront punis.
>> [Les]$_{Det/DefArt}$ [étudiants,]$_{H/N}$ [qui ont triché à l'examen]$_{ApposPostmod/RelCl}$

As a rule of thumb, one can therefore insert the adverb *d'ailleurs* ('incidentally') in a non-restrictive relative clause without changing the basic meaning of the noun phrase, as shown in (53):

(53)   Les étudiants, qui—*d'ailleurs*—ont (tous) triché à l'examen, seront punis.

In speech, non-restrictive relative clauses are separated from their antecedent by an intonation break, and in writing, typically—but by no means always—by a comma.

Non-restrictive relative clauses typically function as **appositional postmodifiers** within noun phrases.

Sentential relative clauses

In some cases, the **antecedent** of a non-restrictive relative clause is not a noun phrase, but a whole finite clause, an infinitival clause, or an adjectival phrase.

In those cases, the relative clause will be introduced by *ce qui, ce que, ce à quoi*, etc. (cf. section 19.3.4 for details), and it functions independently as an adverbial of the main clause. In (54) below, the relative pronoun *ce qui* thus refers back to the whole clause *ça m'a quand meme bien humilié*, which is its antecedent:

(54)   Ça n'a pas duré longtemps, mais *ça m'a quand même bien humilié*_{Ant}, [ce qui est très désagréable.]_{Adv'al/RelCl}

4.2.2.3 Predicative relative clauses

Whereas all the subordinate clause types discussed above have equivalents in English, French has a third type of relative clause besides restrictive and non-restrictive relative clauses. This third type is known as **predicative relative clauses**, and is not found in English. A French predicative relative clause will therefore typically be translated into English using a present participle.

Predicative relative clauses are used in connection with verbs of perception (*voir, entendre*, etc.) or with *avoir, être,* or *rester*. As shown in (55) below, they are always introduced by *qui*, can be separated from their antecedent by one or more other clause constituents, and can function as free indirect attributes:

(55)   [Magali]_{Subj/NP(Antecedent)} restait là [qui regardait les affiches.]_{FIA/PredicativeRelCl}
       'Magali stayed there looking at the posters.'

This construction is rarely used in contemporary French, and the same meaning can be expressed by a prepositional phrase with *à* taking an infinitival clause as its complement, as shown in (56), or by two independent clauses, as in (57):

(56)   Magali restait là [à regarder les affiches.]_{FIA/PP}
       >> [à]_{H/Prep} [regarder les affiches]_{Compl/InfCl}

(57)   Magali restait là. Elle regardait les affiches.

Unlike what is the case with other types of relative clauses, the antecedent of a predicative relative clause may be an unstressed personal pronoun, as shown in (58):

(58) Alexis [l']$_{\text{DirObj/PersPron(Antecedent)}}$ a entendu [qui chantait sous la douche.]$_{\text{FIA/}}$
$_{\text{PredRelCl}}$

Again, the same meaning is more commonly expressed using an infinitival clause, as in (59), or two independent clauses, as in (60):

(59) Alexis [l']$_{\text{DirObj/PersPr}}$ a entendu [chanter sous la douche.]$_{\text{FIA/InfCl}}$

(60) Alexis l'a entendu. Il chantait sous la douche.

Predicative relative clauses can also function as **object attributes**, as in (61) below. In this type of construction, the relative clause cannot be paraphrased by an infinitival clause and, while grammatical, the simple sentence in (62) is not appropriately used in the same types of context:

(61) J'ai [le cœur]$_{\text{DirObj/NP(Antecedent)}}$ [qui bat.]$_{\text{ObjAttr/PredRelCl}}$
'My heart's beating (with fear/excitement/ . . .).'

(62) Mon cœur bat.
'My heart beats.' (i.e. I'm alive.)

4.2.3 Adverbial clauses

Adverbial clauses usually (but not always, see below) function as adverbials inside the main clause. Like other types of adverbials, they are sub-classified according to their meaning (see section 4.2.3.2 below).

4.2.3.1 Conjunctions introducing adverbial clauses

The conjunctions that introduce adverbial clauses can be simple, like *si* in (63) below, or complex, like *pour que* in (64) and they always function exclusively as subordinators:

(63) [*Si* David était ici]$_{\text{Adv'al/ConditionalCl}}$, je lui dirais mes quatre vérités.

(64) Je ne te dis pas ça [*pour que* tu te sentes coupable.]$_{\text{Adv'al/PurposeCl}}$

Complex conjunctions can consist of a frozen combination of:

- a preposition + *que* (e.g. *pour que* in (64) above);
- an adverb + *que*, as in (65):

(65) [*Bien qu'*il soit intelligent]$_{\text{ConcessiveCl}}$, il est trop paresseux pour faire du bon travail.

- a verb form + *que*, as in (66):

(66)   L'industrie automobile est obligée d'innover constamment [*étant donné que* la concurrence est sévère.]CausalCl

- a prepositional phrase + *que/où*, as in (67):

(67)   Tu peux aller à la soirée, [*à condition que* tu rentres avant minuit.]ConditionalCl

It is important to be aware that some conjunctions have more than one possible meaning, and may thus introduce two or more different types of adverbial clause. Thus, the conjunction *comme*, for instance, can introduce comparison clauses, as in (68) below, causal clauses, as in (69), or temporal clauses, as in (70):

(68)   Malheureusement, il n'a pas pu venir nous aider [*comme* il l'avait promis.]ComparisonCl

(69)   [*Comme* Gabriel n'a pas su s'adapter à la nouvelle structure]CausalCl, il s'est fait virer de son poste.

(70)   J'ai vu Laurence [*comme* elle montait dans le bus.]TemporalCl

Conversely, most types of adverbial clause can be introduced by a restricted set of different conjunctions, but these conjunctions do not always have precisely the same meaning, and they are therefore often not freely interchangeable.

To take a few examples, a concessive clause introduced by *bien que* ('although') is a so-called 'real' concessive, which describes something which is actually the case. A concessive clause introduced by *même si* ('even if'), on the other hand, is an 'unreal' concessive (also known as a concessive conditional), which describes a hypothetical state of affairs. See further section 4.2.3.2 below.

4.2.3.2 Subtypes of adverbial clauses

French has a total of eight different subtypes of adverbial clauses, which express different aspects of the circumstances under which the main clause is true. As will be seen in chapters 6–7 below, the use of tense, aspect, and particularly mood in French adverbial clauses is often closely linked to the subtype of the adverbial clause in question, and even to the specific conjunction used.

Temporal clauses

Temporal clauses express aspects that have to do with the timing of the situation described in the main clause, as in (71)–(73) below:

(71)   Luc dormait [quand Sophie est rentrée.]_{Adv'al/TemporalCl}

(72)   Luc dort [jusqu'à ce que Sophie le réveille.]_{Adv'al/TemporalCl}

(73)   Sophie a pris sa douche [pendant que Luc préparait le petit déjeuner.]_{Adv'al/}
    _{TemporalCl}

The exact temporal relation between the main clause and the subordinate clause, for instance whether they take place simultaneously or one before/after the other, is expressed by the specific conjunction introducing the subordinate clause. Temporal conjunctions thus cannot be used interchangeably.

Causal clauses

Causal clauses express the causes of the situation described in the main clause, as in (74) below; the speaker's reasons for believing the main clause to be true, as in (75), or their reasons for uttering the main clause, as in (76):

(74)   Pierre-Henri a épousé Muriel [parce qu'elle est riche.]_{Adv'al/CausalCl}

(75)   Muriel doit être riche, [vu que Pierre-Henri l'a épousée.]_{Adv'al/CausalCl}

(76)   Mais épouse-la, [puisqu'elle est riche !]_{Adv'al/CausalCl}

Causal conjunctions in French are specialized for one or two of these three types of causality, and cannot be used interchangeably.

The conjunction *comme* ('as') can have causal meaning only if the subordinate clause precedes the main clause, as in (77) below. If an adverbial clause introduced by *comme* follows the main clause, it will have either temporal or comparative meaning, as shown in section 4.2.3.1 above:

(77)   [*Comme* Muriel est riche,]_{Adv'al/CausalCl} Pierre-Henri désire l'épouser.

Although the conjunction *car* ('for') has causal meaning, it is a coordinating conjunction (cf. sections 3.2.1.1 and 22.3.2), not a subordinating one. Clauses introduced by *car* are therefore not adverbial clauses, but independent clauses.

Conditional clauses

Conditional clauses express hypothetical circumstances under which the state of affairs described by the main clause will be, might be, or would have been true, for example (78)–(80) below:

(78) [Pour peu qu'Alain ait fait son travail,]$_{Adv'al/ConditionalCl}$ on pourra soumettre le rapport à la fin de la semaine.

(79) [En supposant qu'il fût bien représenté par son avocat,]$_{Adv'al/ConditionalCl}$ l'enquête pourrait être courte.

(80) [Si Fleur était venue,]$_{Adv'al/ConditionalCl}$ on aurait été treize à table.

Conditionals, i.e. the combination of a conditional clause and a main clause, come in three types, which use different tenses (see section 6.4 for details), and possibly different conjunctions, as well:

- **'Real' conditionals**, where the speaker considers it entirely possible that the subordinate clause may be true and that the main clause will thus be true as well. Such a conditional is exemplified by (78) above.
- **'Potential' conditionals**, where the speaker considers it possible, but unlikely, that the subordinate clause is true, and hence also unlikely that the main clause will be true, as exemplified in (79).
- **'Unreal'** (or **counterfactual**) **conditionals**, where the speaker knows that both the main clause and the subordinate clause are untrue, as in (80). Thus, from (80), we can infer that Fleur did not, in fact, come, and so there were not thirteen dinner guests, but only twelve.

Some conjunctions (prominently *si*) can occur in all three types, whereas others tend to prefer a specific subtype.

Concessive clauses

Like conditionals, concessive constructions come in several types:

- **'Real' concessives**, such as (81) below, are related to causal clauses, in as much as they express the fact that some causal relation which might have been expected to obtain, in fact does not obtain. In other words, we might have expected that Pierre-Henri would not want to marry Muriel because of her poverty, but in fact he does intend to marry her:

(81) Pierre-Henri épousera Muriel [bien qu'elle soit pauvre.]$_{Adv'al/ConcessiveCl}$

- **'Unreal' concessives**, such as (82) below, are related to both causal constructions and conditionals, in as much as the concessive clause expresses a hypothetical situation which does not affect the truth of the main clause, although one might have expected it to:

(82)   Pierre-Henri épouserait Muriel [même si elle était pauvre.]$_{Adv'al/ConcessiveCl}$

- Finally, **'alternative' concessives**, such as (83)–(84) below, express that a range of things expressed in the subordinate clause might be the case without affecting the truth of the main clause:

(83)   [Quelle que soit la fortune de Muriel,]$_{Adv'al/ConcessiveCl}$ Pierre-Henri l'épousera.

(84)   [Que Muriel soit riche ou pauvre,]$_{Adv'al/ConcessiveCl}$ Pierre-Henri l'épousera.

Purpose clauses

As the name suggests, purpose clauses express the purpose for which the action or activity described by the main clause takes place, i.e. its **intended results** (whether they were realized or not), for example:

(85)   J'ai traversé la rue [afin que Tiphaine ne me voie pas.]$_{Adv'al/PurposeCl}$

Result clauses

Result clauses express the **actual results** (whether intended or not) of the action or activity described by the main clauses, for example:

(86)   J'ai traversé la rue [si bien que Tiphaine ne m'a pas vu(e).]$_{Adv'al/ResultCl}$

Note that, just like English *so that*, some French conjunctions, such as *de sorte que*, may introduce both purpose clauses and result clauses. In that case, the mood used in the subordinate clause will reveal the intended interpretation: the indicative is used in result clauses, and the subjunctive in purpose clauses, as shown in (87)–(88):

(87)   J'ai traversé la rue [de sorte que Tiphaine ne m'<u>a</u> pas <u>vu(e)</u>.] (→ As a result she didn't see me.)

(88)   J'ai traversé la rue [de sorte que Tiphaine ne me <u>voie</u> pas.] (→ I did not want her to see me.)

While the result clauses in (86)–(87) above function straightforwardly as adverbials of the main clause, some types of result clauses function as postmodifiers within noun phrases, adjectival phrases, or adverbial phrases. In such cases, the superordinate phrase will contain a so-called correlative expression, viz. one of the expressions *tel*, *tellement*, *si*, or *tant*, as a pre-modifier, as shown in (89)–(90):

(89) Louka m'a fait [un *tel* sourire que j'ai fondu comme de la neige.]$_{DirObj/NP}$
>> [un]$_{Det/IndefArt}$ [tel]$_{Premod/IndefPron}$ [sourire]$_{H/N}$ [que j'ai fondu comme de la neige]$_{Postmod/ResultCl}$

(90) Louise est [*si* belle que tous les garçons tombent amoureux d'elle.]$_{SubjAttr/AdjP}$
>> [si]$_{Premod/Adv}$ [belle]$_{H/Adj}$ [que tous les garçons tombent amoureux d'elle]-$_{Postmod/ResultCl}$

Comparison clauses

As the name suggests, comparative constructions compare two or more entities. The entity that is being compared to something is called the first element of the comparison. The entity that is used as a yardstick is called the second element of the comparison.

The second element may be expressed in two ways. It may take the form of a subordinate comparison clause, as in (91)–(92) below:

(91) Stéphane est aussi grand [que l'est Benoît.]

(92) Il parle [comme le ferait un fou.]

Alternatively, and perhaps more frequently, it may simply consist in *que* or *comme* followed by the second element, as in (93)–(94) below. This second type of construction can be considered to be a reduced version of the first type.[9]

(93) Stéphane est aussi grand [que Benoît.]

(94) Il parle [comme un fou.]

Comparative constructions come in two types:

• Those of the first type are called **comparisons of inequality**. They are found after comparative expressions like *aussi*, *autant*, *autre*, *même*, *moins*, *plus*, *plutôt* + adjective/adverb, as in (91)–(93), or following a so-called 'synthetic' comparative, where the form of adjective or adverb expresses comparative degree in itself, e.g. *mieux*, as in (95)–(96) below:

---

[9] An alternative possible analysis of these structures is one where *que/comme* are considered to be prepositions. We will leave that out of consideration here.

(95)   Marc a réussi [*mieux* que (ne)[10] l'a fait Corinne.]$_{Adv'al/AdvPhr}$ >> [mieux]$_{H/Adv}$
[que (ne) l'a fait Corinne]$_{Postmod/ComparisonCl}$

(96)   Stéphane est [*aussi* grand que Benoît.]$_{SubjAttr/AdjP}$ >> [aussi]$_{Premod/Adv}$
[grand]$_{H/Adj}$ [que Benoît]$_{Postmod/ReducedComparisonCl}$

Here, the second element is always introduced by *que*. Note that, even
though (96) tells us that Stéphane and Benoît are equally tall, both (95) and
(96) thus express comparisons of (potential, if not actual) <u>in</u>equality in this
purely grammatical sense.

Comparisons of inequality function as postmodifiers in an adjectival or
adverbial phrase, where the preceding comparative expression (*aussi, plus*,
etc.) functions as a premodifier, as shown in (96) above.

- Comparative constructions of the second type are called **comparisons of
equality**, and are introduced by *comme*. Comparisons of equality function
as adverbials.

(97)   Il parle [comme le ferait un fou.]$_{Adv'al/ComparisonCl}$

It is worth noting that, in reduced comparison clauses, the exact logical role
of the second element, and consequently the nature of the first element, may
be ambiguous. Thus, (98) below can be expanded as in either (99), where
Jean is the subject of the comparison clause and *Il* is the first element of the
comparison, or (100), where *Jean* is the direct object of the comparison
clause, and *Marie* is the first element of the comparison:

(98)   Il respecte Marie *plus* que Jean.

(99)   Il$_{1stElement}$ respecte Marie *plus* que Jean$_{Subj(2ndElement)}$ (ne) le fait.

(100)   Il respecte Marie$_{1stElement}$ *plus* qu'il (ne) respecte Jean$_{DirObj(2ndElement)}$.

Modal clauses
Modal clauses (also known as manner clauses) express that something
happened without something else (which might have been expected) happening as well, as in (101) below:

(101)   Carine est partie [sans que personne s'en rende compte.]$_{Adv'al/ModalCl}$

---

[10]   For an account of the possible uses of so-called 'expletive' *ne*, see section 23.4.

English does not have finite modal clauses, but uses the preposition *without* followed by a gerund-participle clause, as in (102):

(102)   Karin left [without anyone noticing.]_{Adv'al/PP}

4.3 Conclusion

This and the preceding three chapters have provided an overview of the grammatical structure of Modern Standard French. The concepts presented here will be used in the remaining parts of the book as a basis for giving an account of the specific rules that govern different areas of French grammar.

Appendix C contains a full list of subordinate clause types in French, with examples. Examples of how to parse simple and complex sentences down to the level of the individual word are given in Appendix D.

From here on, the book is structured mainly in terms of basic word classes, with the grammatical behaviour of verbs being treated first, in Part II, then nominals in Part III, and particles in Part IV. Grammatical rules relating not to specific word classes, but to the levels of clause- or sentence-grammar, will be treated in Part V.

PART II

The Grammar of French Verbs

5

Finite verb forms: Mood

Learning objectives

- To understand the basic differences between the three moods (indicative, imperative, subjunctive) in French.
- To understand and be able to correctly apply the rules governing the use of the subjunctive mood in French.

5.1 Introduction

Mood is marked on finite verbs in French.[1] It is a form of verbal inflection which at a very basic level reflects the use to which a given sentence is put in discourse. French has three different moods: the indicative, the imperative, and the subjunctive, which will be treated in turn below.

---

[1] For the notion of a 'finite verb', see section 1.1 above.

The Structure of Modern Standard French. First edition. Maj-Britt Mosegaard Hansen.
© Maj-Britt Mosegaard Hansen 2016. First Published 2016 by Oxford University Press

5.2 The indicative

In French, the indicative is the most basic mood. It is prototypically (but very far from exclusively) used **assertively**, i.e. to make assertions. To make an assertion is to communicate a piece of information that the speaker presents as new to the hearer, and as something to whose truth or probability the speaker is committed.

In French, the indicative is found in both independent/main clauses (cf. (1) below) and subordinate clauses (cf. (2) below,[2] which has the indicative mood in both the main clause and the subordinate clause):

(1)   Philippe vient de se faire muter à Grenoble.

(2)   Line est vexée parce que Cyril l'a traitée de nunuche.

In addition, the indicative is the only mood in French that displays the full range of tense/aspect forms.

5.3 The imperative

The imperative is typically used to express that the speaker considers it desirable and/or advisable for the hearer to carry out the action expressed in the clause.

Imperative clauses are used **non-assertively** in the sense defined in section 5.2 above, in as much as they express something that has yet to happen at the time of speaking. In other words, the speaker is not presenting the contents of an imperative clause as new and factual information about the world, nor is she committing herself to the truth of the future state-of-affairs expressed by the imperative clause.

The imperative in French, like its English equivalent, cannot explicitly express its subject. However, a second person subject is normally understood, and so the imperative can be conjugated in the second person singular or plural, depending on the number of addressees or the formality of the relationship between the speaker and the hearer, cf. (3)–(4) below. In other

---

[2] For the distinction between independent/main and subordinate clauses, see chapters 3–4 above.

words, the person/number marking on the verb shows who the implied subject is:[3]

(3) <u>Fais</u> attention !

(4) <u>Disposez</u> les morceaux de lapin dans un plat allant au four.

Unlike English, French also has a **first person plural imperative**, which expresses an **exhortation** including both the speaker and the hearer(s), cf. (5):

(5) Ne nous <u>disputons</u> pas !

This is similar in meaning to the English *let's*-construction in (6):

(6) <u>Let's</u> not argue!

The imperative mood is only ever used in independent/main clauses in French. Imperatives cannot be marked for tense or aspect at all, but only for person, as shown in (3)–(5) above. At the level of meaning (as opposed to morphological form), the temporal reference of an imperative clause is always future.

5.4 The subjunctive

More extensive use of the subjunctive mood is one of the salient differences between French and particularly British English, where the subjunctive has all but disappeared from the contemporary language, except in more or less fixed optative phrases (i.e. expressions of wishes) such as (7) below:[4]

(7) Long <u>live</u> the Queen!

In terms of tense/aspect marking, the French subjunctive is found in a reduced range of forms as compared to the indicative, viz. the present, the

---

[3] If the predicator is a pronominal verb, the form of the reflexive direct or dative object pronoun will of course also give information about the subject, as seen in (i) below. (See section 15.2.2 for the form of direct/dative object pronouns with positive imperatives.)

(i) Dépêche-<u>toi</u> !

[4] The subjunctive survives to a greater extent in at least some varieties of American English, where it is used in ways that are reminiscent of some of its uses in French, e.g.:

(i) It is very important that John <u>be</u> present at the meeting tomorrow.

present perfect, the imperfect, and the pluperfect. Moreover, the latter two are increasingly rare, being largely confined to highly formal, typically written, registers. Even in those registers, the imperfect and the pluperfect subjunctive are hardly used at all in the first and second person in contemporary French. In the subjunctive, the present tense can thus freely refer to events that took place in the past, or are predicted to take place in the future, with respect to the moment of speech, as shown in (8)–(10) below:

(8)   Il *faut* que tu <u>viennes</u> maintenant.

(9)   Je t'avais dit à l'époque qu'il *fallait* que tu <u>viennes</u>.

(10)   L'année prochaine, il *faudra* que tu <u>viennes</u>.

The present perfect subjunctive marks events that are completed with respect to a particular reference point, but as with the present subjunctive, that reference point need not be the moment of speech, cf. (11)–(13) below:[5]

(11)   Tu *es* content(e) qu'il <u>ait fait</u> ça ?

(12)   Tu *étais* content(e) qu'il <u>ait fait</u> ça ?

(13)   Un jour, tu *seras* content(e) qu'il <u>ait fait</u> ça.

Like the imperative, the subjunctive mood is arguably basically used non-assertively, in the sense defined in section 5.2 above. Often, it is found in clauses that express something that is still unreal at the time of speaking, to the truth of which the speaker is therefore not committed. Alternatively, a clause in the subjunctive may express something that is presupposed, i.e. presented as taken for granted, and hence as not new to the hearer.

That said, it must be emphasized that in Modern French it is very rarely the case that speakers can choose freely between the indicative and the subjunctive in order to convey different nuances of meaning. Over time, the use of either the indicative or the subjunctive has essentially become fixed in certain syntactic environments. We therefore say that the subjunctive is grammaticalized in Modern French.

In French, the subjunctive is primarily found in subordinate clauses.[6] Typically—but by no means invariably—clauses in the subjunctive will

---

[5] For further discussion of tense and reference points, see chapter 6.

[6] Hence the name 'subjunctive', which is derived from the Latin verb SUBJUNGO, meaning 'I bind under'; in other words, the subjunctive is seen largely as a subordinating mood.

thus be introduced by the conjunction *que* or by a complex conjunction containing *que*. As sections 5.4.2–5.4.4 below will show, the precise rules governing the use of the subjunctive depend on the particular type of subordinate clause in question.

5.4.1 The subjunctive in independent clauses

Although the subjunctive is typically found in subordinate clauses, we do find a few environments where the French subjunctive is used in independent clauses.

In 'regular' independent clauses, the subjunctive is only used in more or less frozen expressions used to express wishes, as in (14) below. (In this use, the subjunctive is also known as the 'optative' mood.) As we saw in (7) above, Modern English also uses the subjunctive in such cases:

(14)   Vive la France !

The subjunctive is used in a similar way, to express wishes, requests, and the like, in a particular, and rather marginal, type of independent clause introduced by *que*, which is likely to be derived from a complement clause whose main clause has been elided.[7] They are similar in meaning to imperatives, but unlike the latter, they can be used with third-person subjects, cf. (15)–(16):

(15)   *Qu'*il attende dehors !

(16)   *Que* le diable t'emporte !

In English, constructions with the modal verbs *may* and *must*, or with the verb *let*, are used to express similar meanings, as shown in (17)–(18):

(17)   He must wait outside!/Let him wait outside!

(18)   May the Devil take you!

5.4.2 The subjunctive in nominal clauses

It was shown in section 4.2.1 that there are three types of nominal clauses in French: complement clauses, indirect interrogatives, and free relative

---

[7] For the notion of 'complement clauses', see section 4.2.1.1.

clauses. The French subjunctive is only ever used in complement clauses, where it is very common, but never in either indirect interrogatives or free relative clauses. Arguably, the subjunctive is the default mood in complement clauses, whereas the indicative is used only if there is reason to emphasize the assertive nature of the complement clause, i.e. its status as new and factual information.

It is important to understand, however, that as already noted above, the distinction between assertion and non-assertion will not in and of itself allow one to predict where the subjunctive should be used. Thus, the choice of mood in complement clauses depends on three ordered factors, two syntactic and one semantic:

  (i) The **position** of the complement clause with respect to its main clause. This is a syntactic factor.
 (ii) The **grammatical function** of the complement clause. This is likewise a syntactic factor.
(iii) The presence or absence of a **'subjunctive-triggering' modality** in the main clause. Subjunctive-triggering modalities are expressions (for instance, particular kinds of verbs) that suggest either that the contents of the complement clause are not real at the time of speaking, or that they are somehow taken for granted, and are therefore not presented as new information. This is a semantic factor, i.e. a factor that has to do with the meaning of the sentence.

We have to consider each of these factors in the order in which they are listed above. If we do that, we may find that factor (i) is sufficient to determine the use of the subjunctive, without our having to look at the other two. If factor (i) is not sufficient, we then have to look at factor (ii), which will determine which exact rules to consider in connection with factor (iii).

5.4.2.1 Preposed complement clauses

Complement clauses that precede the main-clause predicator normally take the subjunctive irrespective of their syntactic function or the meaning of the main clause. In other words, factor (i) is sufficient to determine which mood to use in such cases, as exemplified in (19)–(20) below, where the complement clause is placed at the beginning of the sentence in both cases. The fact that the complement clauses in these examples have different grammatical functions, or that they both express factual information, is thus of no consequence: the subjunctive must be used in both cases.

(19)   [Qu'Olivier <u>soit</u> rondelet]$_{Subj/ComplCl}$ n'est pas une raison de se moquer de lui.

(20)   [Que Danièle <u>soit</u> intelligente]$_{Left\text{-}dislocatedDirObj}$[8]$_{/ComplCl}$, on le sait très bien.

A complement clause will typically only be preposed if its content is taken for granted in the context, such that the main clause is communicatively more important. In (19), the fact that Olivier is rotund is thus presented as information that is not assumed to be new to the addressee, and which the addressee is therefore not expected to challenge. Similarly, in (20), the fact that Danièle is intelligent belongs to the speaker and hearer's common ground.

If the complement clause is not preposed, i.e. if it follows the main-clause predicator, then we have to look at factor (ii), the syntactic function of the complement clause. There are four different possibilities: postponed subject, direct object, complement of preposition, or subject attribute.[9] While the potential subjunctive-triggering modalities (i.e. factor (iii)) are somewhat similar across these four cases, they are not exactly the same.

5.4.2.2 Complement clauses as postponed subjects

The subjunctive is used if the complement clause functions as a postponed subject and the main clause contains a non-assertive expression of the types discussed below. In other words, factors (ii) and (iii) are relevant in such cases.

Expressions of volition or desire

If the main clause contains an expression of volition or desire (in a broad sense, including for instance necessity), this suggests that the contents of the complement clause are not real at the time of speaking, as there is little communicative point in expressing volition or desire for something to be the case if it already is.

In (21) below, for instance, the complement clause describes a future event, which the subject attribute *nécessaire* in the main clause describes as highly desirable. This triggers the subjunctive in the complement clause:

(21)   Il est *nécessaire* [que tu <u>viennes</u> à la réunion.]$_{PostponedSubj/ComplCl}$

---

[8] See section 26.2 for further details on left-dislocation.

[9] For the notions of direct object and subject attribute, see chapter 1 above; for that of complement of a preposition, see chapter 2, and for that of 'postponed subject', see chapter 3.

Expressions of subjective evaluation

Expressions of subjective evaluation in the main clause come in two basic types:

(a) expressions of how the speaker feels about the contents of the complement clause;

(b) expressions of how possible or likely it is that the contents of the complement clause are true.

Type (a) expressions, i.e. expressions of emotion, indicate that the contents of the complement clause are presupposed, as in (22) below, where it is taken for granted that Juliette did not come. Notice that it would not be meaningful to say something like (23), where the speaker expresses regret with respect to something that may not actually have happened. This shows that complement clauses governed by expressions of emotion in the main clause are not presented as new information that is open to challenge. Such expressions thus always trigger the subjunctive in a complement clause functioning as a postponed subject.

(22)   Il est *regrettable* [que Juliette ne soit pas venue.]

(23)   #It is regrettable that Juliet didn't come, but I don't know if she did.

Some type (b) expressions in the main clause may indicate that the speaker does not want to commit to the truth of the complement clause, because at the time of speaking s/he considers it to be a mere possibility, as opposed to a (probable) fact. In such cases, the subjunctive must be used in the complement clause, as in (24):

(24)   Il est *possible* [que Luc ne soit pas à la réunion.]

Conversely, other type (b) expressions, namely expressions of truth, certainty, and probability, are assertive in meaning (cf. section 5.2), i.e. they are typically used to present information to whose truth the speaker is at least somewhat committed. They are therefore normally followed by a complement clause in the indicative mood, as in (25)–(26) below:

(25)   Il est *probable* [que Luc sera à la réunion.]

(26)   Il est *vrai* [qu'Adèle est malade.]

If, however, an expression of truth, certainty or probability is negated (cf. (27) below) or modified by *peu* (cf. (28)), the complement clause will normally take the subjunctive mood, because the speaker is then not committed to its truth. This is also frequently the case if the governing clause is interrogative or conditional, as in (29)–(30):

(27)   Il *n*'est *pas* probable [que Luc <u>soit</u> à la réunion.]

(28)   Il est *peu* probable [que Luc <u>soit</u> à la réunion.]

(29)   Est-il vrai [qu'Adèle <u>soit</u> malade] *?*

(30)   *S*'il est vrai [qu'Adèle <u>soit</u> malade], alors la réunion ne pourra avoir lieu.

5.4.2.3 Complement clauses as direct objects or as complements of prepositions

If the complement clause functions as a direct object of the main verb or as the complement of a preposition (where the prepositional phrase as a whole is then a prepositional object), it takes the subjunctive if the main clause expresses a non-assertive modality. Again, it is factors (ii) and (iii) that are relevant.

Expressions of volition or desire

As with postponed subjects, if the main clause contains an expression of volition, desire or the like, this suggests that the contents of the complement clause are not real at the time of speaking. In both (31) and (32), the complement clauses thus describe potential future states of affairs:

(31)   Franchement, je *préférerais* [que tu le lui <u>dises</u> toi-même.]$_{\text{DirObj/ComplCl}}$

(32)   Il ne *faut* absolument pas [que vous lui <u>répétiez</u> ce que je viens de vous dire.]$_{\text{DirObj/ComplCl}}$

Note that the verb *espérer* is not treated as a verb of volition/desire in Modern French, but as a verb of saying or opinion.

Expressions of subjective evaluation

As with postponed subjects (cf. section 5.4.2.2), expressions of emotion in the main clause indicate that the contents of the complement clause are presupposed, as in (33)–(34) below:[10]

---

[10]   See section 4.2.1.1 for an explanation of the use of *ce que* rather than *que* in (33), as well as of why a construction like (i) below, in which *de* is omitted, would in fact be more commonly found than that in (34).

(i)   J'étais *content* [que le morceau soit assez copieux.]$_{\text{Compl. of preposition/ComplCl}}$

(33)   Monsieur Dutrillaux *s'est plaint de* [ce que vous n'<u>ayez</u> pas assisté à la réunion.]_{Compl of preposition/ComplCl}.

(34)   J'étais *content* de [ce que le morceau <u>fût</u> assez copieux.]_{Compl. of preposition/ComplCl}

Again as with postponed subjects, expressions of mere possibility in the main clause indicate that the subject of the main clause is not committed to the truth of the complement clause, and thus trigger the subjunctive, as in (35):

(35)   Les chercheurs trouvent *possible* [que cela <u>ait</u> une origine mythique.]_{DirObj/ComplCl}

Expressions of truth, certainty, or probability, on the other hand, trigger the indicative (cf. (36)), unless (as shown in section 5.4.2.2) they are negated or modified by *peu*, cf. (36)–(37):

(36)   Les chercheurs trouvent *vraisemblable* [que cela <u>a</u> une origine mythique.]

(37)   Les chercheurs trouvent *peu* vraisemblable [que cela <u>ait</u> une origine purement mythique.]

Expressions of doubt or denial

Verbs that express doubt or denial are by their very nature non-assertive, as they explicitly state that the subject is not committed to the truth of the complement clause, cf. (38):

(38)   Je *doute* [que Corinne <u>soit</u> déjà partie.]

What is perhaps more surprising is that even when negated these verbs also frequently govern complement clauses in the subjunctive, as shown in (39), where either the indicative or the subjunctive may be found:[11]

(39)   *Personne ne* nie [que Claude <u>soit</u>/<u>est</u> intelligente.]

---

[11] A tentative explanation might be that expressions like *je ne doute/nie pas que* are typically used, not to communicate new information, but to concede what both the speaker and the addressee already take to be facts. In other words, the content of a complement clause like that in (39) above may be presented as something that is taken for granted.

Verbs of saying or opinion
Verbs of saying or opinion are assertive in meaning, and therefore normally govern complement clauses in the **indicative** mood, as shown in (40):

(40)   Luc *croit* [que Corinne est déjà partie.]

Note that, in Modern French (unlike Old French), the verb *espérer* is treated like a verb of saying or opinion, and not as a verb of volition or desire. Thus, as shown in (41) below, it triggers the indicative (normally a future tense form) in direct object complement clauses:

(41)   J'espère [que Corinne sera déjà partie.]

However, if verbs of saying or opinion are negated they take the subjunctive, as shown in (42), because the speaker is then no longer committed to the truth of the complement clause:

(42)   Luc *ne* croit *pas* [que Corinne soit déjà partie.]

If the main clause is interrogative and features verb-subject inversion,[12] this type of verb may likewise govern complement clauses in the subjunctive mood, as in (43) below. Note, however, that if the interrogative is formed without verb-subject inversion, the complement clause will normally take the indicative, cf. (44):

(43)   *Crois-tu* [que Corinne soit déjà partie] *?*

(44)   *Tu crois* [que Corinne est déjà partie] *?*

Verbs of ambiguous modality
In the above-mentioned types of complement clauses Modern French essentially does not allow a choice of mood. Except for the couple of cases mentioned above where we find some slight variation, using the indicative instead of the subjunctive or *vice versa* will thus, in the constructions discussed above, normally result in ungrammaticality rather than a change of meaning (but see section 5.4.5 below). It is in this sense that mood can be said to be grammaticalized in Modern French.

There are, however, some frequently used verbs of saying or opinion that can be followed by a complement clause in either the indicative or the

---

[12] Inversion is when we change the normal order of subject and verb, such that the subject follows the verb. See section 24.3 for details.

subjunctive, and in these cases the choice of mood in the subordinate clause does result in a change of meaning, in as much as the choice of mood will determine the precise meaning of the main-clause predicator.

If, for instance, the verb *répondre* takes a direct-object complement clause in the indicative (as in (45) below), it will mean that somebody made a factual reply. If, however, it takes a direct-object complement clause in the subjunctive, as in (46), it acquires an additional meaning of volition or desire which turns the contents of the complement clause into an indirect request:

(45) *Réponds*-lui$_i$ [qu'il$_j$ attend.]^{13} (= "Tell him$_i$ [e.g. Pierre] that he$_j$ [e.g. Jean] is waiting." = fact)

(46) *Réponds*-lui$_i$ [qu'il$_i$ attende.] (= 'Tell him$_i$ [e.g. Pierre] that he$_i$ [Pierre] must wait.'/'Tell him to wait.' = request)

Similarly, when taking a direct-object complement clause in the indicative, as in (47) below, the verb *suggérer* neutrally expresses opinion. When taking a direct-object complement clause in the subjunctive, as in (48), however, it will express a preference on the part of its subject:

(47) Je me permets de *suggérer* [que vous vous êtes trompé(e)(s).] (→ It is my opinion that you're wrong.)

(48) Elle *suggère* [que nous venions la voir.] (→ It is her wish that we come to see her.)

Other French verbs that are modally ambiguous in this way are, for instance, *dire*, *admettre*, *supposer*, *comprendre*, and *expliquer*.

5.4.2.4 Complement clauses as subject attributes

Finally, complement clauses functioning as subject attributes may take the subjunctive if the subject is a non-assertive expression. In other words, factors (ii) and (iii) are once more of relevance to the choice of mood.

The subject is an expression of volition or desire

If the subject of the main clause is an expression of volition, desire, or the like, such as *mon dernier vœu* in (49), the subjunctive is always used in the complement clause:

(49) *Mon dernier vœu*, c'est [que la famille soit unie.]$_{SubjAttr/ComplCl}$

---

^{13} The indices i and j are added to show whether *lui* and *il* refer to the same individual, as in (46), or to two different people, as in (45).

The subject expresses a subjective evaluation
If the subject of the main clause expresses an emotional reaction, as in (50) below, the complement clause will likewise often take the subjunctive:

(50) *Ce que je trouve inquiétant*, c'est [que Jacques Chirac perde à ce point la mémoire.]_{SubjAttr/ComplCl}

However, in this type of construction, the indicative may be used instead of the subjunctive if the speaker wants to present the contents of the complement clause as communicatively more important than the contents of the subject, as in (51):

(51) *Ce qui m'inquiète*, c'est [qu'il perd peu à peu la mémoire.]_{SubjAttr/ComplCl}

If we compare (50) and (51), the difference is that in (50), the observation that Jacques Chirac is losing his memory (i.e. the subject attribute) is presented as taken for granted, hence not up for discussion. Thus, the adverbial *à ce point* shows that Chirac's failing memory is already part of the speaker and hearer's common ground. What the speaker principally wants to communicate is the contents of the subject clause, namely that s/he finds that fact disturbing under the circumstances. In (51), on the other hand, the content of the subject attribute (i.e. that 'he' is losing his memory) is presented as the principal piece of new information.

5.4.3 The subjunctive in adjectival clauses

Section 4.2.2, showed that adjectival clauses come in three types in French: restrictive, non-restrictive, and predicative. The last type always takes the indicative, as exemplified in (52) below:

(52) J'entends David [qui court derrière moi.]

In **non-restrictive** relative clauses, **the subjunctive is very rarely found**. When it is, it is used in the same way as in independent clauses, i.e. to express **wishes**, cf. (53) below and (15)–(16) in section 5.4.1 above:

(53) L'année dernière, quand mon mari—dont Dieu ait l'âme—était encore vivant, nous nous portions tous bien.
('Last year, when my husband—may God take his soul—was still alive, we were all in good health.', literally: 'Last year, when my husband—whose soul God should have—was still alive...')

5.4.3.1 Restrictive relative clauses

In restrictive relative clauses, on the other hand, the subjunctive is frequently used. The choice of mood depends on the nature of the antecedent, i.e. the main clause constituent that the relative clause postmodifies (see section 4.2.2).

Indefinite antecedent
The subjunctive is used in a restrictive relative clause if the antecedent is presented as non-referential. That is, the antecedent does not refer to a specific entity in the world and the speaker does not commit herself explicitly to the notion that such an entity even exists. This will often be the case if the main clause contains an expression of volition or desire (in a broad sense, including, for instance, seeking).

Thus, there is a difference in meaning between (54) and (55) below, depending on which mood is used:

(54)   Je cherche *une maison* [qui ait une vue sur la mer.] (→ Any such house will do, but I'm not sure if there is such a house.)

(55)   Je cherche *une maison* [qui a une vue sur la mer.] (→ I'm thinking of a specific house, which I know exists.)

In (54), the use of the subjunctive tells us that the speaker is looking for any house that fulfils the condition of having a sea view, and the sentence does not necessarily imply that such a house even exists. (It may be that the speaker is talking to an estate agent because she is hoping to relocate to a particular area, and would prefer to live in a house with a sea view, but is aware that no such house may currently be for sale in that area.)

In (55), on the other hand, the indicative tells us that the antecedent is referential and specific. In other words, the speaker is looking for a particular house which can be identified by the fact that it has a sea view. (It may be that the speaker is asking for directions because she is coming to visit a friend for the first time, forgot to make note of the exact address, but remembers the friend mentioning that their house is the only one in the area that has a sea view.)

Besides verbs of volition, desire, and the like, expressions of negation (cf. (56) below), interrogation (cf. (57)), and condition (cf. (58)) typically also make an indefinite antecedent non-referential. Thus, all three sentences below either state explicitly or imply the possibility that no philosopher exists who is not critical:

(56)   Il *n'*y a *pas* de philosophe [qui ne <u>soit</u> critique.][14]

(57)   Y a-t-il un philosophe [qui ne <u>soit</u> critique] *?*

(58)   *S'*il y a bien un philosophe [qui ne <u>soit</u> critique], montre-le-moi !

Antecedent in the superlative
If the antecedent of a restrictive relative clause is modified by an **adjective in the superlative** (i.e. the form that expresses the highest degree of the adjective in question), or contains a modifier with a quasi-superlative meaning (i.e. an adjective such as *seul* or the cardinal numeral *premier*), the subjunctive will typically be used.

   This is particularly the case if the predicator of the relative clause is either *être, avoir, connaître*, or *pouvoir*, as in (59) below, or if a non-negative *jamais* (= 'ever')[15] can be inserted in the relative clause, as in (60):

(59)   C'est la voiture *la plus rapide* [qui <u>soit</u>.]

(60)   C'est *le seul* homme [que j'<u>aie</u> (jamais) respecté.]

5.4.4 The subjunctive in adverbial clauses

Mood in adverbial clauses is determined by the subordinator, such that specific adverbial subordinating conjunctions are invariably followed by a particular mood, either the indicative or the subjunctive. For definitions of individual types of adverbial clauses, see section 4.2.3.

5.4.4.1 Temporal clauses
Temporal clauses normally take the indicative, but the conjunctions *avant que* and *jusqu'à ce que* trigger the subjunctive, as in (61):

(61)   La réunion a commencé [*avant que* tout le monde (ne) <u>soit</u> arrivé.]$_{\text{TemporalCl}}$[16]

---

   [14] For the use of *ne* without *pas* with negative meaning, see section 23.2.1.1.
   [15] Non-negative uses of indefinites such as *jamais*, which are normally used in negative clauses, are treated in greater depth in section 23.2.1.2.
   [16] For the use of so-called 'expletive' (non-negative) *ne*, see section 23.4.

5.4.4.2 Causal clauses

Causal clauses normally take the indicative, but the subjunctive is used after *non que*, as shown by the two contrasting instances in (62):

(62)   Kerviel est innocent, [*non qu*'il n'<u>ait commis</u> aucune faute,]_{CausalCl} mais [*parce qu*'il <u>a été laissé</u> libre de faire n'importe quoi dans un système criminogène.]_{CausalCl}

5.4.4.3 Conditional clauses

Conditional clauses introduced by *si* take the indicative, as do those introduced by *au cas où*, *pour le cas où*, and *dans le cas où*.[17] All other conditional conjunctions normally trigger the subjunctive, as exemplified in (63):

(63)   Tu peux venir avec nous, [*à moins que* tu (ne) <u>sois</u> trop fatigué(e).]_{ConditionalCl}

5.4.4.4 Concessive clauses

Unreal concessive clauses introduced by *même si* take the indicative. Real and alternative concessive clauses normally take the subjunctive, as in (64) below. (For the distinction between different types of concessive clauses, see section 4.2.3.2)

(64)   Il est allé au bureau, [*bien qu*'il <u>ait</u> la fièvre.]_{ConcessiveCl}

However, real concessives introduced by *encore que*, and which follow the main clause, occasionally take the indicative to express that the content of the concessive clause may, upon reflection, invalidate the content of the main clause. Thus, in (65) below, the indicative signals that the speaker is, after all, not certain that the addressee will be able to find an empty parking space near the town hall:

(65)   Vous pourrez vous garer près de la mairie, [*encore que* c'<u>est</u> souvent très plein.]

5.4.4.5 Purpose clauses

All purpose clauses take the subjunctive, independently of the conjunction used, as in (66):

(66)   Florent a acheté un téléphone portable [*pour qu*'on <u>puisse</u> le joindre à tout moment.]_{PurposeCl}

---

[17] For information about the use of tenses in these types of conditionals, see section 6.4.

5.4.4.6 Result clauses

Result clauses normally take the indicative, except when expressing purpose as well as result. The conjunctions *de façon/manière à ce que* thus always trigger the subjunctive, as in (67):

(67) Être un vrai comédien, c'est savoir se mettre dans la peau du personnage [*de façon à ce que* l'illusion <u>soit</u> parfaite.]_{Result+PurposeCl}

In the case of other conjunctions, such as *de telle manière que*, it will depend on the context whether purpose is expressed in addition to result, and use of the subjunctive will indicate to the hearer/reader which is the intended interpretation, cf. the contrast between (68) below, where earning the respect of others is both a goal and a result of the recommended type of behaviour, and (69), where the speaker does not assume that Bertrand is necessarily consciously intending to communicate that he is happy to see her:

(68) Comportez-vous [*de telle manière que* vous <u>méritiez</u> le respect des autres.]_{Result +PurposeCl}

(69) Bertrand me sourit toujours [*de telle manière que* j'<u>ai</u> l'impression qu'il est très heureux de me voir.]_{ResultCl}

5.4.4.7 Comparison clauses

Comparison clauses take the indicative, except when introduced by the conjunction *(pour) (autant) que*, meaning 'as far as', which triggers the subjunctive:

(70) [*(Pour) (autant) que* je <u>sache</u>,]_{ComparisonCl} on n'est pas obligé(e)(s) de te demander ta permission.

5.4.4.8 Modal clauses

Modal clauses always take the subjunctive:

(71) Adèle est sortie [*sans que* son père s'en <u>aperçoive</u>.]_{ModalCl}

5.4.5 Use of the indicative where the subjunctive would be expected

As explained earlier in section 5.4, the subjunctive in Modern French has a very restricted set of tense forms available. These forms do not include equivalents of the future tenses, nor of the *conditionnel*. In addition, the imperfect and pluperfect subjunctives are avoided in all but the most formal of registers.

For these reasons, speakers may sometimes choose an indicative form in a grammatical context where the subjunctive would otherwise be expected, if they wish to make it clear either that the temporal reference of the clause in question is in the past or the future or that the described situation is hypothetical.

Thus, the 'real' concessive in (72) below should normally take the subjunctive (cf. section 5.4.4.4 above). However, the imperfect subjunctive would be out of place in most registers, particularly with a first person subject, and the present subjunctive would be ambiguous as to whether the speaker has only now decided that the initiative in question was an error. Hence, the indicative is acceptable here:

(72) À l'époque, j'ai donné mon assentiment bien que je <u>trouvais</u> que cette initiative était une erreur.

In (73), we have a restrictive relative clause with an indefinite negative antecedent, which would normally trigger the subjunctive (cf. section 5.4.3.3 above). Here, the reference of the relative clause is meant to be future, however, so the *futur simple* can substitute for the temporally ambiguous present subjunctive:

(73) Il n'y a personne qui t'<u>aidera</u> à faire ça.

Finally, the complement clause in (74) is the direct object of a negated verb of saying (cf. section 5.4.2.3 above), but the *conditionnel* is chosen to emphasize the hypothetical nature of the problematic enterprise:

(74) Je n'ai jamais dit que ça ne <u>poserait</u> pas de problèmes.

6

Finite verb forms: Tense

Learning objectives

- To understand the notions of Speech Time, Reference Time, and Event Time, and the differences between them.
- To understand the notions of primary *vs* secondary tenses.
- To understand the temporal reference of each of the French tenses.
- To understand the distinction between temporal and modal uses of tense forms.
- To understand the differences between the principal types of reported speech/thought and the associated uses of the tenses.

6.1 Introduction

Tense is a grammatical category that has to do with the expression of time in language. Clauses and sentences can express time **lexically**, using particular words and phrases, such as *demain, le 9 juillet 2011, une semaine, dans trois mois*, etc. This is not the only way to express notions of time, however. It can

The Structure of Modern Standard French. First edition. Maj-Britt Mosegaard Hansen.
© Maj-Britt Mosegaard Hansen 2016. First Published 2016 by Oxford University Press

also be done **morphologically**, through the form of finite verbs, in particular, or **morphosyntactically** through the use of compound tenses and constructions such as *devoir* + infinitive. Two morphological categories in French are specialized for the expression of time, viz. tense and aspect.

Tense expresses **'external' time**, i.e. tense forms situate the states, activities, or events referred to by clauses with respect to other states, activities, or events. Tense can therefore be said to view the timing of the former from an outside perspective, namely the perspective of the latter.

In contrast, **aspect**, which will be discussed more fully in chapter 7, expresses **'internal' time**, i.e. aspect is concerned with the internal stages (if any) of the state, activity, or event referred to in the clause.

6.1.1 Tense as a deictic category

Unlike aspect, tense is a so-called **deictic category**.[1] The term comes from the ancient Greek word *deixis*, which means 'pointing' or 'display'. Thus, deictic items in language point outside the text itself, to aspects of the outside world of reference, which must be taken into account when interpreting sentences in which deictic items appear.

Thus, in order to correctly interpret any tensed clause, we need to know (approximately) when that clause was spoken or written. This is a facet of the 'real world' which will be referred to below as 'speech time' (or S, for short). To see why we need to know about S, imagine someone producing the sentence in (1) below:

(1)   La France est une république.

If we assume that this sentence was uttered in, say, 2013, then the statement it expresses would clearly be a true one. If, however, we imagine the same sentence being uttered in 1713, it would just as clearly express a false statement, as France was at that time a monarchy under King Louis XIV. That said, by changing the present tense to a *futur simple*, as in (2)

---

[1] Tense is not the only grammatical category in French that is deictic. Various types of pronoun and articles (e.g. personal pronouns, demonstrative pronouns and articles, etc.) are fundamentally deictic, as well (see section 14.4). In addition, certain lexical expressions may have deictic meaning, for instance adverbs and prepositional phrases such as *ici*, *de l'autre côté de la rue*, *aujourd'hui*, *dans trois mois*, etc.

below, we can make a statement that would have been true in 1713 (although its truth could of course only be verified later). Notice, however, that if uttered in 2013, (2) would be at the very least misleading:

(2)   La France <u>sera</u> une république.

In order to understand the tense system of French, let us start by representing time metaphorically as a line moving from left to right on the page, as in Figure 6.1. On this line, we mark the present moment as a point ('now'). To the left of this point, we have the past, and to the right of it, we have the future.

Figure 6.1. A metaphorical representation of time.

When describing the uses of individual French tenses, it is useful to operate with three different points in time:

- **Speech Time**, or S. This is the time at which a given utterance is produced.
- **Reference Time**, or R. This is the time with respect to which the state, activity or event described by a clause is relevant. R is always located with respect to S, and it may or may not be identical to S.
- **Event time**, or E. This is the time at which the state, activity, or event takes place or is valid. E is always located with respect to R, and it may or may not be identical to R.

With the aid of these three times and the relations that obtain between them, we can distinguish the French tenses from one another, and describe their basic meaning. At the top level, we can distinguish between so-called primary and secondary tenses. Primary tenses are those where R and E are simultaneous, while secondary tenses are those where R and E are located at different points on the timeline.

Appendix E contains an overview of the French tenses and their English equivalents in tabular form.

6.2 Primary tenses

In French, the primary tenses are the *présent*, the past tenses (i.e. the *passé simple*, the *imparfait*, and the *passé composé* in certain of its uses), and the *futur simple*. Each of these will be discussed in turn below. The basic temporal meaning of each tense will be described using the timeline and the three points, S, R, and E. In addition to this basic meaning, most of the tenses have certain uses which differ from the basic one in some way, but which can nevertheless be understood as derived from that basic meaning.

6.2.1 The present tense

In the present tense, expressed in French by the *présent*, R and E are not just simultaneous with one another, but with S as well. We can represent that with the formula in (3) below, where commas indicate simultaneity between points in time, and we can plot it graphically on a timeline as in Figure 6.2.

(3)   Temporal reference of the present tense: S, R, E

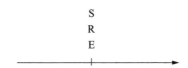

Figure 6.2. Temporal reference of the present tense.

What this means is that the *présent* in a sentence like (4) below tells the hearer that, with respect to the time of utterance (S), the information conveyed by the sentence, namely that the subject, Elizabeth II, is Queen of England, is both relevant (R) and valid (E):

(4)   Elizabeth II est reine d'Angleterre.

In other words, the present tense is normally used about things that are presented as valid at Speech Time. This does not mean, however, that states, activities, or events that are described in the present tense must be valid only at Speech Time. That, in fact, is very rarely the case. On the contrary, their validity typically goes beyond the brief moment it takes to utter a sentence, as (4) shows. Indeed, the present tense is the tense normally used to express eternal truths such as (5) below in both French and English:

(5)   Deux et deux font quatre.

And like the English present tense, the French *présent* may also be used about states, activities, and events that are not actually on-going at the very moment the sentence is uttered, provided the sentence describes a habitual pattern that exists as such at Speech Time. Thus, a sentence like (6) below is perfectly acceptable if uttered on a Wednesday, when Claude is not playing tennis, so long as it is the case that s/he did play tennis on most or all Fridays of the preceding weeks and is expected to do so on most or all Fridays of the weeks to come. This is known as the **habitual use** of the *présent*.

(6)   Claude joue au tennis le vendredi.

In addition, the French *présent* can be used in clauses that describe a change of state which is completed more or less instantly, if that change of state took place immediately prior to Speech Time, as in (7) below, or conversely, to describe planned events which are more or less imminent at S, as in (8):

(7)   Allô, Delphine, je rentre à l'instant et je te téléphone pour te dire que je ne peux pas venir ce soir. ('...I have just arrived home...')

(8)   Moi, je descends aux Halles, et toi ?

To describe events in the immediate past, it is, however, more common to use the present perfect *venir de* + infinitive construction, as in (9) (see further section 6.3.1 below):

(9)   Allô, Delphine, je viens de rentrer...

Similarly, when talking about imminent future events, a common alternative to the *présent* is the *futur composé* (i.e. *aller* + infinitive, see section 6.3.3 below), cf. (10):

(10)   Moi, je vais descendre aux Halles, et toi ?

Finally, the *présent* can be used metaphorically in narrative (i.e. in [hi]stories) to describe past events which the speaker wants to render more interesting and immediate for the hearer, by as it were pretending that these events are taking place as s/he speaks.

This use is known as the '**narrative** (or **historical**) **present**'. It is illustrated in (11) below, where the use of the *passé simple* in the first paragraph (along with the dates given) clearly shows that the described events are, in fact, firmly in the past at S. The switch to the narrative present tense in the second paragraph marks that a more exciting and fateful series of events is now being described:

(11)   Ayant conservé la confiance du roi, le baron de Breteuil *fut* consulté par celui-ci sur l'évolution de la situation à la veille de la Révolution française. Il *s'opposa* à la convocation des états généraux et *conseilla* à Louis XVI une série de mesures répressives énergiques pour venir à bout de l'agitation de juin et juillet 1789.

Lors du renvoi de Jacques Necker et des ministres libéraux le 11 juillet 1789, Louis XVI nomme le baron de Breteuil pour lui succéder comme principal ministre, cent heures à peine avant la prise de la Bastille. Dès le 16 juillet, Louis XVI doit toutefois rappeler Necker et Breteuil émigre le 17 ou 18 juillet 1789 en Allemagne puis en Suisse.

> from 'Louis Auguste Le Tonnelier de Breteuil',
> http://fr.wikipedia.org/wiki/Louis_Auguste_Le_Tonnelier_de_Breteuil.

6.2.1.1 The inclusive use of the *présent*

Unlike the present tense in English, the French *présent* may be used 'inclusively', with an 'up to now' sense, to describe states or activities whose duration spans an interval of the timeline both preceding and including the moment of speech. In such cases, English uses the present perfect (progressive) instead.

The inclusive use of the *présent* is found when the sentence or clause contains an adverbial introduced by *depuis* + an indication of a time span, *il y a* + an indication of a time span + *que*, or alternatively, an adverbial clause introduced by *depuis que*, as in (12)–(14) below:[2]

(12)   Christophe habite à Nantes *depuis deux ans.* (cf. 'Christopher has lived/been living in Nantes for two years.')

(13)   *Il y a une heure qu'*on t'attend ! (cf. 'We have been waiting for you for an hour!')

(14)   *Depuis que Marc travaille ici,* on se voit regulièrement. (cf. 'Since Marc started working here, we have been seeing one another regularly.')

Note, however, that French uses the *passé composé* (with present perfect meaning, see section 6.3.1 below) in such contexts if the state or activity in question has actually ceased prior to S, as shown in (15):

(15)   Gérard va venir demain. On ne s'est pas vu(s) *depuis cinq ans.*

---

[2] Notice that in (14), the inclusive *présent* is used in both clauses.

Verbs describing punctual changes of state, which inherently have no duration, always take the *passé composé*, as in (16):

(16) Il y a trois mois que Jacques <u>est mort</u>.

6.2.2 The past tenses

The past tenses are characterized by the simultaneity of R and E, both of which are located before S on the timeline. This configuration is represented by the formula in (17) below, where > means 'precedes in time'. It can be plotted on the timeline as in Figure 6.3.

(17) Temporal reference of the past tenses: R, E > S

Figure 6.3. Temporal reference of the past tenses.

In other words, a past tense describes a state, activity, or event which is located in the past, and which is not directly relevant to states, activities, or events taking place at Speech Time, but only (possibly) to other past states, activities, or events.

Modern Standard French has three different verb forms which can function as past tenses. In formal writing (and very occasionally in formal speech), the *imparfait* and the *passé simple* are used with this meaning, whereas in less formal writing and almost always in speech, we find the *imparfait* and the *passé composé*. The latter is then used in those past tense contexts where formal written text would use the *passé simple*.

The difference between the *imparfait* on the one hand, and the *passé simple/passé composé* on the other is not temporal, but aspectual, in nature. It will be discussed in depth in chapter 7.

Thus, the sentences in (18)–(20) below all describe past states or events that have no particularly strong link with, or relevance to, the present moment. While (19) and (20) describe the same past event in the same way, they differ in terms of the register in which they are most appropriate.

(18)   Victor Hugo <u>était</u> un grand poète.

(19)   Louis XIV <u>mourut</u> en 1715.

(20)   Louis XIV <u>est mort</u> en 1715.

Although the three past tense forms are represented in the same way in (17) above, the *imparfait* aspectually has more in common with the present tense that the other two past tenses. Thus, both the present and the *imparfait* normally describe states, activities, and events that are on-going at Reference Time. For this reason, the *imparfait* is used with inclusive meaning ($\approx$ 'up until then') in the same types of context where we find the inclusive use of the present tense (see section 6.2.1. above). In English, on the other hand, the past perfect, also known as the pluperfect, (progressive) is used in inclusive contexts when R is located in the past, as shown in (21):

(21)   A l'époque, Catherine <u>était</u> en thèse *depuis un an et demi.* (cf. 'At the time, Catherine <u>had been working</u> on her thesis for 18 months.')

The inclusive *imparfait* is replaced by the *plus-que-parfait* in the same types of context where we find the inclusive *présent* replaced by the *passé composé*, i.e. when the state or activity has ceased prior to R, as in (22) below, or when the clause describes a punctual event with no duration, as in (23) (cf. section 6.2.1. above):

(22)   Il y avait une dizaine d'années que Marie <u>avait visité</u> New York.

(23)   Jacques <u>était mort</u> depuis trois ans lorsque sa veuve s'est remariée.

6.2.3 *The simple future tense*

The temporal reference of the *futur simple* is the mirror image of that of the past tenses: here, both Reference Time and Event Time are situated after Speech Time. This is summarized in the formula in (24) below, and graphically plotted on the timeline in Figure 6.4.

Figure 6.4. Temporal reference of the *futur simple*.

(24)   Temporal reference of the *futur simple*: S > R, E

The fact that R is located to the right of S on the timeline serves to indicate that the *futur simple* describes future states, activities, and events which have no particular direct connection or relevance to Speech Time. In other words, this tense expresses **neutral predictions** about the future. Frequently, the context will contain an explicit future-time adverbial, such as *en l'an 2050* in (25) below, which serves to fix the Reference Time of the tense:

(25)   La troisième guerre mondiale éclatera *en l'an 2050.*

Note that, unlike the English *will/shall* + infinitive-construction,[3] which is ungrammatical in such contexts, the French *futur simple* must be used in temporal clauses if the main clause also has future-time reference:

(26)   Viens me voir *quand* tu seras à Paris. (cf. 'Come (and) visit me when you are in Paris.' *vs* *'Come (and) visit me when you will be in Paris.')

We saw in section 6.2.1 above that the present tense has a narrative use, where it describes past events. In certain genres, particularly history writing, the *futur simple* has a similar narrative use, in which it refers to past events which are, however, situated further to the right along the timeline (i.e. closer to S) than past events previously recounted in the text. The excerpt in (27) below shows such a use. Notice that the preceding clause is in the narrative present tense (or possibly, but contextually less likely, the *passé simple*), and that the text is from 1975, when General de Gaulle had already been dead for five years. Notice further that the adverbial *vingt ans plus tard* serves to change the Reference Time of the preceding clause to one further along the timeline:

(27)   Le général de Gaulle, ses appels, ses commentaires, la manière dont il *unit* à Londres et, vingt ans plus tard réunira à Paris tant de magistratures en une seule, est un autre exemple latin.

      Ch. Morazé, *Le Général de Gaulle et la République* (Flammarion, 1975), 4.

6.2.3.1 Modal uses of the *futur simple*
While the narrative use of the *futur simple* retains future-time reference at least in so far as the past events it describes are seen in relation to the more remote past events described in the preceding text, so-called modal uses of

---

[3] While *will/shall* + infinitive is usually given a future-time interpretation, English has no morphological future tense.

the *futur simple* are further removed from the notion of future-time reference. When a tense form is used with predominantly **modal** meaning, the speaker is instead expressing a particular attitude towards whatever is described by the clause or sentence.

The *futur simple* can be used modally as a politely insistent alternative to the imperative mood, as in (28) below. By ostensibly predicting that the addressee will perform a future action that is in accordance with the speaker's interest, the latter is implicitly communicating a request:

(28)   Vous <u>viendrez</u> bien avec nous. ('Do come with us!')

The *futur simple* may also, less commonly, be used to mark that the utterance represents an inference the speaker is making about a present situation. Thus, in (29), the use of the *futur simple* indicates that the speaker has good reason to believe, but is not 100 per cent certain, that the person calling at Speech Time is Norbert:

(29)   [The phone rings.] Ça <u>sera</u> Norbert. ('That will/must be Norbert.')

6.3 Secondary tenses

In secondary tenses, Reference Time and Event Time do not coincide, unlike in primary tenses. The configuration of S, R, and E may therefore be more complex than in the primary tenses. Indeed, as we will see in section 6.3.6 below, one of the secondary tenses (i.e. the future perfect in the past) requires us to operate with not just one, but two Reference Times. This has consequences for the precision with which situations described by some of the secondary tenses may be situated in time.

6.3.1 The present perfect

In the present perfect, Speech Time and Reference Time coincide, and the Event Time is prior to both of them, as represented in (30) below and in Figure 6.5.

Figure 6.5. Temporal reference of the present perfect.

(30)   Temporal reference of the present perfect: E > S,R

In other words, unlike the past tenses (cf. section 6.2.2 above), the present perfect describes past states, activities and events that have continued relevance at Speech Time, often in the form of concrete present results. Thus, in (31)–(32) below, the past event of eating is currently relevant because it means that the speaker is no longer hungry, which explains why she is not going to the cafeteria.

(31)   Je ne vais pas à la cantine : j'ai déjà mangé.

(32)   Je ne vais pas à la cantine : je viens de manger. (cf. '...I have just eaten.')

To express the present perfect, French uses either the *passé composé* (as in (31)) or the *viens de* + infinitive construction (as in (32)). The latter is more restricted in its use than the former, and will only be used if E is in the immediate past with respect to R and S. In other words, as the translation of (32) shows, it is equivalent to adding the adverbial *just* to an English present perfect.

Both forms have the auxiliary (*avoir/être*[4] or *venir*) in the present tense, which arguably serves to locate R as simultaneous with Speech Time.

We saw in section 6.2.2 that the *passé composé* may also be used with past-time reference, equivalent to the *passé simple*. In formal genres where the *passé simple* is also used, occurrences of the *passé composé* will normally have present perfect meaning, as in (33) below, where the use of the *passé composé* indicates that at the time of writing (i.e. S), the author has still not come to terms with her brother's suicide.

(33)   [In an autobiography:] Mon frère se *suicida* en 1965. Il n'avait que 25 ans. Je n'ai jamais compris ce qui a pu le pousser à faire un tel geste. (cf. 'I have never understood...')

In less formal genres that do not make use of the *passé simple*, the precise value of the *passé composé* will thus be ambiguous and its most appropriate translation into English must be determined by the context.

Notice that, unlike the English present perfect, the *passé composé* can—indeed must—be used with so-called **present perfect adverbials**, i.e. adverbials like *hier*, *la semaine dernière*, etc., which display a close deictic link to Speech Time:

---

[4] For the choice between *avoir* and *être* as auxiliaries, see section 8.2.

(34) J'ai rencontré Alain *hier soir.* (cf. 'I <u>met</u> Alain [for the first time] last night.' *vs*
*'I <u>have met</u> Alain [for the first time] last night.')

6.3.2 The past perfect

In the past perfect (or pluperfect) tense, Event Time precedes Reference
Time which itself precedes Speech Time. This is represented in (35) below
and in Figure 6.6.

(35) Temporal reference of the past perfect: E > R > S

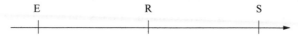

Figure 6.6. Temporal reference of the past perfect.

Thus, the past perfect describes a past event that temporally precedes
another past event, which constitutes its reference point. In (36) below, for
instance, the time when Denis was remembering something constitutes R;
the activity of remembering is marked as past through the use of the
imparfait. The time of his first kiss constitutes E, and is prior to R, which
is why it is described in the past perfect tense:

(36) Denis *se rappelait* la première fois qu'il <u>avait embrassé</u> une fille.

It is worth noting that French uses the past perfect more systematically
than English does when the temporal reference of a clause is as depicted in
Figure 6.6: thus, (37)–(38) below are both possible translations of (36), but
the direct French equivalent of (38), using a past tense in the relative clause,
is unacceptable, as seen in (39):

(37) Denis was remembering the first time he <u>had kissed</u> a girl.

(38) Denis was remembering the first time he <u>kissed</u> a girl.

(39) *Denis se rappelait la première fois qu'il <u>embrassa</u> une fille.

French has three **compound forms** that convey past perfect meaning: the
plus-que-parfait, where the auxiliary is in the *imparfait* (as in (36) above),
the ***passé antérieur*** (cf. (40) below) which has an auxiliary in the *passé
simple*, and the ***passé surcomposé***, whose auxiliary is in the *passé composé*
(cf. (41)):

(40)   Quand Francis <u>eut terminé</u> la lettre, il *alla* se coucher.

(41)   Quand Francis <u>a eu terminé</u> la lettre, il *est allé* se coucher.

Arguably, the past tense forms of the auxiliaries in all three cases serve to mark R as being located in the past.

The *passé antérieur* and the *passé surcomposé* are both relatively rare forms. They are used mainly in temporal adverbial clauses (cf. section 4.2.3.2) introduced by *quand, lorsque, dès que, aussitôt que, après que*, and *à peine . . . que*, and which denote a past event that took place immediately prior to another past event (as illustrated by (40)–(41) above). In most cases, the main clause predicator will be in either the *passé simple* (if the *passé antérieur* is used in the temporal clause) or in the *passé composé* (if the *passé surcomposé* is used).

Even less frequently, the *passé antérieur* or the *passé surcomposé* may be used in main clauses to describe an action that was completed quickly. In the latter case, the clause will typically contain an adverbial indicating speed and/or brevity, as in (42):

(42)   Il <u>eut/a eu</u> *vite* <u>fini</u> son repas.

Because of the form of the auxiliary, the *passé antérieur* is only used in those registers where the *passé simple* is also used, i.e. principally in formal writing. The *passé surcomposé*, on the other hand, is considered substandard and is used mainly in regional dialects and in very colloquial speech.

In a neutral register, it is possible to avoid the use of either of these forms, and yet clearly mark two past events as sequential, by replacing the temporal clause by a non-finite verb phrase, as in (43)–(44):

(43)   <u>Après avoir terminé</u> la lettre, Francis est allé se coucher.

(44)   <u>Ayant terminé</u> la lettre, Francis est allé se coucher.

In addition, the past perfect may be expressed by *venais de* + infinitive. This form is the equivalent of the present perfect construction *viens de* + infinitive discussed in section 6.3.1 above, except that it has its Reference Time in the past, and not in the present. In other words, it describes past events that took place immediately prior to some other past event. As such, it is available as yet another alternative to the *passé antérieur/passé surcomposé* in many cases, as seen in (45):

(45)   Francis <u>venait de terminer</u> sa lettre quand il est allé se coucher.

6.3.3 The compound future tense

Unlike the *futur simple* discussed in section 6.2.3 above, the ***futur composé*** formed with a present tense of the auxiliary *aller* followed by an infinitive is a secondary tense, in as much as its Reference Time precedes the Event Time, while being simultaneous with Speech Time. This is represented in (46) below, and in Figure 6.7:

(46)   Temporal reference of the *futur composé*: S, R > E

Figure 6.7. Temporal reference of the *futur composé*.

What this means is that, unlike the *futur simple*, which is used to predict future events that have no direct relevance at the moment of speech (cf. section 6.2.3 above), the *futur composé* describes future occurrences that are anchored in, or motivated by, present states, activities or events. In (47) below, for instance, the speaker's future action of going to the cafeteria is directly motivated by the fact that s/he is currently hungry:

(47)   Je <u>vais aller</u> à la cantine, car j'ai faim.

Thus, the *futur composé* is usually preferred to the *futur simple* when the clause contains a present time adverbial, whose reference point coincides with S, as in (48):

(48)   *Maintenant* je <u>vais aller</u> voir Cédric.

An occurrence that is anchored in, or motivated by, some present state, activity or event is not necessarily imminent, however, so the term *futur proche*, which is often used for this tense, is inappropriate. It may conceivably take decades before the speaker of (49) below dies as a consequence of the radiation s/he has been exposed to. Nonetheless, the *futur composé* is felicitously used here.

(49)   Nous avons été irradiés, et nous <u>allons</u> tous <u>mourir</u>.

(49) can usefully be contrasted with (50) below, in which the *futur simple* is preferred. Unlike the former, the latter is a neutral prediction

about a future event, which is not directly linked to anything in the present:

(50)   Nous <u>mourrons</u> tous un jour.

6.3.4 The future perfect

With the future perfect tense, expressed in French by the ***futur antérieur***, which consists of an auxiliary in the *futur simple* followed by a past participle, the configuration of S, R and E becomes more complex, in as much as the location of E with respect to S is indeterminate. All we know when interpreting a clause in the future perfect is that S precedes R (which is thus in the future), and that E also precedes R (which is what makes this tense a perfect). This is represented in (51) below:

(51) $S > R$ and $E > R$

Typically, when the *futur antérieur* is used, Reference Time will be expressed by a future-time adverbial, as in (52) below, where R is represented by *dans un an*. The hearer will thus understand that the Event Time, i.e. the time when Fabienne finishes her thesis, will occur before a year has passed:

(52)   Fabienne est en train de rédiger sa thèse. J'espère qu'elle l'<u>aura terminée</u> *dans un an.*

What we cannot know, out of context, is whether E is itself future with respect to Speech Time. In (52), the first sentence tells us that it must be, but in the context of the mini-discourse in (53), the *futur antérieur* is three-ways ambiguous, and even the speaker need not know which interpretation is the factually correct one.

(53)   L'année dernière, Fabienne était déjà en train de rédiger sa thèse. Elle l'<u>aura</u> sans doute <u>terminée</u> *avant l'été.* C'est peut-être déjà fait.

Thus, it may be the case, as in (52), that E is located between S and R, yielding an interpretation whereby Fabienne has not yet finished her thesis, but is predicted to do so before next summer, as illustrated in Figure 6.8.

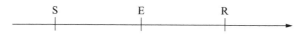

Figure 6.8. A possible interpretation of (53).

However, it could also be the case that, unbeknownst to the speaker, Fabienne has already finished her thesis at Speech Time, yielding the configuration in Figure 6.9, where E precedes not just R, but also S:

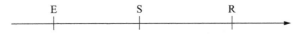

Figure 6.9. A second possible interpretation of (53).

Finally, it may be that Fabienne is in fact finishing her thesis on the very day that (53) is uttered, in which case the correct representation would be that in Figure 6.10, where S and E coincide.

Figure 6.10. A third possible interpretation of (53).

The main point here is not so much the details of the three competing interpretations, but rather the fact that, unlike the tense forms discussed previously, the *futur antérieur* does not in and of itself clearly identify the timing of the state, activity, or event that it describes with respect to Speech Time. Instead, contextual factors may help to guide the hearer's interpretation, but even they will not necessarily allow him/her to determine the precise location of E.

6.3.4.1 Modal use of the *futur antérieur*

Apart from its temporal use described in the section above, the *futur antérieur* may also be used modally, in a way that is analogous to, but more common than, the inferential modal use of the *futur simple* (cf. section 6.2.3.). Whereas the *futur simple* may be used to indicate that something represents an inference about a present state-of-affairs, the *futur antérieur* can indicate that the speaker is making an inference about a past event, as seen in (54) below. In other words, by using the *futur antérieur*, speaker B in that example is presenting the contents of her utterance not as a fact, but as a reasonable conjecture:

(54)   A: On m'a volé mon portemonnaie !
       B: Mais voyons, c'est ridicule ! Tu l'auras oublié à la maison. ('You must have left it at home.')

6.3.5 The future in the past tense

The future in the past is expressed in French chiefly by the **conditionnel** in its **temporal use**.[5] It is worth noting straight away, however, that temporal uses of the *conditionnel* tend not only to be restricted to specific syntactic and discourse contexts, but are also in the minority compared to the various modal uses of this verb form. Those modal uses will be treated below.

The temporal use of the *conditionnel* is principally used in subordinate clauses and in independent clauses that represent so-called free indirect speech (see further section 6.5). In all other types of independent/main clauses, uses of the *conditionnel* will thus normally be modal in nature.

The temporal reference of the *conditionnel* displays a similar sort of ambiguity to what we found in the case of the future perfect: all we can infer from a future in the past tense as such is that the Reference Time precedes both the Event Time (i.e. the described situation is future with respect to R) and the Speech Time (which is why the *conditionnel* denotes a future in the past), as represented in (55):

(55)   R > S and R > E

What such a tense does not tell us is where E is located with respect to S. Depending on the context, the most likely interpretation may thus be one where E is prior to S, as in (56) below. Here, R is the point in the past where the teacher is making his calculation, and E—the event of 'their' arrival— will take place at least half an hour later. Since R is expressed in the *passé simple*, a past tense which—as we saw in section 6.2.2 above is disconnected from the moment of speech, it is most likely that E is also located in the past, as illustrated in Figure 6.11:

(56)   L'instituteur calcula qu'ils ne <u>seraient</u> pas là *avant une demi-heure*.

Figure 6.11. The most likely interpretation of (56).

[5] Traditional grammars have frequently classified the *conditionnel* as a fourth mood in French. Among contemporary grammarians, however, the consensus seems to be that it is an indicative tense, and it will be treated as such in this book.

In (57) below, on the other hand, the adverbial *aujourd'hui* tells us that E (i.e. Damien's leaving) must coincide with S, as shown in Figure 6.12.

(57)   Damien a dit hier qu'il partirait *aujourd'hui*.

Figure 6.12. The temporal reference of the *conditionnel* in (57).

Finally, in an example like (58) below, E (which is still the event of Damien's leaving) must be located after Speech Time: R is located here, as in (57), by the adverbial *hier*, and is thus only one day prior to S. E is located three days after R by the adverbial *dans trois jours*. Three days from R is thus two days after S, yielding the configuration in Figure 6.13.

(58)   Damien a dit hier qu'il partirait *dans trois jours*.

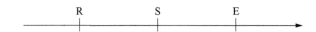

Figure 6.13. The temporal reference of the *conditionnel* in (58).

The above examples all have the temporal *conditionnel* in subordinate clauses, which is probably its most common environment.

Example (59) below shows a temporal use of the *conditionnel* in free indirect speech (see section 6.5 below for a definition). It is useful to compare this example with the one in (60), where the same meaning is expressed using direct speech:

(59)   Il raccrocha tout de suite avant d'avoir composé le numéro de Juliette. Finalement, il ne l'appellerait pas. Il passa à la salle de bain et là fit un peu de toilette.

(60)   Il raccrocha tout de suite avant d'avoir composé le numéro de Juliette. Il pensa : « Finalement, je ne l'appellerai pas. » Il passa à la salle de bain et là fit un peu de toilette.

In both examples, R is located in the past through the use of the *passé simple* in the first sentence. In (60), the second sentence consists of a reporting clause, *Il pensa*, followed by a quote in the *futur simple* supposedly representing the exact wording of the subject's thought. Here, the reporting clause and the quotation marks together signal that the quote (or reported clause) represents the character's rather than the narrator's voice. In (59), on the other hand, the reporting clause has been dispensed with, and it is the fact that the *conditionnel* is used in a main clause with future-in-the-past meaning that tells the reader that this sentence represents a reported clause, i.e. what the subject of the sentence was thinking at Reference Time. In other words, the *conditionnel* in the second sentence of (59) strongly suggests to the reader that, unlike what we find in the first and third sentence, this is not the narrator's, but the character's voice.

If an independent clause is not intended to represented free indirect discourse, the *conditionnel* is not usually used to express future-in-the-past temporal reference. The two main alternatives in finite clauses are:

(i) Use of the modal verb *devoir* in the *imparfait* followed by an infinitive, as in (61) below;
(ii) Use of the auxiliary *aller* in the *imparfait* followed by an infinitive, as in (63) below.

Let us first compare *devais* + infinitive in (61) with (62), where the *conditionnel* is used:

(61) Comme il était pressé, Jean-Pascal but un express au comptoir. Il devait aller chercher sa femme à Roissy. ('He had to go pick up his wife at Roissy Airport') (= narrator's comment, providing an explanation of why J.-P. was in a hurry)

(62) Comme il était pressé, Jean-Pascal but un express au comptoir. Il irait chercher sa femme à Roissy. (= free indirect speech)

The two examples differ in their interpretation, such that the second sentence of (61) will be interpreted as the narrator's explanation of why Jean-Pascal was in a hurry. The corresponding sentence of (62) will—as explained above—tend to be interpreted as indicating that while he was drinking his coffee, it suddenly occurred to Jean-Pascal to go pick up his wife at the airport (i.e. as equivalent in meaning to *Il pensa : « J'irai chercher ma femme à Roissy. »*).

As the translation shows, *devais* + infinitive does not, however, express a neutral future in the past, but conveys a **modal nuance**, namely that Jean-Pascal is under some sort of external obligation to pick up his wife.

If we similarly compare (63) below to (64), we see that the version with the *conditionnel* appears to be simply unacceptable, because it seems impossible in this context to interpret the whole sentence as something someone is saying or thinking at Reference Time:

(63)   Valérie <u>allait gagner</u> la course, mais elle a buté sur une pierre. ('Valérie was going to win the race , . .')

(64)   *Valérie <u>gagnerait</u> la course, mais elle a buté sur une pierre.

Like *devais* + infinitive, *allais* + infinitive expresses more than just temporal meaning. In this case, the additional nuance is an **aspectual** one, namely that something was on the verge of happening, but ultimately did not.

6.3.5.1 Modal uses of the *conditionnel*

In main clauses, uses of the *conditionnel* are thus typically modal, rather than temporal, in nature. Depending on the context, the form may be interpreted in different ways, which have in common that they are about the present (i.e. the time of utterance), rather than about a future in the past.

One common use of the modal *conditionnel*, which is particularly frequent in media discourse, is to mark the contents of the clause as some form of hearsay. In other words, the modal meaning here is that the speaker does not personally vouch for the truth of what s/he is saying. This use, which is exemplified in (65) below, bears some similarity to the use of the temporal *conditionnel* to mark free indirect speech, but the difference is that (65) concerns an alleged state-of-affairs in the present:

(65)   Le Président de la République <u>serait</u> gravement malade. ('The President is allegedly very ill.')

Secondly, the *conditionnel* can be used modally to mark an (unlikely) hypothetical situation, as shown in (66) below. The conditions for that situation to obtain may be explicitly expressed, for instance by a conditional clause or an adverbial, or it may have to be inferred from the context. (For further details about tense in *si*-conditionals, see section 6.4 below.) The hypothetical *conditionnel* concerns either the present or, as in (66), the future, but never the future in the past.

(66)   Qu'est-ce que c'est sympa ici ! (*Si je pouvais,*) je <u>resterais</u> bien encore une semaine.

Finally, the modal *conditionnel* is very frequently used to express politeness in utterances that concern the present, such as (67), where the speaker wishes to speak briefly with the hearer now:

(67)   Tu n'<u>aurais</u> pas deux minutes ? J'<u>aimerais</u> te parler.

6.3.6 The future perfect in the past

The final tense we have to deal with is the future perfect in the past, which in French is expressed by the ***conditionnel passé***. Calculating the temporal reference of a future perfect in the past is even more complex than in the case of the future perfect and the future in the past, for we now need to work with two Reference Times, R1 and R2. As will be seen below, this means that a future perfect in the past is four-ways ambiguous in terms of the location of E.

What the form tells us is that R1 precedes both Speech Time and R2, and that Event Time also precedes R2. This is formally represented in (68):

(68)   R1 > S and R1 > R2 and E > R2

Consider now the example in (69) below, where the event described by the *conditionnel passé* is Patrick's departure. There is essentially no way in which we can determine the time of his departure, i.e. Event Time, out of context.

(69)   Céline *se disait*$_{R1}$ que Patrick serait déjà parti$_E$ *quand ils arriveraient.*$_{R2}$

Here is why. As the added indices in (69) show, R1 is the time when Céline was thinking about Patrick's departure. As indicated by the use of the *imparfait*, R1 is thus in the past. R2, represented by the time of 'their' arrival, is future with respect to R1, hence expressed by the temporal *conditionnel*, which—as we saw in section 6.3.5 has future in the past meaning. If 'they' have already arrived at Speech Time, and R2 is thus in the past, Patrick's departure must also be in the past, as shown in Figures 6.14–6.15. However, the *conditionnel passé* does not tell us that Patrick's departure is necessarily future with respect to R1, as in Figure 6.14. It could be the case that, unbeknownst to Céline, he actually left the day before, which would yield the configuration in Figure 6.15.

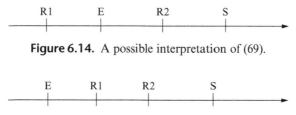

Figure 6.14. A possible interpretation of (69).

Figure 6.15. A second possible interpretation of (69).

Nor does the *conditionnel passé* tells us that R2 is necessarily past with respect to S. It could well be the case that 'their' arrival is still in the future when Céline's thoughts are reported, as in Figures 6.16 and 6.17. If that is the case, E may either have taken place prior to S, as in Figure 6.16, or may itself still be in the future, as in Figure 6.17:

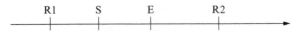

Figure 6.16. A third possible interpretation of (69).

Figure 6.17. A fourth possible interpretation of (69).

As with the other ambiguous tenses discussed above, the speaker of (69) does not actually need to know which of these interpretations is the factually correct one in order to use the *conditionnel passé* appropriately.

The temporal use of the *conditionnel passé* is restricted in the exact same way as the temporal use of the *conditionnel*: it is normally found only in subordinate clauses and in independent/main clauses representing free indirect speech (cf. section 6.3.5 above). In other types of context, there is essentially no means of expressing a future-perfect-in-the-past meaning by a finite verb form.

6.3.6.1 Modal uses of the *conditionnel passé*

Like the *conditionnel*, the *conditionnel passé* is probably more frequently used with modal meanings. Essentially, the same types of modal meaning are found, the difference being that modal uses of the *conditionnel passé* are either about the past, or express situations that are known to be counterfactual.

Thus, we find it used to indicate hearsay about past states-of-affairs, as in (70) below; to express hypothetical, but counterfactual, situations, as in (71); and to convey politeness, as in (72):

(70) Le Président de la République <u>aurait été</u> gravement malade. ('The President has allegedly been very ill.')

(71) (*Si j'avais pu,*) je <u>serais</u> bien <u>resté(e)</u> encore une semaine. (→ but I could not stay)

(72) J'<u>aurais aimé</u> te parler. (→ but it was/is not possible)

6.4 Tense in conditionals

Conditional ('if... then') constructions are by definition modal in nature, as they express hypothetical situations. The tenses used in such constructions therefore do not have their normal temporal reference. While most of the conjunctions that can introduce conditional clauses in French trigger the subjunctive (cf. section 5.4.4.3), the most commonly used conjunction, i.e. *si*, is always followed by the indicative, as are conditionals introduced by one of the compound conjunctions *au cas où*, *pour le cas où*, and *dans le cas où* (cf. section 6.4.4 below).

From the point of view of meaning, there are three basic types of conditional *si*-constructions (see section 4.2.3.2), each of which features a particular combination of tenses in the subordinate clause and the main clause. Each of these combinations expresses a particular attitude of the speaker towards the hypothetical situation described by the sentence.

6.4.1 Real conditionals

Real conditionals concern hypothetical future situations, which the speaker assesses as genuinely possible (although of course not certain). Here the conditional *si*-clause takes the *présent*, and the main clause takes the *futur simple*, as in (73):

(73) Si Loïc n'_est_ pas au rendez-vous, je _piquerai_ une crise.

6.4.2 Potential conditionals

Potential conditionals concern hypothetical situations in either the present (cf. (74) below) or the future, as in (75). The speaker assesses the situation as unlikely to obtain.

In these cases, the conditional *si*-clause takes the *imparfait*, and the main clause takes the *conditionnel*:

(74) Si jamais Camille _était_ déjà rentrée d'Amsterdam, on _pourrait_ éventuellement se voir ce soir.

(75) Si, demain, vous _gagniez_ 500 000 euros, qu'est-ce que vous en _feriez_ ?

6.4.3 Unreal (or counterfactual) conditionals

'Unreal' conditionals concern either the present or the past, and the speaker knows or believes that the hypothetical situation does not or did not obtain.

If the hypothesis concerns the present, the conditional *si*-clause takes the *imparfait*, and the main clause takes the *conditionnel*, as in (76):

(76)   Si tu <u>savais</u> de quoi tu parles, tu ne <u>dirais</u> pas de telles énormités. (→ You clearly don't know what you're talking about.)

If the hypothesis concerns the past, the conditional clause takes the *plus-que-parfait*, and the main clause takes the *conditionnel passé*, as in (77):

(77)   S'il <u>avait épousé</u> Evelyne au lieu de Bérengère, il <u>aurait</u> sans doute <u>été</u> plus heureux. (→ But it is known that he actually married Bérengère.)

6.4.4 Tense use after au cas où, pour le cas où, dans le cas où

These three conjunctions, which introduce potential conditionals, normally trigger the use of the *conditionnel* in both the conditional clause and the main clause, as shown in (78):

(78)   Au cas où Fabien ne <u>pourrait</u> pas venir, il <u>faudrait</u> trouver quelqu'un pour le remplacer.

6.5 Tense in (free) indirect speech and thought

All forms of reported speech and thought centrally involve the notion of deixis (see section 6.1 above). The three main forms of reported speech and thought in language are:

(i) Direct discourse
(ii) Indirect discourse
(iii) Free indirect discourse

Direct discourse involves quotation, i.e. presenting the reported utterances or thoughts as a (more or less) *verbatim* rendering of what the quoted individual said or thought, as in (79):

(79)   (François produces the following sentence:) Pierre répondit : « Je m'en occu-
perai demain. »

Direct discourse reports thus involve two deictic points of view, that of the
reporting speaker and that of the reported speaker. In the case of (79),
François is the reporting speaker, and Pierre is the reported speaker. The
reporting clause *Pierre a dit* assumes the point of view of François at the time
and place where he produced his utterance, whereas the reported clause '*Je le
ferai demain*' assumes Pierre's point of view. This is why the pronoun *je* in the
reported clause refers to Pierre and not to François, and why the verb of the
reported clause can be in the *futur simple* even if Pierre did 'it' a year ago.

In contrast, **indirect discourse** involves only one deictic point of view,
namely that of the reporting speaker. Let us assume that François reports
what Pierre said a year after he said it. An indirectly reported version of (79)
might then look as in (80):

(80)   (François produces the following sentence:) Pierre répondit *qu'il s'*en
occuperait *le lendemain.*

Here, the reported clause takes the form of a complement clause. Unlike
the direct quote in (79), it is thus formally marked as subordinate to the
point of view of François. Because Pierre produced his utterance a year
before François reports it, the *futur simple* of (79) has become a temporal
conditionnel expressing future-in-the-past in (80), and the deictic adverbial
demain has been replaced with the non-deictic *le lendemain* (cf. 22.1.4.1).
Similarly, because Pierre is third person from François's point of view, his
original first person pronoun *je* has been replaced by *il*.

Finally, under the same circumstances, a **free indirect** version of (79)
might look as in (81):

(81)   (François produces the following discourse:) On demanda à Pierre de contacter la mairie. *Il s'*en occuperait *le lendemain.*

Here, there is no reporting clause, and the reported clause is syntactically
independent, which is why this form of reporting is 'free'. However, as in
(80) above, the dominant point of view is that of François.[6]

---

[6] In free indirect discourse, this is strictly speaking true only with respect to the
choice of tense and personal/reflexive pronouns. Adverbials and other types of
pronoun may express the point of view of the reported speaker, as in (i) below:

(i)   (François produces the following discourse:) On demanda à Pierre de contacter
la mairie. *Il s'*en *occuperait* demain.

It is important to realize, however, that any changes made to tense, pronouns, and adverbials when converting direct discourse into (free) indirect discourse are neither automatic nor consistent across all contexts, but are subject to whatever differences and similarities exist between the points of view of the reporting and the reported speaker. Thus, if François reports Pierre's utterance later on the same day, we may get the indirect version in (82) below, which retains the *futur simple* and the adverbial *demain*, but changes the subject to the third-person singular:

(82)   (François utters the following sentence:) Pierre a répondu qu'*il s'*en <u>occupera</u> *demain.*

If Pierre himself reports his own utterance later on the same day, we may get no changes to the tense, pronouns, or adverbials of the reported clause at all, as seen in (83):

(83)   (Pierre utters the following sentence:) J'ai répondu que *je* m'en <u>occuperai</u> *demain.*

In those cases where the two points of view are clearly distinct, the use of tenses in indirect speech will follow the schema in Figure 6.18. The present-time axis represents the 'now' of the reported speaker, and the past-time axis

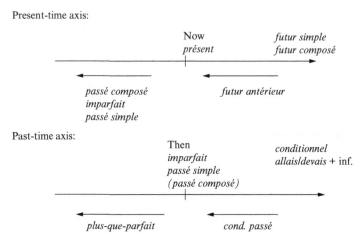

Figure 6.18. Relations between the present- and the past-time axis in indirect speech.

shows the appropriate transpositions of tenses when the reported utterance is adjusted to the point of view of the reporting speaker. Thus, assuming that the two points of view are clearly distinct, a present tense in the original reported utterance will become a past tense in the indirectly reported clause, a past tense form will become a past perfect, a future tense form will become a future in the past, and a future perfect will become a future perfect in the past.

7

Finite verb forms: Aspect

Learning objectives

- To understand the difference between tense and aspect.
- To understand the difference between aspect and mode of action, and how the two interact.
- To understand the difference between the perfective and the imperfective aspect in French.
- To understand the influence of adverbials and clause type on the choice of aspect in French.

7.1 Introduction

As mentioned in section 6.1 above, aspect resembles tense in having to do with the expression of time in language. It differs from tense, however, in expressing internal time, i.e. aspect concerns the **internal temporal structure** (or stages), if any, of events, activities and states. In addition, whereas tense expresses the temporal location of a particular event, activity, or state

The Structure of Modern Standard French. First edition. Maj-Britt Mosegaard Hansen.
© Maj-Britt Mosegaard Hansen 2016. First Published 2016 by Oxford University Press

objectively, as seen in relation to the moment of utterance, aspect expresses the speaker's subjective point of view on that event, activity, or state.

While the difference between the French *présent* and the *futur simple*, for instance, is one of tense, the difference between the *imparfait* on the one hand, and the *passé simple/passé composé*, on the other, is a difference of aspect. The difference between the *passé simple* and the *passé composé* as a past tense form is one of **register**. In the remainder of this chapter, the term *passé simple* will therefore be used to include uses of the *passé composé* as a past tense, as found in spoken and less formal written registers (cf. section 6.2.2 for further details).

Aspect as a grammatical category is not peculiar to French; indeed, it is found across a large number of languages, including English. Thus, in English, the difference between simple and progressive tense forms, as in (1)–(2), is aspectual in nature.

(1)   John <u>plays</u> tennis.

(2)   John <u>is playing</u> tennis.

Note, however, that not all languages grammaticalize the exact same aspectual distinctions. Thus, while the difference between the English simple past and the past progressive overlaps with the distinction between the *passé simple* and the *imparfait* in French, it is not identical to it.

In French, the distinction is between a so-called **perfective** (or **punctual**) aspect, represented by the *passé simple*, and an **imperfective** (or **durative**) aspect, represented by the *imparfait*. Roughly, the *passé simple* describes a given state-of-affairs as delimited in time, an indivisible whole, which is viewed from the outside. The *imparfait*, on the other hand, describes it as not delimited, but rather as unfolding at Reference Time,[1] as something which can be divided into differences phases, and it views the state-of-affairs from the inside.

Importantly, the choice between the two aspects is in principle unrelated to the question of how long a given state-of-affairs lasts in the real world. It is entirely possible to use the *passé simple* about events, activities, and states that last quite a long time, as in (3). Similarly, the *imparfait* may be used felicitously about an event such as commencing one's exercises in (4), which has no duration at all:

(3)   Ensemble, les deux époux <u>passèrent</u> un demi-siècle en parfaite harmonie.

---

[1] For the notion of Reference Time, see section 6.1.1 above.

(4)   À l'instant où Léon <u>commençait</u> ses exercices, Max entra.

In many cases, a speaker/writer can in fact choose freely between the two aspects when describing one and the same situation; depending on his/her choice, however, s/he will be conveying different meanings. Thus, for instance, either aspect may be used in the first sentence of (5)–(6) below, but as the possible continuations show, the *passé simple* in (5) implies that Alain finished the book, whereas the *imparfait* in (6) is neutral on that issue. Notice that the English simple *vs* progressive past function similarly in this respect, as shown in (7)–(8):

(5)   L'été dernier, Alain <u>lut</u> *Guerre et paix.* (Il le termina même en deux semaines./ *Cela dit, il ne le termina pas.)

(6)   L'été dernier, Alain <u>lisait</u> *Guerre et paix.* (Cela dit, il ne le termina pas./Je crois même qu'il le termina.)

(7)   Last summer, Alan <u>read</u> *War and Peace.* (He even finished it in two weeks./ *That said, he didn't finish it.)

(8)   Last summer, Alan <u>was reading</u> *War and Peace.* (That said, he didn't finish it./I think he may even have finished it.)

Before discussing the difference between the two aspects in greater detail, let us first take a look at the closely related notion, 'mode of action'.

7.2 Mode of action

Mode of action has to do with the distinction between events, activities, and states, and with any possible or actual changes of state that may be implied by the meaning of a sentence. It is a property of situations in the abstract. It is thus determined mainly by the meaning of a predicator + its complements (if any), although the subject and certain types of adverbial may also play a role.

While finer distinctions have been drawn in the research literature on the subject, this book will operate with a simple distinction between two basic modes of action:

(i) Telic situations
(ii) Atelic situations

The word 'telic' comes from the Ancient Greek *telos*, which means 'goal'. **Telic situations** are those that have an inherent end point (or goal, in an abstract sense) and which therefore result in a change of state if they are allowed to go to completion. They are necessarily bounded in time, because once the end point has been reached, the original situation no longer obtains. In (9), for instance, *gagner la course* describes a telic situation, as one cannot go on winning a race indefinitely. Once Corinne has crossed the finish line, the race is necessarily over for her:

(9)   Corinne a gagné la course.

Atelic situations, in contrast, have no such inherent end point, and may in principle continue indefinitely. Thus, in (10), *habiter* + locative object describes an atelic situation, because Marc can go on living in Nantes for as long as he pleases:

(10)   Marc habite à Nantes.

Importantly, the same verb may change its telicity depending on whether it takes a complement or not, and on the type of complement if there is one. Compare (11)–(12) below, on the one hand, and (13)–(14), on the other:

(11)   Alain fume une cigarette. (telic)

(12)   Alain fume. (atelic)

(13)   Esther mange une pomme. (telic)

(14)   Esther mange des pommes. (atelic)

Alain cannot continue to smoke the same cigarette forever; at some point, he will have reached the end of it, and the action of smoking it will have been completed, so the situation described by (11), in which *fumer* takes a direct object, is a telic one. The situation described by (12), where there is no complement, on the other hand, is atelic, because Alain can go on being a smoker for as long as he wants, without any inherent limit. The difference between (13) and (14) is analogous, even though *manger* takes a direct object in both sentences. In the telic situation in (13), the amount of apples is finite and is specified by the numeral determiner *une* of the direct object noun phrase *une pomme*. In (14), the partitive plural article *des* does not specify the amount of apples that Esther has at her disposal. For all we know, she may have an infinite supply of them, as well as an infinite appetite for them.

7.3 Choice of aspect: General principles

As such, situations—whether past, present, or future—are thus inherently either telic or atelic. In addition, when talking or writing about any situation that belongs in the past, French language users are obliged to superimpose a particular aspectual viewpoint on that situation, either perfective or imperfective.

We can graphically represent the internal temporal structure of situations as in Figure 7.1. What we have here is a **period of time** represented by the horizontal line. This period has a **starting point** represented by the vertical line at the extreme left-hand side, and an **end point** represented by the vertical line at the extreme right-hand side. In between the two, we may have a number of **phases** or stages of development, represented by the oblique lines.

When we use the **perfective aspect** in French, i.e. the *passé simple*, we impose an **external viewpoint** on the situation. Imposing an external viewpoint implies that we take either the starting point, the end point, or both into consideration, and this implies the idea of a change of state. Figure 7.2 illustrates the possibilities, which are exemplified in (15)–(18):

(15)   Louis XV <u>régna</u> pendant 59 ans.

(16)   Tout d'un coup il <u>eut</u> froid. ('Suddenly he began to feel cold.')

(17)   Nadia <u>travailla</u> jusqu'à dix heures du soir.

(18)   Gilles <u>tomba</u> de l'escabeau.

(15) illustrates the first case in Figure 7.2, where both the beginning and end point of the situation are taken into account: in order to say that Louis XV reigned for exactly 59 years, we have to know both when he became king (the starting point of his reign) and when he died (the end point), so this situation is temporally bounded at both ends.

Figure 7.1. A graphic representation of the internal temporal structure of a situation.

Figure 7.2. Representation of the meanings of the perfective aspect.

In (16), the *passé simple* is used to mark the beginning of the subject's state of feeling cold. In this case, however, we do not know how long that state lasted, so the situation is only bounded at one end.

(17) illustrates the opposite configuration: we do not know when Nadia started to work, but we know at what time she stopped, and because of this terminal boundary, the *passé simple* may be used (but see section 7.4.1.2 below).

Finally, (18) illustrates the case where an event is of such short duration that its starting point and its end point become more or less indistinguishable. Nevertheless, because both are present, the *passé simple* is used.

Perfective aspect is **dynamic**, and figuratively speaking, we can compare uses of the *passé simple* to a film, showing a number of different **events in a sequence**. Due to this inherent dynamicity, the *passé simple* is therefore used to express the basic stages of the plot in narrative texts. Thus, if several clauses in the *passé simple* follow one another in a text, the described events will be understood as similarly following one another in time, in the order in which they are mentioned in the text. This means that, every time a *passé simple* is used, Reference Time and Event Time move (slightly) further to the right on the timeline (i.e. closer to Speech Time).[2] Consider (19), for instance:

(19)   Thérèse se <u>leva</u> et <u>fit</u> un café ; il avait un goût amer et elle le <u>jeta</u> sans le finir. Elle s'<u>habilla</u> et <u>sortit</u> pour acheter le journal.

Here, we have five clauses in the *passé simple*, and one in the *imparfait*. In principle, each of the clauses in the *passé simple*, but not the clause in the *imparfait*, could be preceded by the adverbial *puis* ('then') without changing our understanding of the text.

When we use the **imperfective aspect**, on the other hand, we impose an **internal viewpoint** on the described situation, that is, we abstract from its starting point and end point, as well as from any changes of state, and we focus instead on the situation as it might appear to an eyewitness or a participant at a given moment in time. Graphically, this can be represented as in Figure 7.3, where the vertical lines from Figure 7.1 are missing.

Figure 7.3. Representation of the meaning of the imperfective aspect.

[2] See chapter 6 for the notions of Reference, Event, and Speech Time.

The imperfect aspect is thus a **static** one, which can be compared to a **snapshot** (as opposed to a film), freezing a particular situation as it is unfolding. In (20), for instance, it is not important to know when it began to be warm in the café, nor when it stopped; the sentence merely sets the stage for something else. (21) is similar in as much as the beginning and/or end point of Chantal's sleep is irrelevant: her being in a state of sleep at Reference Time simply frames Olivier's return home.

(20)   Il faisait chaud dans le café.

(21)   Chantal dormait quand Olivier rentra.

If several clauses in the *imparfait* follow one another in a text, the situations they describe will usually be understood to be more or less simultaneous. In such cases, the Reference Time stays constant. Unlike the text in (19) above, the one in (22) would thus be rendered quite strange if we were to insert the adverbial *puis* at the beginning of each clause:

(22)   Dans l'allée sablée, une jeune femme apprenait à marcher à son bébé. L'enfant trébuchait parfois et se cramponnait au doigt de sa mère.

Typically, therefore, the *imparfait* is used to express background information of a primarily descriptive or explanatory nature.

A distinct use of the *imparfait* is to express **iterative** or **habitual aspect**, i.e. situations that are repeated an indefinite number of times (iterative aspect), or even regularly (habitual aspect) during an unspecified period of time. This is exemplified in (23):

(23)   Marie-Pierre jouait au tennis tous les samedis après-midi.

The iterative/habitual use of the *imparfait* is related to its basic imperfective use in as much as a sentence like (23) can be said to describe a temporally unbounded state of Marie-Pierre's at Reference Time, namely the state of being 'someone who plays tennis on Saturday afternoon'.

To more fully appreciate the respective roles of the *passé simple* and the *imparfait*, let us consider the somewhat longer narrative text in (24) below:

(24)   Autrefois, un robot très intelligent rencontra [1] dans un bal à la cour une jeune et jolie dame de la noblesse. Ils dansèrent [2] ensemble. Il lui dit [3] des choses galantes. Elle rougit [4]. Il s'excusa [5]. Ils recommencèrent [6] à danser. Elle le trouvait [a] un peu raide, mais charmant sous ses manières guindées, qui lui donnaient [b] beaucoup de distinction. Ils se marièrent [7] le lendemain. Ils reçurent [8] des cadeaux somptueux et partirent [9] en voyage de noces. La jeune mariée était [c] naïve, et elle n'aperçut [10] pas tout de suite le caractère cybernétique de son conjoint. Cependant, elle voyait [d] bien qu'il faisait [e] toujours les mêmes gestes et qu'il disait [f] toujours les mêmes choses. (Adapted from Alain Robbe-Grillet, *Djinn*, Les Éditions de Minuit, 1981)

In this text, the clauses (numbered [1] through [10]) whose predicators are in the *passé simple* report the main events of the story. These events should be interpreted as occurring in the sequence in which they are mentioned in the text. Thus, for instance, the repeated use of the *passé simple* in [2]–[6] makes it clear that the couple had at least one dance before the robot complimented the lady, who blushed as a result. In response to her blushing, he apologized, and only then did they dance again.

The clauses whose predicators are in the *imparfait* (and which are labelled using letters [a] through [f]) provide background information about the circumstances of the main events, they explain why certain things happened or did not happen, or they describe habits of the characters at Reference Time. There is no specific temporal sequence in these cases; presumably, the lady was naïve even before she met the robot and succumbed to his charms, for instance, and she may well have been aware of the repetitive nature of his behaviour already on the night they met. Notice, moreover, that all the clauses that are in the *imparfait* could be left out without changing our basic understanding of what happened between these two characters.

This text also shows that the choice of aspect in a particular clause tends to correlate with the telicity of the situation described by the clause, such that the situations described by clauses in the *passé simple* are also inherently telic, whereas situations described by clauses in the *imparfait* are inherently atelic.

That is not true in all cases, however: to dance with one another is inherently atelic, but by using the *passé simple* in clause [2], the narrator makes it clear that the dancing should be understood as a bounded event. This shows how the choice of aspect may, in and of itself, have a clear effect on the meaning of the utterance.

In many cases, if an atelic situation is described using the *passé simple*, or a telic situation is described using the *imparfait*, an appropriate translation into English will have to reflect that somehow, for instance by using a different (i.e. not a past) form of the English verb (cf. (25)–(26)) or a different verb altogether (cf. (27)–(28)):

(25) Aline se jeta du pont. ('Aline threw herself off the bridge.')

(26)   Une seconde de plus, et Aline se jetait du pont. ('One second more, and Aline would have thrown herself off the bridge.')

(27)   Quand j'étais petite j'avais peur des chiens. ('When I was little, I was afraid of dogs.')

(28)   En voyant l'énorme chien de garde, j'eus peur. ('When I saw the huge watchdog, I became frightened.')

There is nothing particularly mysterious about examples like (26) or (28). In (26), the *imparfait* indicates that the event is recounted from the point of view of an eyewitness observing Aline standing on the bridge and inferring that she is about to jump; the situation is thus conceived as unfolding before that person's very eyes. (28) is, of course, equivalent to (16) above, and marks the beginning of a state, in this case the state of being afraid of the dog.

7.4 Typical patterns of aspectual use in connection with adverbials and subordinate clauses

In addition to the general rules set out above, certain syntactic environments are strongly associated with the use of either the *passé simple* or the *imparfait*. On the one hand, certain types of adverbial will strongly favour a particular aspect; on the other hand, certain types of subordinate clause are similarly associated with either the *passé simple* or the *imparfait*.

However, it is important to realize that the patterns described below are not exceptions to the general rules. In fact, they essentially follow from those general rules. They are described here mainly as an aid to the non-native speaker. In addition, just like the default associations between telicity and aspect described above, the patterns mentioned below can be overridden if the speaker/writer wishes to express something special.

7.4.1 Adverbials

7.4.1.1 Adverbials that normally trigger the *imparfait*
When used in past-time contexts, a number of different types of adverbial normally co-occur with the *imparfait* rather than the *passé simple*.

Present-time adverbials

Present-time adverbials are adverbials like *maintenant, en ce moment*, etc., which are mostly combined with the present tense. Because the validity of a present tense typically extends beyond Reference Time (cf. section 6.2.1), the present tense is aspectually imperfective, and thus more similar to the *imparfait* than to the *passé simple*. For that reason, these adverbials are almost always combined with the *imparfait* when used in past-time contexts:

(29)   *Maintenant*, il <u>était</u> fatigué.

Adverbials that describe on-going activity

The adverbial *déjà*, as well as *encore* and *toujours* when they mean 'yet/still', usually co-occur with the *imparfait*, because they are used about situations that are on-going at Reference Time:

(30)   Il <u>faisait</u> *déjà* nuit.

Iterative adverbials, when they describe an indefinite number of repetitions

Iterative adverbials, i.e. adverbials which express that something happened on more than one occasion, combine with the *imparfait* if no very definite number of repetitions is expressed. Examples of such adverbials are *toutes les semaines, chaque matin, souvent, parfois, rarement*, etc.:

(31)   Magali <u>venait</u> *rarement* me voir.

7.4.1.2 Adverbials that normally trigger the *passé simple*

Other types of adverbial express meanings that are most naturally combined with the perfective aspect.

Limitative adverbials

Adverbials that denote a limited timespan combine with the *passé simple*. The timespan in question may be delimited on both sides, that is, the adverbial may express both its beginning and its end point, or it may be delimited at only one end, marking either the beginning or the end point. Some adverbials of this type are, for instance, *pendant deux heures, dès son arrivée, jusqu'au soir*. When it is the end point that is marked, the *imparfait* is also regularly used, however, cf. (33):

(32)   Ils l'<u>attendirent</u> *pendant deux heures.*

(33)   Nadia <u>travailla(it)</u> *jusqu'à dix heures du soir.*

Iterative adverbials, when they describe a definite number of repetitions
If an iterative adverbial specifies a more or less precise, limited number of repetitions, the *passé simple* is used, for example *trois fois, à plusieurs reprises*:

(34)   Géraldine <u>rencontra</u> Dominique *trois fois de suite.*

7.4.1.3 Other types of temporal adverbials
Temporal adverbials that do not fit into any of the above categories are freely combined with either aspect in accordance with the general rules, depending on what the speaker intends to express.

7.4.1.4 Clauses containing two or more different types of adverbial
In some cases, a clause may contain two or more adverbials of different types, such that one of them is normally combined with the *passé simple*, and the other with the *imparfait*. In such cases, one of them will express a timespan that encompasses the span expressed by the other adverbial(s), and it is this former adverbial that will determine the choice of aspect. In (35) below, for instance, the limitative adverbial *longuement* would normally be used with the *passé simple*. Here, however, the *imparfait* is used because the timespan marked by *longuement* is subject to an indefinite number of repetitions, marked by the adverbial clause *chaque fois qu'ils se rencontraient*. Similarly, in (36), *deux fois* is a limitative adverbial which on its own would trigger the *passé simple*. Because of the presence of the indefinite iterative adverbial *toujours*, however, the *imparfait* must be used here:

(35)   *Chaque fois qu'ils se rencontraient*, ils s'embrassaient <u>LONGUEMENT</u>.

(36)   Le facteur <u>sonnait</u> *toujours* DEUX FOIS.

7.4.2 Subordinate clauses

The basic meanings of various types of subordinate clause are such that these types of clauses are typically associated with one or the other aspect.

7.4.2.1 Nominal clauses

In nominal clauses, i.e. complement clauses, indirect interrogatives, and free relative clauses,[3] the *imparfait* is normally used if the main clause predicator is in a past tense form, cf. (37) below. This is because the states, activities and/or events described in the main clause and the nominal clause are normally understood to be more or less simultaneous in such cases.

(37)   Norbert *comprit* qu'il ne <u>pouvait</u> rien faire.

However, the *passé simple* is used in complement clauses functioning as postponed subjects[4] of verbs such as *arriver, advenir*, etc., which express the occurrence of an event, if that verb is itself in the *passé simple*, as in (38):

(38)   Il *arriva* qu'un jour, pendant l'entraînement, il se <u>foula</u> la cheville.

7.4.2.2 Adjectival clauses

In adjectival relative clauses, the use of aspect depends, in the first instance, on whether the relative clause is of the predicative, the restrictive, or the non-restrictive subtype.[5]

Predicative relative clauses

Predicative relative clauses take the *imparfait*, if the main verb is in a past tense form, as in (39) below. This is because there is simultaneity between the situations described by the main clause and the relative clause.

(39)   Je l'*entendis* qui <u>chantait</u> sous la douche.

Restrictive relative clauses

Restrictive relative clauses usually take the *imparfait* if the main verb is in a past tense form, as in (40), because the situations described in the main clause and the relative clause are normally more or less simultaneous. Thus, in (40), the taxi is already in the process of stopping when it is hailed:

(40)   Il appela un taxi qui <u>s'arrêtait</u>. (= '. . . a taxi that was stopping')

---

[3] For more details about nominal clauses in French, see section 4.2.1.

[4] See section 3.1.2 for the notion of postponed subject.

[5] For more details about types of relative clauses, see section 4.2.2.

However, the *passé simple* is used if the antecedent and the relative clause together delimit a period of time, as in (41):

(41)   *Les jours* qui <u>suivirent</u> furent angoissants.

Non-restrictive relative clauses

With respect to aspect, non-restrictive relative clauses behave much like independent clauses, which is to say that either aspect may be used in accordance with the general rules, depending on the meaning that the speaker wishes to express. By using the *passé simple* in (42), the speaker will be understood to suggest that the taxi stopped subsequently to, and presumably as a result of, being hailed:

(42)   Il appela un taxi, qui <u>s'arrêta</u>. (= '... a taxi, which (then) stopped')

7.4.2.3 Adverbial clauses

Certain adverbial clause types, and certain subordinators, are strongly associated with use of one or the other aspect.

Temporal clauses introduced by quand or lorsque

Temporal clauses introduced by *quand* or *lorsque* may describe (i) a punctual event, (ii) an identifiable period in someone's life, or (iii) a repeated or habitual occurrence.

When the temporal clause describes a punctual event, it usually takes the *passé simple*. The main clause, however, may be in either the *passé simple* or the *imparfait*, depending on whether it describes a situation that is on-going when the event in the subordinate clause takes place (as in (43) below) or one that occurs subsequently to the event described by the temporal clause (as in (44)):

(43)   Quand il <u>rentra</u>, Amélie *dormait* déjà.

(44)   Quand il <u>rentra</u>, Amélie se *réveilla*.

The *imparfait* is used in the temporal clause if that clause denotes a period in someone's life, as in (45). As before, the main clause may take either aspect, in accordance with the general rules:

(45)   Quand Maman <u>était</u> petite, il n'y avait pas encore internet.

The *imparfait* is also used in the temporal clause if the sentence as a whole describes a habitual relationship between two states of affairs, in (46) below.

In such cases, the main clause must also be in the *imparfait*, and *quand/ lorsque* can be translated as 'whenever' (as opposed to 'when'):

(46) Quand il <u>pleuvait</u>, ils *jouaient* au billard dans le salon.

Temporal clauses introduced by comme, alors que, pendant que, *or* tandis que

The conjunctions *comme*, *alors que*, *pendant que*, and *tandis que* are used when the situation described by the temporal clause is more or less simultaneous with that described by the main clause. They are thus almost always combined with the *imparfait*, as in (47):

(47) J'ai vu Laurence comme elle <u>montait</u> dans le bus.

Temporal clauses introduced by dès que, aussitôt que, *or* tant que

Temporal clauses introduced by *dès que*, *aussitôt que*, or *tant que* may take either aspect. However, the same aspect must normally be used in both the main clause and the subordinate clause, as in (48):

(48) Dès qu'il y <u>avait</u> un brin de soleil, les vacanciers *s'installaient* sur la plage pour en profiter.

(49) Dès qu'ils <u>furent</u> prêts, ils *partirent*.

When the *imparfait* is used, as in (48), its meaning is habitual/iterative. When the *passé simple* is used, as in (49), the sentence as a whole is understood to describe a singular occurrence.

Clauses of cause, comparison, or concession

Adverbial clauses of cause, comparison, and concession typically express the background circumstances of the situation described by their main clause. Usually, they are therefore in the *imparfait*:

(50) Il avait accepté un poste comme professeur en Arabie Saoudite parce que ça lui <u>permettait</u> de mettre beaucoup d'argent de côté.

Result clauses

A result clause may take either aspect, but will normally be in the *passé simple* if the main verb is also in the *passé simple*, as shown in (51):

(51) Elle *poussa* un cri si fort qu'il <u>se réveilla</u>.

Other types of adverbial clause

Purpose clauses and **modal clauses** always take the subjunctive, so the issue of aspect does not arise. See sections 8.4.4.5 and 8.4.4.8 below.

When the verb of a **conditional clause** is in the past tense, it is normally the *imparfait*, as shown in (52) below. For further details about the forms and meanings of verb forms in conditional constructions, see section 8.4.

(52)   Si Jonathan <u>venait</u>, je serais bien content(e).

8

Finite verb forms: Auxiliaries

Learning objectives

- To understand the notions of auxiliary and main verb.
- To understand what verb forms are possible auxiliaries in French compound verb forms.
- To understand the rules governing the choice between *être* and *avoir* as tense/aspect auxiliaries.

8.1 The notion of auxiliary

As explained in section 2.3.1, compound verb forms always contain at least one element functioning as an auxiliary of the main verb. Whereas the main verb provides the basic conceptual meaning of the compound verb, the auxiliary gives information about tense, aspect, and/or voice.[1] Thus, in (1) below, *a* indicates that the action of sending the letter was completed in the past with respect to the moment of speech, whereas *vais* in (2) indicates

---

[1] For more information about tense and aspect, see chapters 6 and 7 above. For voice, see chapter 25.

that the activity of sleeping is in the future with respect to that moment. In (3), *fait* is a causative auxiliary indicating that Max is not painting the house himself, but is making someone else do it. Finally, in (4), *être* is a passive auxiliary indicating that the children are not carrying out the activity of looking-after, but are rather subject to it.

(1)   Pierre <u>a</u> envoyé la lettre.

(2)   Maintenant, je <u>vais</u> dormir.

(3)   Max <u>fait</u> peindre la maison.

(4)   Les enfants <u>sont</u> surveillés par des adultes à tout moment.

French has a total of five verbs that can function as auxiliaries, namely *être*, *avoir*, *aller*, *venir*, and *faire*.[2] Three of these, namely *être*, *avoir*, and *faire*, can take the same range of forms as other verbs, including compound forms, as shown in (5)–(7) below:

(5)   Pierre <u>aurait</u> envoyé la lettre si tu le lui <u>avais</u> demandé.

(6)   Max <u>va faire</u> peindre la maison cet été.

(7)   Que les enfants <u>aient été</u> surveillés par des adultes à tout moment, cela va sans dire.

Aller and *venir* on the other hand, only ever occur as auxiliaries in either the present tense or the *imparfait*, as in (2) above and (8) below. In (2), *va* is an auxiliary in the *futur composé* (see section 6.3.3 above), while in (8), *venais* is a past perfect auxiliary (see section 6.3.2 above):

(8)   Je <u>venais</u> de t'appeler quand Max est rentré.

If any other forms of *aller* or *venir*, such as the *futur simple* in (9) below, are followed by an infinitive, then they function as full motion verbs. Thus, the infinitive in (9) is not the main verb, but an adverbial indicating the purpose of the movement:

---

[2] Some readers may wonder why the modal verbs (principally, *devoir* and *pouvoir*) are not included in the list. In English, it is quite clear that modal verbs are auxiliaries, on a par with *be*, *have*, and periphrastic *do*. The French modal verbs, however, behave differently from their English counterparts in a number of ways, and as a result, their status is controversial: some grammarians consider them to be auxiliaries, while others do not. In this book, the French modal verbs will be treated as full verbs.

(9)   J'<u>irai</u> voir mon père demain. (= I will go [somewhere else in order] to see my
father tomorrow.)

The tenses that take *aller* or *venir* as their auxiliaries are discussed in
sections 6.3.1–6.3.3 and 6.3.5. The use of *faire* as a causative auxiliary, and
of *être* as a passive auxiliary are treated in sections 25.2 and 25.4. The
remainder of this chapter will thus discuss only the choice between *être*
and *avoir* as tense/aspect auxiliaries.

8.2 *Être* and *avoir* as tense/aspect auxiliaries

In French compound tenses, the choice of auxiliary depends on the type of
verb and the construction in which it is used. There are four different
possibilities.[3]

8.2.1 Transitive verbs used non-reflexively

As explained in section 1.2.3.2, transitive verbs are verbs that can take an
object. These verbs always take *avoir* as their auxiliary in French. *Boire* in
(10) below takes a direct object *un chocolat chaud*, which shows us that it is
transitive. Accordingly, the auxiliary used is *avoir*:

(10)   J'ai <u>bu</u> un chocolat chaud aux Deux Magots.

8.2.2 Pronominal verbs and reflexive constructions

Pronominal verbs, such as those in (11)–(12) below (see section 15.1), always
take *être* as their auxiliary, and so do all other verbs whenever they are used
in a reflexive construction (as shown in (13)):

(11)   Evangéline <u>s</u>'est évanouie en entendant ces mots.

(12)   Pierre ne <u>s</u>'était douté de rien. ('Pierre hadn't suspected anything.')

(13)   Corinne <u>s</u>'est lavée.

---

[3] The related issue of past participle agreement is treated in section 10.2.

8.2.3 Intransitive verbs: The general rule

The majority of intransitive verbs in French, i.e. verbs that either take no complement or take only a subject attribute (cf. sections 1.2.2 and 1.2.3.1), likewise take *avoir* as their auxiliary, e.g. (14)–(16) below:

(14)   Pascal a couru pour attraper le bus.

(15)   Frédéric et Germaine ont divorcé.

(16)   Maryse a été danseuse.

8.2.4 Intransitive verbs: The exceptions

Seventeen common intransitive verbs (mainly, but not exclusively, verbs of motion), some of which are (partly) synonymous, take *être* as their auxiliary, however. These verbs are *aller*, *apparaître*, *arriver*, *décéder*, *demeurer*, *descendre*, *entrer*, *monter*, *mourir*, *naître*, *partir*, *passer*, *rester*, *retourner*, *sortir*, *tomber*, and *venir*, cf. (17)–(18):[4]

(17)   Sébastien est né en 1972.

(18)   Ils sont descendus au premier étage.

In most cases, **intransitive derivations**[5] from these 17 intransitive verbs also take *être*. Thus, in (19)–(20) below, the derived verbs *devenir* (from *venir*) and *remonter* (from *monter*) take *être* as their auxiliary.

(19)   Nicolas est devenu tout rouge.

(20)   J'avais oublié mon parapluie ; alors je suis remonté(e) le chercher.

Several of these verbs can also be used **transitively**, in which case they take *avoir*, like all other transitive verbs, cf. (21)–(22) below. When they are used

---

[4] Some of these verbs are sometimes found with *avoir*, even when they function intransitively. This is a fairly marginal phenomenon in Standard French, however, and will not be discussed further.

[5] Derivation is when a new word is formed from an existing one by adding something to the original word form. In French, verbs can be derived from other verbs by adding a **prefix**, i.e. a morpheme that attaches to the beginning of the base verb, as in *[de]venir* and *[re]monter*.

transitively, their meanings will be somewhat (or even very) different from their basic intransitive use. This is unsurprising, given that, as shown in section 1.2.3.10, the same verb will frequently have different meanings when used with different valency structures.

(21) Pascale a sorti le chien cet après-midi. ('Pascale took the dog out for a walk this afternoon.')

(22) La police a descendu le malfrat. ('The police shot down the gangster.')

9

Non-finite verb forms:
The infinitive

Learning objectives

- To understand the difference between infinitives as main verbs, nouns, and heads of infinitival clauses.
- To understand the difference between infinitival clauses with verbal functions and infinitival clauses with nominal functions.
- To understand the difference between de/à as infinitive markers and as prepositions.
- To understand and be able to apply the grammatical rules that determine when infinitive markers are used, and what form they take.

9.1 Introduction

The infinitive is one of four non-finite verb forms in French, the other three being the past participle (cf. chapter 10), the present participle and the *gérondif* (cf. chapter 11). Unlike finite verb forms, non-finite forms in French are not inflected for person, nor for mood or tense. The infinitive

The Structure of Modern Standard French. First edition. Maj-Britt Mosegaard Hansen.
© Maj-Britt Mosegaard Hansen 2016. First Published 2016 by Oxford University Press

may, however, occur in a compound form denoting completion, which is an aspectual notion, as in (1):

(1)   Cela me fait plaisir d'avoir rencontré ta femme.

As parts of speech, non-finite verb forms have an intermediate status, behaving in some ways like verbs, and in other ways like nouns or adjectives.

In French, infinitives may have three different types of function:

(a) An infinitive may function as the **main verb** in a compound verb form which itself functions as the predicator of a finite clause. This is the case when an infinitive forms part of a compound future tense (i.e. *aller* + infinitive), as in (2) below, or of a causative construction (i.e. *faire* + infinitive), as in (3). This is a properly verbal function, which will not be treated further in this chapter.[1]

(2)   Je vais voir Samantha.

(3)   Jacqueline a fait pleurer son frère.

(b) Some infinitives, such as *pouvoir*, have become **nominalized**. As such, they function as heads of noun phrases, taking determiners and potentially also modifiers, as in (4) below. Nominalized infinitives behave like other nouns, and will not be treated further in this chapter.

(4)   Le pouvoir illimité est corrupteur.

(c) Very frequently, however, infinitives in French function as **heads of infinitival clauses**. The remainder of this chapter will concentrate on that function.

9.2 Infinitival clauses

Whenever an infinitive takes, or could potentially take, at least one valency element, then it constitutes the head of an infinitival clause. Like other non-finite clauses, however, infinitival clauses do not normally take a

---

[1] See section 6.3.3 for more information about the compound future tense, and section 25.4 for the causative construction.

grammatical subject of their own. The logical subject of an infinitival clause must therefore—except in one particular case (cf. section 9.2.1.1 below)—be inferred from context.[2]

Infinitival clauses may have a predominantly verbal function or a predominantly nominal function.

9.2.1 Infinitival clauses with predominantly verbal function

There are two types of construction in French where an infinitival clause plays a role that corresponds closely to that of a finite verb. Given that infinitives cannot express information about person, number, tense, or mood, these constructions are found only where such information is either unnecessary or can be inferred from the context.

9.2.1.1 Absolute constructions

Absolute constructions (see section 3.2.3) constitute the one case where an infinitival clause can have a grammatical subject. That subject is the base of the absolute construction, while the infinitival clause is its predicate.

Absolute constructions of this kind can be used as **exclamatives**, as in (5) below, in which case no infinitive marker is used:

(5)   Moi demander pardon à Manu ! ($\approx$ 'Do you really expect me to apologize to Manu?!')
 >> [Moi]$_{\text{Base/PersPron}}$ [demander pardon à Manu !]$_{\text{Pred/InfCl}}$
 >> [demander pardon]$_{\text{H/Infof PhrV}}$ [à Manu]$_{\text{DatObj/PP}}$

They may also be used as so-called '**historical infinitives**', in which case the infinitive marker *de* is used, as in (6) below. A historical infinitive conveys that the state, activity or event it describes is an immediate result of something that was described in the preceding discourse. Often, as in (6), the construction will therefore be linked to the preceding discourse by the conjunction *et*:

(6)   Pour Mgr Di Falco, il est désormais question de transformer ce lieu de pèlerinage et de culte marial en un « Lourdes moderne » ! D'où le projet de cette nouvelle église annoncé à grand renfort d'album musical et plus discrètement de la vente de cinémas. Sauf que les habitants et citoyens de Gap ne l'entendent

---

[2] For the notion of logical subject, see section 3.1.

pas de cette oreille. Pour eux, en effet, ce projet sonne faux car il met en péril une certaine idée de la culture dans les Hautes-Alpes. <u>Et ceux-ci de faire circuler une pétition pour interpeler la population, ses responsables et bien sûr, Mgr Di Falco, l'évêque de la place.</u> ('As a result they sent round a petition...')

Ch. Terras, 'Un album pour quelle église?', *Goli@s news* (13 March 2010), http://golias-news.fr/article3666.html.

>> [Et]$_{Coord/CoordConj}$ [ceux-ci]$_{Base/DemPron}$ [de faire circuler une pétition...]$_{Pred/InfCl}$
>> [de]$_{Premod/InfMarker}$ [faire circuler]$_{H/CompInf}$ [une pétition]$_{DirObj/NP}$ [pour interpeler...]$_{Adv'al/PP}$

In both cases, the absolute construction stands alone, as an alternative to a whole sentence.

9.2.1.2 Clause fragments

Infinitival clauses with verbal function can also be found as both main and subordinate clause fragments, in which case they do not have an expressed subject. Infinitival clauses as **main clause fragments** may convey a range of meanings, including imperative meaning as in (7) below, or interrogative meaning as in (8):

(7)   Après usage, <u>laver la machine</u>. (≈ '...il faut laver la machine/...lavez la machine.')

(8)   <u>Que faire</u> ? (≈ 'Que faut-il faire ?')

As **subordinate clause fragments**, infinitival clauses usually correspond to either an indirect interrogative, as in (9), or to a relative clause, as in (10):

(9)   Je ne savais pas <u>où donner de la tête</u>. (≈ '...où je devais donner de la tête.')

(10)   Il n'avait plus personne <u>à qui parler</u>. (≈ '...à qui il pouvait parler.')

As the above examples suggest, infinitival clauses as clause fragments typically—although not invariably—express some form of modality (necessity, possibility, etc.).

When occurring as clause fragments, infinitival clauses do not take infinitive markers, as the above examples show.

9.2.2 Infinitival clauses with predominantly nominal function

Despite the possible verbal uses treated above, it is far more common in French to use infinitival clauses with a predominantly nominal function.

In such cases, the infinitival clause functions syntactically in much the same way as a noun phrase would.

9.2.2.1 Infinitive markers *vs* prepositions

The main issue with respect to infinitival clause that have a predominantly nominal function is whether or not they take an **infinitive marker**.

English normally uses the infinitive marker *to*, as in (11), where the infinitival clause functions as the subject of the sentence. We can tell that *to* is an infinitive marker here, and not a preposition, by replacing the infinitival clause with a noun phrase, in which case *to* disappears, as seen in (12):

(11)   [To behave like that]$_{Subj/InfCl}$ is bizarre.

(12)   That behaviour$_{Subj/NP}$ is bizarre.

In French, however, an infinitive marker is not always present, and when it is, it does not always take the same form. Depending on their grammatical function and on the meaning of the predicator that governs them, infinitival clauses may be bare (i.e. without an infinitive marker), or they may be marked by either *de* or, more rarely, *à*, as seen in (13)–(15):

(13)   [Fumer]$_{Subj/InfCl}$ provoque des maladies graves.

(14)   J'essaierai [de te téléphoner ce soir.]$_{DirObj/InfCl}$

(15)   Lucie a appris [à lire]$_{DirObj/InfCl}$ à l'âge de 4 ans.

Just as English *to* is sometimes an infinitive marker and sometimes a preposition, so French *de* and *à* can be either infinitive markers or prepositions. We can tell the difference by applying the substitution test (cf. section 2.6.1). Just as we did in the English cases in (11)–(12) above, we can replace a French infinitival clause with a noun phrase or a pronoun playing the same grammatical role. If *de/à* disappear along with the infinitive, they are infinitive markers. If they remain, they are prepositions.

Thus, in (16) and (18) below, *de* and *à* are infinitive markers because they disappear if the predicators *essaie* and *continue* are followed by a pronoun or a noun phrase. In (17) and (19), on the other hand, they are prepositions, which may take different types of complement, incl. infinitival clauses and pronouns:

(16)   Il essaie *de travailler*. → Il essaie Ø cela. (→ *de* is an infinitive marker)

(17) Il parle *de travailler.* → Il parle de̱ cela. (→ *de* is a preposition)

(18) Il continue *à travailler.* → Il continue Ø le travail. (→ *à* is an infinitive marker)

(19) Il aspire *à travailler.* → Il aspire à̱ cela. (→ *à* is a preposition)

9.2.2.2 The use or non-use of infinitive markers

As mentioned above, the use or non-use of infinitive markers in French depends in the first instance on the grammatical function of the infinitival clause.

Infinitival clauses as (dislocated) subjects
When an infinitival clause functions as the (dislocated) subject of a clause,[3] it normally takes no infinitive marker, as illustrated by (20)–(21) below:

(20) [Ø Fumer] provoque des maladies graves.

(21) [Ø Fumer des cigarettes], ça provoque des maladies graves.

However, the marker *de* may be used if the infinitival clause expresses an actual occurrence, as opposed to a virtual one as in (20)–(21). This is so particularly when the head of the infinitival clause is a compound infinitive like *avoir fumé* in (22):

(22) [Ḏ'avoir fumé deux havanes] l'a rendu(e) malade.

Infinitival clauses as postponed subjects
When an infinitival clause functions as a postponed subject, the general rule is that it takes the infinitive marker *de*, as in (23):

(23) Il est dangereux [de̱ fumer.]

However, in clauses that also contain a subject attribute (cf. section 1.2.3.1), the infinitive marker will take the form *que de* if the subject attribute is also an infinitival clause, as in (24) below. If the subject attribute takes the form of a noun phrase, either *de* or *que de* may be used, as in (25):

(24) Ce serait *risquer sa santé*$_{\text{SubjAttr/InfCl}}$ [que de̱ commencer à fumer.]$_{\text{PostponedSubj/}}$
$_{\text{InfCl}}$

(25) Ce serait *une bêtise*$_{\text{SubjAttr/NP}}$ [(que) de̱ commencer à fumer.]$_{\text{PostponedSubj/InfCl}}$

---

[3] For the notion of dislocation, see section 26.2.

As a postponed subject of *il vaut mieux,* the infinitival phrase occurs without an infinitive marker, as in (26):

(26)   Il vaut mieux [Ø ne pas se presser.]

If the predicator is the verb *rester*, *à* is normally used instead of *de*, as in (27):

(27)   Il ne me reste qu'[à̲ écrire la conclusion.]

Infinitival clauses as subject attributes

When an infinitival clause functions as a subject attribute (cf. section 1.2.3.1), two different interpretations are possible, one of them being associated with the use of the infinitive marker *de*, the other with the use of a bare infinitive.

If there is a **relation of equivalence** between subject and subject attribute, such that they can be swapped around without changing the basic interpretation of the clause, then the infinitive marker *de* is used, as in (28) below. Example (29), where the subject and subject attribute have changed places, has essentially the same meaning as (28):

(28)   *Ma tendance naturelle, ce* serait plutôt [d̲'exagérer mes problèmes.]

(29)   Exagérer mes problèmes, ce serait plutôt ma tendance naturelle.

In such cases, the subject will typically take the form of a noun phrase or a pronoun whose referent is represented by a noun phrase elsewhere in the text (as in (28), where the noun phrase represented by the grammatical subject *ce* is dislocated).

If there is a **relation of implication** (i.e. an "if ... then" relation) between subject and subject attribute, no infinitive marker is used on the subject attribute, as seen in (30)–(31) below. Unlike (28)–(29), this pair of sentences evidently does not have the same meaning, (30) meaning something along the lines of 'if you love someone, then you'll forgive them', while (31) means, rather, 'if you forgive someone, then you'll love them'.

(30)   *Aimer, c'*est [Ø pardonner.]

(31)   *Pardonner, c'*est [Ø aimer.]

When the relationship between subject and subject attribute is one of implication, the subject is usually a neutral *ce* representing an infinitival clause (as in (30)–(31)) or a finite clause somewhere in the preceding text.

Infinitival clauses as direct objects

When an infinitival clause functions as a direct object, the default is that it takes the infinitive marker *de*, as in (32):

(32) J'essaierai [de te téléphoner ce soir.]

However, there is a **large number of exceptions** to this, which are outlined below.

For one thing, the marker *à* is used when the governing verb is *apprendre, enseigner, chercher, commencer,* or *continuer,* cf. (33) below. Note, however, that *commencer* and *continuer* are also compatible with the use of *de* as an infinitive marker, as shown in (34):

(33) Lucie *a appris* [à lire] à l'âge de 4 ans.

(34) Elles *continuaient* [à/de bavarder.]

In addition, the verb *demander* may, but need not, trigger the use of *à* when its subject is the same as the logical subject of the infinitive, cf. (35) below. If the subject of *demander* is different from the logical subject of the infinitive, the default rule applies, and *de* is used as in (36):

(35) Je *demande* [à/d'apprendre le français.] (→ I am going to learn French.)

(36) Je lui *demande* [de m'apprendre le français.] (→ He is going to teach me French.)

The following five categories of governing verb take **bare infinitives** as their direct objects:

(i) Verbs of **volition** and **desire**, as in (37):

(37) Je *préférerais* [Ø ne pas y aller.]

(ii) Three verbs expressing **strong emotion**, viz. *adorer, aimer,* and *détester,* as in (38):

(38) Walter *déteste* [Ø aller en boîte.]

(iii) Verbs of **saying** and **opinion**, as in (39):

(39) Isabelle *prétend* [Ø avoir passé l'agrégation de lettres classiques.] ('Isabelle claims to have passed the Classics agrégation exam.')

(iv) **Modal verbs**, such as *devoir, pouvoir, falloir,* or *oser,* as shown in (40):

(40)   Je *peux* [Ø vous aider] ?

(v) Three verbs (*faillir*, *manquer*, and *avoir beau*) whose meaning can be roughly described as **aspectual**, cf. (41):

(41)   Magali *a failli* [Ø se faire virer de son poste.]

Infinitival clauses as complements of prepositions
With one exception, infinitival clauses functioning as complements of prepositions never take an infinitive marker, cf. (42)–(43):

(42)   Henri a réussi à faire une thèse d'Etat *sans* [Ø divorcer.]

(43)   *Pour* [Ø aller à la gare], prenez à gauche après l'église.

The exception is the preposition *avant*, which triggers the use of the infinitive marker *de*, as in (44):

(44)   Avant [de partir], Alexis a pris un café.

Of course, as we saw in section 9.2.2.1 above, and as illustrated by (16)–(19), an infinitival clause may be the complement of one of the prepositions *de* or *à*, as in (45):

(45)   Géraldine rêve *de* [Ø devenir mannequin.] (cf. Géraldine rêve d'une carrière de mannequin.)

Infinitival clauses as purpose adverbials following a motion verb
If an infinitival clause functions as a purpose adverbial following a motion verb, as in (46), it never takes an infinitive marker:

(46)   Noémi *est partie* [Ø vivre dans un ashram.]

Infinitival clauses as object attributes or free indirect attributes
An infinitival clause functions as an object attribute when it occurs as part of the so-called **permissive construction** (i.e. *laisser* + infinitive, see section 25.4.1.1), as in (47) below:

(47)   Frédéric *a laissé* les enfants [Ø jouer sur la Wii pendant des heures.]_ObjAttr

Infinitival phrases may also function as free indirect attributes in construction with a **verb of perception** (*voir*/*entendre* etc.), as in (48):

(48)   J'*ai entendu* les enfants [Ø jouer sur la Wii pendant des heures.]_FIA

These constructions take no infinitive markers.

10

Non-finite verb forms:
The past participle

Learning objectives

- To understand the different uses of the past participle (three in all).
- To be able to accurately explain and apply the rules governing the agreement or non-agreement of French past participles with other clause constituents.

10.1 The past participle

As we saw in section 9.1, non-finite verb forms have certain features that make them similar to one or more other word classes in terms of the grammatical functions they are able to fulfil.

Thus, the past participle has three different uses in French: a genuinely verbal use as a main verb in the passive voice and/or in a compound tense, an adjectival use as the head of a past participle clause, and a nominal use.

The Structure of Modern Standard French. First edition. Maj-Britt Mosegaard Hansen.
© Maj-Britt Mosegaard Hansen 2016. First Published 2016 by Oxford University Press

10.2 Verbal use of the past participle

The past participle may be used as the main verb in a range of compound tenses, as well as in the passive voice. More details on tenses can be found in chapter 6. The passive voice is treated in section 25.2.

As a main verb, the past participle will be accompanied by a finite form of either *être* or *avoir*, which function as auxiliaries. Auxiliaries, and the choice between *être* and *avoir* with the past perfect, are treated in greater depth in chapter 8.

10.2.1 Past participle agreement

When the past participle functions as a main verb, it sometimes agrees in gender and number with another constituent.

In the spoken language, however, the difference is audible only if the written form of the masculine singular ends in a consonant, in which case that consonant will be pronounced in the feminine form. Thus, in (1) below, there is no audible difference between the masculine and the feminine form of the participle, both of which end in an /i/ in the spoken language. In (2)–(3), on the other hand, there is an audible difference, such that—in the spoken language—the masculine form ends in an /i/, while the feminine form ends in a /t/:

(1)   Je suis sorti(e).

(2)   Le livre que j'ai écrit. (/eˈkʁi/)

(3)   La lettre que j'ai écrite. (/eˈkʁit/)

Past participle agreement in French is governed by two rules, a 'subject rule' and a 'direct object rule', the latter of which has two sub-cases.

10.2.1.1 The subject rule

In non-reflexive constructions where *être* is the auxiliary, the past participle agrees in gender and number with the subject of the sentence. This is the case with compound tenses of 17 intransitive verbs and derivations therefrom treated in section 8.2.1.4, cf. (4) below, and in 'canonical' passive constructions like that in (5) (see section 25.2.1):

(4)   *Elles* sont sorties.

(5) *Les portes* ont été ouvertes à 19 heures précises.

The generic subject pronoun *on* is grammatically a third-person masculine singular form. As such, it can always trigger masculine singular agreement. If, however, it functions notionally as a variant of the first-person plural pronoun *nous*, as it frequently does in more informal registers (see section 15.2.3), plural (possibly feminine) agreement is also possible, as shown in (6):[1]

(6) *On* est rentré(e)(s) vers minuit hier soir.

10.2.1.2 The direct object rule

In all other cases (except for a few contexts where the past participle of *faire* is used as an auxiliary, and which are discussed below), the past participle agrees in gender and number with a preceding direct object, if there is one.

The past participle never agrees with a preceding dative object, on the other hand. To determine whether or not a given past participle must be marked for agreement, it is therefore essential to know how to distinguish a direct object from a dative object, even in cases where the two have the same form. (See sections 1.2.3.2 and 1.2.3.5.)

Pronominal verbs and reflexive constructions

When in construction with a reflexive pronoun, verbs always take *être* as their auxiliary in those compound tenses that use the past participle. The participle agrees with the reflexive pronoun in gender and number in two cases:

(i) If the verb is inherently pronominal, i.e. is invariably in construction with a reflexive pronoun, like the verb *s'évanouir* in (7) below. In these cases, the reflexive pronoun is always treated like a direct object for agreement purposes:

(7) Les filles *se* sont évanouies. (cf. the impossibility of *Les filles ont évanoui *quelqu'un.*)

(ii) If the verb is not inherently pronominal, and the reflexive pronoun is a direct object, as in (8):

(8) Les filles *se* sont vues hier. (cf. Les filles ont vu *quelqu'un.*)

---

[1] As shown in section 15.2.3, feminine singular agreement is also possible when *on* has generic reference to females only. This is a rather rare phenomenon, however.

The past participle, however, does not agree with a reflexive pronoun which functions as a dative object, such as the one in (9):

(9)   Les filles *se* sont téléphoné[-Ø] hier. (cf. Les filles ont téléphoné *à quelqu'un.*)

Note that (9) shows quite clearly that it would be a mistake to think that the participle agrees with the subject in these types of construction: the subject of (9) is feminine and plural, yet the participle must be in the neutral (masculine singular) form. The fact that pronominal verbs and reflexive constructions use *être* rather than *avoir* as their auxiliary makes no difference in that respect.

Transitive constructions

Non-reflexive transitive constructions always take *avoir* as the auxiliary in compound tenses using the past participle. In such cases, the participle agrees with a preceding direct object if there is one, as shown by (10)–(12) below.

(10)   Vous n'avez pas encore reçu *ma lettre* ? Mais je *l'*ai envoyée il y a trois jours !

(11)   La lettre *que* j'ai envoyée à Marie il y a trois jours ne lui est pas encore parvenue.

(12)   Mais j'ai envoyé[-Ø] *cette lettre* il y a trois jours !

All three sample sentences contain a direct object and a past participle in the same clause. In (10)–(11), the (italicized) direct object[2] precedes the predicator, and so the participle shows agreement with that direct object. In (12), on the other hand, the direct object follows the predicator, and so the participle does not agree with it.

As before, however, the past participle will not agree with a preverbal dative object (if any), as shown by (13), where the preverbal dative object refers to a feminine singular individual, but the participle shows no agreement:

---

[2] With respect to (11), note that the direct object of the relative-clause predicator *ai envoyée* is the relative pronoun *que*, and not its antecedent *la lettre*. *La lettre* belongs to the main clause and is the subject of the main-clause predicator *est parvenue*. Relative pronouns inherit the number and gender of their antecedents, however.

(13)   Marie, écoute : je *t'*ai envoyé[-Ø] cette lettre il y a trois jours !

If the direct object is *en* representing an indefinite plural noun phrase, as in (14) below, the past participle does not usually agree. That said, examples with agreement may occasionally be found, and are not considered incorrect:

(14)   Des lettres, tu parles si j'*en* ai envoyé(es) ces derniers jours ! ('You'd better believe I've sent some letters these past few days!')

Constructions with *(se) faire* and *se voir*

The verb *faire* functions as an auxiliary followed by an infinitive in the **causative construction** (i.e. a construction that indicates that the subject made someone or something else do something), as in (15):[3]

(15)   Jean <u>fait pleurer</u> Marie. ('Jean makes Marie cry.')

When the causative construction occurs in compound tenses, the past participle of *faire* will be used, but it will not show agreement with a preceding direct object because it acts only as an auxiliary in such cases.

In these constructions, it is the following infinitive that functions as the main verb. Thus, in (16) below, the meaning is not that Jean made (i.e. created) the girl, but that the girl cried because of Jean's behaviour. In (17), on the other hand, Jean did, in fact, create something, so *faire* is the main verb, which therefore agrees with the preceding direct object:

(16)   Voilà la fille *que* Jean [a fait[-Ø] pleurer.]

(17)   Voilà la statue *que* Jean a fait<u>e</u>.

Faire and, to a lesser extent, *voir* can also occur as auxiliaries followed by an infinitive in the **reflexive causative** construction (cf. section 25.4.2), which is similar in meaning to a passive construction in indicating that something was done to the subject. In this construction, similarly to the regular causative construction, neither *faire* nor *voir* will show agreement with a preceding reflexive pronoun, as shown in (18)–(19):

(18)   Les deux étudiantes [*se* sont fait[-Ø] écraser] par un bus.

(19)   Meryl Streep [*s'*est vu[-Ø] décerner] l'Oscar de l'interprétation féminine.

---

[3] For further details on the grammar of causatives, see section 25.4.

10.3 Past participle clauses

When the past participle is not the main verb of a compound tense, it frequently behaves in a similar way to an adjective. In such cases, the participle occurs without an auxiliary, and its function is to ascribe a property to a noun, just as adjectives do. Structurally, the participle is the head of a past participle clause.

10.3.1 The structure of past participle clauses

In its adjectival function, the participle functions like a **reduced passive clause**. It cannot take a grammatical subject or direct object, but it can take other valency elements, as well as adverbials.

In (20) below, for instance, the subject of the sentence as a whole consists of a noun phrase, *le délai de deux ans accordé aux enterprises par le Ministre de l'environnement*. Inside this noun phrase, we find a postmodifying past participle clause (in square brackets), which ascribes a property to the deadline in question. This past participle clause can be paraphrased as the passive sentence in (21). Note that in the past participle clause, the subject and the auxiliary verbs of the passive sentence have been deleted, but the main verb (i.e. the participle), the dative object, and the adverbial remain:

(20) Le délai de deux ans [accordé aux entreprises par le Ministre de l'environne-ment]$_{PastPartCl}$ est à notre avis excessif.

(21) [Quelque chose]$_{Subj}$ [[a été]$_{Aux}$ [accordé]$_{MainV}$]$_{Pred}$ [aux entreprises]$_{DatObj}$ [par le Ministre de l'environnement.]$_{Adv'al}$

10.3.2 The functions of past participle clauses

10.3.2.1 Verbal use

Past participle clauses can function as **predicates of absolute constructions**, as in (22)–(23) below:[4]

---

[4] For the notion of absolute constructions, see section 3.2.3.

(22)   Réflexion <u>faite</u>, je ne regrette rien.

(23)   Son manuscrit <u>envoyé à l'éditeur</u>, elle pouvait enfin se détendre.

In absolute constructions, the past participle clause agrees in number and gender with the base constituent, as the above examples show.

10.3.2.2 Adjectival use

More commonly, however, past participle clauses are used in the same functions as adjectives, namely:

(i) As pre- or postmodifiers within noun phrases, as in (20) above or (24)–(25) below. Note that the use of a past participle phrase as a premodifier, as in (24), is rare.

(24)   [Le <u>très attendu</u> classement mondial des universités] est sorti !

(25)   [La jeune fille <u>morte</u>] continue à hanter la maison.

(ii) As subject attributes, as in (26) below; object attributes, as in (27); or free indirect attributes, as in (28):

(26)   Sébastien est [un peu vexé] parce que Madone a oublié son anniversaire.

(27)   Je trouve cet ouvrage [assez réussi.]

(28)   [Très épuisée par la longue randonnée], elle s'est vite endormie.

As the examples show, past participles can be modified, for instance by degree markers, in the same way as genuine adjectives.

In all these cases, the past participle clause agrees in number and gender with the constituent to which it ascribes a property, just as an adjective would.

10.4 Nominal use of the past participle

Finally, past participles may, in some cases, function as **derived nouns**, in which case they are marked for number and gender, as appropriate.

Thus, in (29)–(30) below, the past participle of the verb *accuser* has been nominalized (i.e. converted into a noun), and depending on the gender and/

or number of the accused person(s) it refers to, it will take an additional feminine *-e* and/or a plural *-s*.

(29)   L'accusé(e) est mon ami(e).

(30)   Les accusé(e)s sont mes ami(e)s.

Nominalized participles behave like other nouns, and no more needs to be said about them here.

11

Non-finite verb forms: The present participle and the *gérondif*

Learning objectives

- To understand the difference between a present participle and a deverbal adjective in *ant*.
- To understand the difference between verbal and adjectival uses of the present participle.
- To understand the differences in meaning and function between the present participle used adjectivally and the *gérondif*.

11.1 Introduction

This chapter discusses non-finite verb forms ending in –*ant*, as well as adjectives ending in –*ant* which are derived from verbs (i.e. so-called deverbal adjectives).

The Structure of Modern Standard French. First edition. Maj-Britt Mosegaard Hansen.

French has two non-finite verb forms ending in –*ant*, viz. the present participle and the *gérondif*. The **gérondif** differs formally from the present participle partly by always being preceded by the preposition *en*, as shown in (1) below, and partly by having no compound form, as shown in (2):

(1)   *parlant* (= present participle)—*en parlant* (= *gérondif*)

(2)   *ayant parlé* (= compound present participle)—*en ayant parlé (not found)

Functionally, the two forms overlap, but are not identical, as discussed below.

Deverbal adjectives ending in –*ant* are formally very similar to the present participle, except for having no compound form. Unlike the participle, however, they can be marked for gender and number agreement like other adjectives. Moreover, the internal structure of a present participle clause is different from that of an adjectival phrase headed by an adjective ending in –*ant*. It is therefore important to be able to distinguish between the two.

11.2 Deverbal adjectives ending in –*ant*

A number of French verbs have been the basis for the formation of adjectives closely resembling the past participles of those same verbs. Thus, for instance, the adjective *intéressant* in (3)–(6) below is closely related in both form and meaning to the verb *intéresser*.

(3)   un plan *très* <u>intéressant</u>

(4)   une idée *moyennement* <u>intéressante</u>

(5)   des plans *furieusement* <u>intéressants</u>

(6)   des idées *toujours* <u>intéressantes</u>

The adjective, however, has certain properties that clearly distinguish it from the present participle of the verb. First, as the formal variation in (3)–(6) shows, the adjective *intéressant* must agree in gender and number with the noun it describes. As will be seen in section 11.3 below, present participles never show agreement, even though they, too, frequently fulfil adjectival functions.

Secondly, deverbal adjectives ending in –*ant* take the same types of modifiers as other adjectives, i.e. degree modification as in (3)–(5), temporal modification as in (6), and postmodifying prepositional phrases indicating what causes the property described by the adjective, as in (7) below:

(7) L'allée était <u>grouillante</u> *de monde*.

As shown by (8)–(10) below, these types of modification are all found with non-deverbal adjectives as well. They cannot, however, be combined with the present participle.

(8) Marie-France est <u>très</u> *sympathique*.

(9) Corinne était <u>encore</u> *jeune*.

(10) Paul devint *rouge* <u>de honte</u>.

In the case of a certain number of *–ant* forms, there are further reasons not to conflate deverbal adjectives and present participles.

First, the base form of some deverbal adjectives is formally different from the corresponding present participle, and seen in (11)–(14) below. Note that in the case of (13)–(14), the forms sound identical when spoken, but are spelled differently, such that the adjective in fact does not end in *–ant* in this case, but in *–ent*:

(11) <u>Sachant</u> la réponse, Audrey a levé la main. (= present participle: 'knowing the answer')

(12) Henri est très <u>savant</u> en cinématographie. (= adjective: 'knowledgeable about cinematography')

(13) <u>Différant</u> sur tous les points, ils ne s'entendent guère. (= present participle: 'differing/disagreeing')

(14) Ludivine est une fille très <u>différente</u> des autres. (= adjective: 'different/unlike')

Secondly, deverbal adjectives are not always directly related to an existing verb; for instance, although the verb *chaloir* ('to be important') existed in Old French, no verb *nonchaloir* corresponding directly to the adjective *nonchalant* in (15) has ever existed.

(15) Il se comporte de manière assez <u>nonchalante</u>.

Thirdly, a deverbal adjective in *–ant* may have a specialized meaning which is different from that of the verb it is derived from, cf. (16):

(16) Madame Bernardin est assez <u>regardante</u>. ('careful with money'/'particular')

Finally, some verbs may have corresponding deverbal adjectives which are not based on the present participle of those verbs, but which have been derived by some other mechanism, cf. (17)–(19) below:

(17)   Un calme <u>trompeur</u> règne en Algérie. (= deverbal adjective)

(18)   Un calme *<u>trompant</u> règne en Algérie. (= non-existent deverbal adjective)

(19)   Cet homme politique a failli, <u>trompant</u> tous ses électeurs. (= present participle)

11.3 The present participle

As a non-finite verb form, the present participle is distinct from finite verb forms by being unmarked for person, tense, and mood. It is distinct from deverbal adjectives in so far as it does not accept gender and number marking.

Thus, as (20)–(21) show, present participles are invariant in form even when their logical subject is feminine and/or plural:[1]

(20)   <u>Fredonnant</u> le dernier tube de Louane, *Chloé* s'est assise à la terrasse d'un café.

(21)   *Deux jeunes filles* <u>fredonnant</u> le dernier tube de Louane étaient assises sur un banc.

However, a compound form denoting completion of a state, activity or event does exist, as shown in (22):

(22)   <u>Ayant terminé</u> ses études de Sciences Po, Christine est partie travailler à l'Ambassade de France à Tokyo.

Because they are verb forms, present participles can take the same types of valency elements and adverbials as finite verb forms, although subjects are confined to absolute constructions. However, because it is a non-finite form, the behaviour of present participles also in some ways resembles that of members of other word classes, principally adjectives.

11.3.1 Present participles with predominantly verbal function

In an **absolute construction**,[2] a present participle clause functioning as the predicate of the construction can co-occur with a grammatical subject, which thus functions as the base of the absolute construction.

---

[1] For the notion of logical subject, see section 3.1.

[2] For the notion of absolute construction, see section 3.2.3.

This type of absolute construction expresses **causal meaning** (cf. (23) below) or **conditional meaning** (cf. (25)). Such constructions can therefore be paraphrased by adverbial clauses of the relevant types, as shown in (24) and (26):

(23) Le professeur étant malade, le cours a été supprimé.

(24) Comme le professeur est malade, le cours a été supprimé.

(25) Les circonstances aidant, nous réussirons.

(26) Si les circonstances nous aident, nous réussirons.

In addition, when co-occurring with one of the concessive conjunctions *bien que* or *quoique*, a present participle phrase may constitute an **adverbial clause fragment**, as in (27):

(27) *Quoique* se prenant très au sérieux, M. Tournier n'arriva pas à convaincre le public. (→ Quoiqu'il se prît très au sérieux . . .)

11.3.2 Present participles with predominantly adjectival function

More commonly, present participle clauses appear without a grammatical subject, in which case their logical subject will be expressed somewhere else in the sentence or clause. In such cases, the present participle clause will describe some property of the logical subject in much the same way as an adjective might.

The constituent of the governing finite clause that is closest to the present participle will normally be understood to be the logical subject of the non-finite clause. Thus, in (28) below, the subject of the finite clause, *je*, will be understood to be the one who is getting off at the Abbesses metro stop, whereas in (29), it is the direct object of the finite clause, Lou, who is alighting at Abbesses:

(28) Descendant à Abbesses, *j*'ai aperçu Lou.

(29) J'ai aperçu *Lou* descendant à Abbesses.

Just like an adjective, a present participle clause may function as a **postmodifier** within a noun phrase, as seen in (30) below. Its logical subject is then constituted by the determiner and head noun, and the present participle clause can be paraphrased in the form of a relative clause, as in (31):

(30)   Il a reçu *une lettre* renfermant un chèque de deux mille euros.

(31)   Il a reçu *une lettre* qui renfermait un chèque de deux mille euros.

Like adjectives, present participle clauses may also function as **free indirect attributes**. In such cases, they typically have one of the following kinds of meanings:

(a) **Causal meaning** as in (32):

(32)   Etant (une) femme, j'ai été obligée de mettre le hijab lors de ma visite en Arabie Saoudite.

(33)   Comme je suis (une) femme, j'ai été obligée de mettre le hijab lors de ma visite en Arabie Saoudite.

(b) **Result meaning** as in (34):

(34)   La police contra brutalement la manifestation, blessant gravement un étudiant.

(35)   La police contra la manifestation si brutalement qu'elle blessa gravement un étudiant.

(c) **Temporal meaning**, as in (36):

(36)   Ayant fait sa valise, il prit un taxi pour l'aéroport.

(37)   Quand il eut fait sa valise, il prit un taxi pour l'aéroport.

As (33), (35), and (37) show, present participle clauses with these three kinds of meaning may be paraphrased by the adverbial clauses of the corresponding types.

In principle, when a present participle clause has temporal meaning, it denotes a state, activity, or event which precedes that described by the finite clause. In other words, with respect to (36) above, 'he' leaves his hotel and then goes to the railway station. As will be seen in section 11.5 below, the temporal sequentiality ideally expressed by the present participle contrasts with the simultaneity ideally expressed by the *gérondif*. In practice, however, this distinction in meaning between the two forms is not systematically observed.

11.4 Deverbal nouns ending in *–ant*

Finally, the present participles of some verbs have been nominalized, as seen in (38) below. In such cases, the deverbal noun can take a determiner as well as pre- and/or postmodifiers, just like any other noun:

(38)   Nous n'utilisons que *des* colorants *non-toxiques*.

11.5 The *gérondif*

The *gérondif* consists of the present participle preceded by the preposition *en*. As mentioned in section 11.1 above, it has no compound form.

A *gérondif*-clause may contain the same types of valency elements and adverbials as a present participle clause, but it cannot have a grammatical subject. In other words, a *gérondif*-clause cannot function as the predicate of an absolute construction.

Normally, the logical subject of a *gérondif*-clause will be identical to the subject of the governing finite clause. In both (39) and (40) below, it is thus Max who is understood to have been watching the news:

(39)   En regardant les infos, *Max* a reconnu un ami d'enfance.

(40)   *Max* a reconnu un ami d'enfance en regardant les infos.

However, if the subject of the finite clause is inanimate, an animate dative object, if there is one, may be understood to represent the logical subject of the *gérondif*-phrase, as in (41) below, where the referent of *me*, and not the idea, is understood to have been speaking:

(41)   L'idée *m*'est venue en parlant.

In rare cases, where there is neither an animate subject nor an animate dative object in the clause, the logical subject may have to be inferred from the non-linguistic context, as in (42), where the addressee (or alternatively, a generic *on*) is understood to be meant:

(42)   C'est la première porte à gauche en sortant.

Gérondif-clauses always function syntactically as adverbials. They can have five different adverbial interpretations, depending on the context:

(a) A *gérondif*-clause may describe the **means** whereby something took place, as in (43):

(43)   Ce matin, en écoutant la radio, j'ai appris qu'il y avait eu des attentats à Paris. (→ 'by (means of) listening to the radio')

(b) A *gérondif*-clause may describe the **manner** in which something took place, as in (44):

(44)   Ils défilèrent dans la rue en chantant.

(c) A *gérondif*-clause may describe a **condition** for something else to take place, as in (45):

(45)   En prenant l'escabeau, vous atteindrez le rayon. (→ 'if you take the stepladder')

(d) A *gérondif*-clause may describe a temporal relation of **simultaneity** with something else, as in (46) below. In such cases, a *tout* may be inserted before the *gérondif*:

(46)   Il regardait, (tout) en rêvant, les tours de la Défense.

In this temporal use, there is frequently little difference between using a *gérondif*-clause and using the corresponding present participle clause, despite the fact that the latter is in principle supposed to denote a temporal relation of sequentiality (see section 11.3.2 above). Thus, (47) and (48) can be used interchangeably:

(47)   En vous remerciant de votre intérêt, nous vous retournons vos certificats.

(48)   Vous remerciant de votre intérêt, nous vous retournons vos certificats.

(e) Finally, a *gérondif*-clause may have **concessive** meaning. In such cases, the *gérondif* will typically be preceded by either *tout* or *même*, as in (49)–(50):

(49)   Il a persisté dans cette voie, tout en sachant que c'était une erreur.

(50)   Même en courant très vite, tu ne le rattraperas pas.

In contrast to present participle clauses (cf. (32) above), a *gérondif*-clause cannot normally be used with causal meaning.

PART III

The Grammar of French Nominals

12

Definite and indefinite determiners

Learning objectives

- To understand the communicative function of determiners in general.
- To understand the basic difference between definite and indefinite determiners.
- To understand the notion of a generic article.
- To be able to explain and correctly apply the principal grammatical rules governing the uses of the indefinite article, the partitive article, the zero article, and the definite article in Modern French noun phrases.

12.1 Introduction

The syntactic function of determiners is to mark the beginning of a noun phrase, principally in connection with **referential noun phrases**, i.e. noun phrases that actually identify an entity or entities in the world. In (1) below, for instance, the subject noun phrase *la pilote* is referential because we can potentially identify the particular pilot in question. In (2), on the other hand,

The Structure of Modern Standard French. First edition. Maj-Britt Mosegaard Hansen.
© Maj-Britt Mosegaard Hansen 2016. First Published 2016 by Oxford University Press

the subject attribute noun phrase *pilote* is non-referential, and only serves to ascribe a property to the referential subject noun phrase *ma sœur*:

(1)   La pilote a 35 ans.

(2)   Ma sœur est pilote.

In terms of meaning, the function of determiners is to indicate the status of the referent as either already known (**definite determiners**) or new to the discourse (**indefinite determiners**), and to point the addressee to the most efficient way of identifying that referent.

Thus, for instance, the first-person singular (1.p.sg.) possessive article *ma* in (2) above tells the addressee that the sister in question can be identified *via* some relation to the speaker/writer. The demonstrative article *cette* in (3), on the other hand, tells the addressee that s/he must look to the immediate physical context in order to identify the referent of *cette robe*:

(3)   [Reading a fashion magazine] Cette robe est superbe !

French principally uses the types of item listed in Table 12.1 as determiners, only a subset of which will be discussed further in this chapter.[1]

Table 12.1. Types of determiner in French.

Definite determiners	Indefinite determiners
Definite article (4)	Indefinite article (5)
Possessive article (7)	Partitive article (6)
Demonstrative article (8)	Numerals (9)
	The interrogative article *quel* (10)
	A number of indefinites (11)

Numbers in parentheses refer to examples below.

(4)   le garçon

(5)   un garçon

(6)   du beurre

(7)   son fils

---

[1] For details on possessive and demonstrative articles, see ch. 9(e). For the interrogative article *quel*, see section 19.2, and for indefinites, see chapter 20 and section 23.2.1.2.

(8)   ce garçon

(9)   trois garçons

(10)   quel garçon ?

(11)   plusieurs garçons

In some cases, different determiners can be combined into a complex determiner. In that case, one of them is regarded as the **central determiner**, and the other(s) as **pre-** and/or **postdeterminers**, as in (12) below. The central determiner will normally be one of the three types of definite determiners.

(12)   Pierre venait [tous$_{\text{PreDet}}$ les$_{\text{CentrDet}}$ cinq$_{\text{PostDet}}$]$_{\text{ComplexDet}}$[2] jours.

12.2 Definiteness and indefiniteness

Indefinite determiners are primarily used to introduce new referents into a particular discourse. Once a given referent has been introduced in this way, it will normally be treated as definite from then on. In the first sentence of (13) below, for instance, both the physician and the stomach pains are marked as indefinite, i.e. new to the discourse, while in the second sentence, they are presumed to be known and therefore marked as definite:

(13)   Damien est allé voir un médecin parce qu'il avait des douleurs à l'estomac. Le médecin lui a donné une injection qui a apaisé les douleurs.

In the following, we will look at the grammatical rules that govern the indefinite articles, the zero article, and the definite article in French.

12.3 Indefinite articles

Unlike English, French has two types of indefinite article: the 'regular' indefinite article *un(e)*, and the 'partitive' article *du, de la, des*.

---

[2] In terms of the list in Table 12.1, *tous* is an indefinite, *les* a definite article, and *cinq* a numeral.

Except for a few cases where French uses a zero article instead (see section 12.3.2 below), the regular indefinite article is used much as in English, i.e. to introduce singular noun phrases that refer to 'discourse-new' entities of which there might in principle be more than one.

In other words, the regular indefinite article is used with countable entities. With respect to (13) above, for instance, physicians, stomachs, and injections are all things that can be counted ('one physician', 'two physicians', 'three physicians', and so on). Moreover, if we take a single countable entity and divide it into smaller entities, the resulting parts can no longer be described using the original noun. Thus, for instance, if we kill a chicken and cut it up with a view to cooking it for dinner, any given piece of it (e.g. a thigh) will not itself be a chicken.

The partitive article in the singular, on the other hand, is used to indicate an indefinite amount of a non-countable entity, i.e. something that is conceived as a mass, as in (14), for instance:

(14)   Tu veux du thé ?

Unlike countable entities, non-countable entities can be divided up in smaller parts while still remaining instances of the original thing. If you have made a pot of tea and pour yourself a cup, the contents of your cup will still be describable as tea, even though they constitute only a part of the total amount of tea available.

In the plural, the partitive article indicates an indefinite number of countable entities, as in (15):

(15)   Sophie a acheté des tulipes.

In both cases, English would frequently use what we may call a 'zero article',[3] as in (16)–(17), but the determiner *some* could also be used, as in (18)–(19):

(16)   Do you want [Ø] tea?

(17)   Sophie bought [Ø] tulips.

(18)   Do you want some tea?

(19)   Sophie bought some tulips.

---

[3] For further details on the use of the zero article in French, see section 12.4.1 below.

An interesting property of countability is that—although a particular interpretation may be statistically preferred—countability or non-countability is not an inherent property of French nouns. In fact, any French noun can be used as either countable or non-countable, depending on the context. Instead, it is the type of determiner used (regular indefinite *vs* partitive article) that tells you what kind of entity is being referred to, and this will contribute to the precise interpretation of the noun phrase in its context. To take a fairly straightforward example, we could, instead of (14), say (20), which would be most naturally translated into English as (21):

(20)   Tu veux un thé ?

(21)   Do you want a cup of tea?

In a different type of context, *un thé* might instead refer, for instance, to a particular type of tea (green, black, Indian, Chinese, etc.). In (13) above, on the other hand, the plural *des douleurs* indicates that the pain is not constant but recurring.

Conversely, even though cats are typically thought of as countable entities, it is perfectly possible (if unusual), in the right kind of context, to say:

(22)   Hier matin, notre pauvre Minou s'est fait écraser par un bus à impériale. C'était horrible : il y avait du chat partout. (>> '. . . there was cat(-stuff) all over the place.')

12.3.1 The partitive article

12.3.1.1 The full partitive article

The partitive article is formally a combination of *de* + definite article. This is known as the **'full' partitive article**. Although historically, the *de* of the partitive article represented the preposition *de*, the two are no longer identical in Modern French.

Thus, in (23) below, the form *du* represents a partitive article (i.e. it has indefinite meaning), and the sentence can be translated as in (24), and parses as in (25). In (26), on the other hand, the form *du* represents the preposition *de* + an actual definite article *le* (i.e. with definite meaning), and that sentence is translated as in (27), and parses as in (28):

(23)   Tu veux du thé ?

(24)   Do you want [Ø] tea?

(25)   [Tu]$_{Subj}$ [veux]$_{Pred}$ [du thé]$_{DirObj/NP}$ >> [du]$_{Det/PartArt}$ [thé]$_{H/N}$

(26)   Je me souviens du thé qu'on a bu chez Michel.

(27)   I remember the tea we had at Michel's.

(28)   [Je]$_{Subj}$ [me]$_{DirObj}$ [souviens]$_{Pred}$ [du thé qu'on a bu chez Michel]$_{PrepObj/PP}$ >> [de]$_{H/Prep}$ [le thé qu'on a bu chez Michel]$_{Compl/NP}$ >> [le]$_{Det/DefArt}$ [thé]$_{H/N}$ [qu'on a bu chez Michel]$_{Postmod/RelativeClause}$

12.3.1.2 The reduced partitive article

In certain contexts, both the full partitive article and the regular indefinite article *un(e)* are replaced by a mere *de*, referred to as a **'reduced' partitive article**.

As mentioned above, this *de* should not be confused with the preposition *de*. In (29) below, for instance, we have a reduced partitive article, which fills the determiner slot of the noun phrase *de cigarettes*, analysable as in (30). This can be demonstrated by using the substitution test (cf. section 2.6.1). Thus, as (31) shows, a reduced partitive article can potentially be replaced by other types of article, with no preposition present:

(29)   Il n'a pas de$_{(Reduced)PartArt}$ cigarettes.

(30)   [Il]$_{Subj}$ [n']$_{Adv'al}$ [a]$_{Pred}$ [pas]$_{Adv'al}$ [de cigarettes]$_{DirObj/NP}$ >> [de]$_{Det/PartArt}$ [cigarettes]$_{H/N}$

(31)   Il n'a pas les/ces/tes cigarettes.

In (32) below, on the other hand, we have the preposition *de* followed by a noun phrase with a zero article, analysable as in (33). As above, the substitution test can be used to show that this is so: in (34), we see that in this case *de* does not disappear if we use a different determiner, so clearly *de* cannot be filling the determiner slot inside the noun phrase in this example:

(32)   Il a lu beaucoup de$_{Prep}$ livres.

(33)   [Il]$_{Subj}$ [a lu]$_{Pred}$ [beaucoup de livres]$_{DirObj/AdvP}$ >> [beaucoup]$_{H/Adv}$ [de livres]$_{Postmod/PP}$ >> [de]$_{H/Prep}$ [livres]$_{Compl/N}$

(34)   Il a lu beaucoup des (= 'of the')/de ces/de mes/ . . . livres.

There are two major syntactic environments where the reduced partitive article is used in preference to the full partitive article: when the noun phrase is a direct object or a postponed subject (but not when it is a subject attribute) following a negated predicator, and when the noun phrase contains a premodifying adjective in the plural.

Direct objects following a negated predicator

When the noun phrase functions as the **direct object of a negated predicator**, we normally get the reduced partitive article. It does not matter if the clause contains the general clause negator *ne . . . pas* or a so-called n-word negation (see section 23.2.1.2) such as *ne . . . rien/personne/jamais*, etc. So if we negate the positive statements in (35) and (37) below, we will normally get the results in (36) and (38):

(35)   Bertrand veut un/des enfant(s).

(36)   Bertrand *ne* veut *pas* d'enfant(s).

(37)   Colette mange de la viande.

(38)   Colette *ne* mange *jamais* de viande.

There are, however, exceptions to this rule, where the full partitive article, and not the reduced article, is used following negation. This happens in three types of case:

• When what is denied is not in fact the direct object, but an adverbial. This is illustrated in (39) below, which can be paraphrased as (40):

(39)   Corinne *ne* boit *plus* du café *le soir*.

(40)   Corinne boit du café, mais pas le soir.

• When what is denied is not the head of the noun phrase itself, but a pre- or postmodifying element. We see this exemplified in (41) below, which can be paraphrased as (42):

(41)   François *ne* porte *pas* des chemises *en coton*.

(42)   François porte des chemises, mais pas en coton.

• When the speaker/writer is objecting to a particular linguistic term,[4] and wishes to replace it by another, related, term. In other words, the speaker/

---

[4] This is known as 'metalinguistic' negation.

writer is correcting an erroneous assumption on the part of the addressee. This is what we find in (43) below, where *écrevisse* and *langouste* both denote types of superficially similar crustaceans:

(43)   A: Alors, elles étaient bonnes, les écrevisses ?
            B: Nous *n'*avons *pas* mangé des écrevisses, *mais des langoustes*.

Postponed subjects following a negated predicator

If the noun phrase that follows the negated predicator is a **postponed subject**, the partitive article will appear in its reduced form.[5] This is the type of construction that we find in (44) below:

(44)   Il *n'*existe *pas* de solution à ce problème. (cf. 'Une solution à ce problème n'existe pas.')

The exception: subject attributes following a negated predicator

When a noun phrase following a negated predicator functions as **subject attribute**, the partitive article is never reduced, but always appears in its full form, as in (45) below:

(45)   Tous les maris *ne* sont *pas* des monstres.

The noun phrase contains a premodifying plural adjective

Finally, the partitive article will normally appear in its reduced form when introducing a noun phrase containing a **premodying adjective** in the **plural**. This is what we see in (46):

(46)   Haydée a fait de *grands* progrès.

Note that it is only premodifying adjectives that have this effect, not postmodifying ones (as (47) below shows), and only adjectives in the plural, not in the singular (as (48) shows):

(47)   Haydée a fait des progrès *exceptionnels*.

(48)   Luc fait du *bon* café.

Although reduction is the general rule, very short, common adjectives, such as *petit* or *bon*, may, however, allow the full partitive article to appear, cf. (49)–(50) below. This is particularly common when the adjective and the

---

[5] For the notion of postponed subject, see section 3.1.2.

noun together constitute a more or less 'frozen' combination, such as *petits pains* ('breakfast rolls').

(49) Ça se vend comme des *petits* pains.

(50) Il y avait des *jeunes* filles partout.

12.3.2 The zero article

In some cases, indefinite noun phrases are not introduced by any determiner (indefinite or partitive) at all. In such cases, we speak of a 'zero' article. Compared to English, there are, however, very few contexts in which noun phrases are used with a zero article in French.

12.3.2.1 The noun phrase functions as a subject attribute

If the subject is a personal pronoun or a noun phrase referring to a human being, no article is used if the function of the subject attribute is simply to neutrally describe the subject as being of a certain type.

Thus, in (51)–(52) below, the underlined noun phrases simply classify Jocelyne in (51) as a member of the category 'lawyer', and Philippe in (52) as a member of the category 'grandfather':

(51) Jocelyne est [Ø] avocate.$_{\text{SubjAttr}}$

(52) Philippe est devenu [Ø] grand-père$_{\text{SubjAttr}}$ la semaine dernière.

If, however, a pre- or postmodifier is added to the noun phrase, as in (53) below, that noun phrase will typically express a more individualizing meaning, typically a subjective evaluation on the part of the speaker/writer.[6] In such cases, an article will be used:

(53) Jocelyne est une avocate *très douée.*

(54) Philippe est vraiment un grand-père *gâteau.*

---

[6] In some cases, the combination of noun + pre- or postmodifier is a 'frozen' expression indicating a well-known category. In such cases, no article is needed, cf. (i)–(ii), where 'only child' and 'good pupil' are conventional categories whose defining features everyone (or at least most people) can be expected to agree on:

(i) Béatrice est [Ø] fille unique.

(ii) Marc a toujours été [Ø] bon élève.

The indefinite article can also be used where there is no pre- or postmodifier, if the noun phrase is clearly intended to denote a subjective evaluation. Thus, (55) below is a well-known quote from an essay by Jean-Paul Sartre, about his fellow novelist François Mauriac:

(55)   Monsieur Mauriac n'est pas un romancier.

What Sartre meant by (55) was not that Mauriac was not objectively speaking a member of the category 'novelist'. That would have been factually incorrect, given that Mauriac was a Nobel Prize laureate and author of some 20 novels. Rather, Sartre meant that Mauriac did not write his novels in the way that Sartre believed that novels should be written. In other words, (55) does not translate simply as (56) below, but rather as something along the lines of (7):

(56)   Mr Mauriac is not a novelist.

(57)   Mr Mauriac is not a 'proper' novelist.

If the subject is a noun phrase that does not refer to a human being, use of the indefinite article on the subject attribute is the norm, as in (58) below:

(58)   Le chat de Christine est un Siamois.

The indefinite article is likewise normally used when the subject is the neutral pronoun *ce*. This is always the case when the pronoun refers to a human being, as shown in (59) below. If *ce* does not refer to a human being, the zero article is occasionally used if the subject attribute is an abstract noun, as in (60):[7]

(59)   Vous connaissez Georges Lainé ? *C'*est un ami.

(60)   Ecoutez, *ce* serait [Ø] folie de faire cela.

12.3.2.2 The noun phrase functions as an object attribute, a free indirect attribute, or an apposition

Noun phrases that function as **object attributes**, as in (61) below, or **free indirect attributes**, as in (62),[8] normally occur with the zero article after any type of subject:

---

[7] See section 15.2.2, for more information about the use of *ce* as a neutral subject.

[8] See section 1.2.3.8 for the notion of object attribute, and section 3.2.4.1 for free indirect attributes.

(61)   On a nommé Madame Magdelénat [Ø] <u>directrice du service</u>._{ObjAttr}

(62)   [Ø] <u>Homme d'expérience</u>_{FIA}, il sait traiter une telle affaire.

Appositions[9] take the **zero article** if they neutrally and parenthetically describe the head noun in a way that does not constitute important new information, but could be left out without hampering the comprehensibility of the text as a whole, as in (63) below. If, on the other hand, the apposition provides information that explains another part of the text, as in (64) (where the fact that the speaker's father is an artist explains how he was in a position to teach him/her to draw), then the **indefinite article** is used:

(63)   Nous sommes arrivés à Trebiano, [Ø] <u>petit village proche de La Spezia</u>._{Appos}

(64)   C'est mon père, [<u>un</u> artiste connu]_{Appos}, qui m'a appris le dessin.

12.3.2.3 The noun phrase is the complement of a preposition

After a number of prepositions, indefinite noun phrase complements will normally take the zero article.

This is the case for the preposition *en*, as in (65) below, and *sans*, as in (66). It is also true of *avec* if the meaning of the prepositional phrase is equivalent to that of an adverb ending in *–ment*, as in (67):

(65)   Caroline a passé sa jeunesse <u>en</u> [Ø] province.

(66)   Emile est rentré d'Egypte <u>sans</u> [Ø] argent et <u>sans</u> [Ø] bagages

(67)   On a traité l'affaire <u>avec</u> [Ø] discrétion (= 'discrètement')

However, if the complement of a manner adverbial with *avec* contains a modifying adjective, particularly a postmodifying one, the regular indefinite article will normally be used, as seen in (68):

(68)   On a traité l'affaire avec <u>une</u> discrétion *admirable*.

As we have already seen above, the partitive article is distinct from, and can never be combined with, the preposition *de*, cf. the contrasts in (69)–(71) below:

(69)   Yann a <u>de</u> l'argent. (= full partitive article) >> Yann has (some) money.

(70)   Yann a besoin <u>d'</u>[Ø] argent. (= preposition + zero article) >> Yann needs (some) money.

---

[9]   See section 3.2.4.2 for appositions.

(71)   Yann a besoin <u>de</u> l'argent que tu lui dois. (= preposition + definite article) >>
        Yann needs <u>the</u> money that you owe him.

This includes the preposition *de* as part of quantifying expressions of various
kinds, as in (72)–(74):

(72)   Claire a fumé *un paquet* <u>de</u> [Ø] cigarettes. (= preposition + zero article)

(73)   Raphaël a fumé *beaucoup* <u>de</u> [Ø] cigarettes hier soir. (= preposition + zero
        article)

(74)   Claire a fumé *un paquet* <u>des</u> cigarettes que j'avais achetées à l'aéroport.
        (= preposition + definite article >> 'a pack of <u>the</u> cigarettes . . .')

12.3.2.4 Coordinated noun phrases

Noun phrases coordinated by *et*, *ou*, or *ni* often occur with the zero article,
as in (75)–(76):

(75)   Il m'a promis [Ø] monts et [Ø] merveilles.

(76)   Le pauvre enfant n'avait ni [Ø] père ni [Ø] mère.

This is particularly the case if the individual noun phrases are seen as parts
of a more encompassing concept, for instance 'parents' in (76).

Determiners will be used if the speaker/writer wants to put more emphasis
on the individuality of each element. Thus, in (77) below, the specific nature
of the items dropped is not really seen as terribly important by the speaker/
writer: what is important is simply that "she" dropped whatever she was
carrying. In (78), on the other hand, there is more of a focus on each item:

(77)   [Ø] Sac à main, [Ø] clé, [Ø] parapluie : elle a tout laissé tomber quand elle a vu
        Frédéric dans l'entrée.

(78)   <u>Son</u> sac à main, <u>sa</u> clé, <u>son</u> parapluie : elle a tout laissé tomber quand elle a vu
        Frédéric dans l'entrée.

12.4 The definite article

As already discussed above, use of the definite article suggests that the
speaker/writer believes that the addressee can unproblematically identify
the referent of the noun phrase.

There are various ways in which a referent can be easily identifiable. One obvious way is if the referent has already been introduced in previous discourse, as in (79):[10]

(79)   Sabine a *un chat* et deux chiens. <u>Le</u> chat est très méchant.

Another is if the referent constitutes a part or a subset of another, already introduced entity or concept, as in (80) below. We know that country houses are usually equipped with bedrooms, and so it comes as no surprise to us when the bedroom of the particular country house mentioned in the first sentence is introduced by a definite article:

(80)   On vient d'acheter *une nouvelle maison de campagne*. <u>La</u> chambre à coucher donne sur un lac.

A referent can also be easily identifiable if it is in some way salient in the immediate real-world context. Thus, if we are sitting at a restaurant table, we will not be surprised if a diner at the next table makes the request in (81) below, even if salt has not been mentioned previously:

(81)   Pourriez-vous me passer <u>le</u> sel, s'il vous plaît ?

If a referent is more or less unique, given the communicative situation, such that ambiguity is not deemed possible or likely, it can be introduced into the discourse with a definite article. Thus, (82) below would be a perfectly natural first utterance because, even though there are many suns in the universe, there is only one that is directly relevant to our planet. Similarly, although most countries have a Prime Minister, the context (usually the particular country in which the speaker/writer finds him-/herself at the moment of utterance) will normally suffice to identify a particular Prime Minister as the relevant one in (83):

(82)   <u>Le</u> soleil se lève à l'est.

(83)   <u>Le</u> premier ministre a prononcé un discours à la télévision hier soir.

Finally, a noun phrase may contain certain types of postmodifiers, such as genitive constructions,[11] which serve to uniquely identify the referent. This is what makes (84) below acceptable as a first utterance even if the

---

[10] But see section 18.2.1.2 for differences between English and French in this respect.

[11] See section 14.3, for the notion of a genitive construction.

addressee may never have heard of this particular woman before, for in Western societies, at least, men do not normally have more than one wife at any given time:[12]

(84)   La femme *de mon frère* vient du Nicaragua.

12.4.1 *Generic use of the definite article*

The uses of the French definite article described above all have exact equivalents in English.

However, the French definite article may also be used generically, i.e. to refer to a species as a whole or to a concept in the abstract. In such cases, the hearer is not expected to identify a specific referent.

Thus, the sentence is (85) below will very often be most appropriately translated into English as (86), meaning not that a particular bottle of cognac is more expensive than a particular bottle of whisky (although (85) could, of course, have that meaning in the right kind of context), but that, in general, cognac is more expensive than whisky:[13]

(85)   Le cognac est plus cher que le whisky.

(86)   [Ø] Cognac is more expensive than [Ø] whisky.

Similarly, the English sentence in (87) below translates into French as (88), using a generic article, because both sentences refer to whales as a species. The French sentence in (89), on the other hand, appears odd because the use of the partitive article suggests that only some whales are mammals, which we know is factually incorrect:

(87)   [Ø] Whales are mammals.

(88)   Les baleines sont des mammifères.

---

[12]   By implication, (84) will be less than fully acceptable if the speaker/writer hails from a society where polygamy is regularly practiced.

[13]   As shown in (i)–(ii) below, the English definite article, particularly in the singular, can sometimes be used generically, too. Thus, neither of those sentences is intended to describe a particular tiger, but rather to make a statement about tigers in general. Nevertheless, generic noun phrases in English usually take a zero article.

 (i)   Le tigre est un fauve.

(ii)   The tiger is a wild animal.

(89)   #Des baleines sont des mammifères.

In French, the generic article is used, among other things, in referring to:

* abstract entities, as in (90)–(93):

(90)   Pascal aime la musique.

(91)   Pascal likes [Ø] music.

(92)   L'amour triomphe de tout.

(93)   [Ø] Love conquers everything.

* many (although not all) diseases (cf. (94)–(95)):

(94)   Dominique a la rougeole.

(95)   Dominique has [Ø] measles.

* technical installations (cf. (96)–(97)):

(96)   Je n'ai pas l'eau courante.

(97)   I don't have [Ø] running water.

* academic disciplines, skills and activities (cf. (98)–(103)):

(98)   La linguistique est la discipline la plus intéressante.

(99)   [Ø] Linguistics is the most interesting discipline.

(100)   Aude joue au tennis tous les vendredis après-midi.

(101)   Aude plays [Ø] tennis every Friday afternoon.

(102)   Cécile est partie en Afrique chasser l'éléphant.

(103)   Cécile has gone to Africa to hunt [Ø] elephant.

Note that in all the examples given above, the French generic article is appropriately translated into English as a zero article.

13

Adjectives within the noun phrase

Learning objectives

- To understand the communicative function of modifiers within noun phrases.
- To understand the meaning difference between pre- and postmodifying adjectives in French.
- To be able to correctly apply and explain the rules governing adjective placement in Modern French.

13.1 The forms of French adjectives

In French, adjectives can be marked for gender, number and degree of comparison. Adjectives normally agree in gender and number with the (pro)noun they describe (but see section 13.4.1.2 below). As shown by

The Structure of Modern Standard French. First edition. Maj-Britt Mosegaard Hansen.
© Maj-Britt Mosegaard Hansen 2016. First Published 2016 by Oxford University Press

(1)–(2) below, this is so irrespectively of whether the adjective (phrase) fulfils a clause-level function (i.e. subject attribute, object attribute, or free indirect attribute), or a phrase-level function as a pre- or postmodifier of a noun phrase.

(1)   *Les filles/Elles* étaient [blond<u>es</u>.]_{SubjAttr}

(2)   [*Trois filles* blond<u>es</u>_{Postmod}] étaient assises à la terrasse d'un café.

13.1.1 Adjectives with irregular masculine forms

Standard monolingual dictionaries will provide both regular and irregular feminine and plural forms of adjectives. Five adjectives, however, also have irregular masculine forms that are used in premodifying position before head nouns starting in a vowel or a silent 'h'. These are the adjectives *beau*, *nouveau*, *vieux*, *fou*, and *mou*, whose forms are summarized in Table 13.1, and examples are given in (3)–(7).

(3)   Un beau garçon—un bel été—une belle fille—de beaux garçons—de beaux étés—de belles filles

(4)   Un vieux manoir—un vieil homme—une vieille femme—de vieux manoirs—de vieux hommes—de vieilles femmes

(5)   Un nouveau fauteuil—un nouvel espoir—une nouvelle robe—de nouveaux fauteuils—de nouveaux espoirs—de nouvelles robes

(6)   Un homme fou—un fol espoir—une histoire folle—des hommes fous—de fols espoirs—des histoires folles

(7)   Un coussin mou—un mol oreiller—une molle protestation—des coussins mous—de mols oreillers—de molles protestations

Table 13.1. Adjectives with irregular masculine forms.

| Head N | Masc. | | Fem. | Masc. | | Fem. | Masc. | | Fem. | Masc. | | Fem. |
	Cons.	Vowel or silent 'h'		Cons.	Vowel or silent 'h'		Cons.	Vowel or silent 'h'		Cons.	Vowel or silent 'h'	
Sing.	*beau*	*bel*	*belle*	*vieux*	*vieil*	*vieille*	*nouveau*	*nouvel*	*nouvelle*	*fou, mou*	*fol, mol*	*folle, molle*
Plur.	*beaux*		*belles*	*vieux*		*vieilles*	*nouveaux*		*nouvelles*	*fous, mous*	*fols, mols*	*folles, molles*

13.1.2 Degree marking

If two or more entities are being compared with the respect to the property described by an adjective, **degree marking** becomes relevant, as in (8) below:

(8)   Camille est <u>plus grande</u> que Charlotte.

There are three degrees of comparison, as exemplified by the adjective *grand* below:

(a) **Absolute** or **positive degree**: *grand*. This is the base form of the adjective, which is normally used when there is no explicit comparison between two or more entities.

(b) **Comparative degree**: *plus/moins grand*. The comparative degree is used to indicate that an entity or group of entities possess(es) a higher or smaller degree of a given property than some other entity or entities, that are seen as belonging to a different set, as in (8) above and (9) below (where the speaker's sons and daughters are conceived as two different sets):

(9)   Pour le moment, mes filles sont toutes <u>plus grandes</u> que leurs frères.

(c) **Superlative degree**: *le plus/moins grand*. The superlative is used to indicate that one entity or group of entities out of two or more possess(es) the highest or smallest degree of a property compared to one or more other entities that are seen as belonging to the same set, as seen in (10)–(11) below. In (10), the speaker's two daughters are seen as constituting a set, and in (11), all his/her children are thought of as one set:

(10)   Camille est <u>la plus grande</u> de mes deux filles.

(11)   Louis est <u>le moins grand</u> de mes enfants.

As these examples show, degree of comparison is normally expressed with the aid of the degree adverbs *plus* and *moins*, with the addition of a definite article in the superlative degree. Only three adjectives, *bon, mauvais*, and *petit*, have irregular comparative and superlative forms, as seen in (12)–(14) below. As shown, *mauvais* and *petit* also have regular comparative and superlative forms, however:

(12)   bon—meilleur—le meilleur

(13)   mauvais—pire/plus mauvais—le pire/le plus mauvais

(14)   petit—moindre/plus petit—le moindre/le plus petit

(Le) pire will normally only be chosen to compare entities both/all of which are inherently bad, as in (15) below. *(Le) moindre* is usually used in an abstract sense (≈ 'negligible'), as in (16), whereas *(le) plus petit* will tend to be chosen to express a more concrete sense having to do with physical size, cf. (17):

(15)   C'est sans aucun doute le pire de ses *mensonges.*

(16)   Ce procédé permet de fabriquer de l'acier à un moindre coût.

(17)   Une équipe de chercheurs américains affirment avoir identifié la plus petite forme de vie sur Terre.

French makes frequent use of *moins* as an alternative to *plus* when expressing degrees of comparison. Often, the preference is to use an adjective that may also be applied to the entity described in the positive degree. Thus, if the speaker's grandfather and grandmother are, respectively, 75 and 78 years of age, a comparison between them will tend to be expressed as in (18) below, rather than as in (19), because neither would normally be described as young:

(18)   Mon grandpère est moins âgé que ma grandmère.

(19)   Mon grandpère est plus jeune que ma grandmère.

13.2 The use of adjectives within the noun phrase

Pre- and postmodifiers make the reference of a noun phrase more precise, thus making it easier for the hearer/reader to identify the intended referent.

For instance, if we compare (20)–(23) below, the range of potential referents of the underlined noun phrase is quite broad in (20), but it is progressively narrowed down in (21)–(23) with each new modifier that is added to the noun phrase, given that the number of handsome clean white shirts, while still considerable, is only a small subset of the total number of shirts in the world:

(20)   Patrice portait [une chemise].

(21)   Patrice portait [une chemise blanche].

(22) Patrice portait [une belle chemise blanche].

(23) Patrice portait [une belle chemise blanche propre].

In French, as in English, a variety of constituent types are potential noun phrase modifiers, for example genuine and deverbal adjectives, nouns, participles and participial clauses, prepositional phrases, and subordinate clauses. Normally, however, only genuine adjectives can premodify a head noun.[1] The other constituent types mentioned are normally found only as postmodifiers, as shown in (24)–(28) below.

(24) Il m'a dit ça sur [un ton rassurant.] (Deverbal adjective)

(25) Myriam ne mange que [la glace vanille.] (Noun)

(26) [Une femme portant une robe bleue] entra. (Present participle clause)

(27) Je voudrais [une tarte aux pommes], s'il vous plaît. (Prepositional phrase)

(28) Celle-là est [la robe que je préfère]. (Subordinate clause)

13.3 The position of modifying adjectives

In French noun phrases, there are slots for adjectival modifiers on either side of the head noun. Statistically speaking, the postmodifying slot is very clearly preferred. That said, the distribution has been shown to vary across different adjectives, across different types of noun phrases, as well as across different text genres.

To understand the variation in question, it is important to realize that the premodifying and postmodifying slots have distinct communicative values. It is likely that these different values are linked to the prosodic structure of spoken French, whereby stress will normally fall on the last syllable of an intonation unit. Thus, except in relatively slow speech, there would be a total of seven intonation units in (29) below, and only the underlined syllables would be stressed:

---

[1] In relatively rare instances, deverbal adjectives ending in –ant (but not genuine present participles, cf. chapter 11 for the distinction between them), and to a lesser degree past participles, may be preposed as well, e.g.:

(i)   une amusante anecdote
(ii)   ce maudit chat

(29) [L'année dernière,] [je suis allée rejoindre Laurie] [dans un minable quartier de
      Liverpool,] [avant qu'elle ne s'embarque] [pour le Canada] [avec le garçon du
      moment,] [qui n'est pas l'homme de sa vie.]
      M. Clément, *Le vent sur la maison* (Gallimard, 1976), 48.

As most noun phrases will constitute only a single intonation unit, it is
only postmodifiers that can normally be stressed, whereas premodifiers will
be unstressed.

(i) The **premodifying slot** contains adjectives whose information value is
     comparatively less significant and/or distinctive. In other words, pre-
     modifying adjectives typically convey information that is less new to/
     more expected by the hearer and/or less important to the text. This slot
     typically contains adjectives that are more abstract, more figurative,
     and/or more subjective in meaning, and the precise interpretation of
     those adjectives seems to be less stable than that of postmodifying
     adjectives, varying according to the nature of the head noun. These
     features are summarized in Table 13.2 below.

(ii) The **postmodifying slot**, on the other hand, contains adjectives that
     express important new information about the referent of the noun
     phrase. Typically, adjectives placed here will have a more contrastive,
     more concrete, and/or more objective meaning, and their interpretation
     will tend to be independent of the nature of the head noun. These
     features are summarized in Table 13.2.

Accordingly, we get contrasts such as the following:

(30) un grand homme ('great' = subjective, figurative, abstract, more dependent on
      meaning of head noun)—un homme grand ('tall') = objective, concrete,
      literal, less dependent on meaning of head noun)

(31) une verte pelouse (expected property, less distinctive)—une pelouse jaune
      (unexpected property, contrastive, more distinctive)

(32) de la pure fiction ('nothing but' = non-contrastive, abstract)—de l'alcool pur
      ('undiluted' = contrastive, concrete)

(33) un vrai discours/une vraie femme ('a real speech'/'a real woman' = subjective,
      more dependent on the meaning on the meaning of the head noun)—une histoire
      vraie ('a true story' = objective, less dependent on the meaning of the head noun)

(34) un cruel tyran (expected, non-contrastive)—un garçon cruel (unexpected,
      contrastive)

Table 13.2. Influence of the premodifying position *vs* the postmodifying position on the interpretation of a given adjective.

Premodifying slot	Postmodifying slot
Less distinctive	More distinctive
Less new to the hearer	More new to the hearer
More expected	Less expected
Less contrastive	More contrastive
More abstract	More concrete
More figurative	More literal
More subjective	More objective
More dependent on the meaning of the head noun	More independent of the meaning of the head noun
Less stable across different head nouns	More stable across different head nouns

(35) [As parts of the same text] Au fond, Durand était un individu <u>méprisable</u> [new information]...Ce <u>méprisable</u> individu [old information] se croyait tout permis.

(36) Un <u>bon</u> morceau ('large')/une <u>bonne</u> grippe ('bad')/un <u>bon</u> repas ('tasty') = more dependent on the meaning of the head noun, less stable across different head nouns

In French, modifying adjectives can be roughly partitioned into two groups: those that are typically placed in the premodifying slot, and those that are typically placed in the postmodifying slot. Crucially, however, all adjectives can change their slot if the context calls for it, and the properties shown in Table 13.2 give us some understanding of the reasons why a given adjective may change its default position.

13.3.1 Normally premodifying adjectives

A small group of eleven adjectives, listed in (37) below, are typically placed before the head noun, as shown in (38)–(42). These adjectives are short, highly frequent, and they give information about very basic properties of noun phrase referents. In terms of their meaning they can be paired as shown in (37):

(37)   bon—mauvais
       grand/gros—petit
       vieux—jeune
       vrai—faux
       beau/joli

(38)   un <u>bon</u> dîner

(39)   un <u>petit</u> garçon

(40)   une <u>vieille</u> maison

(41)   une <u>fausse</u> facture

(42)   un <u>bel</u> été

However, as already suggested above, all of these adjectives can be found in postmodifying position under certain circumstances. This will be discussed further in section 13.3.3.1 below.

13.3.2 Normally postmodifying adjectives

As exemplified in (43)–(45) below, all other adjectives are typically used as postmodifiers:

(43)   une robe <u>verte</u>

(44)   une terrasse <u>agréable</u>

(45)   un peintre <u>italien</u>

There are, however, a range of circumstances under which they may be—and frequently are—used in premodifying position (cf. section 13.3.3.2 below).

13.3.3 'Unusual' word orders

Both normally premodifying adjectives and normally postmodifying adjectives can change their default position to convey specific nuances of meaning.

13.3.3.1 Normally premodifying adjectives in postmodifying position
If a normally premodifying adjective is itself the head of an adjective phrase containing one or more modifiers, that adjective phrase will usually move

into the postmodifying slot of the noun phrase, as shown in (46)–(47) below. In fact, if the modification takes the form of a prepositional phrase, as in (47), postposition of the adjective phrase is the only grammatical option. Modification will normally make the meaning of the adjective phrase more contrastive and information-rich, and thus more suitable for the postmodifying slot:

(46)   une étude remarquablement bonne
   >> [une]$_{Det/IndefArt}$ [étude]$_{H/N}$ [remarquablement bonne]$_{Postmod/AdjP}$
   >> [remarquablement]$_{Premod/Adv}$ [bonne]$_{H/Adj}$

(47)   une expérience bonne pour la morale
   >> [une]$_{Det/IndefArt}$ [expérience]$_{H/N}$ [bonne pour la morale]$_{Postmod/AdjP}$
   >> [bonne]$_{H/Adj}$ [pour la morale]$_{Postmod/PP}$

If an unmodified adjective from the group of normally premodifying adjectives goes into the postmodifying slot, that will usually effect a change in meaning compared to the same adjective used in the premodifying slot. In conformity with the general value of the postmodifying slot, the meaning of the adjective will tend to become more distinctive, concrete and/or contrastive in that position, as compared to the premodifying slot.

Thus, the expression *un jeune homme* in (48) below is not a very precise description of Loïc. It merely informs the hearer that Loïc is (roughly) between 12 and 40 years of age, and most likely unmarried, but it does not otherwise single him out from any other men that the speaker may know. In contrast, *un homme jeune* in (49) describes Serge as a man who appears youthful for his age compared to others, and this expression will therefore typically be used about a man who is middle-aged or older. Along similar lines, *cette bonne femme* in (50) does not provide any kind of precise description of the woman in question, but rather corresponds more or less to 'this woman here/that woman there' in English. In (51), on the other hand, *une femme bonne* describes Mme Dupont in implicitly contrastive moral terms, as a woman who is kind-hearted:

(48)   Loïc est un jeune homme de ma connaissance.

(49)   Serge est encore un homme jeune.

(50)   Elle m'énerve, cette bonne femme.

(51)   Mme Dupont n'est pas seulement une femme importante, c'est aussi une femme bonne.

13.3.3.2 Normally postmodifying adjectives in premodifying position

When an adjective that would normally be used in the postmodifying slot is put into the premodifying slot, the change in position likewise affects its meaning to a greater or lesser extent. Four different types of case are distinguished below. In practice, however, these frequently overlap, and in all cases the meaning differences noted can ultimately be attributed to the distinct information values of the two modifier slots.

Distinct meaning difference between pre- and postmodifying position
With certain adjectives, there is a very notable difference in meaning between the two modifier positions.

In these cases, the meaning relation between the head noun and the adjective in postmodifying position can be paraphrased by a clause where the head noun is the subject and the adjective is a subject attribute, as shown in (52) below, where *pauvre* as a postmodifier describes the family as having little money. In keeping with the general value of the postmodifying slot, this interpretation is a fairly concrete and objective one, which implicitly contrasts the family with other wealthier ones:

(52) Il est né d'une famille pauvre qui n'avait pas les moyens de payer pour qu'il fasse des études. (→ La famille était pauvre.)

The meaning relation between the head noun and the adjective in premodifying position cannot be paraphrased in this way, as seen in (53) below. Here, *pauvre* takes on a more abstract and subjective meaning along the lines of 'unfortunate', and there is no sense that the boy is implicitly contrasted with more fortunate boys. Notice also that it is possible to combine premodifying *pauvre* with postmodifying *riche* without any sense of contradiction, as in (54):

(53) Le pauvre garçon était tout désemparé. (≠ Le garçon était pauvre.)

(54) un pauvre petit garçon riche

Other adjectives of this type are, for instance, *propre*, *sacré*, *sale*, and *simple*, cf. (55)–(58) below:

(55) ta propre voiture ('your own car') *vs* une chemise propre ('a clean shirt')

(56) un sacré connard ('a damn idiot') *vs* un devoir sacré ('a sacred duty')

(57) une sale besogne ('a nasty job') *vs* une chemise sale ('a dirty shirt')

(58) une <u>simple</u> demande ('a mere request') *vs* une devinette <u>simple</u> ('an easy riddle')

Weakening of the meaning of a normally postmodifying adjective to resemble that of a normally premodifying adjective

In the case of **evaluative adjectives** that are normally placed in postmodifying position, putting them in the premodifying slot may attenuate their meaning so that it comes to resemble the meaning of one of the normally premodifying adjectives (cf. section 13.3.1 above). As a result of its premodifying position in (59) below, for instance, *brillant* becomes essentially a synonym for *grand*. Likewise, in (60), the meaning of *fâcheux* is weakened so as to become largely just another word for *mauvais*:

(59) On a beaucoup parlé de la <u>brillante</u> réussite de ce jeune cinéaste. ≈ On a beaucoup parlé de la <u>grande</u> réussite de ce jeune cinéaste.

(60) Fernand a une <u>fâcheuse</u> propension à se disputer avec tout le monde. ≈ Fernand a une <u>mauvaise</u> propension à se disputer avec tout le monde.

Weakening of the meaning of a normally postmodifying adjective to resemble that of a determiner

Apart from the premodifying adjective slot, French noun phrases also contain a determiner slot which precedes the head noun. As shown in section 12.1, the determiner slot can be filled by articles of various types, by numerals, and by indefinite pronouns.

In some cases, premodifying adjectives take on meanings involving quantifying or sequencing that resemble those of determiners, particularly numerals or indefinite pronouns:

(61) Je me trouvais aux prises avec de <u>multiples</u> difficultés. ('many')

(62) Odette était l'<u>unique</u> femme de l'assemblée. ('only')

(63) Ses <u>rares</u> amis disent tous du bien de lui. ('few')

(64) La <u>prochaine</u> fois, il faut que tu emmènes Sophie ! ('next')

(65) L'<u>ancien</u> maire était de droite. ('previous')

Use of a normally postmodifying adjective to describe a supposedly natural or inherent property of the referent

Finally, the use of a normally postmodifying adjective in the premodifying slot may serve to suggest that the property described by the adjective is somehow inherent to, or at least naturally occurring in, referents described by the head noun. Thus, as in other cases discussed above, the premodifying adjective is non-contrastive in meaning, whereas the same adjective in postmodifying position would imply the existence of a contrast.

If we compare the pairs of examples in (66)–(71) below, we see that in each case, the premodifying adjective implies that the referent of the head noun in its totality possesses the property in question, whereas the post-modifying adjective implies that only a subset or part of the referent(s) of the head noun has that property. For reasons of politeness, the use of (70), with *aimable* in the premodifying slot, will therefore normally be preferred over (71) in a sales brochure, for instance:

(66)   la libre Amérique (→ Toute l'Amérique est libre.)

(67)   l'Amérique libre (→ Une partie de l'Amérique n'est pas libre.)

(68)   les élégantes Françaises (→ Toutes les Françaises sont élégantes.)

(69)   les Françaises élégantes (→ Certaines Françaises ne sont pas élégantes.)

(70)   notre aimable clientèle (→ Toute notre clientèle est aimable.)

(71)   notre clientèle aimable (→ Une partie de notre clientèle n'est pas aimable.)

13.4 More than one modifier within a noun phrase

A noun phrase may, of course, contain two or more modifiers. If both/all modifiers are adjectives, this raises, in the first instance, the issue of their relative positions. Secondarily, in a limited number of cases, a plural head noun may be modified by adjectives in the singular. This is discussed in section 13.4.1 below.

Alternatively, one of the modifiers may be a prepositional phrase whose complement is a noun, such that the structure as a whole corresponds to a compound noun. The relative positions of a postmodifying adjective and the prepositional phrase in such cases is treated in section 13.4.2.

13.4.1 Two or more adjectives within a noun phrase

13.4.1.1 Relative position
In many cases, a balanced distribution around the head noun will be attempted, with one adjective going into the premodifying slot and another adjective into the postmodifying slot. This is particularly straightforward

when the former belongs to the category of normally premodifying adjectives and the latter to the category of normally postmodifying ones, as in (72) below:

(72)   une belle église gothique

When two modifying adjectives belong to the same basic category, they may still be distributed around the head noun, but with a change of meaning in one of them, according to the principles described in section 13.2.3 above. This is illustrated in (73)–(76) below:

(73)   un vieil homme beau (→ notably handsome for his age)

(74)   une merveilleuse église gothique (→ attenuated sense of *merveilleux* ≈ *beau*)

(75)   un certain succès populaire (→ attenuated determiner-like sense of *certain* ≈ 'some degree of'; cf. *un succès populaire certain* ≈ 'definite')

(76)   l'éternelle lumière céleste (→ the heavenly light is inherently eternal)

Not infrequently, however, two or more adjectives may together occupy either the premodifying or the postmodifying slot. If so, they can be either coordinated (by a coordinating conjunction or a comma) or simply juxtaposed.

In the premodifying slot, juxtaposition is rare unless one or preferably both of the adjectives belong(s) to the category of normally premodifying items, as in (77)–(78) below. Notice that in (77), it is the normally preposed adjective *petit* that is placed closest to the head noun:

(77)   mon cher petit papa

(78)   une belle jeune fille

If neither adjective is normally preposed, coordination (normally by means of a conjunction) is preferred, as shown in (79):

(79)   la blonde et gentille Madeleine

In the postmodifying slot, coordination is used if the adjectives modify the head noun individually. In that case, as shown in (80)–(83) below, the order of the two adjectives can be changed around. Juxtaposition, on the other hand, is used if the second adjective modifies the combination of the head noun + the first adjective, as in (84). In this type of case, the order of the two adjectives cannot be changed without altering the meaning of the noun phrase or rendering it ungrammatical, as shown in (85):

(80)   un couloir long *et* étroit

(81)   un couloir long, étroit

(82)   un couloir étroit *et* long

(83)   un couloir étroit, long

(84)   la politique économique allemande

(85)   *la politique allemande économique

If the second of the two adjectives is itself premodified by a degree adverb, juxtaposition can be used even if each adjective independently modifies the head noun, as shown in (86):

(86)   un couloir long *très* étroit

Combinations of more than two adjectives are relatively infrequent, but both coordination and juxtaposition remain possible, with the meaning differences described above:

(87)   un couloir long, gris, sale *et* étroit

(88)   la politique économique allemande contemporaine

Finally, a combination of pre- and postposition of several adjectives is possible (if infrequent). Both coordination and juxtaposition may be used:

(89)   un curieux petit poème romantique français

(90)   un sombre *et* merveilleux tableau expressioniste *très* célèbre

(91)   une jolie petite table noire *et* sale

13.4.1.2 Number agreement

The norm is that modifying adjectives agree in number and gender with the head noun. However, if more than one adjective modifies a plural head noun, number agreement may vary along the following lines. If both adjectives modify the plural noun in its entirety, plural agreement is used, as in (92) below, where all the corridors in question are both long and narrow:

(92)   *des couloirs* longs et étroits

In some cases, however, two or more adjectives may modify distinct subsets of the plurality described by the noun. In that case, those adjectives will show singular agreement, as seen in (93) below, where there are two royal families in total (accordingly, the adjective *royales* is plural), but each country has only one:

(93)   *Les familles royales* <u>danoise</u> et <u>suédoise</u> ont assisté à la cérémonie.

13.4.2 Adjectives in compound-like noun phrases

When a head noun is modified by a prepositional phrase with a noun complement in the compound-like type of structure seen in (94) below, postmodifying adjectives may follow either of the two nouns, as shown in (95)–(97):

(94)   head N + preposition + N

(95)   un *camarade d'école* <u>sympathique</u> ('a nice school mate')

(96)   mon *professeur de français* <u>médiéval</u> ('my Medieval French teacher')

(97)   la *ministre* <u>française</u> *de la santé* ('the female French Health Minister')

If the adjective is intended to modify either the 'compound' as a whole, as in (95), or only the complement of the preposition, as in (96) (where the teacher is not himself Medieval, but is someone who teaches Medieval French), then it will normally follow the second noun, as those examples show.

If, on the other hand, the adjective is intended to modify only the head noun, and not the complement of the preposition, as in (97), then it will frequently follow the head noun immediately, in particular if that noun bears the same number and gender as the complement of the preposition. Thus, the preferred interpretation of (98) below would be that seen in (99), while the preferred interpretation of (100) would be that in (101):

(98)   une prof de linguistique <u>allemande</u>

(99)   'a female teacher of German linguistics'

(100)   une prof <u>allemande</u> de linguistique

(101)   'a female German teacher of linguistics'

If the two nouns differ in their gender and/or number, an adjective which is intended to modify only the head noun may follow the 'compound' as a whole if its form is audibly or visibly different from the form of an adjective modifying the complement of the preposition. This is exemplified in (102) below, where the head noun *prof* is masculine singular, while the complement of the preposition, *linguistique*, is feminine singular. Thus, no ambiguity is possible:

(102) un *prof de linguistique* <u>allemand</u> ('a German teacher of linguistics')

14

Pronouns: Overview

Learning objectives

- To understand the grammatical notion 'pronoun'.
- To understand the difference between genuine *vs* clitic pronouns.
- To understand the difference between pronouns and articles.
- To understand the difference between deictic and anaphoric uses of pronouns.
- To understand the notion of a genitive and the different types of basic meaning that genitives can express.

14.1 Introduction

Pronouns are a class of grammatical items which typically stand in for a different type of phrase (or, sometimes, for a clause) in its entirety. Thus, in (2) below, the **neutral pronoun** *ce* replaces the entire noun phrase *le nouveau* *roman de Jean Durand* in (1) (see chapter 1, in particular, for further examples of pronominalization of different types of constituent):[1]

(1)   Le nouveau roman de Jean Durand est un pur chef-d'œuvre.

(2)   C'est un pur chef-d'œuvre.

The term 'pronoun' itself is thus somewhat misleading, as pronouns rarely stand in for just a noun. If, for instance, we were to replace just the noun *roman* in (1) by *ce*, the result would be ungrammatical, as seen in (3) below. A more appropriate term would therefore be 'pro-NP'. However, given that the term 'pronoun' is traditional and has been around for a very long time, it will be retained in this book.

(3)   *Le nouveau ce de Jean Durand est un pur chef-d'œuvre.

Pronouns come in a range of different sub-types, the traditional names for which largely reflect their meanings and/or uses in discourse. Each of these sub-types is treated in turn in chapters 15–20.

14.2 Genuine *vs* clitic pronouns

The French pronominal system includes several types of so-called 'clitic' pronouns (or clitics, for short), viz. the personal and reflexive clitics (e.g. *je*, *tu*, *il/elle*, *se*, etc.; cf. sections 15.2 and 15.4), the neutral clitics *il* and *ce* (chapter 16), and the pronominal adverbs *en* and *y* (chapter 17).

Clitics are in several respects very different from genuine pronouns. To illustrate the difference, we may compare French personal clitics like *je*, *tu*, *il*, etc., to the English personal pronouns *I*, *you*, *he*, etc. Unlike the latter, the French personal clitics are not actually independent words, but rather valency markers that can be attached to verbs. In other words, the personal clitics cannot occur in isolation, but need another word of a particular type (in this case, a verb) to 'lean against'. This explains why clitic pronouns are also known as 'bound' pronouns.

Thus, while the English personal pronoun *I* (or, in less formal registers, *me*) can occur in elliptical contexts, such as (4) below, neither the French

---

[1] Further details about the forms and uses of neutral pronouns can be found in chapter 16.

subject clitic *je* nor the direct object clitic *me* can do so, as shown in (5). Instead, the French translation of (4) must use the non-clitic first person singular (1.p.sg.) pronoun *moi*, as in (6):[2]

(4)   John is taller than I/me.

(5)   Jean est plus grand que *je/*me.

(6)   Jean est plus grand que moi.

Moreover, personal clitics can only be separated from the predicator by other clitic forms. Thus, while it is perfectly possible in English to separate the subject pronoun *I* from the predicator by an intervening relative clause,[3] as in (7) below, the French example in (8) is ungrammatical with a relative clause directly following the subject clitic *je*. Instead, the non-clitic pronoun *moi* must be inserted before the relative clause and resumed by *je* before the predicator, as in (9):

(7)   I, who cannot stand Oriental cuisine, nevertheless *had* Vietnamese food last night.

(8)   *Je, qui déteste la cuisine orientale, *ai* néanmoins *mangé* vietnamien hier soir.

(9)   Moi qui déteste la cuisine orientale, j'*ai* néanmoins *mangé* vietnamien hier soir.

In French, the personal clitics can normally only be attached to one verb at a time.[4] Thus, whereas (10) below is perfectly acceptable in English with the 3.p.pl. pronoun *them* functioning as the direct object of both predicators (*sees* and *hears*) simultaneously, (11) is not possible in French, where both predicators must have their own direct-object clitic, as in (12):

(10)   Peter sees and hears them.

(11)   *Pierre les voit et entend.

(12)   Pierre les voit et les entend.

---

[2] See section 15.1, for person/number marking in pronouns.

[3] For the term 'relative clause', see section 4.2.2.

[4] In more formal registers, one subject clitic can sometimes attach itself to two predicators if there are no other clitic forms attached to those predicators, as in (i). The structure in (ii) is, however, always possible, and indeed more common. Direct-object and dative-object clitics must always be repeated.

(i)   Je mange et bois.

(ii)   Je mange et je bois.

Finally, as the alternative term 'unstressed pronouns' indicates, clitics cannot normally receive emphatic stress in French. Again, this is unlike English, where it is perfectly possible to mark the contrast between Sophie and the speaker/writer of (13) below by stressing the pronoun *I*. In French, on the other hand, we must make use of a combination of a non-clitic and a clitic pronoun in order to express that contrast, cf. (14)–(15), where capitals indicate emphatic stress:

(13)   Sophie would like to come, but I wouldn't.

(14)   *Sophie veut bien venir, mais JE ne veux pas.

(15)   Sophie veut bien venir, mais moi, je ne veux pas.

14.3 Pronouns *vs* articles

When discussing certain types of items in French, in particular possessives and demonstratives, but also certain indefinites, and interrogative *quel*, it is important to distinguish pronouns from articles. The examples in (16)–(18) below illustrate the difference:

(16)   [Mon manteau]$_{Subj/NP}$ est beige.

(17)   Le manteau beige, c'est [le mien.]$_{SubjAttr/PossPron}$

(18)   [Ce manteau]$_{Subj/NP}$ ne me plaît pas. Je préfère [celui-là.]$_{DirObj/DemPron}$

Thus, in (16), *mon* is a possessive article, which functions as the determiner of the noun phrase *mon manteau*. Determiners are phrase-level, not clause-level, constituents (cf. section 2.3.2). *Le mien* in (17), on the other hand, is a possessive pronoun, which functions as a subject attribute, i.e. a clause-level constituent (cf. section 1.2.3.1). Similarly, in (18), *ce* is a demonstrative article functioning as the determiner of the noun phrase *ce manteau*, whereas *celui-là* is a demonstrative pronoun, which functions as the direct object of the second clause.

Pronouns can stand on their own syntactically, i.e. they can constitute a clause-level constituent by themselves. Articles, on the other hand, cannot; they occur in the determiner slot of a noun phrase. For ease of reference, however, the two types of constituent will be treated together in several of the chapters below.

14.4 Deixis and anaphoricity

Sometimes a pronoun represents an entity that is not necessarily mentioned elsewhere in the text. Instead, the pronoun points to something outside the text, typically something in the real world. This means that, in order to work out what the pronoun refers to, the addressee must look at the world, rather than at the text itself. In such cases, the pronoun functions **deictically**.[5]

First and second person clitics like *je* and *te* in (19) below always function in this way:

(19) Je t'ai vu(e) hier soir, à St-Germain.

Who or what a deictic pronoun or clitic refers to will depend on who the speaker/writer and the addressee are, and on their respective locations: if Jacques utters (19) in a conversation with Françoise, the personal subject clitic *je* will refer to Jacques while the personal direct-object clitic *te* will refer to Françoise. If, on the other hand, it is Frédérique who utters the sentence in a conversation with Stéphane, then *je* will refer to Frédérique and *te* to Stéphane.

Third person pronouns/clitics may likewise be used deictically, but more often they are used **anaphorically**, i.e. they point back to something that has already been mentioned in the text.

In (20) below, we have an example of a deictic use of a third person direct-object clitic: Dominique may not have been mentioned previously in the conversation between A and B, but they both know that they are waiting for her, and so the personal direct-object clitic *la* can be used unproblematically to refer to her. This deictic use of *la* may be accompanied by actual physical pointing.

(20) [Two people, A and B, are waiting for a third person, Dominique] A to B: La voilà ! (= deictic use)

In (21), on the other hand, we have an anaphoric use of the personal dative-object clitic *lui*. Dominique is not present in the context, but she has been mentioned in the immediately preceding sentence. Note that, unlike

---

[5] The adjective 'deictic' comes from the ancient Greek noun *deixis*, which means 'pointing' or 'showing'. In linguistics, the term 'deixis' covers all the ways in which linguistic items and constructions may be used to point to something outside the text. See also section 6.1.1.

(20), no physical pointing can meaningfully accompany the use of *lui* in this context:

(21)   J'ai rencontré *Dominique* hier. Je lui ai dit que tu voulais lui parler. (= anaphoric use)

14.5 Genitives

Several subtypes of pronouns and related determiners can express so-called genitive meanings. In languages like Latin, from which French is descended, the term 'genitive' is the name of a morphological case form.[6] In French, as in English, the types of meaning conveyed by Latin genitives are not expressed morphologically, but by certain types of grammatical constructions. Arguably, the most basic genitive construction in French takes the form of the preposition *de* followed by a complement, and functions as a postmodifier of a noun phrase, as in (22) below:

(22)   J'ai trouvé [le frère d'Antoine] très sympathique.

Genitives are of four different types, depending on their meaning and on the nature of the head noun: possessive, subjective, objective, and partitive.

14.5.1 Possessive genitives

Possessive genitives express some kind of often quite abstract relationship between two distinct entities, such that the entity denoted by the head noun can be identified via its relation to the entity represented by the genitive. In (23) below, for instance, *voiture* is the head noun, Pierre is the entity represented by the genitive, and the construction as a whole tells the addressee that the car in question can be identified as one that stands in a salient relation to Pierre:

(23)   *La voiture* de Pierre est bleue. → Pierre a une voiture.

Often, but far from always, the relationship in question is one that involves some kind of loosely defined possession, as in (23), which will

---

[6] For the notion of case, see section 15.2.1.

typically suggest that Pierre owns, or at least has use of, the car in question. For this reason, the meaning of a possessive genitive can often be paraphrased by a clause using the verb *avoir* where the complement of *de* becomes the subject and the head noun the direct object, as seen in (23).

14.5.2 Subjective and objective genitives

Subjective and objective genitives are found with so-called **deverbal nouns**, i.e. nouns that are derived from verbs. For instance, the noun *conquête* is derived from the verb *conquérir*, the noun *proclamation* from the verb *proclamer*, the noun *arrivée* from the verb *arriver* etc. The meaning of a noun phrase with a deverbal noun as its head can be paraphrased as a finite clause in which the corresponding verb is the predicator.

A **subjective genitive** can thus be paraphrased as a clause in which the complement of *de* becomes the subject, as shown in (24):

(24)   *La promesse* de Thierry était peu sincère. → Thierry$_{Subj}$ a promis quelque chose.

An **objective genitive** can be paraphrased as a clause in which the complement of *de* becomes the direct object:

(25)   *L'accusateur* d'Arlette reste anonyme. → Quelqu'un a accusé Arlette$_{DirObj}$ de quelque chose.

14.5.3 Partitive genitives

Finally, in partitive genitives, the head noun denotes a part of the complement of *de*. The meaning of a partitive genitive can thus typically be paraphrased by a clause using the phrasal verb *faire partie de*, with the head noun as its subject, and the complement of the genitive *de* as its prepositional object, as shown in (26):

(26)   *Le nord* de l'Italie est une région prospère. → Le nord fait partie de l'Italie.

14.5.4 Pronouns and articles with genitive meaning

In French, **possessives** (pronouns and articles), which are treated further in section 18.1, always express genitive meanings. While the name might suggest that they always represent possessive genitives, they may in fact represent any of the four subtypes of genitive. In (27) below, for instance, the possessive article *sa* expresses a subjective genitive (cf. (24) above):

(27)   Sa promesse était peu sincère.

The **relative pronoun** *dont*, treated further in section 19.3.3.2 and exemplified in (28) below, can likewise represent any subtype of genitive. The pronominal adverb *en*, on the other hand, seen in a genitive use in (29), is limited to three of the subtypes, viz. possessive, objective, and partitive genitives (see section 17.2.1.3, for details).

(28)   Ma tante Sophie, dont tu connais le mari, est l'auteure de ce roman.

(29)   Quand on parle du loup, on en voit la queue. ('Speak of the Devil, and he appears', lit.: 'When you speak of the wolf, you see its tail.')

15

Personal and reflexive pronouns

Learning objectives

- To understand the difference between personal and reflexive pronouns.
- To understand and be able to accurately apply the rules governing the use of personal and reflexive clitics, as well as non-clitic personal and reflexive pronouns in French.
- To understand the notion of a generic pronoun, and to understand the rules governing its use in French.

15.1 Personal *vs* reflexive pronouns

Personal pronouns are used by default (i.e. when there is no particular reason to use any other pronominal form) to represent the three types of entity that are relevant to any text or discourse, viz. the speaker/writer, the addressee, and any other entities mentioned in the discourse. All three types may be either singular or plural, as the speaker and addressee may be perceived as

The Structure of Modern Standard French. First edition. Maj-Britt Mosegaard Hansen.
© Maj-Britt Mosegaard Hansen 2016. First Published 2016 by Oxford University Press

members of a group of similar individuals. That gives us a total of six options, which are also found in English, as shown in Table 15.1.

Table 15.1. Types of entity represented by personal pronouns.

	Singular	**Plural**
1st person	The speaker ('I')	Group of which the speaker is a member ('we')
2nd person	The addressee ('you')	Group of which the addressee is a member ('you')
3rd person	Entity that is being talked about ('he', 'she', 'it')	Group of entities that are being talked about ('they')

In addition, French has a so-called 'generic' third-person singular personal pronoun, *on*, which has no single direct equivalent in English (see section 15.2.4 below).

The third-person singular neutral subject clitic *ce* is sometimes used to refer to non-neutral, incl. human, entities, as in (1) below, where *ce* refers to the woman Paule, who is mentioned in the preceding sentence. Such uses are treated in chapter 16.

(1)   J'aimerais te présenter *Paule* un jour. C'est une chercheure vraiment brillante.

A **reflexive pronoun** has the same reference as the (implied) subject of the verb it belongs with. In (2) below, the subscript indices 'i' and 'j' indicate that the proper nouns *Pascale* and *Laurent* refer to two different individuals.[1] If we want to paraphrase that sentence representing Laurent by a pronoun, we have to use a personal clitic, as in (3):

(2)   Pascale$_i$ regardait Laurent$_j$.

(3)   Pascale$_i$ le$_j$ regardait.

---

[1] As with many other notational conventions within linguistics, this one has its origins in mathematics, where subscript indices are used to keep track of variables.

In (4) below, on the other hand, both *Pascale* and the reflexive direct-object clitic *se* are marked by the index $_i$ to show that the two refer to one and the same individual. In other words, Pascale is looking at herself in the mirror:

(4)   Pascale$_i$ s̲e̲$_i$ regardait dans la glace.

If a verb with a particular meaning is always found in construction with a reflexive clitic, it is a **pronominal verb**.[2] Thus, *s'évanouir* in (5) below is a pronominal verb, because *évanouir* cannot be used in the absence of a reflexive clitic. Similarly, *se douter de qc.* is a pronominal verb in (6), because although *douter de qc.* can be used non-reflexively (as in (7)), the two constructions have very different meanings:

(5)   Evangéline s̲'évanouit en entendant ces mots.

(6)   Pierre ne s̲e̲ doutait de rien. ('Pierre didn't suspect anything.')

(7)   Franck [Ø] doute de tout. ('Franck has doubts about everything.')

In addition, many verbs are sometimes constructed reflexively, with essentially the same meaning as in their non-reflexive uses. Thus, for instance, the only difference between (8) and (9) below is that the subject and direct object represent two different entities in (8), while in (9), the direct object *se* refers to the same entity as the subject. It would not be meaningful to say that the verb *laver* has different senses in the two constructions:

(8)   Capucine a lavé s̲o̲n̲ b̲é̲b̲é̲.

(9)   Capucine s̲'est lavée.

In French, unlike English, there are two different kinds of both personal and reflexive pronouns, called 'clitic' and 'non-clitic', respectively (cf. section 14.2). Of the two, the clitics are the more frequently used forms. Personal clitics are treated in section 15.2 below, and non-clitic personal pronouns in section 15.3. Section 15.4 discusses reflexive clitics and non-clitics.

---

[2] Note that, while *se* is always reflexive, *me*, *te*, *nous*, and *vous* frequently function non-reflexively (see section 15.4 below). Thus, in (i) *me* is non-reflexive because the speaker (referred to by *me*) is a different individual from the subject Sylvie:

(i)   Sylvie m̲'a longuement regardé(e).

15.2 The personal clitics

The three series of pronouns in Table 15.2 below are known as **personal (non-generic) clitics** in French. Some grammars use the terms 'unstressed', 'bound', or 'conjunctive' personal pronouns to describe what this book calls personal clitics. For more information on the notion of clitics, see section 14.2.

15.2.1 Case inflection

The French personal clitics are subject to **case inflection**. This means that each person/number combination may have different forms, whose uses depend on the precise grammatical role of the pronoun within its host clause, cf. Table 15.2. Thus, **nominative** clitics are used as **subjects**, **accusative** clitics are used as **direct objects**, and **dative** clitics are used as **dative objects** (see sections 1.2.2, 1.2.3.2, and 1.2.3.5).[3]

Note that the 1.p.pl. and 2.p.pl. forms of the pronouns are identical across all three cases, and that the 1.p.sg. and 2.p.sg. forms are identical in the accusative and the dative case. To be able to determine whether one of these forms is in the accusative or the dative case, you therefore need to know the valency structure of the verb they are associated with.

Table 15.2. The forms of the personal, non-generic, clitics.

		Nominative (subject case)	Accusative (direct-object case)	Dative (dative-object case)
1st person	Singular	*je*	*me*	*me*
	Plural	*nous*	*nous*	*nous*
2nd person	Singular	*tu*	*te*	*te*
	Plural	*vous*	*vous*	*vous*
3rd person	Singular	*il, elle*	*le, la*	*lui*
	Plural	*ils, elles*	*les*	*leur*

[3] As explained in section 1.2.3.1, the form *le* may be used to represent a subject attribute. This *le*, however, is an oblique case form of the neutral pronoun *il* (cf. section 16.5)

15.2.2 The relative position of personal clitics

The personal clitics are always **valency elements**, and, as explained above, their grammatical role is indicated by the case form they take in any given clause.

Except in clauses where inversion is used (cf. section 24.3), subject clitics always precede all other clitic forms, incl. personal and reflexive clitics in the accusative or dative case.[4]

If there is both an accusative and a dative clitic attached to a given predicator, these occur in a specific order. There are two different cases to consider:

(a) The general rule is that personal and reflexive clitics are placed before the verb (including non-finite verb forms), and the complements occur in the order shown in Table 15.3.

Table 15.3. The order of unstressed complement pronouns.

1. Accusative or dative	2. Accusative only	3. Dative only
me		
te	le	lui
(se)[5]	la	leur
nous	les	
vous		

In Table 15.3, there are three columns of forms. The forms in the first column may be in either the accusative or the dative case. Those in the second column are accusative forms, and those in the third column are dative forms. The larger of the two overlapping squares in Table 15.3 unites the forms from columns 1 and 2, while the smaller square contains those from columns 2 and 3.

---

[4] For the position of pronominal adverbs and the negative clitic *ne*, cf. chapters 17 and 23.

[5] The reflexive clitic *se* is included in Table 15.3 for simplicity's sake.

The rule that Table 15.3 illustrates is that only two complement clitics can occur with any one verb. These clitics must be chosen from two different columns, and only from within one and the same square.

In other words, either one clitic from column 1 + one from column 2, or one clitic from column 2 + one from column 3 may be used. It is never possible to combine a clitic from column 1 with one from column 3, or two clitics from the same column.

Accordingly, the examples in (10)–(11) below illustrate possible combinations, while those in (12)–(13) illustrate impossible combinations:

(10)   Tu me le présentes. (1st + 2nd column) ('You introduce him to me.')

(11)   Je la leur présente. (2nd + 3rd column) ('I introduce her to them.')

(12)   *Tu me lui présentes. (1st + 3rd column) ('You introduce me to him.')

(13)   *Il me te présente. (1st + 1st column) ('He introduces me to you.')

To express the intended meaning of (the ungrammatical) (12) or (13) above, the dative object must take the form of a prepositional phrase instead, as shown in (14)–(15) below:

(14)   Tu me présentes à lui. ('You introduce me to him.')

(15)   Il me présente à toi. ('He introduces me to you.')

These general rules represented in Table 15.3 also apply to negated imperative clauses,[6] as shown in (16)–(17) below:

(16)   *Ne le lui dis pas* !

(17)   *Ne me le donne pas* !

(b) In positive imperative clauses, on the other hand, the clitics always follow the verb, and in the first, second, and third person alike, accusative clitics always precede dative clitics, as shown in (18)–(19) below. In other words, the order of personal clitics prescribed by Table 15.3 does not apply to positive imperative clauses.

(18)   Dis-le-lui !

---

[6] For further details on imperative clauses, see section 5.3.

(19)   Dis-le-nous !

Positive imperatives do, however, observe the ban against combinations of two clitics from the same column or of clitics from columns 1 + 3 of Table 15.3, as shown by the unacceptability of (20)–(21):

(20)   *Présentez-vous-moi !

(21)   *Présente-me-lui !

   As (22) below shows, if a first or second person singular form occurs as the last clitic following a positive imperative, the forms *moi* and *toi* are used instead of *me* and *te*:

(22)   Donnez-le-moi !

However, *me* and *te* are used if followed by one of the pronominal adverbs *en* and *y*, as in (23)–(24):[7]

(23)   Va t'*en* !

(24)   Donnez-m'*en* quelques-uns !

15.2.3 The generic clitic on

In addition to the personal clitics in Table 15.1 above, for which English equivalents exist, French possesses a **generic nominative (= subject) clitic**, *on*, which cannot be translated literally, but which in its most basic meaning corresponds variably to expressions such as 'people in general', 'some people', indefinite 'they'/'you'/'one', 'someone', or indeed a passive construction in English, as exemplified in (25)–(28) below:[8]

---

[7] In informal spoken registers, *moi* and *toi* may be used even in this environment, as in (i). In such cases, a /z/ will be inserted between the personal clitic and the pronominal adverb. Examples like (i) will normally only be found in writing that deliberately mimics speech; elsewhere, the construction exemplified in (24) above is preferred.

(i)   Donnez-moi-z-*en* !

[8] *On* is historically a nominative form of the noun *homme*, and is thus not unlike the (rather old-fashioned) generic use of *man* in English, as in (i):

(i)   Man is a creature of habit. (≈ 'Human beings in general are creatures of habit.')

(25) <u>On</u> ne *peut* pas faire ça ! ('You/One can't do that!' → For people in general, it is not acceptable to do that.)

(26) <u>On</u> *va* construire un nouvel hypermarché ici. ('They're going to build a new giant supermarket here.')

(27) <u>On</u> t'*a* apporté des fleurs. ('Someone brought you flowers.')

(28) <u>On</u> *vient* d'attraper l'assassin du Président ! ('The President's killer has just been caught!')

Although *on* in this basic indefinite use thus typically refers to a plurality of individuals which may include both genders, the form is grammatically third person singular and masculine. Accordingly, it always combines with a third person singular finite verb, as in (25)–(28) above.

However, any associated constituents other than the finite verb (such as past participles or adjectives, nouns, or indefinite pronouns functioning as subject attributes or free indirect attributes of the subject) will very often reflect the **notional plurality** of *on*, as shown in (29) below. More rarely, such elements may reflect the intended feminine reference of an indefinite *on*, as in (30). Masculine singular agreement is always possible, however, as seen in (31)–(32):

(29) On est <u>tous</u> <u>mortels</u>. (≈ 'All human beings are mortal.')

(30) On n'est pas toujours <u>jeune</u> et <u>belle</u>. (≈ 'Women in general aren't young and beautiful forever.')

(31) On est <u>mortel</u>, après tout. (≈ 'Human beings in general are mortal, after all.')

(32) On n'est pas toujours <u>jeune</u> et <u>beau</u>. (≈ 'Human beings in general aren't young and beautiful forever.')

The reference of *on* is not necessarily generic, however. In fact, given an appropriate context, *on* may stand in for any other person, as shown in (33)–(37) below:

(33) 1.p.sg.: Quand ma femme m'a tapé dessus, je porte toujours des lunettes noires. <u>On</u> n'a tout de même pas envie que ça se sache. (→ I don't want it to be known.)

(34) 1.p.pl.: Dépêche-toi, <u>on</u> t'attend ! (→ We're waiting)

(35) 2.p.sg./pl.: Dis donc, <u>on</u> est bien pâlotte(s) ce matin ! (→ You're rather pale.)

(36)   3.p.sg.: J'ai demandé au secrétariat, et on m'a dit qu'il était absent aujour-
d'hui. (→ A single identifiable individual working in the secretariat told me
this.)

(37)   3.p.pl.: Il paraît qu'on s'est disputé au labo ce matin. (→ Some identifiable
people working in the lab had an argument.)

On is used with **non-generic reference** for a variety of reasons. The speaker
may not think it communicatively important to identify the subject more
explicitly, as in (36) above; s/he may avoid identifying the subject explicitly
for reasons of politeness, as in (37); s/he may use *on* due to embarrassment,
as in (33); or *on* may take on an affectionate nuance, as in (35).

Most commonly, however, particularly in relatively informal registers, *on*
with definite reference is used as a first-person plural subject clitic, in place
of *nous*, as in (34). Arguably, this is a way of simplifying the morphology of
the finite verb. Thus, when *on* replaces *nous*, the endings of regular verbs
of the first conjugation (i.e. those whose infinitives end in *–er*) will, in
some of the most commonly used tenses, take the same phonetic form in
all cases except the second person plural cf. (38)–(39) below.[9]

(38)   je parle, tu parles, il parle, on parle, vous parlez, ils parlent

(39)   /ʒəˈpaʁl/, /tyˈpaʁl/, /ilˈpaʁl/, /õˈpaʁl/, /vupaʁˈle/, /ilˈpaʁl/

The grammatical rules governing agreement are the same for non-generic
uses of *on* as for generic uses.

On exists only in the nominative case, and has no accusative or dative
forms. Nor does it have its own non-clitic equivalent. When *on* is used with
generic reference, or with non-generic reference to something other than the
first person plural, the second-person plural personal clitic *vous* is used as an
accusative/dative form in non-reflexive contexts like (40) below, and the
reflexive clitic *se* is used in reflexive contexts like (41):

(40)   Cela peut être gênant que quelqu'un vous dévisage. ('...if someone stares at
you/one.')

[9] First conjugation verbs constitute not only by far the largest group of verbs in
the language, but also the only one that is productive, i.e. which accepts new
members, so the morphological simplification achieved by using *on* instead of *nous*
is of considerable importance.

(41) On *se* tait quand quelqu'un d'autre parle. ('You/One must be silent when someone else is speaking.')

When *on* replaces *nous*, the accusative/dative form used in non-reflexive contexts is *nous*, as in (42) below. Reflexive *se* is used in reflexive contexts (cf. (43)):

(42) *On* sait que quelqu'un *nous* a vus.

(43) Richard et moi, *on se* dispute souvent.

In writing, the form *l'on* is not infrequently used instead of the plain *on*. While there are no very systematic rules governing the use of *l'on*, it often serves to avoid a clash of two successive vowels (i.e. a hiatus), as in (44) below, where the absence of *l'* would result in a clash between the final /i/ of the relative pronoun *qui* and the /õ/ of *on*. The form *l'on* is, however, also often used after the conjunction *que*, as in (45), where a hiatus would equally be avoided by contraction to *qu'on*:

(44) C'est quelqu'un à *qui* l'on s'est déjà adressé.

(45) Il est important *que* l'on se prépare le mieux possible.

15.3 Non-clitic personal pronouns

Unlike their clitic counterparts, the non-clitic personal pronouns of French are genuine pronouns, i.e. independent words which are not directly attached to a verb form, and which therefore do not have to function as valency elements (cf. section 14.2).

For this reason, the non-clitic pronouns are not marked for case in French. Like the personal clitics, they are, however, morphologically marked for person, number and, in the third person, also gender.

These pronouns can have a variety of different functions, which are not open to their unstressed counterparts.

(a) They can be **subject attributes**, as in (46) below:

(46) C'*est* bien lui.

(b) They can be **complements of a preposition**, as in (47):

(47) Je ne voterai pas pour toi.

In this use, the non-clitic pronouns normally only occur with reference to human beings. If reference is being made to entities other than human beings, one of the pronominal adverbs *en* and *y*, the neutral pronoun *cela*,[10] or certain adverbs or prepositions are used instead, as exemplified in (48) below:

(48)   Je ne voterai pas pour <u>cela</u>.

(c) They can occur after the **restrictive marker** *ne . . . que*, as in (49):[11]

(49)   Je *n'*inviterai *qu'*<u>eux</u>.

(d) They can occur in **clause-** or **sentence fragments** (i.e. elliptical clauses/ sentences), such as B's reply in (50):

(50)   A: Qui veut venir ?
       B: <u>Moi</u>.

(e) They can either precede or follow the core clause in so-called **dislocation** constructions,[12] such as that in B's reply in (51):

(51)   A: Tu as parlé à Max et à Isabelle ?
       B: <u>Elle</u>, je *lui* ai téléphoné, mais pas à lui.

(f) They can occur in **coordination** with another pronoun or noun phrase, as in (52), where the plural subject of the sentence consists in a coordination of *moi* and the proper noun *Alexandre*:

(52)   [*Alexandre et* <u>moi</u>]$_{Subj}$ sommes allés voir le dernier film de François Ozon l'autre soir.

When the generic clitic *on* is used with first-person plural reference, the corresponding non-clitic form is always *nous*, as seen in (53) below:

(53)   Il est tard : *on* va rentrer chez <u>nous</u>.

15.4 Reflexive pronouns

Because they depend on the subject for their reference (cf. section 15.1 above), **reflexive clitics** have no nominative (i.e. subject-case) forms, but

---

[10] For details on neutral pronouns, see chapter 16.
[11] For details on the use of restrictive markers, see section 23.5.
[12] For details on dislocation, see section 26.2.

are found only in the accusative (i.e. direct-object) or dative case. Like the non-clitic personal pronouns, non-clitic reflexives are unmarked for case. The available forms, both clitic and non-clitic, are seen in Table 15.4.

Table 15.4. Clitic and non-clitic reflexives.

		Clitic: accusative+ dative	**Non-clitic**
1st person	Singular	*me*	*moi*
	Plural	*nous*	*nous*
2nd person	Singular	*te*	*toi*
	Plural	*vous*	*vous*
3rd person	Singular	*se*	*soi*
	Plural	*se*	*soi*

As Table 15.4 shows, only two pronominal forms in French are overtly marked as reflexive, namely the accusative/dative clitic *se* and the non-clitic *soi*, which are both third-person singular/plural forms. In first- and second-person reflexive uses, the personal pronouns double as reflexive pronouns. Thus, in (54) below, the form *te* is a personal clitic, because it refers to a different person from the subject of the sentence. In (55), on the other hand, *te* is a reflexive clitic, as its reference in that sentence is identical to that of the subject:

(54)   Fais comme si de rien n'était : *on* te regarde !

(55)   Faut-il vraiment que *tu* te regardes dans toutes les vitrines ?

The position of reflexive clitics is governed by the same set of rules as the position of personal clitics. For details, see section 15.2.3 above.

The choice between clitic and non-clitic reflexives is subject to the same basic set of rules that govern the choice between personal clitics and non-clitics, i.e. the clitics can only occur in the immediate vicinity of a verb form.

The non-clitic, inherently reflexive pronoun *soi* is used only when referring to a non-specific entity or group (i.e. when an expression such as indefinite *on*, *chacun, tout le monde*, etc. is the subject of the clause). If the reference is specific, a personal pronoun (*lui, elle, eux*, or *elles*) is used instead.

Thus, *soi* can be used in (56) below because the generic subject *on* refers to people in general, rather than to any specific group of people that we can identify.

(56)   *On* a souvent tendance à s'occuper exclusivement de <u>soi</u> et de ses proches.

In (57) below, on the other hand, where the subject *Justine* refers to a particular woman, we must use a non-clitic personal pronoun, even though the construction is clearly reflexive (i.e. Justine is thinking of herself, not of some other woman, as shown by the fact that we can attach *–même* to the stressed pronoun *elle*):

(57)   *Justine*$_i$ a souvent tendance à s'occuper exclusivement d'<u>elle</u>$_i$(-même) et de ses proches.

15.4.1 Uses of the reflexive construction in French

Reflexive constructions in French can have three different meanings depending on the context.

15.4.1.1 Standard reflexive use

In this use, the subject of the clause or sentence is directing an action or activity at him-/her-/itself/themselves. We thus have a standard reflexive use (expressing middle voice, cf. section 25.1) in example (4), section 15.1 above, as well as in (58) below:

(58)   Nous <u>nous</u> lavons chaque matin.

15.4.1.2 Reciprocal use

The reciprocal use is a variant of the regular reflexive use. It is found only with plural subjects who direct an action or activity, not at themselves, but at one another. Thus, on a reciprocal interpretation, (59) below tells you that the speaker/writer knows Muriel and Muriel knows the speaker/writer. In a standard reflexive interpretation, on the other hand, it would mean that both women knew themselves.

(59)   <u>Muriel et moi</u>, on <u>se</u> connaît depuis des années.

Because the reflexive construction with a plural subject may be potentially ambiguous between these two interpretations, the reciprocal meaning can be made explicit by adding one of the following expressions:

• *l'un* [preposition] *l'autre*,[13] as in (60)–(61):

(60)   Ils *se* détestent l'un l'autre.

(61)   Elles *se* parlent souvent les unes aux autres.

• *entre* + non-clitic personal pronoun, as in (62):

(62)   Elles *se* parlent souvent entre elles.

• *mutuellement*, as in (63):

(63)   Ils *se* détestent mutuellement.

In all these cases, the 'bare' reflexive construction has two potential meanings: besides the reciprocal interpretations 'They hate each other' and 'They were talking to each other', *Ils se détestent* might mean 'They hate themselves', and *Elles se parlent* might be interpreted as 'They are talking to themselves'. The use of expressions such as those found in (60)–(63) disambiguates the clause, such that only the reciprocal interpretation is possible.

15.4.1.3 Passive use

Finally, the French reflexive construction can be used with a meaning akin to that of a passive sentence, as in (64)–(65) below. For more information about the reflexive passive and the reflexive causative construction, which likewise has passive meaning, see sections 25.3.2 and 25.4.2.

(64)   A l'époque, le dollar s'échangeait à 0,85 euros. (> On échangeait le dollar à 0,85 euros.)

(65)   Louise s'est fait couper les cheveux. (> On lui a coupé les cheveux.)

---

[13] See further section 20.2.5.

16

Neutral pronouns

Learning objectives

- To understand the difference between neutral pronouns as 'regular' and as anticipatory subjects.

- To understand and be able to correctly apply the grammatical rules governing the choice between neutral (anticipatory) subject pronouns in French.

- To understand and be able to correctly apply the rules governing the uses of the neutral complement clitic *le*.

16.1 Introduction

Neutral pronouns are largely empty of meaning, hence the term 'neutral'. They are used principally because standard French (like English, but unlike its sister languages Spanish or Italian, for instance) requires all finite clauses to have an explicit grammatical subject, cf. the contrast between (1) below and the Italian example in (2), which has the same meaning:

The Structure of Modern Standard French. First edition. Maj-Britt Mosegaard Hansen.
© Maj-Britt Mosegaard Hansen 2016. First Published 2016 by Oxford University Press

(1)   <u>Il</u> pleut.

(2)   [Ø] Piove.

French has four pronominal forms that are used neutrally, namely *ce, ceci, cela*, and *il*. For the purposes of this book, the informal pronoun *ça* will be subsumed under *cela*, as there are only minor differences between them that are unrelated to register. *Ce* and neutral *il* are clitics, which normally function as subjects or anticipatory subjects,[1] and which take the same position in the clause as other clitic subjects (see sections 14.2 and 15.2 for details). *Ceci* and *cela* are non-clitic pronouns, which can have a variety of grammatical functions. In addition, the invariant complement clitic *le* is used neutrally.

The different neutral subject pronouns cannot be used interchangeably. Rather, the choice between them depends partly on whether they function as 'regular' or as anticipatory subjects, partly on the type and form of the predicator they combine with, and partly on the presence and nature of other valency elements in the clause.

16.2 The neutral pronoun is the subject of the clause

When there is no postponed subject in the clause and the neutral pronoun is thus a 'regular' subject, (i.e. not an anticipatory subject), the forms *cela/ça, ceci, ce*, or *il* may be used. The choice between them depends principally on the nature and form of the predicator.

16.2.1 Cela *and* ceci

The general rule is to use *cela* as a 'regular' neutral subject. This is exemplified in (3)–(4) below. As these examples show, *cela* can refer to something that is assumed to exist outside the text, as in (3) where *cela* refers to a real-world situation that the speaker finds annoying, or it may be empty of reference, as in (4), where there is no particular 'it' in the kitchen that can be identified as smelling of gas:

---

[1] For the notions of anticipatory *vs* postponed subjects, see section 3.1.2.

(3)   Cela m'ennuie.

(4)   Cela sent le gaz dans la cuisine.

Ceci can only be used to refer. It may be used neutrally to refer forward[2] to something that has not been mentioned yet, as in (5) below:

(5)   Jean a ceci de sympathique *qu'il ne sait pas du tout mentir.*

Perhaps more typically, however, *ceci* is used in contrast to *cela*, as in (6) below. In such cases, both pronouns take on a more demonstrative sense (cf. section 18.2)

(6)   *Cela* est une écrevisse. Ceci est une langoustine.

16.2.2 Ce

Ce is normally only used if the predicator is *être*, as in (7) below:

(7)   C'est ouvert jusqu'à 8 heures.

Although *ce* is formally third person singular, *être* must—in neutral and more formal registers—be in the third person plural if the clause also contains a subject attribute in the plural, as seen in (8) below. In colloquial speech, however, the verb is often in the singular, as in (9):

(8)   Ce sont des imbéciles.

(9)   C'est des imbéciles.

When *être* is in the *futur simple* or the *conditionnel*, as in (10) below, or governed by a modal verb, as in (11), *cela* is frequently used instead of *ce*. If a non-subject complement clitic intervenes between the subject and the predicator, as in (12), *cela* is almost always preferred:

(10)   Ce/Cela *sera* pour une autre fois.

(11)   Ce/Cela *peut être* difficile.

---

[2] Forward reference is also known as 'cataphoric' reference, in contrast to the more common backwards, or 'anaphoric', form of pronominal reference (cf. section 14.2).

(12) Cela *m'*est égal.

Because clitic *ce* cannot be stressed, *cela* must be used with all forms of *être* if the speaker wishes to place emphasis on the subject, as in (13) below. Note that, before the forms *est* and *était*, *cela* is never reduced to *ça*:

(13) Non, vraiment, cela est impossible !

16.2.3 Il

Il is used as a neutral subject only where the context precludes its interpretation as a personal clitic, i.e. where it cannot be understood to refer to a concrete entity. Compare (14) and (15) below:

(14) Take this train. It (= taking this train) is faster than taking the bus.

(15) Take this train. It (= this train) is faster than the other train.

In (14), we have a neutral use of English *it*, to refer to something abstract, namely the action of taking a particular train. In (15), on the other hand, it is used as a personal pronoun, to refer to the train as such. When translating (14) into French, we disambiguate the meaning of *it* by using *ce*, as in (16) below. Only the concrete meaning of *it* in (15) can be rendered by *il*, as in (17):

(16) [Prenez ce train]$_i$. C$_j$'est plus rapide.

(17) Prenez [ce train]$_i$. Il$_i$ est plus rapide.

Thus, *il* is used as a neutral subject clitic only in impersonal constructions, where the subject is devoid of reference. The constructions in question are of three types:

(i) **Temporal expressions** such as those in (18)–(19) below:

(18) Il est *minuit et quart*.

(19) Il est *trop tard* maintenant.

Note that when naming parts of the day, days of the week, or seasons, *ce*, and not *il*, is used as a neutral subject:

(20) C'est *le printemps* déjà.

In addition, *ce* may be used as a subject in less formal registers when *tôt* or *tard* is a subject attribute, as in (21) below. Formal registers prefer *il*, however, as in (19) above.

(21)   C'est *trop tard* maintenant.

(ii) **Weather/ambience** expressions like those in (22)–(23):

(22)   Il *neige* sur Liège.

(23)   En Suède, il *fait jour* jusqu'à minuit en été.

(iii) A few **set impersonal expressions**, mainly *y avoir* (as in *il y a*), *falloir*, and *s'agir de*, as in (24):

(24)   Il ne *s'agit* pas de toi maintenant.

16.3 The neutral pronoun is an anticipatory subject

In clauses with an anticipatory and a postponed subject (see section 3.1.2 for details), *cela*, *ce*, and *il* may be used as anticipatory subjects depending on the type of predicator and the nature of other valency elements in the clause.

16.3.1 The clause contains a non-reflexive direct object

Cela is used as an anticipatory subject when the predicator takes a non-reflexive direct object, as in (25)–(26) below. The verb is typically one which describes a psychological effect of the postponed subject on the direct object. Thus, in (25), speaking at length has the psychological effect of tiring the speaker (represented by the direct object *me*):

(25)   Cela *me* fatigue [de parler longtemps.]PostponedSubj

(26)   Cela *m'*étonne [qu'elle n'ait pas consulté un médecin.]PostponedSubj

16.3.2 The clause contains a subject attribute

If the clause contains a subject attribute, either *ce* or *il* may be used, depending on the linguistic form of the subject attribute.

If the subject attribute takes the form of a noun phrase or an infinitival phrase, *ce* is always used, as shown in (27)–(28) below:

(27)   C'est *une honte* [de penser à l'argent avant tout.]_{PostponedSubj}

(28)   Ce n'est guère *vivre* [que de³ passer ses jours avec de vieux livres.]_{PostponedSubj}

If the subject attribute takes the form of an adjectival phrase, *il* is used in neutral and more formal registers, as in (29) below. More colloquial, particularly spoken, registers, often use *ce*, however, as shown in (30):

(29)   Il est *facile* [de se tromper.]_{PostponedSubj}

(30)   C'est *facile* [de se tromper.]_{PostponedSubj}

16.3.3 The postponed subject is a complement clause or an infinitival phrase

If the postponed subject takes the form of a complement clause, as in (31) below, or an infinitival phrase, as in (32), *il* is used as the anticipatory subject in neutral and more formal registers:

(31)   Comment se fait-il *que vous parliez si bien le français*?

(32)   Il suffit *de téléphoner à mon bureau.*

More colloquial, particularly spoken, registers, often use *cela* (usually in its shortened form *ça*), however, as shown in (33)–(34):

(33)   Comment ça se fait *que vous parliez si bien le français*?

(34)   Ça suffit *de téléphoner à mon bureau.*

If the predicator is in the passive voice, as in (35) below, *il* is always used as the anticipatory subject:

(35)   Il est écrit *que les derniers seront les premiers.*

---

³ See section 9.2.2.2 for the form of the infinitive marker here.

16.3.4 The postponed subject is a noun phrase

If the postponed subject is a noun phrase, as in (36)–(37) below, *il* is always used as the anticipatory subject:

(36) Il ne me reste que *quelques francs.*

(37) Il est arrivé *un accident.*

Typically, in this type of construction, the predicator will belong to the small group of intransitive verbs which take *être* as their auxiliary,[4] and it will broadly speaking serve to describe something as existing (e.g. *rester* in (36)) or coming into existence (e.g. *arriver* in (37)) in some form. The postponed subject is normally an indefinite noun phrase, often referring to an inanimate entity (as in both the examples above), and the construction with anticipatory and postponed subject serves to avoid having such an indefinite noun phrase in the regular subject position.

Constructions where the postponed subject is a noun phrase may, however, also be impersonal passives, as in (38) below. This is a relatively rare construction type, however, and it is largely confined to more formal, bureaucratic registers:

(38) Il sera élu *deux représentants* au comité.

16.4 Different functions of neutral pronouns with the same verb

With many verbs, neutral pronouns can be used as either regular or postponed subjects. It follows from the rules given in sections 16.2–16.3 above that the same pronoun will not necessarily be used with the same verb in the two types of construction, even when those constructions occur sequentially in a discourse. Thus, in (39)–(41) below, the utterances produced by speaker A in all cases feature constructions with an anticipatory and a postponed

---

[4] See section 8.2.1.3 for details.

subject, while those produced by speaker B have neutral pronouns as 'regular' subjects.

(39)   A: On m'a dit qu'il suffisait [de signer en bas de la page].
    B: En effet, ça suffit.

(40)   A: Vous est-il arrivé [de vous tromper de train en rentrant tard de votre travail ?]
    B: Oui, cela m'est arrivé une fois ou deux.

(41)   A: Est-ce qu'il est *difficile* [de trouver un exemplaire de ce livre ?]
    B: Mais non, ce n'est pas difficile du tout.

16.5 The neutral pronoun is a complement

The invariant neutral complement clitic *le* can be used to represent any kind of **subject attribute**, as in (42) below.

(42)   Elle a été membre du parti, mais elle ne l'est plus.

In addition, *le* can represent a **neutral direct object**, i.e. one that refers to something abstract. In (43) below, for instance, speaker B's *le* represents the hypothetical situation mentioned in A's utterance:

(43)   A: Esther voudrait *passer ses vacances à faire de l'autostop à travers les États-Unis.*
    B: Ses parents ne le permettront sûrement pas.

Just as with the subject clitic *il* (cf. section 16.2.3 above), *le* can be used neutrally only in contexts that preclude its interpretation as referring to a concrete entity. With verbs like *aimer*, *adorer*, *oublier*, etc., direct object *le* would preferentially be interpreted as referring to a person or thing. Instead, *cela* or zero-pronominalization must be used if the direct object is to be understood as referring to something more abstract, as shown in (44)–(46):

(44)   A: Qu'est-ce que tu penses de *la linguistique* ?
    B: Je n'aime pas [Ø].

(45)   A: Vous aimez *aller au cinéma* ?
    B: Oui, j'adore ça.

(46)   A: Tu es *allé(e) chercher ma veste chez le teinturier* ?
    B: Non, j'ai oublié [Ø].

16.5.1 Translation of the English anticipatory direct object construction into French

Parallel to constructions with an anticipatory and a postponed subject, English has a commonly used construction with an anticipatory and a postponed direct object. This construction type is illustrated in (47):

(47)   We find it$_{AnticipDirObj}$ important [to keep you informed.]$_{PostponedDirObj}$

This construction is not found in French,[5] so when rendering examples like (47) into that language, the English anticipatory direct object is not translated, as shown in (48), where the infinitival phrase functions as a 'regular' direct object:

(48)   Nous [Ø] trouvons important [de vous tenir au courant.]$_{DirObj}$

---

[5] While *ceci* in example (5) in section 16.2.1 above does function as an anticipatory direct object, this construction does not correspond to the English construction in (47). Instead, (5) would be rendered into English along the lines of (i):

(i)   The nice thing about Jean is that he's incapable of lying.

17

Pronominal adverbs

Learning objectives

- To understand the nature of pronominal adverbs and the different kinds of expression they may represent.
- To understand the nature of the variation between *en* and the possessive article when expressing genitives.

17.1 Introduction

French has two pronominal adverbs, *en* and *y*. These items resemble adverbs in as much as they often—although far from always—fulfil adverbial functions inside their host clause. In (1)–(2) below, for instance, they function as place adverbials:

(1)   Benoît mange souvent *au resto U*. Il y retrouve la plupart de ses copains.

(2)   Isabelle a passé l'année dernière *en Espagne*. Elle en a ramené un fiancé.

On the other hand, they are pronominal forms in as much as they usually stand in for a constituent of some other type which is mentioned elsewhere

The Structure of Modern Standard French. First edition. Maj-Britt Mosegaard Hansen.
© Maj-Britt Mosegaard Hansen 2016. First Published 2016 by Oxford University Press

in the text. This is the case not only in (1)–(2), but also, for instance, in (3)–(4) below, where *en* and *y* function as prepositional objects, i.e. a type of complement:

(3) A: Tu te sers *de la photocopieuse* en ce moment ?
   B: Non, je ne m'en sers pas.

(4) A: Tu as pensé *à acheter un cadeau d'anniversaire pour Colette* ?
   B: Ah non, je n'y ai pas pensé.

Like the personal pronouns and the preverbal negative marker *ne*, the pronominal adverbs are clitics, hence constrained to occur in close proximity to a verb form.[1] As shown in (5) below, the pronominal adverbs follow other clitics in a sequence. If both pronominal adverbs occur together in a clause, *y* precedes *en*, as shown in (6):

(5) Je *ne lui* en ai pas parlé.

(6) A: Je peux prendre un petit gâteau ?
   B: Bien sûr, s'il y en a encore.

Generally speaking, the pronominal adverbs do not refer to individual human beings. In such cases, it is normally preferable to use a prepositional phrase with a non-clitic personal pronoun[2] as its complement, cf. the contrast between (7) and (8) below:

(7) J'ai peur *de rater mon examen*. → J'en ai peur.

(8) J'ai peur *de mon prof*. → J'ai peur de lui.

In neutral registers, *en* may, however, refer to a non-specific group of human beings (as opposed to one or more specific individuals). This is often the case in clauses where *en* represents the postmodifier of a quantifying expression, such as *beaucoup*. This is exemplified in (9), where *les femmes* in the first sentence is used with generic reference:[3]

(9) Olivier semble aimer *les femmes*. ('Olivier seems to like women.') En tout cas, il en a connu *beaucoup*. (= Il a connu [beaucoup *de femmes*].)

---

[1] For more on clitics, see section 14.2.
[2] For further details on non-clitic personal pronouns, see section 15.3.
[3] For the notion of noun phrases with generic reference, see section 12.51.

In colloquial registers, the pronominal adverbs can be used to refer to specific human beings, as shown in (10):

(10)   A: Tu as eu des nouvelles de Frédéric depuis votre rupture ?
B: Non, en fait, je n'<u>y</u> pense jamais, *à ce type.*

Section 17.2 below discusses the uses of *en* in greater detail. *Y* will be treated in section 17.3.

17.2 *En*

En can represent two different types of constituent, either a prepositional phrase headed by *de* or (elements of) an indefinite noun phrase. In the former case, it may have different types of grammatical function. Additionally, *en* occurs as part of a number of frozen expressions (incl. phrasal verbs), in which it does not represent a precisely definable constituent. As a result, it does not have a specifiable grammatical function in such expressions, either.

17.2.1 En *represents a prepositional phrase*

When representing a prepositional phrase, *en* functions either as a prepositional object or as a postmodifier of a larger phrase. Such larger phrases may be of different types. The preposition involved is always *de*.

17.2.1.1 *En* as a prepositional object
En frequently functions as a prepositional object. This use is exemplified in (3), section 17.1 above, and (11) below:

(11)   Bertrand est très préoccupé par la situation actuelle en Syrie. Il <u>en</u> parle tout le temps. (= Il parle tout le temps *de la situation actuelle en Syrie.*)

17.2.1.2 *En* as a postmodifier of quantifying expressions
(nouns or adverbs)
Representing the postmodifier of a quantifying expression is another frequent function of *en*. It may represent the postmodifier of a noun phrase, as

in (12) below, or that of an adverbial phrase as in (9), section 17.1 above, or (13) below:

(12)   Tous les exemplaires n'ont pas été vendus, il <u>en</u> reste encore *un grand nombre*. (= un grand nombre *d'exemplaires*)

(13)   Léa adore le chocolat et elle <u>en</u> mange *pas mal*. (= pas mal *de chocolat*)

17.2.1.3 *En* as a genitive postmodifier of a noun phrase

When *en* represents a postmodifier of a non-quantifying noun (phrase), it functions as a genitive (see section 14.3 for details on genitives and the types of meaning they can express). When representing a genitive, *en* may translate into English as a possessive article (*his*, *her*, *its*, *their*) or as a prepositional phrase typically headed by *of*.

En is commonly used to represent possessive genitives (cf. (14) below), objective genitives (cf. (15)), and partitive genitives (cf. (16)):

(14)   J'admire la qualité technique de *ce tableau*.—Moi, j'<u>en</u> apprécie plutôt l'originalité. (= l'originalité *de ce tableau*; → Ce tableau a une certaine originalité.)
'I chiefly appreciate <u>its</u> originality.'

(15)   *Cette décision* ne me surprend pas du tout. En fait, l'annonce <u>en</u> a déjà été faite hier. (= l'annonce *de cette décision*; → On a annoncé cette décision hier.)
'In fact, it was announced yesterday.' Literally: '. . . the announcement <u>of it</u> was made yesterday.'

(16)   J'admire beaucoup *le dernier roman de Modiano*. Je vais t'<u>en</u> lire quelques extraits. (= quelques extraits *du dernier roman de Modiano*; → Ces extraits font partie du dernier roman de Modiano.)
'I'm going to read you some excerpts <u>from it</u>.'

There are several restrictions on the kinds of context in which *en* may be used to represent a genitive, however. Thus, in a number of cases, a possessive article must be used instead.

First, *en* can never represent a subjective genitive:

(17)   *Ce peuple* est fort érudit. Mais j'admire plutôt <u>ses</u> conquêtes./*Mais j'<u>en</u> admire plutôt les conquêtes. (= les conquêtes *de ce peuple*; → Ce peuple a conquis quelque chose.)
'But I admire their conquests more.'

Secondly, if a possessive, objective, or partitive genitive refers to specific human individuals, the norm is likewise to use a possessive article instead of *en*, as seen in (18), which features a possessive genitive:

(18)   J'admire les capacités intellectuelles *de nos deux nouvelles doctorantes.*—Et moi, j'admire <u>leur</u> énergie./*Et moi, j'<u>en</u> admire l'énergie. (→ Nos deux nouvelles doctorantes ont de l'énergie.)

Thirdly, if the noun phrase of which the genitive forms a part is itself the complement of a preposition, *en* can never be used, no matter what type of genitive is involved. Thus, in (19) below, the possessive genitive *de l'enseignement des langues modernes* functions as a postmodifier inside the noun phrase *la crise actuelle de l'enseignement des langues modernes*. That noun phrase is itself the complement of a preposition, namely *de*. As shown, *en* cannot represent a prepositional phrase that belongs inside another prepositional phrase:

(19)   Je ne souhaite pas parler [*de* la crise actuelle [de l'enseignement des langues modernes]$_{PP}$]$_{PP}$. Je souhaite parler *de* <u>son avenir</u>./*Je souhaite <u>en</u> parler *de* l'avenir.

Finally, *en* can be used to represent a genitive only if the subject of the host clause is not identical to the referent of the genitive. Thus, while both (20) and (21) can translate into English as 'Certain animals eat their young', (20) is acceptable only if the possessive 'their' refers to some other kind of animal that has been mentioned in the previous discourse. If the intended meaning is 'Certain animals eat their own young', a possessive article must be used, as in (21):

(20)   Certains animaux$_i$ <u>en</u>$_j$ mangent les petits. (= les petits d'un autre type de bête.)

(21)   Certains animaux$_i$ mangent <u>leurs</u>$_i$ (propres) petits.

17.2.1.4 *En* as a postmodifier of an adjective phrase

En can also represent a prepositional phrase functioning as the postmodifier within an adjective phrase, as in (22) below. Postmodifiers of this type usually indicate the reason why an entity has the property described by the adjective. In (22), the postmodifier thus serves to explain why the subject of the sentence feels proud:

(22)   Il est fier *d'avoir gagné le match* ?—Oui, il <u>en</u> est très fier.

17.2.1.5 *En* as a locative object or adverbial

The last type of prepositional phrase that *en* can represent are prepositional phrases that function as adverbials or locative objects.[4] Often, *en* will denote a place, as in (2), section 17.1 above, or (23) below. It may also represent other types of adverbial, however, for instance adverbials denoting causes, as in (24), or adverbials denoting the logical subject of a verb in the passive voice, as in (25):[5]

(23) Marc n'est-il pas sorti *de son bureau* de la journée ?—Si, il en est sorti une fois, vers 15 heures.

(24) Elle en étouffait presque, *de colère*.

(25) Au zoo, un enfant est tombé parmi les lions, et il en a vite été entouré. (→ 'Il a vite été entouré *de lions*.' → 'Les lions l'ont vite entouré.')

17.2.2 En *represents (the head of) an indefinite noun phrase*

Because the partitive article is historically derived from the preposition *de*, *en* can be used to represent an indefinite noun phrase in Modern French, as in (26)–(27):

(26) Tu as trouvé *des fautes* ?—Ah oui, j'en trouve toujours. (= Ah oui, je trouve toujours *des fautes*.)

(27) Vous voyez *une solution* ?—Non, je n'en vois pas. (= Non, je ne vois pas *de solution*.)

If the determiner of an indefinite noun phrase is not the partitive article, but rather a numeral (incl. the regular indefinite article *un(e)*, which is historically derived from the numeral), *en* will represent just the head noun + any modifiers as in (28) below. Note that, as that example shows, both *en* and the determining numeral (in this case *cinq*) must be present in the clause. The version without *en* in (29) is therefore ungrammatical:

---

[4] For the notion of locative objects, see section 1.2.3.6.
[5] For further details about the passive voice in French, see section 25.2. For the notion of logical subject, see section 3.1.

(28)   A: Voulez-vous encore un *verre de champagne*, Madame ?

B: Merci, j'<u>en</u> ai déjà bu cinq. (= Merci, j'ai déjà bu [cinq verres de champagne.])

(29)   A: Voulez-vous encore un *verre de champagne*, Madame ?

B: *Merci, j'ai déjà bu cinq.

In addition, *en* is frequently used to represent only the head noun of an indefinite noun phrase, leaving both the determiner and any modifiers behind, as shown in (30)–(31) below. This is possible no matter what kind of indefinite determiner is used:

(30)   Un *train* peut <u>en</u> cacher un *autre*. (= Un train peut cacher [un autre *train*.])

(31)   A: Je pourrais te piquer une cigarette, s'il te plaît ?

B: Oui, mais je n'<u>en</u> ai que des *légères*. (= Oui, mais je n'ai que [des *cigarettes légères*.])

17.2.3 En *in frozen expressions*

Finally, *en* is used as a component of a number of more or less frozen expressions, where it is not clear what it contributes at the levels of both grammatical constituency and meaning. Examples are given in (32)–(33) below:

(32)   Où <u>en</u> étions-nous ? ('Where were we?')

(33)   Je ne dis rien, mais je n'<u>en</u> pense pas moins. ('I don't say anything, but I do have an opinion.')

Other such expressions are, for instance, *en vouloir à quelqu'un* ('to be angry with someone'), *s'en faire* ('to be upset'), *ne pas en croire ses yeux* ('to not believe one's own eyes'). These frozen expressions are probably best learned on a case-by-case basis.

17.3 Y

The uses of *y* are considerably more limited than those of *en*. Whenever *y* represents another type of constituent, that constituent will be a prepositional phrase. The preposition involved is typically *à*, but various other

locative prepositions (*sur, sous, dans, devant*, etc.) are possible as well. The functions of *y* in such cases are described below. Like *en*, *y* also occurs as a component of several frozen expressions.

17.3.1 Y represents a prepositional phrase

When representing a prepositional phrase, *y* may have three different grammatical functions.

17.3.1.1 Y as a prepositional object
Just like *en*, *y* often represents a prepositional object, as in (4), section 17.1 above, and (34)–(35) below:

(34)   A: Les ouvriers obéissent-ils *aux nouvelles consignes de sécurité*?
   B: Non, malheureusement, tout le monde n'y obéit pas encore.

(35)   A: Je peux compter *sur votre venue*?
   B: Bien sûr que vous pouvez y compter.

17.3.1.2 Y as a locative object or adverbial
Again like *en*, *y* may represent a locative object or a locative adverbial, as in (36)–(37) below. Unlike *en*, however, *y* does not normally represent other types of adverbial.

(36)   A: On peut s'installer *sous les platanes*?
   B: Oui, vous pouvez vous y installer s'il fait assez chaud.

(37)   A: Vous laissez les enfants jouer *dans le jardin*?
   B: Oui, on les laisse y jouer toute la journée.

17.3.1.3 Y as a postmodifier of an adjective phrase
Finally, like *en*, *y* may represent the postmodifier of an adjective phrase, as in (38):

(38)   A: Êtes-vous sensible *au froid*?
   B: Non, je n'y suis pas très sensible.

17.3.2 Y in frozen expressions

In the same way as *en*, *y* forms part of a number of frozen expressions, in which it is unclear what it contributes, at the levels of both grammar and meaning. Some examples of the expressions in question, which are probably best learned on a case-by-case basis, are *y avoir* (as in *il y a*), *ne plus y tenir* ('to not be able to take it any longer'), and *s'y prendre* (as in (39) below):

(39)   Merci, je sais comment m'y prendre. ('Thanks, I know what to do.')

18

Possessives and demonstratives

Learning objectives

- To understand the distinction between possessive and demonstrative pronouns and the corresponding articles.

- To understand the differences in use between the French possessives and their English counterparts.

- To understand the differences between deictic and anaphoric uses of the demonstratives, and to master the grammatical rules governing the appropriate choice of form.

18.1 Possessives

Both French and English have distinct forms for possessive articles and possessive pronouns,[1] cf. (1)–(2) below and their English equivalents in (3)–(4):

(1) <u>Mon</u> manteaux est beige.

(2) <u>Le mien</u> est beige.

---

[1] For the distinction between pronouns and articles, see section 14.3.

The Structure of Modern Standard French. First edition. Maj-Britt Mosegaard Hansen.
© Maj-Britt Mosegaard Hansen 2016. First Published 2016 by Oxford University Press

(3)   My coat is beige.

(4)   Mine is beige.

However, neither the articles nor the pronouns are used in quite the same way across the two languages. The articles will be treated in section 18.1.1 below, and the pronouns in the subsequent section 18.1.2.

18.1.1 Possessive articles

Possessive articles combine the meaning of the definite article with that of a personal pronoun. As already noted in section 12.1, the possessive article is thus a type of definite determiner.

The forms of the French possessive article can be seen in Table 18.1.

In terms of their meaning, possessive articles can express the same types of relationship as genitives (see section 14.4). In the following, the terms 'possessor' (the entity referred to by the article) and 'possessee' (the entity referred to by the head noun) are thus used in a loose sense, which does not necessarily reflect a relationship of actual ownership between the two.

An important difference between English and French is that, in English, the form of the third-person possessive article reflects the number and, in the singular, also the 'real-world' gender, of the possessor(s), as seen in (5)–(8):

(5)   John put on his coat/jacket/gloves/shoes.

(6)   Jane put on her coat/jacket/gloves/shoes.

Table 18.1. Forms of the possessive article.

	Masculine sg. + feminine sg. before a vowel	**Feminine sg. before a consonant**	**Plural**
1.p.s.	*mon*	*ma*	*mes*
2.p.s	*ton*	*ta*	*tes*
3.p.s.	*son*	*sa*	*ses*
1.p.p.	*notre*		*nos*
2.p.p.	*votre*		*vos*
3.p.p.	*leur*		*leurs*

(7)   The android put on <u>its</u> coat/jacket/gloves/shoes.

(8)   The men/women/androids put on <u>their</u> coats/jackets/gloves/shoes.

In French, on the other hand, the form of the third-person possessive article reflects the grammatical number, and in the singular also the grammatical gender, of the possessee, as shown in (9)–(11) below:

(9)   Jean a mis <u>son</u> manteau/<u>sa</u> veste/<u>ses</u> gants/<u>ses</u> chaussures.

(10)   Jeanne a mis <u>son</u> manteau/<u>sa</u> veste/<u>ses</u> gants/<u>ses</u> chaussures.

(11)   L'androïde a mis <u>son</u> manteau/<u>sa</u> veste/<u>ses</u> gants/<u>ses</u> chaussures.

(12)   Les hommes/femmes/androïdes ont mis <u>leur(s)</u> manteau(x)/<u>leur(s)</u> veste(s)/ <u>leurs</u> gants/<u>leurs</u> chaussures.

If the gender/number of the possessor is potentially ambiguous, it can be made clear by adding *à lui/elle*, as in (13) below; by replacing the possessive article by a combination of a definite article + a demonstrative pronoun (see section 18.2.2 below), as in (14); or by reinforcing the possessive article by the adjective *propre*, as in (15):

(13)   Abigaël et François viennent de partir en vacances aux Seychelles. Ce sont *ses* parents <u>à elle</u> qui leur ont offert le voyage. ('Her parents bought them the trip.')

(14)   Louis a invité sa femme et <u>la</u> mère de <u>celle-ci</u> au restaurant. ('...his wife and her mother...')

(15)   Marie-Paule préfère que chacun s'occupe de *ses* <u>propres</u> affaires. ('...their own business...')

In French, as in English, possessive articles can be used with so-called **distributive meaning**, where each of several possessors has a possession of the same type as the others have. An English example of this is given in (16) below, where we infer that the people in question had one umbrella each. In English, both the possessive article and the head noun take the plural form in such cases. As shown by the equivalent example in (17), however, French allows the possessive noun phrase to be either singular, reflecting the fact that each person has only one umbrella, or plural, reflecting the fact that there is more than one umbrella in total:

(16)   It started to rain and they all opened <u>their</u> umbrellas.

(17)   Il a commencé à pleuvoir et ils ont tous ouvert leur(s) parapluie(s).

Unlike English (cf. (18) below), French does not allow two possessive articles to be coordinated before the same head noun. If the meaning is distributive, as in (18), a combination of a noun phrase with a possessive article and a possessive pronoun may be used in French, as shown in (19). If there are two possessors and only one possessee, a possessive article in the plural reinforced by two coordinated prepositional phrases headed by *à* is used, cf. (20)–(21):

(18)   There are viruses on his and my computers.

(19)   Il y a des virus sur son ordinateur et sur le mien.

(20)   The day before yesterday, I met his and my old French teacher.

(21)   Avant-hier, j'ai rencontré notre ancien prof de français à lui et à moi.

When the head noun describes a body part or some other entity or concept that is intimately and inalienably associated with a particular individual, the norm in French is to use a combination of a definite article and a personal or reflexive pronoun in the dative case in preference to the possessive article, cf. the contrast between the English and French examples in (22)–(25) below:

(22)   Peter broke his leg skiing.

(23)   Pierre s'est cassé la jambe en faisant du ski.

(24)   The shock has disturbed his memory.

(25)   Le choc lui a perturbé la mémoire.

18.1.2 Possessive pronouns

The forms of the French possessive pronoun are found in Table 18.2.

Possessive pronouns are normally used only contrastively in French. Thus, if (26) below is used non-contrastively, simply to assert that a particular book belongs to the speaker, its most appropriate translation into French will be (27). While the sentence using a possessive pronoun in (28) is fully grammatical, it is felicitously used only in a context where there are at least two books present and it is known that only one of them belongs to the speaker:

Table 18.2. Forms of the possessive pronoun.

	Masculine sing.	Feminine singular	Masculine plural	Feminine plural
1.p.s.	*le mien*	*la mienne*	*les miens*	*les miennes*
2.p.s	*le tien*	*latienne*	*les tiens*	*les tiennes*
3.p.s.	*le sien*	*la sienne*	*les siens*	*les siennes*
1.p.p.	*le nôtre*	*la nôtre*	*les nôtres*	
2.p.p.	*le vôtre*	*la vôtre*	*les vôtres*	
3.p.p.	*le leur*	*la leur*	*les leurs*	

(26) This book is <u>mine</u>.

(27) Ce livre-ci est <u>à moi</u>.

(28) Ce livre-ci est <u>le mien</u>. (→ The other book(s) belong(s) to someone else.)

Accordingly, possessive pronouns are typically used in coordinations with a preceding possessive noun phrase, as in (29) below, and in other explicit comparisons and contrasts, like those in (30)–(31):

(29) Mon frère et <u>le sien</u> ne s'entendent pas.

(30) Mon père est plus fort que <u>le tien</u>.

(31) Ma fille est rousse, alors que <u>les leurs</u> sont toutes blondes.

18.2 Demonstratives

Like the possessives, the French demonstratives can be divided into articles and pronouns, which have different forms, as shown in (32) below.[2] The demonstrative article is treated in section 18.2.1 below, and the demonstrative pronoun in section 18.2.2.

(32) <u>Ce</u> manteau ne me plaît pas. Je préfère <u>celui-là</u>.

18.2.1 The demonstrative article

The forms of the demonstrative article are seen in Table 18.3.

---

[2] For this difference, see section 14.3.

Table 18.3. Forms of the demonstrative article.

Masc.sg. before a consonant	Masc.sg. before a vowel	Fem.sg.	Plural
ce	*cet*	*cette*	*ces*

As the table shows, there is no morphological distinction in the French demonstrative article corresponding to the English distinction between *this* and *that*. Where relevant, that distinction may be expressed by attaching one of the locative clitics *–ci/–là* to the end of the noun phrase.

18.2.1.1 Deictic use of the demonstrative article

As in English, noun phrases introduced by a demonstrative article can be used either deictically or non-deictically (cf. section 14.4 for details). When they are used **deictically**, i.e. to refer to something in the extra-linguistic context, the addition of *–ci/–là* may be used to contrast two demonstrative noun phrases within the same sentence or short paragraph, corresponding to the difference between the two English demonstratives, as shown in (33)–(34) below:

(33)   this blue dress—that blue dress

(34)   *cette* robe bleue-ci—*cette* robe bleue-là

In this type of contexts, the noun phrase with *–ci* refers to an entity which is closer to the speaker in physical space, while the one with *–là* refers to an entity that is further removed from speaker. This is illustrated in Figure 18.1.

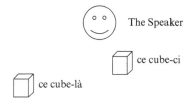

The Speaker

ce cube-ci

ce cube-là

Figure 18.1. The deictic contrast between *ce* + N-*ci* and *ce* + N-*là*.

If no such contrast between two similar entities is being expressed, it is normally either *ce* + N or *ce* + N + *–là* that are used to single out a referent that is present in physical space, as shown in (35) below. *Ce* + N + *–ci*, on the other hand, is rare in such contexts.

(35)   Ce piano(-là) me donne envie de jouer.

With temporal nouns, the norm is to use just *ce* + N when referring deictically (i.e. to the period or point in time that is closest to the moment of utterance), as in (36) below. *Ce* + N + *–ci* is used to signal implicit contrast (cf. (37)), except in the fixed expression *ces jours-ci*, seen in (38):

(36)   cet automne, ce soir, cette année

(37)   Cet été-ci, on n'aura pas les moyens de partir en vacances. (→ Next year, it'll be different.)

(38)   Qu'est-ce que tu fais de beau ces jours-ci ? ('What are you up to these days?')

18.2.1.2 Non-deictic uses of the demonstrative article
Anaphoric use

When a demonstrative noun phrase is used **anaphorically** (cf. section 14.4), it refers back to something mentioned in the previous discourse.

Ce + N is widely used in French in anaphoric contexts where English would tend to use a simple definite article. Compare (39) and (40) below. In both examples, a man is introduced in the first sentence, and then mentioned again in the second sentence. No other referent is introduced in the first sentence. Here, unlike English,[3] French will normally use the demonstrative article at the second mention to mark anaphoric reference.

(39)   *A man* came in. The man was wearing a grey coat.

(40)   *Un homme* entra. Cet homme était vêtu d'un manteau gris./?L'homme était vêtu d'un manteau gris.

On the other hand, if two new referents of different kinds[4] are introduced in the previous sentence, as in (41)–(42) below, the definite article must be used, as in English:

---

[3] When the English demonstrative article is used anaphorically, as in (i) below, it sets up an implicit contrast, which is not the case with the French demonstrative:

(i)   *A man* came in. That man was wearing a grey coat.

[4] Examples like (i) below, where four new referents of the same kind are introduced in the first sentence, follows the same rule as (40), the anaphoric noun phrase in the second sentence taking the demonstrative rather than the definite article:

(i)   *Quatre hommes* entrèrent. Ces/?Les hommes étaient vêtus de manteaux gris.

(41)   *A man* and *a woman* came in. The man was wearing a grey coat.

(42)   *Un homme* et *une femme* entrèrent. L'homme était vêtu d'un manteau gris./ *Cet homme était vêtu d'un manteau gris.

Ce + N + *–là* may be used anaphorically as an alternative to the simple *ce* + N, as shown in (43) below. *Ce* + N + *–ci*, on the other hand, is not used anaphorically.

(43)   *Un homme* entra. Cet homme-là était vêtu d'un manteau gris.

With temporal nouns, *ce* + N + *–là* always indicates anaphoric reference to a period or point in time that is removed from the present, either in the past or in the future, as shown in (44)–(45) below. *Ce* + N + *-là* must be used about past times even if the predicator is in the historical present tense (cf. section 6.2.1), as in (46):

(44)   Je suis allé(e) au Groënland *en 2007*. Cette année-là l'hiver était précoce.

(45)   *Un jour* je te manquerai, mais ce jour-là ce sera trop tard.

(46)   *En 1958*, un déficit important est enregistré pour tous les fleuves. Le débit moyen du Niger cette année-là *est* de 1318 m^3 à Niamey.

Cataphoric use
Less frequently, the demonstrative article may also be used so-called **cataphorically**, i.e. to refer to something that is first mentioned in the immediately following text, as in (47), where the demonstrative noun phrase *cette chance* points forward to the infinitival phrase *de pouvoir vivre sans travailler*. As the example shows, however, the definite article may also be used in such contexts:

(47)   Raphaël a cette/la chance de pouvoir vivre sans travailler.

18.2.2 Demonstrative pronouns

Table 18.4 summarizes the forms of the French demonstrative pronoun. The demonstrative pronoun is never used all by itself, but is always postmodified either by one of the locative clitics *–ci* and *–là*, as in (48) below, or by a relative clause, a prepositional phrase, or (more rarely) a participial clause, as illustrated in (49)–(51):

(48) *Ceux*-<u>ci</u> sont plus beaux que *ceux*-<u>là</u>.

(49) J'ai acheté *celle* <u>que tu m'as recommandée</u>.

(50) *Celui* <u>d'à gauche</u> me plaît davantage que *celui* <u>d'à droite</u>.

(51) Cette inondation n'est pas aussi grave que *celle* <u>provoquée l'année dernière par le Rhône</u>.

Like noun phrases introduced by a demonstrative article, demonstrative pronouns are used either deictically or anaphorically.[5] In both cases *celui-ci* and *celui-là* may be used contrastively within the same sentence or short paragraph.

Similarly to demonstrative noun phrases marked by –*ci* and –*là*, in such contexts, a deictic *celui-ci* refers to an entity which is closer to the speaker in physical space, while *celui-là* refers to one that is further removed from the speaker (cf. Figure 18.1 above).

Analogously, when used anaphorically in contrastive contexts, a demonstrative pronoun + -*ci* refers back to the more recent of two entities previously mentioned in the text, whereas a demonstrative pronoun + –*là* refers to the entity that was mentioned first, i.e. the entity that is further removed in terms of the progression of the text. In other words, they translate, respectively, as *the latter* and *the former* in English. Thus, in (52) below, *celui-ci* designates ballet, and *celui-là* designates opera, as indicated by the subscripts:

Table 18.4. Forms of the demonstrative pronoun.

Masc.sg.	Fem.sg.	Masc.pl.	Fem.pl.
celui	*celle*	*ceux*	*celles*

(52) Je préfère de loin l'opéra$_i$ au ballet$_j$. Celui-ci$_j$ ['the latter'] me fait ronfler, alors que <u>celui-là</u>$_i$ ['the former'] me passionne.

If no contrast is being expressed, demonstrative + -*là* is normally used, as in (53) below:

(53) Il y a *des gens* qui disent que la nourriture bio est plus chère ; <u>ceux-là</u> ont tort.

---

[5] See section 14.4 for this distinction.

19

Interrogative and relative pronouns and adverbs

Learning objectives

- To understand the difference between interrogative pronouns/adverbs and relative pronouns/adverbs.
- To understand the grammatical rules governing the choice of interrogative pronouns/adverbs in both direct and indirect interrogatives.
- To understand the grammatical rules governing the choice of relative pronouns/adverbs.

19.1 Introduction

To a large extent, the French interrogative and relative pronouns and adverbs resemble one another formally, just as is the case with their English equivalents. However, even when the forms are superficially the same, their use is governed by different principles, set out in sections 19.2 and 19.3 below.

The Structure of Modern Standard French. First edition. Maj-Britt Mosegaard Hansen.
© Maj-Britt Mosegaard Hansen 2016. First Published 2016 by Oxford University Press

Their meanings are likewise quite different. As pronominal forms, they share the common feature of being placeholders for some other, typically nominal, constituent mentioned elsewhere in the discourse. However, in the case of **interrogative pronouns** and **adverbs**, i.e. question words, the nature of that constituent is normally unknown to the speaker at the time of utterance, and is expected to be supplied by another speaker, in the following discourse, as shown in (1):

(1)   A: Qui est venu à la réunion ?
      B: Seulement *trois collègues.*

In the case of **relative pronouns** and **adverbs**, on the other hand, the constituent in question (i.e. the antecedent of the relative pronoun/adverb)[1] is known to, and will normally have been mentioned in the immediately preceding discourse of, the speaker who utters the relative clause, as shown in (2):

(2)   Il n'y a que *trois collègues* qui sont venus à la réunion.

19.2 Interrogative pronouns and adverbs

The form of question words will differ, in the first instance, depending on whether they are used in a **direct interrogative**, which takes the form of an independent clause, or in an **indirect interrogative**, i.e. a subordinate clause.[2]

Secondly, when question words are used in independent clauses, language users will in some cases have a choice between short forms and long forms of the relevant pronouns. To a large extent, the choice is determined by register, the short forms being preferentially associated with more formal registers, and the long forms with less formal ones, where speakers can avoid having to use subject–verb inversion by choosing the long form of a question word.[3]

Thirdly, within the different groups of forms, the choice of a specific pronoun is governed, on the one hand, by the intended grammatical function of the pronoun within its host clause, and on the other hand, by whether its referent is human or non-human.

---

[1] For the notion of antecedent, see section 4.2.2.
[2] For further details about direct *vs* indirect interrogatives, see section 4.2.1.2.
[3] For further details on the types and uses of inversion, see section 24.3.

Table 19.1. Summary of the main forms and functions of interrogative pronouns.

	Direct interrogative (independent clause)	Indirect interrogative (subordinate clause)
Human referent	All functions, short: *qui*	*qui*
	Subject attribute, short: *quel*	
	Subject, long: *qui est-ce qui*	
	Non-subject, long: *qui est-ce que*	
Non-human referent	Subject: *qu' est-ce qui*	*ce qui*
	Direct object, short: *que*	*ce que*
	Direct object, long: *qu'est-ce que*	
	Complement of preposition, short: *quoi*	*quoi*
	Complement of preposition, long: *quoi est-ce que*	
	Subject attribute, short: *que, quel*	*ce que, quel*
	Subject attribute, long: *qu'est-ce que*	

The uses are summarized in Table 19.1, and treated in greater depth in sections 19.2.1–19.2.2.

19.2.1 Interrogative pronouns in independent clauses

In direct interrogatives, the form of question words is determined by a combination of the nature of their referents (**human** *vs* **non-human**) and their grammatical function.

It is only in direct interrogatives that 'long' forms, i.e. forms including *est-ce qui/que*, are appropriately used, and where language users thus have a choice between short and long forms.[4]

19.2.1.1 The interrogative pronoun is the subject of the clause

When an interrogative pronoun is the subject of a direct interrogative clause, and when the referent of the pronoun is human, the short form used is *qui* and the long form is *qui est-ce qui*, as shown in (3)–(4) below:

(3)   Qui est venu ?

(4)   Qui est-ce qui est venu ?

If the referent is non-human, the long form *qu'est-ce qui* is always used, as in (5):

(5)   Qu'est-ce qui s'est passé ?

19.2.1.2 The interrogative pronoun is a direct object

When an interrogative pronoun is the direct object in a direct interrogative clause, and when the referent of the pronoun is human, the short form used is *qui* and the long form is *qui est-ce que*, as shown in (6)–(7) below:

(6)   Qui as-tu vu ?

(7)   Qui est-ce que tu as vu ?

If the referent is non-human, the short form of the pronoun is *que*, while the long form is *qu'est-ce que*, as in (8)–(9):

(8)   Qu'as-tu vu ?

(9)   Qu'est-ce que tu as vu ?

19.2.1.3 The interrogative pronoun is the complement of a preposition

When an interrogative pronoun is the complement of a preposition within a direct interrogative clause, and when the referent of the pronoun is human,

---

[4] While indirect interrogative clauses using long forms, such as that in (i) below, are found, particularly in colloquial speech and writing, such usage is considered sub-standard:

(i)   Je lui ai demandé qui est-ce qui est venu.

qui is used as the short form, and *qui est-ce que* as the long form, as seen in (10)–(11) below:

(10)   A qui as-tu parlé ?

(11)   A qui est-ce que tu as parlé ?

If the referent is non-human, the short form is *quoi* and the long form is *quoi est-ce que*, as in (12)–(13):

(12)   De quoi parles-tu ?

(13)   De quoi est-ce que tu parles ?

19.2.1.4 The interrogative pronoun is a subject attribute

When an interrogative pronoun is a subject attribute in a direct interrogative clause, and when its referent is human (i.e. when it corresponds to the English interrogative pronoun *who*), the short form *qui* is normally used if the subject is a personal clitic, as in (14) below:

(14)   Qui est-*il* ?

The long form *qui est-ce que* may in principle be used, but tends to be avoided, particularly if it means that a simple tense of the verb *être* will thereby become the last word in the clause, cf. (15):

(15)   ?*Qui est-ce qu'*il* est ?

Qui may also be used about human referents if the subject is a noun phrase, as in (16) below. However, the form *quel(le)(s)* is a common alternative in such cases, as seen in (17). The long form *qui est-ce que* is only rarely used when the subject is a noun phrase, and never when a simple tense form of *être* would thereby become the last word in the clause, cf. (18):

(16)   Qui sont *ces gens* ?

(17)   Quels sont *ces gens* ?

(18)   *Qui est-ce que *ta sœur* est ?

If the subject attribute is non-human (i.e. if it corresponds to the English interrogative pronoun *what*), *que* may be used as the short form, and *qu'est-ce que* as the long form, cf. (19)–(20) below. Note that, as (19) shows, the reference of the subject attribute may be non-human, even when the subject itself refers to a human being (compare with (15) and (18) above):

(19)   Que devient notre ami Thierry ? (i.e. 'What's become of our friend Thierry?'
→ What's going on in his life?)

(20)   Qu'est-ce que ça va faire comme facture à la fin ? ('What sort of bill will that
turn out to be?' → How much will we end up getting billed?)

However, the typical use of both *que* and *qu'est-ce que* is when asking for
a definition of the subject expression, as in (21)–(23) below. In such cases,
qu'est-ce que is usually expanded by *c'est que* in colloquial speech, as seen in
(23). Note that the use of the short form *que* (as in (21)) when asking for a
definition is appropriate principally in very formal registers:[5]

(21)   Qu'est un écran tactile ?

(22)   Qu'est-ce qu'un écran tactile ?

(23)   Qu'est-ce que *c'est qu'*un écran tactile ?

When the speaker is not asking for a definition, *quel(le)(s)* is the form
more commonly used as a subject attribute, as shown in (24)–(25):

(24)   Quelle est votre profession ?

(25)   Quel était le titre du film que tu as vu ?

19.2.1.5 The interrogative article *quel*
When the question word functions as a determiner inside a noun phrase, the
form used is always *quel(le)(s)*, as in (26):

(26)   [Quel film]~NP~ avez-vous vu hier soir ?

19.2.1.6 The interrogative pronoun *lequel*
The form *lequel* (*laquelle, lesquel[le]s*) is used when the addressee is asked to
make a choice between a restricted number of options. It may be used as a
subject, a direct object, or the complement of a preposition, and with both
human and non-human reference, cf. (27)–(29) below:

---

[5] In addition, in colloquial spoken registers, postverbal *quoi* may be used in a
dislocation construction (see section 26.2 for the notion of dislocation), as in:

(i)   C'est quoi, un écran tactile ?

(ii)   C'est quoi, votre profession ?

(iii) C'était quoi, le titre du film que tu as vu ?

(27) [Lequel de ces trois candidats]$_{Subj}$ est celui que vous préférez ?

(28) Il semble y avoir deux lignes de métro qui vont d'ici aux Halles. Laquelle$_{DirObj}$ vaut-il mieux prendre ?

(29) Quand vous dites que vous n'aimez pas les idées de ce philosophe, auxquelles $_{PrepObj/PP\ (=\ à\ +\ lesquelles)}$ pensez-vous plus particulièrement ?

19.2.1.7 Interrogative adverbs

Finally, French has a range of interrogative adverbs, the choice of which depends on the adverbial meaning (time, place, manner, cause, quantity etc.) the speaker intends to express. All of these can be expanded by *est-ce que* to avoid the use of inversion. Some examples are given in (30)–(34):

(30) Quand est-ce qu'ils arriveront ?

(31) Où est Fernand ?

(32) Comment est-ce qu'on fait pour faire une tarte Tatin ?

(33) Pourquoi n'es-tu pas venu(e) plus tôt ?

(34) Combien en avez-vous acheté ?

For the most part, French interrogative adverbs behave like their English equivalents. The main problem is how to render the meaning of English *how* in French, where there is no direct translation available of expressions with *how* + adjective/adverb (e.g. *how tall, how much*, etc.). Often *combien* will be used, either on its own, as in (35) below, in combination with *en*, as in (34) above, or with the meaning of the English adjective being further specified by some other (non-adjectival/adverbial) element of the clause, as in (36). In other cases, a noun phrase with the interrogative article *quel* will be preferred, cf. (37):

(35) Cela coûte combien ? ('How much does that cost?')

(36) Combien *mesure*-t-elle ? ('How tall is she?')

(37) Quel âge a-t-il ? ('How old is he?')

However, *combien*, or one of the adverbials *à quel point* and *dans quelle mesure*, may be used in connection with an adjective or adverb, as in (38)–(40) below. As these examples show, the interrogative adverb(ial) is placed at the beginning of the clause. The associated adjective/adverb, on the other hand, occurs in the position where it would be found in a declarative clause, and is thus usually separated from the interrogative element:

(38) Tu ne te rends pas compte <u>combien</u> c'est *dangereux*, ça ! ('... how dangerous that is.')

(39) Cela montre <u>à quel point</u> les choses peuvent changer *vite*. ('... how quickly things can change.')

(40) <u>Dans quelle mesure</u> cette question est-elle *légitime* ? ('How legitimate is that question?')

19.2.2 Interrogative pronouns in subordinate clauses

In indirect interrogative clauses, the form of question words is determined in the first instance by the nature of their referent, and secondly by their grammatical function.

19.2.2.1 The referent is human

When the referent of an interrogative pronoun occurring in an indirect interrogative clause is human, the form used is normally always *qui*, irrespective of the grammatical function of the pronoun, cf. (41)–(44) below:

(41) Je me demande [qui$_{Subj}$ viendra.]

(42) Je me demande [qui$_{SubjAttr}$ était cet homme.]

(43) J'aimerais savoir [qui$_{DirObj}$ tu as rencontré hier.]

(44) J'aimerais savoir [à qui$_{ComplPrep}$ tu as parlé de cette affaire.]

The form *quel(le)(s)* may be used when the pronoun functions as a **subject attribute**, as in (45):

(45) Je me demande <u>quel</u> était cet homme.

19.2.2.2 The referent is non-human

When the referent of a question word occurring in an indirect interrogative clause is non-human, its form depends on its grammatical function inside the host clause.

If the pronoun functions as a **subject**, the appropriate form is *ce qui*, as in (46):

(46) Je me demande [<u>ce qui</u>$_{Subj}$ est arrivé.]

If the pronoun functions as a **direct object**, it normally takes the form *ce que*, as in (47) below. However, if it is a direct object inside an **infinitival clause** functioning as an indirect interrogative clause fragment, as in (48), the form used is *quoi*:

(47)   J'aimerais savoir [ce que$_{DirObj}$ tu as dit à Laurence.]

(48)   Je ne sais vraiment pas [quoi$_{DirObj}$ vous dire.]

If the pronoun functions as a **subject attribute**, it may take the form *ce que* or *quel(le)(s)*, as in (49)–(51) below. The choice between the two follows the same principles as the choice between *quelqu'est-ce que* and *quel(le)(s)* in direct interrogatives (cf. section 19.2.1.4 above):

(49)   Je me demande [ce qu'$_{SubjAttr}$ est devenu notre ami Thierry.]

(50)   J'aimerais savoir [ce que$_{SubjAttr}$ c'est qu'un écran tactile.]

(51)   Je n'ai aucune idée [quelle$_{SubjAttr}$ était sa profession.]

If the pronoun functions as the **complement of a preposition**, the form *quoi* is used, as in (52)–(53):

(52)   Si seulement je savais [de quoi$_{ComplPrep}$ il se plaint.]

(53)   Je n'ai aucune idée [à quoi$_{ComplPrep}$ tu penses.]

The pronoun *lequel/laquelle/lesquel(le)s*, interrogative adverbs, and the article *quel(le)(s)* are used as in direct interrogatives, cf. sections 19.2.1.5–19.2.1.6 above, and (54)–(55) below:

(54)   Je te demande [comment il s'appelle.]

(55)   J'aimerais savoir [quel film tu as vu hier soir.]

19.3 Relative pronouns and adverbs

The distribution of the relative pronouns and adverbs depends principally on their grammatical function, and only secondarily on the nature of their referents. Importantly, the grammatical function of a relative pronoun or adverb is not necessarily identical to that of its antecedent. Thus, in (56) below, the antecedent of the relative pronoun *qui* is the noun phrase *un ancien collègue*. While *qui* is the subject of the relative clause, the noun phrase is the direct object of the main predicator *ai rencontré*:

(56)   J'ai rencontré *un ancien collègue*_{DirObj}, <u>qui</u>_{Subj} te souhaite le bonjour. (→ Cet ancien collègue te souhaite le bonjour.)

19.3.1 The relative pronoun is the subject

When a relative pronoun is the subject of its clause, *qui* is normally used, whether the antecedent is human or not. Thus, the relative pronoun *qui* in (56) above has a human antecedent, whereas that in (57) below has a non-human antecedent, namely *une lettre*:

(57)   J'ai reçu *une lettre* <u>qui</u>_{Subj} m'a fait pleurer. (→ La lettre m'a fait pleurer.)

In **non-restrictive relative clauses**,[6] one of the forms *lequel, laquelle*, or *lesquel(le)s* may be used, particularly in more formal registers, as in (58) below, and/or if the identity of the antecedent is potentially ambiguous as in (59), where the speaker wishes to make it clear that it is specifically the first version of the film that s/he found moving:

(58)   L'ambassadeur a présenté *ses lettres de créance*, <u>lesquelles</u> ont été reçues par le Président de la République.

(59)   J'ai n'ai vu que *la première version de ce film*, <u>laquelle</u> m'a beaucoup ému(e).

19.3.2 The relative pronoun is a direct object or a subject attribute

When a relative pronoun functions as either a direct object or a subject attribute inside the relative clause, the form *que* is used, irrespectively of the nature of the antecedent, as shown in (60)–(61) below, in which the antecedents are non-human and human, respectively:

(60)   Merci de *ta lettre*, <u>que</u>_{DirObj} j'ai reçue il y a deux jours. (→ J'ai reçu ta lettre il y a deux jours.)

(61)   Autrefois, j'aimais beaucoup Bernard, mais j'avoue que je n'apprécie pas trop *le petit-bourgeois* <u>qu'</u>_{SubjAttr}il est devenu depuis son mariage avec Cécile. (→ Bernard est devenu un petit-bourgeois depuis son mariage avec Cécile.)

---

[6] For the distinction between restrictive and non-restrictive relative clauses, see sections 4.2.2.1–4.2.2.2.

19.3.3 The relative pronoun is the complement of a preposition

When a relative pronoun functions as the complement of a preposition, its form depends in the first instance on the specific preposition it is governed by.

19.3.3.1 The relative pronoun is governed by a preposition other than *de*

If the preposition is not *de*, the nature of the antecedent will determine the form of the relative pronoun.

The antecedent is human

If the antecedent refers to a human being, the pronoun *qui* is normally used, as in (62):

(62) Pascal est *un type* avec qui on s'amuse bien. (→ On s'amuse bien avec ce type.)

Lequel/laquelle/lesquel(le)s is occasionally found as well, particularly if the subject of the relative clause is the subject clitic *il*, in which case it serves to avoid a hiatus (i.e. a clash of two successive vowels) as in (63):

(63) Hier soir, Michel a fait la connaissance de Clément, auquel *il* n'avait jamais parlé avant. (→ Michel n'avait jamais parlé à Clément avant.)

The antecedent is non-human

When the antecedent of the relative pronoun is non-human, *lequel/laquelle/lesquel(le)s* is used, except for those cases that are covered in the subsection below, cf. (64):

(64) C'est *une éventualité* à laquelle je préfère ne pas penser. (→ Je préfère ne pas penser à cette éventualité.)

The antecedent is a whole clause, a neutral pronoun,
or an indefinite pronoun

When its antecedent is non-human, but takes the form of a clause, a neutral pronoun[7], or an indefinite pronoun[8], the appropriate relative pronoun is *quoi*, as shown in (65)–(66):

---

[7] On neutral pronouns, see chapter 16.

[8] On indefinite pronouns, see chapter 20 and section 23.2.1.2.

(65)   *Prêtez-moi un peu d'argent*, sans quoi je ne pourrai pas payer le taxi. (→ Je ne pourrai pas payer le taxi sans que vous me prêtiez un peu d'argent.)

(66)   Il n'avait plus *rien* à quoi il pouvait s'accrocher. (→ Il ne pouvait s'accrocher à rien.)

19.3.3.2 The relative pronoun is governed by the preposition *de*

If the preposition governing the relative pronoun is *de*, the form *dont*, which incorporates both *de* and its complement, is normally used, whether the antecedent is human or not, as shown in (67)–(68):

(67)   *La jeune femme* dont il s'agit est jouée par Audrey Tautou. (→ Il s'agit d'une jeune femme.)

(68)   Frédéric vient de vendre *la toile* dont tu as tant admiré L'AUDACE. (→ Tu as tant admiré l'audace de cette toile.)

(69)   Frederick just sold *the painting* whose AUDACITY you so admired. (→ You so admired its audacity./You so admired the audacity of that painting.)

When *dont* represents a **genitive[9] postmodifier**, it will typically translate into English as *whose*, as shown in (69) above. Notice that because relative *whose* is a determiner in English, the head noun will move to the start of the relative clause along with it. In French, however, the head noun stays in the position that it would occupy in an independent clause, and it is only the postmodifier, represented by *dont*, that will move, as (68) shows.

Dont may represent any type of genitive construction: a possessive genitive, as in (68) above; a subjective genitive, as in (70) below; an objective genitive, as in (71); and a partitive genitive, as in (72):

(70)   C'est *un peuple* dont j'admire les conquêtes. (→ J'admire les conquêtes de ce peuple.)

(71)   *Arlette*, dont l'accusateur reste anonyme, s'est avérée innocente. (→ L'accusateur d'Arlette reste anonyme.)

(72)   L'Italie est *un pays* dont le nord est plus prospère que le sud. (→ Le nord de ce pays est plus prospère que le sud.)

There is one type of syntactic context in which *dont* cannot be used to represent a postmodifier. Instead, it must be replaced by one of the forms

---

[9] For more details on genitives, and types of genitive constructions, see section 14.5.

duquel, de laquelle, or *desquel(le)s*. This is so when the noun phrase containing the postmodifier itself functions as the complement of a preposition, as in (73) below. In such cases, *duquel* etc. must be used in the normal postmodifying position, and the superordinate prepositional phrase moves as a whole, as shown in (74) below:

(73) Stéphane a été très impressionné [*par* [la profondeur de cet ouvrage_{Postmod}]_{NP}]_{PP}

(74) C'est un ouvrage [*par la profondeur* duquel Stéphane a été très impressionné.]_{RelCl}

The sentence in (73) cannot be turned into a relative clause introduced by *dont*, in which the superordinate preposition and the head noun and determiner of its complement stay in their normal place, as shown by the ungrammaticality of (75):

(75) *C'est un ouvrage [dont Stéphane a été très impressionné *par la profondeur*.]_{RelCl}

19.3.4 *The forms* ce qui, ce que, ce dont, ce + *preposition* + quoi

The forms *ce qui, ce que, ce dont*, and *ce* + preposition + *quoi* are used in two types of circumstances:

(a) These forms may function as **free relative pronouns**, to introduce free relative clauses, which—unlike adjectival relative clauses—do not have an antecedent (cf. section 4.2.1.3), as in (76)–(78) below:

(76) [Ce qui s'est passé] était une erreur regrettable.

(77) [Ce que tu dis là] m'étonne.

(78) [Ce dont nous avons le plus besoin], c'est de votre compréhension.

(b) These forms may function as normal (i.e. non-free) relative pronouns if the antecedent of an adjectival relative clause is a whole clause or an infinitival phrase, i.e. in so-called **sentential relative clauses** (cf. section 4.2.2.2)

In these cases, *ce qui* is used if the relative pronoun functions as the subject of its clause, as in (76) above or (79) below. *Ce que* is used if the pronoun is a subject attribute or a **direct object**, as in (77) above and (80) below. Finally, *ce dont* or *ce* + preposition + *quoi* may be used if the pronoun is the **complement of a preposition**, as shown in (78) above and (81) below (but cf. (65) in section 19.3.3.1 above):

(79)   Léa m'a fait attendre une demi-heure sous la pluie, ce qui m'a bien embêté(e).

(80)   Léa m'a fait attendre une demi-heure sous la pluie, ce que j'ai trouvé peu avenant de sa part.

(81)   Léa me fait toujours attendre, ce à quoi je peine à m'habituer.

19.3.5   The relative pronoun or adverb functions as an adverbial

When a relative pronoun or adverb functions as an adverbial, its form depends partly on the type of adverbial involved, and partly on nuances of its meaning.

19.3.5.1   A relative adverb functions as a locative adverbial

If a relative adverb designates a place where something is happening, it takes the form *où*, as shown in (82) below:

(82)   J'ai oublié le nom de *l'endroit* où l'on devait se retrouver. (→ On devait se retrouver à cet endroit.)

If the relative adverb designates a place which functions as a point of departure for something (i.e a 'place from where'), it takes the form *d'où*, as in (83), where the living room is the point of departure from which the town can be viewed:

(83)   Je suis entrée dans *le salon*, d'où l'on voyait toute la ville. (→ On voyait toute la ville depuis le salon.)

19.3.5.2   A relative pronoun/adverb functions as a temporal adverbial

If a relative clause is introduced by a temporal adverbial, and the **antecedent is definite**, the relative adverb *où* is normally used, as in (84):

(84)   *Le jour* où tu décideras de faire quelque chose, tu me feras signe.

If, on the other hand, the **antecedent is indefinite**, the relative pronoun *que* is used, as in (85):

(85)   *Un jour* que Paul est rentré plus tôt que d'habitude, il a retrouvé sa femme en train d'embrasser le facteur.

Que is likewise used after definite antecedents if the head noun is *fois* and/or if the antecedent is premodified by an ordinal numeral, as in (86) below:

(86)   Je me souviens de *la première fois* que j'ai rencontré mon mari comme si c'était hier.

20

Indefinites

Learning objectives

- To understand the difference between polarity-neutral and negative-polarity indefinites.

- To understand the different syntactic functions that polarity-neutral French indefinites may have.

- To master the grammatical rules governing the uses of polarity-neutral indefinites in French.

20.1 Introduction

At the most basic level, we can distinguish between two types of indefinite:

(a) **Polarity-neutral indefinites,** i.e. indefinites that can occur in any kind of context, negative as well as positive. These are exemplified by *quelque chose* in (1)–(3) below:

(1) J'ai vu quelque chose. (= positive context)

The Structure of Modern Standard French. First edition. Maj-Britt Mosegaard Hansen.
© Maj-Britt Mosegaard Hansen 2016. First Published 2016 by Oxford University Press

(2) Avez-vous vu <u>quelque chose</u> ? (= so-called 'weak negative polarity' context, cf. section 23.2.1.2)

(3) *N'avez-vous pas* vu <u>quelque chose</u> ? (= negative context)

(b) Negative-polarity indefinites, such as *rien*, which do not occur in positive contexts, and often only in genuinely negative ones, as shown by the fact that of (4)–(6) below, only (6) is grammatical on the intended interpretation:

(4) *J'ai vu <u>rien</u>. (= positive context; intended meaning: 'I saw something.')

(5) *Avez-vous vu <u>rien</u> ? (= weak negative polarity context; intended meaning: 'Did you see something/anything?')[1]

(6) *N'avez-vous <u>rien</u> vu ? (= negative context; intended meaning: 'Didn't you see anything?/Did you see nothing?')

The present chapter is concerned only with polarity-neutral indefinites. Negative-polarity indefinites are treated in section 23.2.1.2.

As with possessives and demonstratives (see chapter 18 above), not all indefinites are actually pronouns. Many function as determiners, while others have adverbial or adjectival functions. As seen in Table 20.1 below, most items can function syntactically in several different ways.[2] The term 'indefinite' is thus a bit of a grammatical catch-all category, used for items that are not always easily classifiable, but among which there are perceived to be family resemblances. However, because 'indefinite pronoun' is a traditional term for the items in question, it is retained in this book for parsing purposes.

When they are functioning (pro)nominally, indefinites are peculiar, in as much as most of them refer neither deictically nor anaphorically in a straightforward sense.[3] Instead, they may refer, for instance, to a subset of a group of referents mentioned previously, as in (7) below, or to an entity

---

[1] Examples (4)–(5) are, of course, possible utterances in colloquial French, where the *ne* of negation is often dropped. In that case, however, they would translate, respectively, as 'I saw nothing' and 'Did you see nothing'. See further section 23.1.

[2] For the notion of pre-, post-, and central determiners, see section 12.1.

[3] See section 14.4 for this distinction.

Table 20.1. Syntactic functions of non-negative indefinites.

Determiner (incl. pre-, post-, and central determiner)	Adjectival functions	Nominal functions	Adverbial functions
	autre	*autre*	
certain(e)(s)	*certain(e)*	*certain(e)s*	
différent(e)s	*différent(e)(s)*		
divers(es)	*divers(es)*		
	même(s)	*même(s)*	*même*
plusieurs		*plusieurs*	
quelque(s)			*quelque*
		quelqu'un(e) / *quelques-un(e)s*	
		quelque chose	
tel(le)(s)	*tel(le)(s)*	*un(e) tel(le)*	
tout(e)(s) / *tous*		*tout(e)(s)* / *tous*	*tout(e)(s)*
un(e)	*un(e)*	*un(e)(s)*	

that is of the same type as, but not referentially identical to, a previously mentioned one, as in (8):

(7) Il est venu *une vingtaine de gens* à la réunion. Cependant, plusieurs sont partis avant la fin.

(8) Eric a mangé *un gâteau*, et puis un autre.

Despite their fundamental heterogeneity, the category of indefinites can arguably be subdivided into three broad types, which will be discussed in turn below:

(i) Quantifying indefinites: *certain(e)s*, *différent(e)s*, *divers(es)*, *plusieurs*, *quelque(s)*, *quelqu'un(e)/quelques-un(e)s*, *quelque chose*, and *un(e)*.

(ii) Indefinites with holistic or distributional meanings: *tout(e)(s)/tous*, *chaque*, and *chacun(e)*.

(iii) Adjective-like indefinites: *autre(s)*, *même(s)*, and *tel(le)(s)*.

20.2 Quantifying indefinites

The first subtype of indefinites indicate an indefinite quantity of a referent or group of referents.

20.2.1 Certain(e)(s)

In its adjectival function, *certain(e)(s)* functions just like any other adjective. Thus, it may be used as a pre- or postmodifier[4] within a noun phrase, as in (9) below, or as a subject/object/free indirect attribute.

(9)   Max a [des qualités certaines.]$_{\text{DirObj/NP}}$ ('definite qualities')
  >> [des]$_{\text{Det/PartArt}}$ [qualités]$_{\text{H/N}}$ [certaines]$_{\text{Postmod/Adj}}$

The plural forms *certain(e)s* have two separate uses as indefinite quantifiers: a pronominal use illustrated in (10) below, and a use where *certain(e)s* fills the determiner slot of a noun phrase (cf. (11)):

(10)   Certains$_{\text{Subj/IndefPron}}$ se croient tout permis. ('some'/'certain people')

(11)   [Certains cas spéciaux]$_{\text{Subj/NP}}$ ont été omis.
  >> [Certains]$_{\text{Det/IndefPron}}$ [cas]$_{\text{H/N}}$ [spéciaux]$_{\text{Postmod/Adj}}$

20.2.2 Différent(e)(s) *and* divers(es)

Différent(e)(s) and *divers(es)* may similarly function much like other adjectives, as shown in (12)–(13) below:

(12)   Je pensais à [des choses différentes.]$_{\text{ComplOfPrep/NP}}$ ('things of a different kind')
  >> [des]$_{\text{Det/PartArt}}$ [choses]$_{\text{H/N}}$ [différentes]$_{\text{Postmod/Adj}}$

(13)   Luc préfère [les faits divers]$_{\text{DirObj/NP}}$ à la politique. >> [les]$_{\text{Det/DefArt}}$ [faits]$_{\text{H/N}}$ [divers]$_{\text{Postmod/Adj}}$

The plural forms of these items may be used as indefinite determiners (cf. (14)–(15)):

(14)   A Chicago, j'ai visité [différents musées.]$_{\text{DirObj/NP}}$ ('various museums')
  >> [différents]$_{\text{Det/IndefPron}}$ [musées]$_{\text{H/N}}$

---

[4] For the meaning difference between the two positions, see section 13.2.3.2.

(15) [Diverses raisons]$_{Subj/NP}$ me poussent à prendre ces mesures. ('various reasons')
>> [Diverses]$_{Det/IndefPron}$ [raisons]$_{H/N}$

As these indefinites are very similar in meaning to the plural form of the partitive article (cf. section 12.3.1), the plural forms of the adjectives are never used in premodifying position after the partitive article, as shown by the ungrammaticality of (16)–(17) below:

(16)   *A Chicago, j'ai visité [de différents musées].

(17)   *[De diverses raisons] me poussent à prendre ces mesures.

20.2.3 Plusieurs

Plusieurs has the same form in both the masculine and the feminine. It may function pronominally, as in (18) below:

(18)   Il est venu une vingtaine de gens à la réunion. Cependant, plusieurs sont partis avant la fin.

or as a determiner, as in (19):

(19)   Elle l'a laissé tomber [plusieurs fois].

20.2.4 Quelque(s), quelqu'un(e), quelques-un(e)s, *and* quelque chose

Quelque(s) mostly functions as a determiner (cf. (20) below) or a postdeterminer (cf. (21)) within a noun phrase:

(20)   Il y a déjà [quelques fleurs] dans le jardin. ('a few')

(21)   [Ces quelques poèmes] que j'ai lus de lui, m'ont profondément marqué(e). ('these few')
>> [Ces]$_{CentrDet/DemArt}$ [quelques]$_{PostDet/IndefPron}$ [poèmes]$_{H/N}$

The singular form *quelque* may, in addition, be used as an adverbial premodifier of numerals (as in (22) below) or adverb phrases (as in (23)):

(22)   A mon avis, Noé doit gagner quelque *10 000* euros par mois. ('some 10 000 euros')

(23) J'ai été [quelque peu surpris(e)]$_{\text{SubjAttr/AdjP}}$ par l'attitude de Lucas. ('rather surprised')

>> [quelque peu]$_{\text{Premod/AdvP}}$ [surpris(e)]$_{\text{H/Adj}}$

>> [quelque]$_{\text{Premod/IndefPron}}$ [peu]$_{\text{H/Adv}}$

Quelqu'un(e) and its plural forms *quelques-un(e)s* ('a few') always function pronominally, as exemplified in (24) below. Unlike English *some(one)/some(body)*, none of these forms can be directly modified by an adjective. Instead, a postmodifying prepositional phrase with *de* as the head and the adjective as its complement must be used, as shown in (25)–(26):

(24) Il y a beaucoup de fleurs dans le jardin. <u>Quelques-unes</u> sont vraiment très belles.

(25) John is hoping to find *somebody* <u>nice</u> on that dating site.

(26) Jean espère trouver *quelqu'un* <u>de sympathique</u> sur ce site de rencontres.

As (26) shows (assuming Jean is heterosexual), the masculine singular form *quelqu'un* is normally used rather than the feminine singular, even when the intended reference is feminine. The feminine singular form is used only if the speaker/writer wishes to insist on the gender of the referent, as in (27) below. The feminine plural, on the other hand, is freely used about feminine referents, as seen in (24) above.

(27) Jean a rendez-vous avec *quelqu'un* ce soir. Ou plutôt avec <u>quelqu'une</u>.

Quelque chose similarly is always pronominal, as illustrated in (28) below. Despite being transparently derived from the feminine noun *chose*, the indefinite pronoun is masculine, as shown by past participle agreement (cf. (29)) and by the form of postmodifying adjectives, cf. (30). Notice that, unlike English *something*, *quelque chose* cannot be directly postmodified by an adjective. Instead a prepositional phrase with *de* as its head must be used, just as is the case with *quelqu'un*, cf. the contrast between (30) and (31):

(28) Il fallait bien dire <u>quelque chose</u>.

(29) Tous mes amis parlent de *quelque chose* que Véronique a <u>mis</u> sur Instagram l'autre jour.

(30) J'ai envie d'écouter *quelque chose* <u>de beau</u>.

(31) I feel like listening to *something* <u>beautiful</u>.

20.2.5 Un(e)(s)

Un(e) mostly functions as an indefinite article or numeral, as in (32)–(33) below (see section 12.3, for its use as an indefinite article):

(32)   Tu as envie d'aller voir un film ?

(33)   On a vu pas un, mais deux films hier soir.

It may, however also be used as an adjective (although never in premodifying position), as in (34) below:

(34)   Il faut que l'église reste une. ('unified')

Finally, it may function pronominally. When singular *un(e)* appears on its own in this function, it may or may not be preceded by a definite article, as illustrated in (35) below. As that example shows, singular pronominal *un(e)* is frequently postmodified by a prepositional phrase headed by *de*, whose complement describes a larger set of entities which includes the entity represented by *un(e)*, i.e. in this case, the set of four students who sat the exam:

(35)   Quatre étudiants ont passé cet examen. (L')un *des quatre* a été recalé.

In both the singular and the plural, *l'un(e)/les un(e)s* is often found alongside *l'autre/les autres*. The two may be used contrastively, as in (36) below:

(36)   Karine portait une paire de chaussures dont (l')une était rouge et l'autre verte.

However, the collocation *l'un(e)* [preposition] *l'autre/les un(e)s* [preposition] *les autres* is frequently used (often in combination with a reflexive construction, cf. section 15.4.1.2) in a reciprocal sense corresponding to English *each other/one another*, as in (37) below. Note that, in contrast to (36), the coordinating conjunction *et* is not used in this type of case:

(37)   Ces frères et sœurs se détestent les uns les autres. ('These siblings hate each other.')

When reciprocal *l'un(e)* [preposition] *l'autre/les un(e)s* [preposition] *les autres* is used in connection with a preposition, a simple preposition is always placed between *l'un(e)/les un(e)s* and *l'autre/les autres*, as shown in (38) below. If the preposition is a complex one ending in *de*, it is possible to place only that element between *l'un(e)/les un(e)s* and *l'autre/les autres*, as shown in (39)–(40):

(38)   Ils se parlaient *les uns <u>aux</u> autres.*

(39)   Ils étaient assis *l'un* <u>à</u> côté de *l'autre.*

(40)   Ils étaient assis à côté *l'un* <u>de</u> *l'autre.*

20.3 Indefinites with holistic or distributional meanings

The second type of indefinite indicate either the totality or individual parts of a greater whole or group.

20.3.1 Tout(e)(s) *and* tous

Tout and its feminine and/or plural variants may function as predeterminers, as in (41) below:

(41)   Cyril passe [<u>toute</u> sa journée]$_{DirObj/NP}$ au lit.
　　　　>> [toute]$_{Predet/IndefPron}$ [sa]$_{CentrDet/PossArt}$ [journée]$_{H/N}$

These items may also function as determiners on their own, as in (42) below. In this function, *tout(e)* is normally singular. The plural forms *tous/toutes* are found mainly in frozen expressions such as that in (43):

(42)   <u>Tout</u> *étudiant* devra payer des frais d'inscription s'élevant à 500 euros par an. ('every student')

(43)   Je vous prie d'écrire votre prénom en <u>toutes</u> *lettres*. ('in full')

Tout(e)(s)/tous may be used as a pronoun, in which case the masculine plural form *tous* is always pronounced with a final /s/, i.e. /tus/. Examples of the pronominal use are given in (44)–(45):

(44)   Il avait <u>tout</u> oublié.

(45)   Je les ai <u>tous</u> rencontrés. ('I met them all.')

Notice that only the masculine singular form *tout* can function as a direct object (as in (44) above). The feminine and particularly the plural forms, on the other hand, are frequently used as free indirect attributes, as in (45), but are ungrammatical in direct object position, as shown in (46):

(46) *J'ai rencontré tous.

In addition, the plural forms must refer to a specific group of entities that the hearer can identify. If the intended reference is to a non-specific group of people, *tout le monde* is used instead, as in (47) below. Masculine singular *tout* can be used to refer to a non-specific group of things, as seen in (48):

(47) J'ai rencontré tout le monde. ('I met everybody.')

(48) J'ai tout vu. ('I've seen everything./I've seen it all.')

Pronominal *tout(e)(s)/tous* cannot by itself be the antecedent of an adjectival relative clause, as shown by the ungrammaticality of (49) below.[5] Whereas English offers a choice between the two constructions in (52)–(53), French only allows *tout(e)(s)/tous* to premodify a demonstrative pronoun, which then functions as the antecedent of a relative clause (as in (50)), or to premodify a free relative pronoun,[6] as in (51):

(49) *Tous *qui* pensent que la grammaire est ennuyeuse devraient lire ce livre.

(50) Tous ceux *qui* pensent que la grammaire est ennuyeuse devraient lire ce livre.

(51) Tout *ce qui* m'intéresse, c'est la grammaire.

(52) All *who* think grammar is boring should read this book.

(53) All those *who* think grammar is boring should read this book.

Tout(e)(s), but not *tous*, is often used to premodify the head of an adjective phrase, as in (54) below:

(54) Il est tout *essoufflé*.

In this function, the standard written norm prescribes that when the adjective is masculine, *tout* must be used as a premodifier in both the singular and the plural. If the adjective is feminine, on the other hand, *toute* and *toutes* are used before adjectives starting in a consonant (incl. an aspirated 'h'), whereas *tout* is used before adjectives starting in a vowel (incl. a silent 'h'), as set out in Table 20.2.

---

[5] For the notion of antecedent, see section 4.2.2.

[6] For the notion of free relative pronouns, see section 4.2.1.3.

Table 20.2. Forms of *tout(e)(s)* when premodifying an adjective.

	Masculine	**Feminine**
Before a consonant: singular	*Il est <u>tout</u> pâle.*	*Elle est <u>toute</u> pâle.*
Before a consonant: plural	*Ils sont <u>tout</u> pâles.*	*Elles sont <u>toutes</u> pâles.*
Before a vowel: singular	*Il est <u>tout</u> agité.*	*Elle est <u>tout</u> agitée.*
Before a vowel: plural	*Ils sont <u>tout</u> agités*	*Elles sont <u>tout</u> agitées.*

20.3.2 Chaque *and* chacun(e)

Chaque and *chacun(e)* have distributional meaning, i.e. they focus on invidual elements out of a larger whole.

Chaque is only used as a determiner, as in (55) below:

(55)   <u>Chaque</u> *appartement* dans cet immeuble a deux salles de bain.

Chacun(e), on the other hand, is a pronoun, which may occur on its own, as in (56) below, or postmodified by a prepositional phrase headed by *de*, as in (57):

(56)   Cet immeuble a 100 appartements. <u>Chacun</u> a deux salles de bain.

(57)   <u>Chacun</u> *des appartements* a deux salles de bain.

20.4 Adjective-like indefinites

20.4.1 Autre(s) *and* autrui

Autre(s) can function adjectivally, as a pre- or postmodifier within noun phrases (cf. (58) below), or as a subject or object attribute, cf. (59):

(58)   Je préférerais voir un <u>autre</u> film.

(59)   Son problème est tout <u>autre</u>. ('of a completely different nature')

Autre(s) can be nominalized, in which case it is always preceded by a determiner, as in (60) below:

(60)   Philippe et Delphine sont là depuis une heure, mais où sont *les* autres ?

If the determiner is the partitive article, it always occurs in its reduced form *d'* (cf, section 12.3.1), as in (61) below. The form *des autres* (cf. (62)) thus always represents the preposition *de* + the definite/generic article (cf. section 12.4):

(61)   Certains sont partis, mais d'autres sont venus prendre leurs places.

(62)   Les problèmes des autres lui semblent toujours moins importants que les siens.

For the reciprocal expression *l'un l'autre*, see section 20.2.5 above.

Autrui is a somewhat archaic and predominantly literary form, which is used pronominally, as in (63) below. While *autrui* may refer generically to either one person ('the other') or a plurality of people ('others'), it is always grammatically singular:

(63)   Autrui en tant qu'autrui n'est pas seulement un *alter ego*. Il est ce que moi je ne suis pas. ('The other as other is not just an *alter ego*.') (Lévinas)

20.4.2 Même(s)

Même(s) can function adjectivally, in which case it may pre- or postmodify a noun phrase. Adjectival *même(s)* does not occur as a subject attribute, an object attribute, or a free indirect attribute.

Adjectival *même(s)* has different meanings according to its position within the noun phrase (cf. (64)–(65) below):

(64)   C'est le même artiste qui a peint ces deux tableaux. ('The same artist painted these two pictures.')

(65)   Cet homme est la mesquinerie même. ('This man is petty-mindedness itself/ incarnate.')

If the head noun is a temporal expression, postposed *même(s)* corresponds to English *very* or *the selfsame*, as seen in (66) below. If the head noun refers to a person, postposed *même(s)* normally combines with a non-clitic personal pronoun, as in (67):

(66)   Il est mort *le jour* même de son 80e anniversaire.

(67)   C'est Jean Reno *lui*-même qui fait les cascades. ('Jean Reno himself is doing the stunts.')

Like *autre* (cf. section 20.4.1 above), *même(s)* may be nominalized, in which case it is always preceded by the definite article, as seen in (68) below:

(68)   Pourquoi est-ce que tu ne veux pas de ces chaussures ? Ce sont *les* mêmes que celles de Sarah, que tu as admirées l'autre jour.

Finally, *même* may function adverbially, as in (69) below. As that example shows, adverbial *même* is invariable in form and never takes a plural marker:

(69)   Ce problème est très difficile. Même les filles ne savent pas le résoudre.

20.4.3 Tel(le)(s)

Tel(le)(s) may function as a determiner, cf. (70) below. In this use, it marks that the noun phrase serves as an example in the context:

(70)   Faites-leur savoir que j'arrive tel *jour* à telle *heure*. ('Tell them that I'll arrive on such-and-such a day at such-and-such a time.')

It may function adjectivally, as a pre- or postmodifier of a noun phrase (cf. (71) below) or as a subject attribute, object attribute, or free indirect attribute, cf. (72) below. Pre- or postmodifying *tel(le)(s)* is incompatible with definite determiners, and co-occurs only with the indefinite or the partitive article:

(71)   Je n'ai jamais vu une telle insolence !

(72)   Son insolence est telle qu'on en reste bouche bée.

As (72) shows, *tel(le)(s)* is often found in construction with a subordinate clause, either a result clause, as in (72), or a comparison clause, as in (73) below.[7] In the latter type of use, *tel(le)(s)* is equivalent in meaning to *comme*. In somewhat more formal registers, it is thus found in the construction exemplified in (74), which amounts to a reduced comparison clause:

(73)   Si les activités de Dupont sont telles *que vous dites*, alors la situation est grave.

---

[7] For the notions of result clauses and comparison clauses, cf. section 4.2.3.2.

(74)   Tel *Moïse face à la Mer Rouge*, les invités ont pu traverser le bassin de la Villette, en ayant la sensation d'ouvrir les eaux.

The frozen expression *tel(le)(s) quel(le)(s)* compares an entity to itself, as it were, with the meaning 'such as it is', cf. (75) below. *Tel(le)(s) quel(le)(s)* may be used as a subject attribute, an object attribute, or a free indirect attribute as in (75):

(75)   Je n'ai plus envie de travailler sur ce problème : je vous donne ma solution telle quelle.

Finally, *tel(le)(s)* has a nominalized form, in which it is preceded by the indefinite article, as in (76) below. In this use, it represents a person whom the speaker cannot or will not name explicitly ('somebody', 'so-and-so').

(76)   *Un* tel m'a dit que Christiane sort avec son secrétaire.

PART IV

The Grammar of French Particles

21

Prepositions

Learning objectives

- To understand the distinction between items that function only as prepositions and items that can function as either prepositions or adverbs.
- To understand the distinction between 'light' and 'heavy' prepositions.
- To understand the general syntactic and semantic principles governing the choice between competing prepositions expressing largely similar meanings.
- To understand how the syntax of French prepositions may differ from that of English prepositions.

21.1 Introduction

In French, as in many other languages, prepositions are a heterogeneous subject in the sense that there are few general rules governing this area of the grammar. The appropriate use of prepositions must therefore to a large extent be learned on a case-by-case basis. For reasons of space, this chapter

The Structure of Modern Standard French. First edition. Maj-Britt Mosegaard Hansen.
© Maj-Britt Mosegaard Hansen 2016. First Published 2016 by Oxford University Press

will therefore restrict itself to discussing a relative small number of rules that have some generality.

21.2 Criteria for classifying prepositions

Various criteria may be applied when distinguishing between different types of preposition in French.

21.2.1 Meaning

We can classify prepositions according to their meanings. Thus, we might say, for instance, that *chez* has locative meaning (cf. (1) below), whereas *avec* has instrumental meaning (cf. (2)):

(1)   Pendant les vacances, on va laisser le chien chez mon frère.

(2)   J'ai ouvert la boîte avec un couteau.

However, a number of prepositions have more than one meaning. *Dans*, for instance, may have either locative or temporal meaning, as shown in (3)–(4) below:

(3)   On s'est promenés dans Biarritz.

(4)   On partira pour Biarritz dans 15 jours.

21.2.2 Form

Prepositions may also be classified according to their form, such that a distinction is made between **simple prepositions** like *chez*, *avec*, or *dans* (cf. (1)–(4) above), and **complex prepositions** like *en face de*, *par rapport à*, or *à travers*, cf. (5)–(7) below:

(5)   A Biarritz, on était logés en face du casino.

(6)   Par rapport à son frère, Corinne est plutôt sympathique.

(7)   Philippe a dû écouter notre conversation à travers la porte.

Complex prepositions are clearly frozen combinations of simple prepositions with items from other word classes. However, even among the simple prepositions, some items have their origins in other word classes, for instance the past participle *vu*, which may be used as a preposition (cf. (8) below). In that case, it is never inflected for number and/or gender:

(8) Vu les problèmes que j'ai eus avec ce logiciel, je ne pense pas continuer à m'en servir.

21.2.3 Functional range

In terms of their possible syntactic functions, we may distinguish between items that can function only as prepositions, i.e. items such as *dans*, which—as shown by (9)–(10) below–can never occur without a complement, and items such as *contre*, which can have both a **prepositional function**, as in (11), and an **adverbial function**, as in (12):

(9) Mets la lampe dans la boîte.

(10) *Mets la lampe dans.

(11) J'ai voté contre cette proposition.

(12) J'ai voté contre.

Items with dual functions like *contre* are considerably less common in French than in English, where many items may be used for both purposes, as shown in (13)–(14) below. Most French prepositions, on the other hand, are like *dans* and must be followed by a complement.[1]

(13) Put the lamp in the box.

(14) Put the lamp in.

Moreover, if the complement moves (as it may do in a relative clause, for instance), the preposition must move with it, unlike English, where the preposition typically stays behind in all but the most formal registers.

---

[1] That said, the four prepositions *dans*, *hors*, *sur*, or *sous*, are the basis for derived adverbs, e.g. *dedans* in (i) below. These derived adverbs are quite restricted in their uses, however.

(i) Tu mets la boîte là, et puis, la lampe, tu la mets dedans.

Thus, while both the English examples in (15)–(16) below are grammatical, a direct French translation of (16) is impossible, as shown by the ungrammaticality of (18):

(15)   This is the box <u>in</u> *which* he put the lamp.

(16)   This is the box *that/which* he put the lamp <u>in</u>.

(17)   Ceci est la boîte <u>dans</u> *laquelle* il a mis la lampe.

(18)   *Ceci est la boîte *qu'*il a mis la lampe <u>dans</u>.

21.2.4 Form + meaning

If we take into account a combination of form and meaning, we may subdivide the French prepositions into two groups, namely 'light' *vs* 'heavy' prepositions. (These terms are to be understood in a figurative sense, and nothing much hinges on the precise choice of terms as such.) The general rules governing the choice between light and heavy prepositions with a given complement will be treated in sections 21.3.1–21.3.4 below.

21.2.4.1 Light prepositions

The group of light prepositions comprises *de, à*, and *en*. Formally, these three prepositions are short, monosyllabic and phonologically insubstantial. From the point of view of meaning, they are quite abstract and vague, and their interpretations may vary quite significantly from one context to another. Thus, depending on the context, (19) below may translate as 'the train from Paris', 'the train to Paris', 'the train in Paris', 'the train made in Paris', and probably in yet other ways besides:

(19)   le train <u>de Paris</u>

Within the group of light prepositions, *de* is the lightest, most frequent, and most abstract of the three, while *à* and *en* are comparatively heavier and more concrete.

21.2.4.2 Heavy prepositions

All other prepositions belong to the group of heavy prepositions. Heavy prepositions are generally speaking longer than the three light prepositions, i.e. they are phonologically more substantial and often polysyllabic.

In addition, their meanings are more concrete and less contextually variable than those of the light prepositions.

21.3 General principles for choosing among different prepositions

In many cases, the choice of an appropriate preposition to express a particular meaning will depend on the complement, with superficially rather similar types of complement triggering different prepositions, as in (20)–(21) and (22)–(23) below. As a result, correct preposition use, in French as in many other languages, must to some extent be learnt on a case-by-case basis.

(20)   Patrick est <u>dans</u> la cuisine.

(21)   Jocelyne est <u>aux</u> toilettes.

(22)   La circulation <u>dans</u> cette rue est dense.

(23)   La circulation <u>sur</u> ce boulevard est dense.

However, in a number of cases, the same complement will be compatible with different prepositions, one light and one heavy, both combinations expressing much the same meaning. Within the group of light prepositions, *de* may in addition substitute for either *à* or *en* in a variety of contexts. In such cases, there are various general syntactic and semantic criteria which may determine the choice.

21.3.1 The role of determiners and modifiers in the complement

If the complement consists in a noun phrase with a definite or a zero article and no modifiers, and if the combination of preposition + complement and its interpretation is a relatively stereotypical one, a lighter preposition will typically be preferred, as in (24) and (26) below. If the intended interpretation is less stereotypical, and particularly if the complement contains modifiers or any type of determiner other than the definite article or the zero article, a heavier preposition is likely to be used, cf. (25) and (27)–(28):

(24)   Bénédicte écrit toujours à *la main*.

(25)   Bénédicte s'est cassé les deux bras. Elle a donc été obligée d'écrire cette lettre avec *la bouche*.

(26)   On est dimanche. Claire est à l'église.

(27)   J'ai retrouvé Claire assise toute seule dans *une* église.

(28)   J'ai retrouvé Claire dans la *vieille* église *romane que nous avons vue hier*.

21.3.2 Syntactic distance

If the preposition links its complement to another constituent, a heavier preposition may be preferred if there is syntactic distance between that constituent and the prepositional phrase, cf. (29)–(30):

(29)   On a beaucoup *discuté* de ces questions importantes.

(30)   On a beaucoup *discuté*, lors du colloque d'avril, sur ces questions importantes.

21.3.3 Prepositional phrases as postmodifiers vs adverbials

If a prepositional phrase is used as a postmodifier within a noun phrase, a light preposition is typically used. That is normally (but not only) the case when the combination of head noun and modifier corresponds to an English compound noun, cf. (31)–(33) below:

(31)   une chambre d'hôtel ('a hotel room')

(32)   une machine à écrire ('a typewriter')

(33)   un poêle en porcelaine ('a porcelain stove')

Conversely, if the prepositional phrase functions as an adverbial or a locative object, a heavier preposition may be preferred, as shown by the contrast between (34) and (35) below:

(34)   Joseph préfère l'appartement du boulevard Malesherbes. (postmodifier)

(35)   Joseph a acheté un appartement sur le boulevard Malesherbes. (adverbial)

Postmodifiers and adverbials/locative object can be distinguished using the following tests: If a prepositional phrase functions adverbially or as a locative object, it can be the answer to a question by itself. Postmodifying prepositional phrases, on the other hand, can normally only answer a question as part of a full noun phrase or pronominal phrase, cf. (36)–(38) below:

(36)   A: Où Joseph a-t-il acheté un appartement ?
       B: <u>Sur</u> le boulevard Malesherbes.

(37)   A: Que préfère Joseph ?
       B: L'appartement <u>du</u> boulevard Malesherbes.

(38)   A: Quel appartement Joseph préfère-t-il ?
       B: Celui <u>du</u> boulevard Malesherbes.

For this reason, it will normally be possible to move a prepositional phrase with adverbial function to a different position in the clause. This is not possible if the prepositional phrase functions as a postmodifier, cf. the contrasts in (39)–(48):

(39)   *Sur* <u>le boulevard Malesherbes</u>, Joseph a acheté un appartement.

(40)   *Du <u>boulevard Malesherbes</u>, Joseph préfère l'appartement.

(41)   On va mettre le canapé *dans* <u>le salon</u>. (locative object)

(42)   *Dans* <u>le salon</u>, on va mettre le canapé.

(43)   Je n'aime pas le canapé <u>du salon</u>. (postmodifier)

(44)   *Du <u>salon</u>, je n'aime pas le canapé.

(45)   J'ai pris le train *à* <u>minuit</u>. (adverbial)

(46)   *À* <u>minuit</u>, j'ai pris le train.

(47)   Le train *de* <u>minuit</u> me convient. (postmodifier)

(48)   *De <u>minuit</u>, le train me convient.

21.3.4 Locative prepositions: static vs dynamic senses

In English, different prepositions may often be used with the same complement in order to distinguish between a static 'position' sense and a dynamic 'direction' sense, as in (49)–(54) below:

(49)   Sue is <u>in</u> the parlor. (= static sense)

(50)   Come into my parlor! (= dynamic sense)

(51)   Jane is at the dentist's. (= static sense)

(52)   Jane is going to the dentist's. (= dynamic sense)

(53)   Paul lives on the French Riviera. (= static sense)

(54)   Come to the French Riviera with us! (= dynamic sense)

As the French equivalents in (55)–(60) show, that language typically uses the same preposition with both senses, such that the intended sense is determined by the context:

(55)   Suzanne est dans le salon.

(56)   Viens/Venez dans le salon !

(57)   Jeanne est chez le dentiste.

(58)   Jeanne va chez le dentiste.

(59)   Paul habite sur la Côte d'Azur.

(60)   Viens/Venez sur la Côte d'Azur avec nous !

21.4 The syntax of prepositions

21.4.1 The position of prepositions

In French, prepositions usually immediately precede their complement. Whereas English allows modifying adverbials to be inserted between a preposition and its complement, that is not normally possible in French, cf. (61)–(62) below:

(61)   He reacts in *exactly* the same way every time.

(62)   Il réagit *exactement* de la même façon à chaque fois.

There are, however, a few exceptions to this rule:

(a)   The adverb *même* is regularly (although not always) inserted between a preposition and its complement, as in (63) below:

(63)   Elle est partie sans *même* me regarder.

(b) The adverb *presque* usually follows the preposition if it modifies a complement containing a quantifying expression such as a numeral, but not otherwise, cf. (64)–(65):

(64) On t'attend <u>depuis</u> *presque* deux heures.

(65) Un SDF est mort *presque* <u>dans</u> l'indifférence.

(c) If the complement is an infinitival clause, the prepositions *sans* and *pour* can be followed by an adverbial, as in (66):

(66) Les gouvernements de l'UE souhaitent réduire les rejets, <u>sans</u> *toutefois* les interdire.

(d) The preposition *avec* is frequently separated from its complement, irrespective of the nature of the latter, cf. (67):

(67) Le labo organisera l'année prochaine un colloque <u>avec</u> *pour thème* la communication interculturelle.

21.4.2 Repetition of prepositions

The three light prepositions *de*, *à*, and *en* are normally repeated before coordinated complements, unlike their English equivalents, cf. (68)–(73):

(68) [Novel by Kenizé Mourad:] In the City <u>of</u> Silver *and* [Ø] Gold.

(69) [Novel by Kenizé Mourad:] Dans la ville <u>d'</u>or *et* d'argent.

(70) I have friends <u>in</u> Paris *and* [Ø] Rome.

(71) J'ai des amis <u>à</u> Paris *et* <u>à</u> Rome.

(72) That grammatical construction is the same <u>in</u> French *and* [Ø] English.

(73) Cette construction grammaticale est pareille <u>en</u> français *et* <u>en</u> anglais.

If the two complements together form a unit of meaning, as in (74)–(76), the preposition does not need to be repeated:

(74) Eugénie a fait l'École <u>des</u> Arts *et* [Ø] Métiers.

(75) Accès interdit <u>aux</u> autos *et* [Ø] motos.

(76) J'adore les vieux films <u>en</u> noir *et* [Ø] blanc.

If the preposition used in a coordination is a complex one that incorporates either *de* or *à*, only these elements will normally be repeated, as shown in (77):

(77)   La nouvelle s'est répandue très vite <u>grâce à</u> Facebook *et* <u>à</u> Twitter.

Other prepositions can be repeated in coordinations, but need not be. Repetition normally signals individualization of each of the coordinated elements, cf. (78)–(79) below. It is therefore the norm if the two elements are in opposition, as in (80):

(78)   Être bien <u>dans</u> son corps *et* [Ø] sa tête permet de profiter plus encore de la vie.

(79)   La pratique du yoga permet de se sentir bien <u>dans</u> son corps *et* <u>dans</u> sa tête.

(80)   Répondez-moi <u>par</u> un oui *ou* <u>par</u> un non !

The coordinating conjunction used with the preposition *sans* is *ni*, if the preposition is not repeated, and *et* if the preposition is repeated, as shown in (81)–(82):

(81)   Luc a fait un discours *sans* queue <u>ni</u> [Ø] tête.

(82)   Salomé laisse ses enfants jouer dans la neige *sans* manteau et *sans* gants.

21.4.3 Non-use of prepositions in French

In certain contexts where English standardly uses a preposition, French does not necessarily do so.

(a) When a street name is used as an address, no preposition is used, as shown in (83)–(84):

(83)   Harry lives <u>on</u> *Oak Street.*

(84)   Marc habite [Ø] *rue Charles V.*

When street names are used to indicate a location which is not an address, a preposition is optional, cf. (85):

(85)   La circulation est dense (<u>sur</u> le) *boulevard St-Germain.*

(b) When stating the price of something, a preposition is optional in French, as shown in (86)–(88):

(86)   John sold this house <u>for</u> *£500 000.*

(87)   Jean a vendu cette maison [Ø] *500 000 euros.*

(88)   Jean a vendu cette maison <u>pour</u> *500 000 euros.*

(c) Finally, as shown in (89)–(90) below, absolute constructions of Type 2
(see section 3.2.3) don't take a preposition, although they will often be
translated into English by means of a prepositional phrase:

(89)   Elle apparut à la porte, déjà toute habillée, [Ø] *son sac à la main.*

(90)   She appeared at the door, already fully dressed, <u>with</u> her handbag in her hand.

22

Adverbs, interjections, and coordinating conjunctions

Learning objectives

- To understand the rules governing the derivation of manner adverbs.
- To understand the rules governing the uses of adverbs of degree and quantity.
- To understand the difference between deictic and non-deictic time adverb(ial)s.
- To understand the differences in use between the deictic space adverbs *ici*, *là*, and *là-bas*.
- To understand how motion events are expressed differently in French and English.
- To understand the meanings and uses of the French response interjections *oui*, *si*, and *non*.
- To understand the syntax, meanings, and uses of the French coordinating conjunctions *et*, *ou (bien)*, *soit*, *mais*, and *car*.

The Structure of Modern Standard French. First edition. Maj-Britt Mosegaard Hansen.
© Maj-Britt Mosegaard Hansen 2016. First Published 2016 by Oxford University Press

22.1 Adverbs

The category of adverbs is quite heterogeneous, and includes elements with different morphological status.

At the most basic level, we can make the following two-way distinction:

(i) **'Genuine'** adverbs, i.e. items that have not been created by a productive morphological process on the basis of another part of speech.

(ii) **Derived** adverbs, mainly those ending in *–ment*, which are derived from adjectives. These adverbs do not actually belong to the category of particles, but they will be treated in this part of the book for ease of reference.

Genuine adverbs can be further subdivided into:

(a) **Simple** adverbs, such as *hier, ici, tard, très*, etc., which consist of a single morpheme.

(b) **Complex** adverbs, such as *avant-hier, là-bas, tout à coup*, etc., which involve frozen combinations of two or more morphemes, which are not necessarily themselves adverbs.

Finally, adverbs can be subdivided by meaning and function, into five main groups:

I. **Manner** adverbs. These are often derived from adjectives, and describe the manner in which something takes place, as in (1) below. Manner adverbs modify the predicator.

(1) Paul m'a demandé <u>gentiment</u> si je pouvais l'aider.

II. Adverbs of **degree** and **quantity**. These are treated further in section 22.1.3.

III. Adverbs of **time** and **place**. These are treated further in section 22.1.4.

IV. **Interrogative** adverbs. These are treated in section 19.2.

V. **Sentence adverbs**. These adverbs modify the sentence or utterance as a whole, either expressing the speaker's attitude to the contents of the utterance (cf. (2) below), his/her comments on the style or form of the utterance (cf. (3)–(4)), or marking the connection between the host utterance and the surrounding discourse (cf. (5)):

(2) <u>Malheureusement</u>, je ne pourrai pas venir.

(3)   Franchement, tu es un porc !

(4)   Bref, il faut qu'on paye 100 000 euros avant la fin du mois.

(5)   Ainsi, je resterai à votre disposition.

22.1.1 The formation of derived adverbs

Adverbs can be derived morphologically from a corresponding adjective. The standard procedure is to add *–ment* to the feminine singular form of the adjective, as shown in (6)–(8) below:

(6)   long—longue—longuement

(7)   sérieux—sérieuse—sérieusement

(8)   fou—folle—follement

There are a number of exceptions to this, however.

If the adjective ends in *–ant* or *–ent*, the derived adverb will end in *–amment/-emment* (both pronounced /amã/, as in (9)–(10) below:

(9)   constant—constamment

(10)   évident—évidemment

If the adjective ends in a stressed vowel (i.e. a vowel other than the silent 'e', or schwa: /ə/), the masculine form of the adjective is the basis for the derived adverb, as shown in (11)–(12) below, the adverb *gaiement* (< *gai*) being the exception:

(11)   poli—poliment

(12)   vrai—vraiment

A number of adverbs[1] take the ending *–ément*, as in (13)–(14) below. This is particularly, but not exclusively, the case with adverbs that are derived from first conjugation past participles (i.e. past participles of verbs whose infinitive ends in *–er*), as in (15)–(16):

---

[1] Standard monolingual dictionaries, such as *Le Petit Robert*, will give information about the exact items involved.

(13)   commun—communément

(14)   précis—précisément

(15)   assuré—assurément

(16)   décidé—décidément

Three adverbs ending in *–ment* are irregular, cf. (17)–(19) below:

(17)   bref—brève—brièvement

(18)   gentil—gentille—gentiment

(19)   impuni—impunie—impunément

Finally, the adverbs *bien* and *mal* may be considered irregular derivations from the adjectives *bon* and *mauvais*.

22.1.2 Comparative and superlative forms of adverbs

Like adjectives (see section 13.1.2), most adverbs—both genuine and derived—form comparatives and superlatives with the use of *(le) plus/moins*, as seen in (20)–(21) below:

(20)   tôt—plus/moins tôt—le plus/moins tôt

(21)   poliment—plus/moins poliment—le plus/moins poliment

Four adverbs, however, have irregular comparative and superlative forms, as seen in (22)–(25) below. As (23) shows, *mal* also has competing regular comparative and superlative forms. However, the irregular form *(le) pis* is rarely used in contemporary French, except in frozen expressions such as *tant pis* ('never mind', 'too bad'), *un pis-aller* ('a last resort'), or the like.

(22)   bien—mieux—le mieux

(23)   mal—pis/plus mal—le pis/le plus mal

(24)   beaucoup—plus—le plus

(25)   peu—moins—le moins

22.1.3 Adverbs of degree and quantity

Adverbs of degree and quantity—only a commonly used subset of which are treated here—may differ along two parameters, shown in Table 22.1 and (26)–(36) below:

(a) The type(s) of grammatical role they can fulfil. Some function exclusively as premodifiers of adjective or adverb phrases, others exclusively as adverbials, and some can have either function.

(b) Whether or not they can be followed by a result clause or a comparison clause.[2] Those that can are called 'correlative' adverbs.

(26)   Frédéric mange beaucoup.

(27)   Patricia est très sympathique.

(28)   On nous a accueilli(e)s très chaleureusement.

(29)   Ici, on travaille peu.

(30)   J'ai trouvé ça bien/fort embêtant.

(31)   Frédéric a tant/tellement mangé *qu'il en est malade.*

(32)   Patricia est si/tellement sympathique *qu'on ne peut pas ne pas l'aimer.*

(33)   Vas-y, mange autant *que tu veux* !

(34)   Patricia est aussi sympathique *que son frère est antipathique.*

Table 22.1. Uses of the most common adverbs of degree and quantity.

	Non-correlative adverbs	Correlative adverbs	
		Followed by result clause	Followed by comparison clause
Adverbial	*beaucoup* (26)	*tant* (31)	*autant* (33)
Premodifier	*très* (27)–(28)	*si* (32)	*aussi* (34)
Adverbial or premodifier	*bien, fort, (un) peu* (29)–(30)	*tellement, (assez), (trop)*(31)–(32)	*plus, moins* (35)–(36)

Note: Numbers in parentheses refer to examples below.

---

[2] See sections 4.2.3.2 for result and comparison clauses.

(35) Finalement, j'ai dépensé <u>moins</u> *que je (ne)*[3] *pensais.*

(36) On nous a accueilli(e)s <u>plus</u> chaleureusement *que je (ne) le craignais.*

Note that the correlative adverbs may occur without a following subordinate clause, as in (37)–(38) below. In such cases, *autant, aussi, plus*, and *moins* will be understood to imply a comparison clause. *Si, tant*, and *tellement*, on the other hand, will give the utterance an exclamative meaning:

(37) Frédéric n'a jamais <u>autant</u> mangé. (→ 'Frédéric never ate as much as he did on this occasion.')

(38) Elle est <u>si</u> sympathique, Patricia !

Assez and *trop* are commonly used as both premodifiers and adverbials, as shown in (39)–(40) below. Both are sometimes followed by the preposition *pour* + a correlative element, either a result clause or an infinitival phrase, as shown in (41):

(39) Patricia est <u>assez</u> sympathique.

(40) Frédéric a <u>trop</u> mangé.

(41) Je ne gagne pas <u>assez</u> *pour pouvoir arrondir mes fins de mois.*

Although normally used as an adverbial, *beaucoup* may be used as a premodifier of the degree adverbs *plus* and *moins*, often in connection with adjectives in the comparative degree, as shown in (42) below. If the adjective is in the superlative degree, *de beaucoup/de loin* is used, as in (43):

(42) Patricia est <u>beaucoup</u> *plus sympathique* que son frère.

(43) Patricia est <u>de beaucoup</u> *la plus sympathique* des deux.

Unlike its closest English equivalents *much* and *many, beaucoup* cannot be premodified, as shown by the ungrammaticality of (44) below. Other expressions must therefore be used to render the meanings of *so/how/as much/many* in French, viz. *tant/tellement, combien*, and *autant*, cf. (45)–(47) below:

(44) *Je t'aime <u>si</u> beaucoup !

(45) Je t'aime <u>tant/tellement</u> ! ('so much')

(46) <u>Combien</u> est-ce que tu m'aimes ? ('how much')

(47) Je t'aime <u>autant</u> que Paul. ('as much')

---

[3] For the uses of the so-called 'expletive' *ne*, see section 23.4.

22.1.4 Adverbs of time and place

As with adverbs of degree and quantity, only certain commonly used adverbs of time and place will treated in this section.

22.1.4.1 Deictic *vs* non-deictic time adverb(ial)s

French has two sets of adverb(ial)s designating a particular day as seen from a particular perspective, a deictic set and a non-deictic set. (For the notion of deixis, see sections 6.2.1 and 14.4.) As the name suggests, the deictic set of adverbs designate a day by taking the day the utterance is produced (itself designated by the deictic term *aujourd'hui*) as their point of departure. The non-deictic set of adverb(ial)s, on the other hand, take a previously mentioned day, in either the past or the future, as their point of departure. The two sets correspond as shown in Table 22.2, and their uses are illustrated in (48)–(51):

(48)   Daniel *pense* qu'il verra Line <u>après-demain</u>. ('...the day after tomorrow.')

(49)   Daniel *pensait* qu'il verrait Line <u>le surlendemain</u>. ('...two days later.')

(50)   Noé *affirme* avoir envoyé la lettre <u>hier</u>. ('...yesterday.')

(51)   Si quelqu'un lui pose la question, Noé *affirmera* avoir envoyé la lettre <u>la veille</u>. ('...the day before.')

Similarly, *maintenant* and *en ce moment* are deictic in nature, while *alors* and *à ce moment-là* are their non-deictic equivalents, as shown in (52)–(53) below:

(52)   Ce n'est que <u>maintenant</u> que je *comprends* pleinement de quoi il s'agit.

(53)   Ce n'est qu'<u>alors</u> que j'*ai compris* pleinement de quoi il s'agissait.

Table 22.2. Deictic *vs* non-deictic time adverb(ial)s.

	Two days prior to point of departure	One day prior to point of departure	Point of departure	One day after point of departure	Two days after point of departure
Deictic	*avant-hier*	*hier*	*aujourd'hui*	*demain*	*après-demain*
Non-deictic	*l'avant-veille*	*la veille*	*ce jour-là, un jour*	*le lendemain*	*le surlendemain*

22.1.4.2 *Ici, là,* and *là-bas*

The locative adverbs *ici* and *là-bas* are inherently deictic in nature; the related adverb *là*, on the other hand, is deictic in some of its uses, but not in others. The particular location referred to by all uses of *ici* and *là-bas*, and by deictic uses of *là* is determined by taking the location of the speaker as the point of departure.

Ici designates a location that includes the speaker's location, whereas *là-bas* designates one that is distinct from the speaker's location, as seen in (54) below. As shown by (54)–(55), *là-bas* may designate a space that is either different from or identical to the hearer's location:

(54) Les chaussures, ce n'est pas ici, Monsieur ; c'est là-bas.

(55) Allô, bonjour, Noémi, Emile me dit que tu es en Indonésie en ce moment. Comment ça va, là-bas ?

Là, on the other hand, is unspecified in this respect, and may refer either to the speaker's location, as shown by (56)–(57), or to a location that is different from it, as in (58):

(56) Viens ici, à côté de moi !

(57) Viens là, à côté de moi !

(58) Ôte-toi de là, que je m'y mette !

When *là* is used about the speaker's location, it often takes on a more figurative sense of availability for interaction, as opposed to *ici*, which always refers concretely to a space, cf. (59)–(60) below:

(59) Secretary: « Oui, la présidente est là aujourd'hui. Je vous la passe. » ('Yes, the president is here/in today. I'll put you through to her.')

(60) Je suis ici, mais je ne suis pas là. (≈ 'I'm here physically, but I'm not seeing anybody.')

22.1.4.3 Expressing directional motion in French *vs* English

When describing events involving motion, English often combines a predicator that expresses the manner of motion with an adverb or a prepositional phrase expressing the direction of motion, as in (61)–(64) below:

(61) Jane *put* her hand up.

(62) Peter *carried* the bottles downstairs.

(63)   John *swam* into the cave.

(64)   The children *ran* out of the classroom.

In French, on the other hand, the typical pattern of distributing information about motion events within the clause is largely the mirror image of the English pattern illustrated above. Thus, French tends to express the direction of motion in the predicator, and to express the manner of motion by an adverbial, if indeed it is expressed at all, as seen in (65)–(68) below:

(65)   Jeanne a levé la main.

(66)   Pierre a descendu les bouteilles.

(67)   Jean est entré dans la caverne *en nageant*.

(68)   Les enfants sont sortis de la classe *en courant*.

22.2 Interjections

22.2.1 Definition

Interjections are words that may constitute an utterance all by themselves without the need for a predicator, even in non-elliptical contexts, as exemplified in (69)–(70) below.

(69)   Après la fumée de cet atelier, ouf ! ça fait du bien de marcher un peu. ('whew')
           A. Gide, *Geneviève* (Gallimard, 1936, 1372)

(70)   A: Est-il vrai que Jules est mort ?
           B: Hélas ! ('alas')

Unlike clause- or sentence-fragments such as those seen in (71)–(72), interjections cannot easily be expanded into a clause- or sentence-like structure.

(71)   A: Elodie dit qu'elle ne viendra pas ce soir.
           B: Pourquoi ? (= Pourquoi ne viendra-t-elle pas ?)

(72)   Bien que fatiguée, Valérie a continué à travailler jusqu'à minuit. (= Bien qu'elle soit fatiguée ...)

Some interjections, such as those in (69)–(70) above, only ever function as such. However, in French as in English, many interjections, such as those in (73)–(74) below, are derived from other word classes:

(73) [On seeing a friend's fancy car for the first time:] <u>Putain</u> ! ($\approx$ 'Wow!', lit. 'whore')

(74) <u>Enfin</u>, ça va pas, non ? ($\approx$ 'Jeez', lit. 'finally')

In the rest of this section, we will be concerned only with the conventional response words *oui*, *si*, and *non*.

22.2.2 The response words oui, si, and non

While the use of *non* largely corresponds to that of English *no*, French has two words corresponding to *yes*. *Oui* is used in positive responses to utterances taking the form of a non-negative sentence, as in (75) below. *Si*, on the other hand, is used in positive responses to utterances taking the form of a negated sentence, as in (76):

(75) A: Est-ce que Elodie viendra ?
      B: <u>Oui</u>.

(76) A: Elodie *ne* viendra-t-elle *pas* ?
      B: <u>Si</u>.

When the preceding utterance is not a question, *oui* thus marks agreement with a preceding positive statement, as shown in (77) below. *Non* marks either disagreement with a preceding positive statement, as in (78), or agreement with a preceding negative statement, as in (79). In the latter case, however, *oui* may also be used. Finally, *si* marks disagreement with a preceding negative statement, as shown in (80):

(77) A: Il est bon, ce vin.
      B: <u>Oui</u>. Je suis d'accord.

(78) A: Il est bon, ce vin.
      B: <u>Non</u>. Moi, je n'aime pas.

(79) A: Il *n*'est *pas* bon ce vin.
      B: <u>Non/Oui</u>. Je suis d'accord.

(80) A: Il *n*'est *pas* bon, ce vin.
      B: <u>Si</u>. Moi, j'aime bien.

Responses to the formally negative (but frozen) tag questions *n'est-ce pas* and *non* constitute an exception: here, *oui*, and not *si*, is the appropriate answer, as seen in (81):

(81)   A: Elodie viendra, *n'est-ce pas*/*non* ?
     B: <u>Oui</u>.

In contrast to English *yes* and *no*, when functioning as direct objects of a speech act verb, French *oui*, *si*, and *non* may be introduced by the subordinating conjunction *que*, as seen in (82)–(83) below:

(82)   Mary answered [Ø] *yes*.

(83)   Marie a répondu <u>que</u> *oui*.

In addition, all three items may be used in construction with a noun phrase or a non-clitic pronoun, to indicate contrast with a preceding element, as seen in (84)–(85) below. As (85) shows, either *si* or *oui* may be used in contrast to a preceding negative statement:

(84)   Aurélie a réussi son bac. Sa sœur, <u>non</u>. ('Her sister didn't.')

(85)   Aurélie *n'a pas* réussi son bac. Sa sœur, <u>si</u>/<u>oui</u>. ('Her sister did.')

22.3 Coordinating conjunctions

French has six coordinating conjunctions: *et*, *ou (bien)*, *soit*, *mais*, *car*, and *ni*.[4] The negative coordinating conjunction *ni* is treated in section 23.2.2. This section will discuss only the five non-negative conjunctions.

22.3.1 Et, ou (bien), *and* soit

Et, *ou (bien)*, and *soit* can in principle coordinate any type of constituents at any level of syntactic structure, as exemplified in (86)–(90) below.

(86)   <u>Soit</u> *tu pars*, <u>soit</u> *tu restes*. (Coordinated independent clauses)

(87)   Faut-il *que je parle* <u>ou</u> *que je me taise* ? (Coordinated subordinate clauses)

(88)   *Louis* <u>et</u> *Myriam* sont déjà partis. (Coordinated subjects)

(89)   Hara-Kiri. Journal *bête* <u>et</u> *méchant*. (Coordinated postmodifiers within a noun phrase)

---

[4] Some grammarians consider *or*, *donc*, and *puis* to be coordinating conjunctions as well. In this book, these items are considered to be adverbs.

(90)   Voulez-vous votre sandwich *avec* ou *sans* beurre ? (Coordinated heads of prepositional phrase.)

These three conjunctions may also coordinate more than two elements, cf. (91)–(93) below:

(91)   J'ai acheté des pommes et des poires et des oranges.

(92)   Veux-tu que j'achète des pommes ou des poires ou des oranges ?

(93)   Je lui ai demandé d'acheter soit des pommes, soit des poires, soit des oranges.

Soit is always repeated before each conjunct (cf. (86) and (93) above). *Ou (bien)* may be repeated in a similar way, as shown in (94) below. When *ou (bien)* is repeated before each conjunct, it tends to be interpreted as **exclusive** in meaning, i.e. as meaning that only one of the options can be chosen: thus, in (94), the preferred interpretation is that Hector should buy only one of the three kinds of fruit mentioned. When *ou (bien)* occurs only before the last conjunct, as in (95), the intended interpretation may be **inclusive**, i.e. more than one option may be chosen. Thus, in (95), Hector may buy two or all three kinds of fruit. *Soit... soit* is always interpreted exclusively.

(94)   J'ai demandé à Hector d'acheter ou (bien) des pommes, ou (bien) des poires, ou (bien) des oranges.

(95)   J'ai demandé à Hector d'acheter des pommes, des poires, ou (bien) des oranges.

Et may likewise be repeated before each conjunct, in which case it gets a 'both... and' interpretation, as in (96) below. *Et... et* cannot coordinate two predicators, however, so the English example in (97) must be translated with a single *et*, as in (98):

(96)   J'ai acheté et des pommes et des poires.

(97)   Dr Smith both listens to and asks questions of his patients.

(98)   Le Dr Smith écoute ses patients et il leur pose des questions.

Unlike repetition of *ou (bien)*, repetition of *et* is not very common, however. Instead, speakers tend to prefer the expressions *à la fois... et* or *aussi bien... que*, as in (99)–(100):

(99)   J'ai acheté à la fois des pommes et des poires.

(100)   J'ai acheté aussi bien des pommes que des poires.

If the second conjunct is negated or otherwise opposed to the first, *et* can be used with the adversative meaning otherwise signalled by *mais*. In such cases, it is best rendered in English by *but*, as shown in (101) below:

(101)   La garde meurt <u>et</u> *ne* se rend *pas*. ('The guard dies, <u>but</u> does not surrender.')

22.3.2 Mais *and* car

Due to their more specific meanings, the adversative conjunction *mais* and particularly the causal conjunction *car* are more limited than *et, ou (bien)*, and *soit* in terms of the elements they can conjoin. Thus, for instance, coordinating subjects by means of *car* is impossible, as shown in (102) below, and coordination with *mais* works only if the negative adverb *pas* is inserted before the second conjunct, as in (103). Notice that the singular verb agreement in (103), as opposed to the plural agreement in (88) above, suggests that *mais* always coordinates at the clause(-fragment) level. In addition, neither *mais* nor *car* can coordinate more than two elements.

(102)   *Louis, <u>car</u> Myriam, est déjà parti.

(103)   Louis – <u>mais</u> *pas* Myriam – est déjà parti.

Mais conveys emphatic meaning if coordinating two identical elements, as in (104) below. When introducing a response to a preceding utterance by a different speaker (typically, but not exclusively, a question), as in (105), it marks that response as more or less self-evident according to the speaker:

(104)   Il est *bête*, <u>mais</u> *bête*, ce type ! ('This guy is SO stupid!')

(105)   A: Tu m'en veux ? (A: 'Are you angry with me?')
            B: <u>Mais</u> non ! (B: 'Of course not.')

Although *car* seems superficially similar to the subordinating conjunction *parce que*, only clauses introduced by the latter can ever be the answer to a question, as shown by the contrast in (106)–(107) below:

(106)   A: Pourquoi Antoine est-il parti ?
            B: <u>Parce qu</u>'il était fatigué.

(107)   A: Pourquoi Antoine est-il parti ?
            B: *<u>Car</u> il était fatigué.

Whereas *parce que*-clauses give the reason why the situation described in the main clause obtains, *car*-clauses give the reason why the speaker chose to say what s/he said in the first conjunct, cf. (108)–(109):

(108)   Antoine est-il parti <u>parce qu</u>'il était fatigué ? (→ I ask if the reason Antoine left was that he was tired.)

(109)   Antoine est-il parti ? <u>Car</u> il était fatigué. (→ The reason I ask if Antoine left is that I know he was tired.)

PART V

The Grammar of French Clauses and Sentences

23

Negation and restriction

Learning objectives

- To understand the difference between clause negation and constituent negation.
- To understand the difference between general negation and n-word negation.
- To understand the difference between negative and non-negative uses of n-words.
- To understand the difference between a negative *ne* and an expletive *ne*, and to be aware of the different syntactic contexts in which each of the two may be used.
- To understand the relation between negation and restriction in French.

23.1 Introduction

Like many languages, including English, French can express different forms of negation. Thus, an initial distinction can be made between clause negation and constituent negation.

The Structure of Modern Standard French. First edition. Maj-Britt Mosegaard Hansen.
© Maj-Britt Mosegaard Hansen 2016. First Published 2016 by Oxford University Press

As these terms suggest, clause negation denies that the situation expressed by the clause as a whole obtains, as in (1) below. Thus, if (1) is true and is uttered without emphatic stress on any of its constituents, the non-negated version of the sentence (i.e. the version seen in (2)) can simply be assumed to be false.[1]

(1)   Claude n'a pas acheté de pommes. (Compatible with Claude buying nothing of any kind.)

(2)   Claude a acheté des pommes.

Constituent negation, on the other hand, denies only a specific aspect of a situation, such that the meaning of the sentence as a whole remains positive. The aspect of the situation that is denied may be replaced by something else, as in (3) below, where the speaker is not denying that a buying event took place, but only that it involved apples. Instead she specifies that the items actually purchased were pears:

(3)   Claude a acheté non pas des pommes, mais des poires. (→ Claude did actually buy some kind of fruit.)

As shown by (4) below, which also contains an instance of constituent negation, the negated element is not necessarily replaced by an alternative one. (4) is similar to (3), however, in as much as it does not deny that a man called, but only specifies that he was not a very pleasant man:

(4)   Un homme pas très sympathique vient de téléphoner. (→ A man called.)

French has different ways of expressing both clause negation and constituent negation, depending on the syntactic context and on where the speaker wishes to focus attention. Clause negation will be treated in the following section, and constituent negation in section 23.3.

In addition to its regular use in negated clauses, the preverbal negative marker *ne* is occasionally used with non-negative meaning, particularly in formal registers. This phenomenon is known as 'expletive' negation, and will be discussed in section 23.4.

Finally, the expression of restriction, i.e. the meaning expressed by the English word *only*, is closely related to clause negation in French. Restriction is discussed in section 23.5 below.

---

[1] For the role of prosody, see section 23.3 below.

23.2 Clause negation

Clause negation in standard French has two parts, one of which is the **preverbal clitic *ne*.**[2] In finite clauses, *ne* must occur immediately before the finite verb, from which it can only be separated by other clitics, i.e. personal pronouns in the accusative or dative case, and the pronominal adverbs *en* and *y*, cf. (5) below:

(5)   Je <u>ne</u> le lui *ai* pas dit.

In a present participle/*gérondif* clause, *ne* occurs immediately before the *–ant* form, from which it can only be separated by other clitics, as shown in (6):

(6)   Il est parti en <u>n'</u>y *répondant* pas.

In infinitival clauses, *ne* likewise occurs before the infinitive, but may be separated from it by the second negator, as well as by other clitics, as in (7) below (for further details, see section 23.2.1.1 below):

(7)   <u>Ne</u> pas lui en *parler* serait une erreur.

In colloquial speech, *ne* is frequently omitted, particularly if the subject is a personal pronoun rather than a noun phrase, cf. (8):

(8)   J'[Ø]sais pas, moi.

The position of the second negator depends partly on the specific item, and partly on its grammatical function. The following section will provide details.

23.2.1 The second negator

There are two kinds of second clause negators in French: general negators (see section 23.2.1.1) and so-called 'n-words' (see section 23.2.1.2).

23.2.1.1 General negation

The main general negator is *pas*, whose use in clause negation is illustrated in (1) and (5)–(8) above. In addition, the items *guère*, *point*, *nullement*, and *aucunement* may be used, particularly in more formal registers.

---

[2] For the notion of clitics, see section 14.2.

As clause negators, *pas*, *point*, *nullement*, and *aucunement* negate the situation described by the clause in its entirety. *Nullement* and *aucunement*, and to a lesser extent *point*, are perceived as more emphatic negators than *pas*, along the lines of English *not at all* or *in no way*.[3]

Guère strictly speaking has an intermediate status between general negator and n-word, but almost always functions as a general negator in Modern French. Corresponding to English *hardly*, it in fact does not fully negate the clause; as such, *guère* is compatible with the non-negated situation being true to a very limited extent, as in (9):

(9)   [Marie has eaten only two spoonfuls of broth.] Marie n'a guère mangé.

All the general negators, except *pas*, may occur on their own in clause fragments such as (10):

(10)   A: Pierre a-t-il fait son devoir ?
  B: Nullement/Aucunement/Point/Guère/*Pas.[4]

General negators cannot normally be combined, either with one another or with any of the n-words. There are two exceptions to this rule: one is combinations of *guère* with either *plus* or *rien*, as in (11):

(11)   C'est un vieux médecin qui n'exerce plus guère.[5] ('...who hardly practices anymore.')

The other exception is the frozen combination of *pas + rien*, as in (12):

(12)   Ce n'est pas rien. ('It's (quite) something.' Lit.: 'It's not nothing.')

Note that in the combination *pas + plus*, exemplified in (13)–(14) below, *plus* never has the temporal meaning ('no more/longer') found in clauses negated by *ne...plus*. Instead, it is always an adverb of quantity or degree

---

[3] The meaning of *not at all* is, however, more commonly rendered in contemporary French by *ne...pas du tout*.

[4] *Pas* may occur in clause fragments if followed by *du tout*, as in (i) below. The latter can occur on its own with the same meaning, as shown in (ii):

(i)   A: Pierre a-t-il fait som devoir ?
  B: Pas *du tout*. ('Not at all.')

(ii)   A: Pierre a-t-il fait son devoir ?
  B: Du tout. ('Not at all.')

[5] The order *plus guère* is more common, but *guère plus* is also possible.

('not . . . more'). Thus, as an adverb of quantity, *plus* is often pronounced with a final /s/ even when the following word starts with a consonant. This is never the case with the negative temporal *plus*, which shows that, while they have the same historical source, the two are separate words in Modern French:

(13)   Je n'ai pas plus d'argent que toi. ('I don't have more money than you.')

(14)   Luc n'est pas plus beau qu'Alexis. ('Luc is not more handsome than Alexis.')

The position of general negators

When used in **finite clauses**, general negators are normally placed after the finite verb, but before the non-finite main verb if the clause is in a compound tense, as in (1), (5), (8), (9), (10), and (11) above.

Preposing of *pas* is possible only in connection with a pronoun or a noun phrase (typically in subject position), as in (15):[6]

(15)   Pas *un seul voyageur* n'a survécu au naufrage.

In **present participle** and *gérondif*-**clauses**, the general negators are placed after the *–ant* form, as shown in (6) above. If the head of a present participle phrase is a compound form, the general negator goes before the main verb, as seen in (16):

(16)   N'*ayant* pas encore *obtenu* une augmentation appréciable, les cheminots continuent à faire grève.

In **infinitival clauses** on the other hand, the norm in Modern French is for the two parts of a general negation to occur together before the infinitive, as in (17):

(17)   Tu m'avais pourtant promis de ne pas *parler* sexualité avec le curé !

The verbs *avoir* and *être* constitute an exception, however, particularly when they function as auxiliaries inside a compound infinitive. With these two verbs, the second part of a general clause negation may (but need not) be placed after the infinitive, and before the past participle in a compound form, as shown in (18)–(19):

(18)   L'accusé a soutenu ne pas *être sorti* de la journée.

---

[6] In very formal registers, *point* can be preposed on its own, as in (i) below:

(i)   Point n'est besoin de nous le rappeler.

(19) L'accusé a soutenu n'*être* pas *sorti* de la journée.

Constructions with a **modal verb** followed by an infinitive constitute a special case. Here *ne...pas* may go either around the modal verb, or together between the modal verb and the infinitive. These two different positions correlate with a difference in meaning, which may be more or less perceptible depending on the specific modal verb in question.

If *ne...pas* embraces the modal verb, it is specifically that verb which is negated. If the two parts of the negation are placed together between the modal and the infinitive, the negation targets the infinitive.

The difference in interpretation is most obvious in the case of the modals *pouvoir*, *savoir*, and *oser* as exemplified in (20)–(21):

(20) Charles ne *peut* pas assister à la réunion. (= 'Charles is unable/not allowed to...')

(21) Charles *peut* ne pas assister à la réunion. (= 'Charles is allowed not to.../It's possible that Charles won't...')

With the modals *devoir* and, in particular, *falloir*, the meaning difference is often minimal, as in (22)–(23) below. In some cases, however, the position of the negation may be exploited to favour an interpretation involving either probability or obligation, as in (24)–(25):

(22) Elle ne *devrait* pas y aller. (≈ 'It wouldn't be the best thing for her to go.')

(23) Elle *devrait* ne pas y aller. (≈ 'It'd be the best thing for her not to go.')

(24) Cette situation ne *doit* pas être facile pour lui. (Favoured interpretation: 'This situation is probably not easy for him.')

(25) Ce test *doit* ne pas être trop facile pour lui. (Favoured interpretation: 'You must not allow this test to be too easy for him.')

Negative ne

French did not always need a second postverbal negator to express general negation. In Medieval French, the preverbal *ne* alone could convey the same meaning as contemporary French *ne...pas*. Vestiges of this can still be found in formal registers, where certain syntactic contexts allow *ne* to express negation on its own. Apart from some frozen expressions, it is always possible, in such cases, to insert a postverbal *pas* without changing the meaning of the clause or making it grammatically unacceptable.

While the non-native speaker thus in principle does not need to use the negative *ne*, it is, however, essential for comprehension to be aware of the specific syntactic contexts in which it appears, in order to avoid confusing it with the so-called expletive *ne* (discussed in section 23.4 below). The expletive *ne* crucially does not negate its host clause, and it is found in a different set of syntactic contexts.

Negative *ne* is always used, even in less formal registers, in a range of (often archaic-sounding) **frozen expressions** such as those in (26)–(28) below, where *pas* cannot be felicitously inserted. These expression types are probably best learned on a case-by-case basis.

(26)   N'empêche que ça m'a tout de même bien embêté(e). ('Nonetheless that really annoyed me.')

(27)   Janine ne disait mot. ('Janine didn't say a word.')

(28)   Ce type dit n'importe quoi. ('This guy is talking nonsense.')

The principal **productive** (i.e. non-frozen) **environments** in which the negative *ne* can be used are the following:

(i) With the verbs *pouvoir*, *oser*, *cesser*, and *savoir* followed by an infinitival phrase, as in (29):

(29)   Je ne *saurais* vous le dire. ('I wouldn't be able to say.')

(ii) Relative clauses when the main clause is itself negated or interrogative, as in (30)–(31):

(30)   Il *n* 'y a *personne* qui ne le sache. ('There's no-one who doesn't know.' → Everyone knows.)

(31)   Que dire qui *n*'ait déjà été dit ?

(iii) Conditional clauses introduced by *si*, particularly if the main clause is also negated, as in (32):

(32)   Je *ne* le croirais *pas*, *si* je ne l'avais vu de mes propres yeux. ('I wouldn't believe it if I hadn't seen it with my own eyes.')

(iv) Exclamations and rhetorical questions, particularly if introduced by *que*, as in (33):

(33)   *Que* ne m'avez-vous dit cela avant ? ('Why did you not tell me before ?')

(v) After temporal expressions of the type *il y a longtemps que*, when the verb is in a compound tense, as in (34):

(34)   *Voilà des années qu'on* ne *s'est vu(e)(s).* ('We haven't seen each other in years.')

23.2.1.2 N-word negation

N-word, or quantifier, negation in French uses *ne* in combination with one or more of the **indefinites** *jamais*, *plus* (temporal[-aspectual] adverbs), *nulle part* (a locative adverb), *personne*, *rien* (indefinite pronouns),[7] *aucun*, or *nul* (indefinite pronouns/determiners). Very rarely in Modern French, *guère* can also function as an n-word with the meaning 'almost nothing'/'hardly anything', i.e. a downtoned version of *rien*, as in (35) below. Because of its marginal status, this use of *guère* will not be discussed further.

(35)   Il n'a guère été fait pour les sauver. ('Almost nothing/Hardly anything was done to save them.')

This form of negation involves the quantification of a central element of the described situation as zero, meaning that the situation as a whole does not obtain. N-word negation is therefore a form of clause negation, rather than constituent negation. Thus, for instance, in (36) below, the use of *personne* as the dative object means that the number, or quantity, of people that Elisabeth spoke to at Anne's party was zero. That being so, it can normally be inferred that she didn't speak at all:

(36)   Elisabeth n'a parlé à personne à la soirée d'Anne. ('Elisabeth didn't speak to anyone/spoke to no-one at Anne's party.')

Similarly, in (37), the number of times Franck speaks during meetings is quantified as zero by the use of *jamais*, such that we can again infer that he does not speak at all:

(37)   Franck ne parle jamais dans les réunions. ('Franck never speaks/doesn't ever speak in meetings.')

---

[7] Note that although the noun *(une) personne* is feminine, as is the archaic noun *(une) rien* ('a trifle'), the n-words *rien* and *personne* are grammatically masculine, as shown by past participle agreement:

(i)   Une personne seulement est venue.
(ii)   Personne n'est venu.

Whereas the general negators always have an adverbial function, the n-words *personne* and *rien* are normally valency elements (subject, direct object, etc.). The same may be true of *aucun* and *nul*, although the latter more frequently function as determiners inside noun phrases.

Notice that in both (36)–(37) above the n-words have two different possible translations in English. This is because the systems of quantifier negation in French and English are fundamentally different. As shown in Table 23.1, English has a very clear three-part system of indefinite quantifiers comprising negative indefinites, so-called negative polarity items, and polarity-neutral items. French, on the other hand, essentially has a two-part system, the uses of n-words being intermediate between those of negative indefinites and negative polarity items.

The French n-words resemble English negative indefinites, but differ from English negative polarity items in four ways:

(a) Like the general negator *pas*, they can express negation in the absence of preverbal *ne* in less formal registers, cf. (38) below:

Table 23.1. Indefinite quantifiers in English and French.

English

Negative indefinites	Negative polarity items	Polarity-neutral items
Nobody/no-one	*Anybody/Anyone*	*Somebody/Someone*
Nothing	*Anything*	*Something*
Nowhere	*Anywhere*	*Somewhere*
Never	*Ever*	*Always*
No more/No longer	*Anymore/Any longer*	*Still*
None/no	*Any*	*Some*

French

N-words	Polarity-neutral items
Personne	*Quelqu'un*
Rien	*Quelque chose*
Nulle part	*Quelque part*
Jamais	*Toujours*
Plus	*Encore/Toujours*
Aucun/Nul	*Quelque*

(38)   Pierre (n')a rien fait.
'Pierre did nothing.'/*'Pierre did anything.'

(b) When used in verbless clause/sentence fragments, where *ne* cannot occur, they always express negation, cf. (39):

(39)   A: Qu'est-ce qui s'est passé ? ('What happened?')
B: (*Ne) Rien. ('Nothing.'/*'Anything.')

(c) In standard French, they cannot combine with the general negator *pas* without giving rise to a doubly negative interpretation, i.e. one where the two negators mutually cancel one another out, resulting in an overall positive interpretation. This is illustrated in (40):

(40)   Je n'ai *pas* vu personne.
'I didn't see nobody.' → I saw somebody. ≠ 'I didn't see anybody.'

(d) They may appear at the very beginning of a clause or sentence (preceding the *ne*, if there is one), cf. (41):

(41)   Jamais Max n'aurait fait une telle chose.
'Never would Max have done such a thing.'/*'Ever would Max not have done such a thing.'

Preposing of an n-word as in (41) is possible for purposes of emphasis in the case of *jamais* and *nulle part*. *Rien, personne, aucun*, and *nul* are normally only preposed when functioning as (part of) the subject of the clause, as in (42) below.

(42)   Rien ne l'intéresse.

On the other hand, the French n-words resemble English negative polarity items, and differ from English negative indefinites in two ways:

(i) Two or more n-words can be combined within one and the same clause. In that case, they will normally express only a single negation, cf. (43) below:

(43)   Louise n'a rien dit à personne.
'Louise didn't say anything to anybody.'/*'Louise didn't say nothing to nobody.'/≠ 'Louise said nothing to nobody.' → Louise said something to everybody.

(ii) In the absence of a preverbal *ne*, the n-words may have non-negative meaning in a range of so-called weak negative polarity contexts (listed Table 23.2 below), cf. (44):

(44)   Demande-lui si ce train se remettra <u>jamais</u> en marche.
'Ask him if this train will ever start moving again.'

As shown in (45), it is in principle possible to combine up to five n-words in a single negative clause, but combinations of more than three are rare:

(45)   <u>Personne</u> ne fait <u>plus</u> <u>jamais</u> <u>rien</u> pour <u>personne</u>.
'Nobody ever does anything for anyone anymore.'

N-words in non-negative contexts

The different n-words occur in weak negative polarity contexts, where they have non-negative meaning, to varying extents. As shown in Table 23.2, *jamais* can occur in all such contexts, whereas *plus* essentially occurs in only one, the remaining n-words being in-between. The range of relevant non-negative contexts is exemplified in (44) above and (46)–(54) below.

(46)   Corinne a démissionné *sans que* <u>personne</u> s'y oppose. ('...without anyone objecting.')

Table 23.2. Non-negative uses of the French n-words.

N-word Weak negative-polarity context	*jamais*	*rien/aucun/ personne*	*nulle part*	*nul*	*plus*
After *sans(que)*, cf. (46)	√	√	√	√	√
In comparisons, cf. (47)	√	√	√	√	×
After *trop pour*, cf. (49)	√	√	√	×	(√)
After a superlative, cf. (48)	√	×	×	×	×
In a subordinate clause or infinitival clause governed by a negated main clause, cf. (50)	√	√	√	×	×
In a subordinate clause or infinitival clause governed by an implicitly negative expression in the main clause, cf. (51)	√	√	×	×	(√)
After *avant que/de*, cf. (52)	√	√	×	(√)	×
After *peu*, cf. (53)	√	×	×	×	×
In direct (rhetorical) questions, cf. (55)	√	(√)	×	×	×
In conditional clauses, cf. (54)	√	×	×	×	×
In indirect interrogative clauses, cf. (44)	√	×	×	×	×

Note: Numbers in parentheses refer to examples in the text.
Source: Adapted from Cl. Muller, *La négation en français* (Droz, 1991), 265.

(47)   Il est *plus compréhensif* qu'<u>aucun</u> autre médecin. ('... than any other doctor.')

(48)   Adrien est *trop* calculateur *pour* inspirer <u>aucune</u> confiance. ('... to inspire any confidence.')

(49)   Cette ville est *la plus belle* que j'aie <u>jamais</u> vue. ('... that I've ever seen.')

(50)   Je *ne* pense *pas* [que <u>rien</u> ait été fait]. ('... that anything has been done.')

(51)   Pascal *refuse* [de parler à <u>personne</u>]. ('... to speak to anyone.')

(52)   Il faut vérifier ça *avant* d'en parler à <u>personne</u>. ('... before telling anyone about it.')

(53)   Il y a *peu* de chances qu'on le revoie <u>jamais</u>. ('... that we'll ever see him again.')

(54)   A-t-on <u>jamais</u> vu pareille obstination ? ('Did you ever see such stubbornness?')

(55)   *Si* <u>jamais</u> vous gagniez un million d'euros, qu'est-ce que vous en feriez ? ('If ever you were to win a million euros...')

In contemporary French, the frequency with which the n-words are found in these types of context appears to be decreasing in favour of alternative ways of expressing the same thing (e.g. (56)–(58) below). Only *jamais* remains regularly used non-negatively.

(56)   Corinne a démissionné sans que <u>quiconque</u> s'y oppose.

(57)   Il est plus compréhensif que <u>n'importe quel</u> autre médecin.

(58)   Adrien est trop calculateur pour inspirer <u>la moindre</u> confiance.

23.2.1.3 The relative positions of second clause negators

Table 23.3 below provides a schema of the relative positions of second clause negators in French.

As already explained in section 23.2.1.1 above, the general negators normally always go immediately after the finite verb and before any non-finite forms. Combinations of *plus* and *guère* are an exception to this rule, as the two elements can occur in either order, the more common one being to have *guère* in second position, as in (11) above.

Table 23.3. The position of the French general negators and n-words.

ne FiniteVerb	*pas*	*plus*	*jamais*	*rien*	PastParticiple/ Infinitive	*personne*	*nulle part*
	point	*jamais*	*plus*			*aucun*	
	guère		*guère*			*nul*	

Depending on the specific term, n-words go either before or after any non-finite verb form present in the clause. Moreover, n-words combine in a specific order, except for combinations of *plus* and *jamais*, which can occur indifferently in either order.

Finally, as explained in section 23.2.1.2 above, n-words can also occur in preverbal position in certain circumstances. In the case of *plus*, this is only possible in combination with another n-word, however, as exemplified in (59):

(59)   Plus *personne* ne s'intéresse à ce genre de chose.

23.2.2 *The negative coordinating conjunction* ni

When coordinating constituents in negated clauses, French makes use of the negative conjunction *ni*.

Usually, *ni* occurs before each of the coordinated constituents, along with a preverbal *ne*, as in (60) and (61) below. Note that when *ni...ni...* coordinates two subjects, as in (60), plural verb agreement is the norm. When *ni...ni...* coordinates two direct objects, these very frequently occur without determiners, as in (61):[8]

(60)   Ni Georges ni Suzanne *ne* sont venus.

(61)   Francis *n'*a ni femme ni enfants.

If the first (or both) of two coordinated subjects is an n-word, *ni* is used only once, before the second conjunct, as in (62):

(62)   *Rien* ni *personne* ne me fera changer d'avis.

Following the negative preposition *sans*, a second complement is often coordinated with a previous one by *ni*, as in (63):

(63)   Luc a fait un discours *sans* queue ni tête.

In some cases, speakers/writers may wish to add a coordinated constituent as an afterthought. In that case, *ne...pas* is used, followed by *ni* + the second conjunct, as in (64) below:[9]

---

[8]   See also section 12.4.1.4.

[9]   Notice that in (64), as opposed to (61) above, both of the coordinated direct objects take a reduced partitive article.

(64)   Francis *n'*a *pas* de femme, n̲i̲ d'enfants (d'ailleurs).

Two negated predicators can be coordinated by *ni* if they are both in a simple tense form and have similar complements. In that case, *ne . . . ni ne . . .* is used, without *pas*, as in (65) below:

(65)   Je n̲e̲ l'aime n̲i̲ n̲e̲ le respecte.

If one or both predicators are in a compound tense and/or have different types of complement, they are negated by *ne . . . pas*/n-word and coordinated by *et*, as in (66):

(66)   Je *n'*ai *jamais* aimé cet homme et *ne* souhaite *pas* lui adresser la parole.

Finally, if two compound tense forms using the same auxiliary and sharing the same complement are coordinated, *ne . . . ni . . . ni* is used, with *ni . . . ni* preceding the two main verbs, as in (67):

(67)   Je *ne* l'ai n̲i̲ aimé n̲i̲ respecté.

In Modern French, independent clauses are not normally coordinated by *ni*, but rather by *et*, as in (68) below. Subordinate clauses, on the other hand, which are constituents of their main clause, may be coordinated by a single *ni* if the main clause is negated, as in (69):

(68)   Anne *n'*aime *pas* Patrick, e̲t̲ Félicie *ne* veux même *pas* lui adresser la parole.

(69)   Je n̲e̲ pense p̲a̲s̲ qu'Anne aime Patrick, n̲i̲ même qu'elle le respecte.

Like the n-words, and in the same types of environment, *ni* may sometimes be used with non-negative meaning, as shown in (70), where the conjunction occurs in a subordinate clause governed by a negated main clause (cf. (50) above):

(70)   Je *ne* peux *pas* dire que Patrick soit aimé n̲i̲ même respecté. ('I cannot say that Patrick is liked or even respected.')

23.3 Constituent negation

It is possible in French to express constituent negation using the general negator *(ne) . . . pas*; however, the expressions *non, pas* (without *ne*) and *non pas* are specialized for constituent negation.

In the spoken language, *(ne)...pas* can be used in combination with **prosodic emphasis** on the negated constituent, as in (71)–(73):

(71)   Olivier n̠'a pa̠s embrassé *SYLVIE* (, mais Zoé).

(72)   *OLIVIER* n̠'a pa̠s embrassé Sylvie (, mais Grégoire l'a fait).

(73)   Olivier n̠'a pa̠s *EMBRASSÉ* Sylvie (; il lui a donné la main).

Because stress in French is not as freely mobile as it is in English, there is, however, a strong tendency for so-called **(pseudo-)cleft sentences** (see section 26.3) to be used instead when *ne...pas* expresses constituent negation, as in (74)–(76):

(74)   Ce n̠'est pa̠s Sylvie (mais Zoé) qu'Olivier a embrassée.

(75)   Ce n̠'est pa̠s Olivier (mais Grégoire) qui a embrassé Sylvie.

(76)   Ce qu'a fait Olivier, ce n̠'est pa̠s d'embrasser Sylvie (mais de lui donner la main).

If the point of the utterance is to replace the negated constituent with another one, the specialized constutuent-negation construction *non (pas)..., mais* can be used, as in (77)–(79) below. This construction is explicitly **corrective** in meaning, and is used when the speaker has reason to believe that the hearer is making an erroneous assumption.

When the negated constituent is an adjective or a verb, as in (79), the full form *non pas* is preferred over *non* alone:

(77)   Olivier a embrassé non (pas) Sylvie, mais Zoé.

(78)   Sylvie a été embrassée non (pas) par Olivier, mais par Grégoire.

(79)   Olivier a non pas embrassé, mais donné la main à, Sylvie.

Correction by way of constituent negation can also be expressed mentioning the correct option first, followed by the incorrect one, as in (80)–(82):

(80)   Olivier a embrassé Zoé, (et) non (pas) Sylvie.

(81)   Sylvie a été embrassée par Grégoire, (et) non (pas) par Olivier.

(82)   Olivier a donné la main à, (et) non pas embrassé, Sylvie.

When constituent negation is used for **non-corrective** purposes, as in (83)–(85) below, the choice between *pas* and *non* depends on register and the type of constituent being negated. *Non* is used mainly in more formal registers, *pas* in less formal ones (cf. (83)). In addition, *pas* is used quite regularly across registers with relatively short, common adjectives like that in (84) below, and with adjectival phrases containing a premodifier, as in (85):

(83)   Jean habite <u>non/pas</u> loin d'ici.

(84)   J'ai dû me contenter d'un café <u>pas</u> *chaud*.

(85)   Un homme <u>pas</u> *très sympathique* vient de téléphoner.

23.4 Expletive *ne*

We saw in section 23.2.1.1 above that formal registers allow preverbal *ne* to negate a clause on its own (i.e. without being accompanied by *pas*) in certain syntactic contexts. Potentially confusingly for the non-native speaker, the same registers also allow occurrences of a **lone preverbal *ne*** to occur in a clause without carrying negative meaning. This use of *ne* is known as expletive negation.[10]

The contexts in which expletive *ne* occurs are distinct from those in which we find the negative *ne*, however, reducing the risk of actual confusion between the two radically different meanings.

The following contexts can accommodate an expletive *ne*:

(i) Comparative clauses following a positive comparative, as in (86) below:

(86)   Jacques est beaucoup *plus fort* que je <u>ne</u> le croyais. ('...than I thought.')

(ii) Complement clauses governed by a non-negated verb of fear, as in (87):

(87)   Je *crains* que Paul <u>ne</u> soit trop bête pour pouvoir nous être utile. ('I fear that he is too stupid...')

(iii) Complement clauses governed by a non-negated verb of prevention, avoidance, etc. (e.g. *empêcher*, *éviter*, etc.), as in (88):

(88)   Elle a *empêché* qu'il <u>ne</u> fasse une bêtise. ('She prevented him from making a mistake.')

(iv) Complement clauses governed by a negated *douter* or *nier*, as in (89):

---

[10] The term 'expletive' in this context means 'filler'. In other words, the negative marker is used redundantly in such cases.

(89) Il *ne nie pas* que le problème <u>ne</u> soit difficile à résoudre. ('... that the problem is difficult to solve.')

(v) Conditional clauses introduced by the conjunction *à moins que*, as in (90) :

(90) Je viendrai, *à moins que* vous <u>ne</u> me le déconseilliez. ('... unless you advise me against it.')

(vi) Temporal clauses introduced by the conjunction *avant que*, as in (91):

(91) Dépêche-toi de rentrer *avant qu*'il <u>ne</u> pleuve ! ('... before it starts raining.')

(vii) Modal clauses introduced by the conjunction *sans que*, as in (91) below. This is relatively rare, and is considered substandard by some.

(92) Muriel est partie *sans qu*'Alain <u>ne</u> s'en soit rendu compte. ('... without Alain noticing.')

The use of expletive *ne* is arguably not completely arbitrary in these contexts, which can all be said to implicitly involve a form of negation. Thus, (86), for instance, implies that the speaker thought Jacques was not as strong as he actually is; (87) implies that the speaker would have wished that Paul was not too stupid to be useful; (88) implies that the subject of the main clause ('she') made sure that the subject of the complement clause ('he') did not make a mistake, and so on.

In none of these contexts is *ne* obligatory, however; it can always be left out without affecting either the meaning or the grammaticality of the clause. Conversely, if *pas* is inserted after the verb in the examples above, the clause will become ungrammatical (as in (93) below) or its meaning will change radically, from non-negative to negative, as in (94):

(93) *Jacques est beaucoup plus fort que je <u>ne</u> le croyais <u>pas</u>.

(94) Elle a empêché qu'il <u>ne</u> fasse <u>pas</u> une bêtise. ('She prevented him from not making a mistake.' → She made sure he did make a mistake.)

23.5 Restriction

Restriction, i.e. the kind of meaning that is expressed by the adverb *only* in English, can be expressed in different ways in French, in large part depending on the syntactic position of the constituent that is the object (or focus) of the restriction.

If the focus of restriction follows the predicator of the clause, restriction is preferentially expressed using so-called 'exceptive' negation, i.e. the expression *ne . . . que* (lit.: 'not . . . except') as in (95), where the adverbial *l'après-midi* is the focus of restriction:

(95)   Caroline ne travaille que *l'après-midi*. ('Caroline works only in the afternoon.' ≈ Caroline doesn't work, except in the afternoon.)

When used in exceptive negation, *ne* is placed in the standard preverbal position used also for clausal and expletive negation. The second element *que*, on the other hand, is mobile and is always placed immediately before the constituent that is the focus of restriction, as shown by the contrast between (96) and (97):

(96)   Pierre n'a dit que *cela* à Céline. ('Pierre told Céline only that.' → He didn't tell her anything else.)

(97)   Pierre n'a dit cela qu'*à Céline*. ('Pierre told that only to Céline.' → He didn't tell anyone else.)

However, *que* can never occur before the verb, and is thus incapable of restricting constituents that precede the predicator, or the finite verb itself. Thus, if the intended focus of restriction is the predicator +/– its complements (if any), as in the English examples in (98) and (100) below, then a construction with the pro-verb *faire*, *ne faire que* + infinitive, may be used, as shown in (99) and (101):

(98)   John only *looked at Mary*. (→ He didn't do anything else.)

(99)   Jean n'a fait que *regarder Marie*.

(100)   A: Did John speak to Mary?
B: No, he only *looked* at her.

(101)   A: Jean a-t-il parlé à Marie ?
B: Non, il n'a fait que la *regarder*.

If the intended focus of restriction is a constituent preceding the verb (typically the subject), as in the English example in (102) below, then *ne . . . que* can only be used in clefts or presentative constructions (see sections 26.3–4) such as (103)–(104).

(102)   Only *Caroline* works in the afternoon.

(103) Ce n'est que *Caroline* qui travaille l'après-midi.

(104) Il n'y a que *Caroline* qui travaille l'après-midi.

Otherwise, the indefinite pronoun *seul* or, more rarely, the adverb *seulement* must be used, as in (105)–(106) below. *Seulement* is used mainly with constituents containing numerals, like that in (106):

(105) Seule *Caroline* travaille l'après-midi.

(106) Seulement *deux assistants* travaillent l'après-midi.

Because *ne... que* is not a clause negator on a par with the general negators and the n-words, it can be used in combination with any of those clause negators, as shown in (107)–(108):

(107) Je n'ai pas que ça à faire, vous savez. ('I don't have only that to do you know.' → I have other things to do as well.)

(108) Je n'ai plus personne que lui. ('I no longer have anyone but him left.')

24

Word order

Learning objectives

- To understand the notion of clause topology.
- To understand the difference between complex, simple, and stylistic inversion.
- To understand the grammatical rules governing the choice of inversion type in interrogative and non-interrogative independent clauses and in subordinate clauses.
- To understand the notion of focalizable *vs* non-focalizable adverbial.

24.1 Introduction

Standard French has relatively fixed word order, the basic order of major clause constituents being Subject—Predicator—Complement.

Changing the basic order of subject and predicator is known as **inversion**. Because word order normally serves as a clue to the grammatical role of

The Structure of Modern Standard French. First edition. Maj-Britt Mosegaard Hansen.
© Maj-Britt Mosegaard Hansen 2016. First Published 2016 by Oxford University Press

different constituents in a French clause, inversion cannot be freely used, but is constrained to occur in certain very specific syntactic contexts. Inversion is treated in sections 24.3–24.6 below.

In general, adverbials have greater freedom of position, but are nevertheless constrained to a greater or lesser degree by their specific function. The position of adverbials is treated in section 24.7.

24.2 Topology

Topology concerns the study of spaces. In an abstract sense, French clauses can be seen as consisting of three different spaces, or 'fields', with different properties, namely a pre-field, a verbal field, and a post-field.

As the names suggest, the **verbal field** is the **central** space, which is always present in a French clause. The verbal field contains the predicator, and may in addition contain clitic pronouns[1] (i.e. unstressed personal and reflexive pronouns, the neutral pronouns *il* and *ce*, and pronominal adverbs), the preverbal clitic negative marker *ne*, and certain adverbials.

As such, the **pre-field** is in principle **optional**. If present, it precedes the verbal field and may contain conjunctions, non-pronominal valency elements (particularly noun phrase subjects), non-clitic pronouns, and certain types of adverbial.

The **post-field** is similarly **optional** in principle. If present, it follows the verbal field and may contain non-pronominal valency elements, non-clitic pronouns, and certain types of adverbial.

The relevant types of constituent are exemplified in Table 24.1. All things being equal, clauses with a balanced distribution of constituents in the pre- and post-fields, or with comparatively more and/or lengthier constituents in the post-field, are preferred in French. **'Top-heavy' clauses**, i.e. clauses with more and/or lengthier constituents in the pre-field than in the post-field, are thus normally avoided, particularly if the verbal field contains only comparatively light elements, such as simple tense forms and no or very short adverbials.

---

[1] For the notion of clitics, see section 14.2.

Table 24.1. The topology of French clauses.

Pre-field	Verbal field	Post-field
Les services secrets	viennent de démanteler	un important réseau de terrorisme.
Le député PS	a été chaleureusement accueilli	à l'Assemblée.
Lœ autorités	avaient gardé	une attitude prudente.
	Servez-vous !	
	Tu as vu	celui-là ?
À son frère, Aude	a donné	le dernier roman de Houellebecq.
Mais	je l'ai fait	hier.
Lequel	préfères-tu ?	
À la fin	elle a compris	le problème.

24.3 Types of inversion in French

Unlike English, which only has one, French has three different types of inversion. The different types, known as complex inversion, simple inversion, and stylistic inversion, respectively, are used in different types of context, although the uses of the first two overlap in certain cases. Sections 24.3.1–24.3.3 set out the formal differences between the three inversion types. Their uses are dealt with in sections 24.4–24.6.

24.3.1 Complex inversion

In complex inversion, a **clitic subject pronoun** must be placed in the verbal field immediately after the finite verb. If the subject is in the third person, a **full noun phrase** or **non-clitic pronoun** sharing the same referent as the pronoun may additionally be inserted in the **pre-field**. Thus, in sentences like (1) below, the subject is in effect expressed twice, which is why this type of inversion is termed 'complex':

(1)   Sandrine_{Subj/NP} est-elle_{Subj/PersPron} arrivée ?

However, no full noun phrase subject need be present in complex inversion. Thus, (2) below features complex inversion just like (1), because we could insert the proper noun *Sandrine* before the verb in (2) without affecting the meaning or grammaticality of the sentence. As shown in (3), however, the noun phrase subject cannot be inverted in this construction:

(2)   (Sandrine) Est-elle arrivée ?

(3)   *Est arrivée Sandrine ?

If the subject is in the first or second person, there is, of course, no full noun phrase equivalent that could be inserted. Nevertheless, constructions like (4)–(5) are considered to be instances of complex inversion because they are found in the exact same types of context as (1)–(2):

(4)   Puis-je vous rappeler plus tard, peut-être ?

(5)   Veux-tu encore un café ?

In sum, in complex inversion, only clitic subject pronouns can be inverted, but the clitic subject may be doubled by a non-clitic subject.

24.3.2 Simple inversion

We have simple inversion in French when either a clitic subject or a full noun phrase/non-clitic pronoun subject may be placed after the verb. This type of inversion is simple, because only one of the two types of subject can be present in the clause. Clitic subject pronouns are placed in the verbal field immediately following the finite verb, while non-clitic subjects are placed in the post-field. This is exemplified in (6)–(7):

(6)   Qu'a dit Sandrine ?

(7)   Qu'a-t[2]-elle dit ?

In sum, in simple inversion, both clitic subject pronouns and full noun phrase/non-clitic pronoun subjects can be inverted.

24.3.3 Stylistic inversion

In stylistic inversion, a subject in the form of a full noun phrase or a non-clitic pronoun is placed in the post-field, as in (8) below. If the subject of the

---

[2] In inversion, a '-t-' is inserted between the finite verb and a clitic subject if a hiatus (i.e. a clash of two successive vowels) will thereby be avoided.

clause is a clitic pronoun, stylistic inversion cannot be used, as shown by the ungrammaticality of (9). In such cases, the clitic subject must stay in the normal subject position before the verb, as in (10), where no form of inversion is used:

(8)   Le village [où habitent Jacques et Maïté$_{Subj/NP}$] est assez loin d'ici.

(9)   *Le village [où habitent-ils$_{Subj/PersPron}$] est assez loin d'ici.

(10) Le village [où ils habitent] est assez loin d'ici.

In sum, in stylistic inversion, only subjects in the form of a full noun phrase/non-clitic pronoun can be inverted.

24.4 Inversion in direct interrogatives

One of the main functions of inversion in French, as in English, is to mark the communicative function of a clause. Thus, while we will normally understand the English sentence in (11) below, in which the subject precedes the predicator, as a statement, the sentence in (12), which features inversion, will be understood as a question. The same is true of the equivalent French sentences in (13)–(14):

(11) Jane has left.

(12) Has Jane left?

(13) Jeanne est partie.

(14) Jeanne est-elle partie ?

(12) and (14) above are examples of direct yes/no interrogatives.[3] In both languages, however, inversion is also used to mark sentences as WH-interrogatives, although in those cases the question function is additionally signalled by the presence of the WH-word, cf. the statements in (15) and (17) below *vs* the WH-interrogatives in (16) and (18):

---

[3] For the difference between direct and indirect interrogatives, as well as for that between yes/no and WH-interrogatives, see section 4.2.1.2.

(15) Sandra is in Alexander's office.

(16) Where is Sandra?

(17) Sandrine est dans le bureau d'Alexandre.

(18) Où est Sandrine ?

French direct interrogatives may use complex or simple inversion, depending of the specific type of interrogative (see sections 24.4.1–24.4.2 below). **Stylistic inversion**, on the other hand, is never used in direct interrogatives.

24.4.1 Yes–no interrogatives

Complex inversion is the only type used in yes/no interrogatives in standard French, as shown in (19) below and (1), (4), (5), and (14) above. Simple inversion is never used in this type of sentence.

(19) (Luce) a-t-elle lu *Mémoires d'une jeune fille rangée* ?

(20) Tout s'est-il passé comme prévu ?

24.4.2 WH-interrogatives

In WH-interrogatives, either complex or simple inversion may be used, depending on the specific question word and its grammatical role.

   Simple inversion is used in WH-interrogatives when *que* is a direct object or a subject attribute (cf. (21)–(22) below), and when *quel* or *qui* is a subject attribute (cf. (23)–(24)):

(21) *Que*$_{\text{DirObj}}$ veut ce monsieur ?

(22) *Qu'*$_{\text{SubjAttr}}$ est devenu votre cadet ?

(23) *Quel*$_{\text{SubjAttr}}$ est votre numéro de téléphone ?

(24) *Qui*$_{\text{SubjAttr}}$ est ce monsieur ?

Complex inversion is used when the WH-word is *pourquoi*, as in (25) below, and when *qui* is a direct object, as in (26):

(25) *Pourquoi* Janine a-t-elle renoncé à faire des études ?

(26) *Qui*_{DirObj} les libraires ont-ils choisi comme le meilleur auteur de l'année ?

In addition, complex inversion is preferred in any type of WH-question if *cela* is the subject, as in (27):

(27) Que cela peut-il vous faire ?

(28) A qui cela profite-t-il ?

After WH-words other than the ones mentioned above, either simple or complex inversion may in principle be used, as seen in (29)–(32) below.

(29) A qui s'est plaint Alain ?

(30) A qui Alain s'est-il plaint ?

(31) Quand arrivera ton cousin ?

(32) Quand ton cousin arrivera-t-il ?

Note, however, that simple inversion is excluded if there are complements in the post-field, cf. the grammaticality contrasts between (33)–(34) and (35)–(36) below. It remains possible if the post-field contains only adverbials, as in (37)–(38):

(33) A qui Alain s'est-il plaint *de son travail*_{PrepObj} ?

(34) *A qui s'est plaint Alain *de son travail*_{PrepObj} ?

(35) Depuis combien de temps ton cousin habite-t-il *à Manchester*_{LocObj} ?

(36) *Depuis combien de temps habite ton cousin *à Manchester*_{LocObj} ?

(37) Où va ta sœur *à cette heure-ci*_{Adv'al} ?

(38) Où ta sœur va-t-elle *à cette heure-ci*_{Adv'al} ?

In addition, simple inversion is preferred if the predicator is in a simple tense. Compound tenses, on the other hand, favour the use of complex inversion, as seen in (39)–(42) below:

(39) Quand *commence* la fête ?

(40) Quand la fête *a*-t-elle *commencé* ?

(41) De quoi *discuteront* nos collègues lors de leur réunion ?

(42) De quoi nos collègues *ont*-ils *discuté* lors de leur réunion ?

24.4.3 Alternatives to inversion in direct interrogatives

Complex inversion in particular, but also to a lesser extent simple inversion, is largely a feature of relatively formal, mainly written, registers in contemporary French, and will tend to be avoided in less formal registers.

In yes/no questions, the use of complex inversion can be avoided either by the insertion of the interrogative *est-ce que* at the beginning of the sentence, as in (43)–(44) below, or by the use of sharply rising intonation at the end of a sentence with regular subject-predicator word order, as in (45)–(46) (where the upward arrows indicate rising intonation on the following syllable):

(43)   Est-ce que Luce a lu *Mémoires d'une jeune fille rangée* ?

(44)   Est-ce que tout s'est passé comme prévu ?

(45)   Luce a lu *Mémoires d'une jeune fille ran↑gée* ?

(46)   Tout s'est passé comme pré↑vu ?

The use of rising intonation is by far the most commonly used strategy for asking yes/no questions in spoken French, irrespective of register. *Est-ce que* is not very frequently used and is favoured in particular for emphatic purposes, for instance if the question has already been asked, but not answered, previously.

Note, however, that if a direct yes/no interrogative functions as a rhetorical question, only *est-ce que* is a viable alternative to complex inversion. Rising intonation is appropriate only for genuine questions, as shown by its infelicity in a context like (47):

(47)   A: Maman, Sylvain et moi, on a décidé de se marier le 18 août. Qu'est-ce que tu en penses ?
            B: Oh voyons, est-ce que je suis libre ?/#Oh voyons, je suis ↑libre ?

In direct WH-interrogatives, simple inversion is relatively common even in informal registers if the subject is a clitic pronoun, the predicator is in a simple tense, and the post-field is empty, as in (48)–(49):

(48)   Où vas-tu ?

(49)   Qui est-il ?

Otherwise, the use of inversion is avoided principally by employing the long forms of interrogative pronouns and adverbs (see section 19.2), as in (50)–(51) below:

(50)   Qu'est-ce que vous avez fait hier soir ?

(51)   Où est-ce que tu l'as rencontré(e) ?

In colloquial speech, it is possible, and not infrequent, to leave the WH-word in the slot where a corresponding non-interrogative constituent would be in a declarative sentence, as in (52)–(53):

(52)   Vous avez fait quoi hier soir ? (cf. Vous avez fait *quelque chose* hier soir.)

(53)   Tu l'as rencontré(e) où ? (cf. Tu l'as rencontré(e) *quelque part*.)

Finally, in very colloquial speech, WH-words other than *que* or *quoi* may be placed at the beginning of the sentence and followed by regular subject-predicator word order. In such cases, *que* is sometimes inserted between the WH-word and the rest of the clause, as in (54)–(55) below. Note that the versions with *que* are considered substandard:

(54)   Pourquoi (*que*) t'as fait ça ?

(55)   Où (*que*) tu vas ?

24.5 Inversion in non-interrogative independent clauses

In non-interrogative independent clauses, all three forms of inversion are found, albeit in very different syntactic environments.

24.5.1 Complex inversion

Complex inversion is or may be used in formal registers when certain so-called **conjunctive adverbials** appear in the pre-field at the very beginning of a clause. Conjunctive adverbials indicate either the nature of the connection of the host clause to the preceding discourse or the speaker's commitment to the truth of what is expressed in the clause.

The adverbials that usually trigger complex inversion are *à peine*, *encore* ('yet', 'nevertheless'), *encore moins*, *peut-être*, *sans doute*, and *tout au plus*, as in (56)–(57):

(56)   *Peut-être* la radio a-t-elle déjà annoncé la nouvelle.

(57)   Nous avons longuement réfléchi à cette problématique. *Encore* <u>plusieurs</u> <u>détails</u> restent-<u>ils</u> à éclaircir.

Additional items which frequently trigger complex inversion when placed at the beginning of a clause are *ainsi* ('thus'), *au moins*, *aussi* ('as a result'), *aussi bien* ('incidentally'), *de même*, *du moins*, *en vain*, *plus encore*, and *probablement*, as in (58):

(58)   Elle n'a pas pu mettre assez d'argent de côté au cours de l'année. *Aussi* a-t-elle été obligée de renoncer à son voyage. ('As a result, she had to give up on her trip.')

24.5.1.1 Alternatives to complex inversion after conjunctive adverbials

In some cases, the use of complex inversion can be avoided in less formal registers by placing the adverbial inside the clause, rather than initially, as in (59) below. With some adverbials, however, that will change the meaning (contrast (58) above with (60) below):

(59)   La radio a <u>peut-être</u> déjà annoncé la nouvelle.

(60)   Elle a <u>aussi</u> été obligée de renoncer à son voyage. ('She was also forced to give up on her trip.')

In other cases, such as (61) below, it may be sufficient to detach the adverbial from the rest of the clause by a comma. Finally, in less formal registers, *que* is often inserted after the adverbs *peut-être*, *probablement*, and *sans doute* to avoid the use of inversion, as exemplified in (61):

(61)   <u>Aussi</u>, elle a été obligée de renoncer à son voyage.

(62)   <u>Peut-être</u> *que* la radio a déjà annoncé la nouvelle.

24.5.2 Simple inversion

In standard French, simple inversion must be used in **reporting clauses** that follow the reported clause[4] (cf. (63)–(64) below), or which are inserted into the reported clause (cf. (65)–(66)). If the reporting clause precedes the

---

[4] For the notion of reported speech and the difference between reporting and reported clauses, see section 6.5.

reported clause in its entirety, as in (67), regular subject-predicator word order is used:

(63)   « En 1914, la Grande Guerre a éclaté », dit <u>Louise</u>.

(64)   « En 1914, la Grande Guerre a éclaté », dit-<u>elle</u>.

(65)   « En 1914 », dit <u>Louise</u>, « la Grande Guerre a éclaté. »

(66)   « En 1914 », dit-<u>elle</u>, « la Grande Guerre a éclaté. »

(67)   Louise/Elle dit : « En 1914, la Grande Guerre a éclaté. »

In addition, simple inversion is used in cases where a subject attribute, whose normal place would be the post-field, is instead placed in the pre-field, as shown in (68)–(70) below. Examples like (69), where the subject is a clitic pronoun, appear to be little used outside a few very specific types of context, such as religious discourse, and in more or less frozen constructions like the concessive [*si* + Adj + *être*_{Subjunctive} + Subj] construction exemplified in (70). Constructions with lengthy noun phrase subjects like that in (68) are more common, in as much as French generally prefers to place comparatively 'heavy' constituents in the post-field.

(68)   *Nombreux* sont ceux que la crise a obligés à ne pas partir pendant les vacances.

(69)   *Nombreux* sont-ils.

(70)   *Si intelligente* soit-elle, Clarisse n'obtient pas toujours les meilleures notes. ('However intelligent she may be . . . ')

24.5.3 Stylistic inversion

In independent clauses, stylistic inversion is or may be used where a constituent (other than a subject attribute, cf. section 24.5) that would normally appear in the post-field has been moved up to the pre-field.

If the constituent in question is a **complement** (which is relatively rarely the case), stylistic inversion is obligatorily used, as shown in (71)–(72) below. Note that the ungrammaticality of both (73) and (74) shows that we are indeed dealing with stylistic inversion in such cases, and not with simple inversion:

(71)   *À la diversité géographique* correspond <u>la diversité des crus</u>.

(72)   **À la diversité géographique* <u>la diversité des crus</u> correspond.

(73) **À la diversité géographique ele correspond.*

(74) **À la diversité géographique correspond-ele.*

If an **adverbial** has been moved to the pre-field, leaving the post-field empty, stylistic inversion is optional, but common, cf. (75)–(78):

(75) *Le 3 juin sera lancée une nouvelle fusée spatiale.*

(76) *Le 3 juin une nouvelle fusée spatiale sera lancée.*

(77) *Le 3 juin ele sera lancée.*

(78) **Le 3 juin sera-t-ele lancée.*

24.6 Inversion in subordinate clauses

In subordinate clauses, neither complex nor simple inversion can be used. Stylistic inversion is common, however, even in less formal registers, including speech.

Thus, stylistic inversion is optionally, but frequently, used if there is no complement in the post-field of the subordinate clause, as shown in (79)–(84) below.

(79) On ne savait pas du tout [ce que voulait la nouvelle direction.]

(80) On ne savait pas du tout [ce que la nouvelle direction voulait.]

(81) Renée l'accompagnait poussant un landau [où se trouvaient les deux derniers.]

(82) Renée l'accompagnait poussant un landau [où les deux derniers se trouvaient.]

(83) [Quand vint le moment du départ,] il regretta presque sa décision.

(84) [Quand le moment du départ vint,] il regretta presque sa décision.

As implied above, stylistic inversion is incompatible with the presence of complements in the post-field, as shown in (85)–(86) below. The presence of **adverbials** in the post-field, on the other hand, does not affect its use, as seen in (87)–(90):

(85) Je me demande [quand Pierre achetera *ce livre*$_{\text{DirObj}}$.]

(86) *Je me demande [quand achetera Pierre *ce livre*$_{\text{DirObj}}$.]

(87) Ils ont parlé de leur vie, de [ce qu'était l'Amérique *pour eux*$_{\text{Adv'al}}$.]

(88) Ils ont parlé de leur vie, de [ce que l'Amérique était *pour eux*_{Adv'al}.]

(89) Il faut d'abord [que s'établisse <u>un climat de confiance</u> *entre les négociateurs*_{Adv'al}.]

(90) Il faut d'abord [qu'<u>un climat de confiance</u> s'établisse *entre les négociateurs*_{Adv'al}.]

Finally, stylistic inversion is obligatorily used in subordinate clauses in all registers if the post-field would otherwise be empty following a simple tense form of the verb *être*, cf. (91)–(92):

(91) Il ne voyait pas [où *était* <u>le problème</u>.]

(92) *Il ne voyait pas [où <u>le problème</u> *était*.]

24.7 The position of adverbials

When considering the place of adverbials within the clause, it is useful to make a distinction between so-called **focalizable** *vs* **non-focalizable adverbials**.

The main criterion underpinning this distinction is whether or not a given adverbial appears natural as the focus of a cleft sentence, i.e. a sentence of the form *c'est X qui/que Y*, where the constituent taking the place of X is the focus constituent.[5] An adverbial which can take the place of X in such a construction is a focalizable adverbial.

Thus, as shown in (93)–(96) below, *hier* is a focalizable adverbial, as it appears completely natural as the focus of the cleft sentence in (94). *Déjà*, on the other hand, is not natural in this position, and could only occur in the construction shown in (96) in very special circumstances. *Déjà* is thus a non-focalizable adverbial. As (97)–(100) show, adverbials with the same contextual meaning will be focalizable or not in both French and English:

(93) Simon est revenu <u>hier</u>.

(94) C'est <u>hier</u> que Simon est revenu.

(95) Simon est <u>déjà</u> revenu.

(96) *?C'est <u>déjà</u> que Simon est revenu.

---

[5] For further details about cleft sentences, see section 26.3.

(97) Simon came back <u>yesterday</u>.

(98) It was <u>yesterday</u> that Simon came back.

(99) Simon has <u>already</u> come back.

(100) *?It's <u>already</u> that Simon has come back.

As shown in (101) below, focalizable adverbials cannot normally occur in the verbal field in French, whereas non-focalizable adverbials are frequently found in that position, cf. (95) above.

(101) *Simon est <u>hier</u> revenu.

24.7.1 Types of non-focalizable adverbials

There are four main types of non-focalizable adverbials, and one type of normally focalizable adverbial which in some uses is treated like non-focalizable adverbials with respect to position.

24.7.1.1 Stance adverbials
Non-focalizable stance adverbials bear on (i) the truth or validity of what is expressed by the sentence as a whole (e.g. *sans doute, peut-être, probablement*, etc.), (ii) the speaker's attitude to the situation expressed in the sentence or the way it is worded (e.g. *malheureusement, pour ainsi dire, . . .*), or (iii) on how the contents of the sentence relate to the context in which it appears, principally the preceding discourse (e.g. *donc, ainsi* ['thus'], *en effet*, etc.).

This type of adverbial can occur in the pre-field (cf. (102) below), the verbal field (cf. (103)), or the post-field, cf. (104):

(102) <u>Malheureusement</u>, Paul a été muté à Grenoble.

(103) Paul a <u>malheureusement</u> été muté à Grenoble.

(104) Paul a été muté à Grenoble, <u>malheureusement</u>.

24.7.1.2 Indefinite time adverbials
As the name suggests, non-focalizable indefinite time adverbials do not specify the precise timing of the event, activity or state described by the host clause in the way that focalizable definite time adverbials like *hier* or *le 18 mai 2011* do. Rather, indefinite time adverbials indicate such temporal notions as **succession** (*d'abord, ensuite*, etc.), **repetition/iterativity** (*souvent, de*

nouveau, etc.), **imminence/speed** (*bientôt, tout de suite*, etc.), or **precocity/ lateness** (*déjà, encore* ['still'], etc.).

This type of adverbial can likewise occur in all three fields, cf. (105)–(107):

(105)   Céline a d'abord téléphoné à Nathalie.

(106)   D'abord, Céline a téléphoné à Nathalie.

(107)   Céline a téléphoné à Nathalie d'abord.

24.7.1.3 Adverbials of degree and quantity
Adverbials of degree and quantity are items like *bien* ('much', 'very'), *beaucoup, tant, terriblement* etc. (see also section 22.1.3).

They may occur in the verbal field or in the post-field, as in (108)–(109), but not normally in the pre-field, as shown in (110):

(108)   Ils ont beaucoup hésité avant de se lancer dans cette aventure.

(109)   Ils ont hésité beaucoup avant de se lancer dans cette aventure.

(110)   *Beaucoup, ils ont hésité avant de se lancer dans cette aventure.

24.7.1.4 Negative adverbials
The clitic negative marker *ne* and the negative adverbs *pas, point, nullement, aucunement, guère, plus, jamais*, and *nulle part* normally occur in the verbal field. For further details, see chapter 23.

24.7.1.5 Non-focalizable manner adverbials
Manner adverbials are normally placed in the post-field, as shown in (111) and (113) below. However, in some cases, the meaning of a manner adverbial is weakened so that it comes to resemble an adverbial of indefinite time or degree. In the latter type of case, it may occur in the verbal field, as in (112) and (114):[6]

(111)   Delphine a répondu brusquement à ma question. ('brusquely')

(112)   Marc s'est brusquement levé. ('suddenly')

---

[6] Moving a manner adverb into the verbal field puts it into a slot where it cannot normally receive prosodic stress. The kind of attenuation of meaning that takes place in such cases is thus reminiscent of what happens to normally postmodifying adjectives when they are moved into the premodifying slot inside a noun phrase (cf. section 13.3.3.2).

(113)   Jean a mangé légèrement. ('Jean ate a light meal')

(114)   Je pense qu'Alice a été légèrement blessée par ta remarque. ('slightly')

24.7.1.6 The relative position of non-focalizable adverbials

Although, as detailed above, some types of non-focalizable adverbials can occur in the pre-field and/or the post-field, their default position is in all cases the verbal field. Inside the verbal field, their normal positions with respect to one another and to different parts of the predicator are as shown in Table 24.2 below.

Table 24.2. The place of non-focalizable adverbials.

Nadia	n'	a	sans doute	pas	toujours	été	bien	comprise
	neg.		stance	neg.	indef.	time	degree	
							(manner)	

In some cases, indefinite time adverbials may occur either before or after a negative adverb, with a corresponding change in meaning, as in (115)–(116):

(115)   Maryse ne reviendra plus bientôt. ('Maryse will not come back again any time soon.')

(116)   Maryse ne reviendra bientôt plus. ('Maryse will soon not come back anymore.')

25

Voice

Learning objectives

- To understand the notion of voice alternations and how they relate to verb valency.

- To understand the difference between passive and active uses of *être* + past participle.

- To understand the difference between medial and passive uses of the reflexive construction.

- To understand and master the grammatical rules governing the expression of the logical subject in causatives.

25.1 Introduction

Voice is a verbal category which can to a large extent be seen as being a matter of what one might call the **'direction'** of an activity or an action, i.e. whether that activity/action is described as being performed by the grammatical subject of the clause, or whether that subject is rather the undergoer of the activity/action. On that conception, we can operate with a distinction

The Structure of Modern Standard French. First edition. Maj-Britt Mosegaard Hansen.
© Maj-Britt Mosegaard Hansen 2016. First Published 2016 by Oxford University Press

between three different voices, namely an active voice, a passive voice, and a middle voice. This book will consider the causative construction as a fourth voice in French, but let us initially consider the first three.

On the rough definition given above, we may say that in transitive clauses in the **active voice**, the activity/action is seen from the perspective of the logical subject,[1] i.e. the entity that performs an activity/action. The logical subject is therefore also the grammatical subject of the clause. If the clause has a direct object, that constituent is normally the entity that undergoes the activity/action, i.e. the logical direct object. Thus, in the active sentence in (1) below, Alain is both the logical subject, who performs the action of washing, and the grammatical subject, while the baby undergoing the washing is both the logical direct object and the grammatical direct object.

In the **passive voice**, on the other hand, the action/activity is seen from the perspective of the logical direct object, which therefore becomes the grammatical subject of the clause. The logical subject is grammatically demoted to an adverbial. It is thus no longer a valency element, and may indeed be left out of the clause altogether.[2] In the passive sentence in (2) below, it is still Alain who performs the washing action, and the baby who undergoes it, but the baby is now the only valency element in the clause, while Alain is mentioned only in the optional *par* + complement adverbial:

(1)   [Alain]$_{Subj/LogSubj}$ a lavé [le bébé.]$_{DirObj/LogDirObj}$

(2)   [Le bébé]$_{Subj/LogDirObj}$ a été lavé (par Alain.)$_{Adv/LogSubj}$

Notice that in both the active and the passive voice, the two entities involved in the activity/action are referentially different, i.e. they are different entities in the real world.

As its name suggests, the **middle voice**, which in French is expressed by one of the uses of the reflexive construction (cf. section 25.3.1 below), represents a sort of middle ground between the active and the passive voice, in as much as the grammatical subject simultaneously performs and undergoes the activity/action described. Thus, in (3) below, the same referent, namely Alain, is simultaneously washing and being washed, i.e. both the logical subject and the logical direct object:

---

[1] For the notion of 'logical' constituents, see section 3.1.

[2] For the distinction between valency elements and adverbial, see chapter 1.

(3) [Alain]$_{Subj/LogSubj}$ [se]$_{DirObj/LogDirObj}$ lave.

If we take the active voice to be the basic one, from which others are derived, we observe that **voice alternations** result in changes in the valency pattern of the verb, as shown in Figure 25.1.

When considering voice from this valency-based perspective, it becomes relevant to operate with a fourth voice in French, namely the so-called **causative voice** (i.e. the *faire* + infinitive construction), seen in (4) below:

(4) [Mathilde]$_{Subj/Causer}$ fait laver [le bébé]$_{DirObj/LogDirObj}$ [à Alain.]$_{DatObj/LogSubj}$

This construction is called 'causative' because the grammatical subject of the clause, in this case Mathilde, does not perform the action of washing herself, but causes some other entity, in this case Alain, to perform it. The distribution of the roles of logical subject and logical direct object is thus the same in the causative as in the active voice, but the causative voice adds a new logical valency element, namely a 'causer', to the verb, and it is this element that becomes the grammatical subject. The logical subject of the main verb becomes either a grammatical direct object or a grammatical dative object, depending on the total number of valency elements in the clause (see section 25.4.1 below for details). Configurations where both a logical subject and a logical object are expressed are illustrated in Figure 25.2.

Active voice

Reference	Referent 1	≠	Referent 2
Semantics	Logical subject		Logical direct object
Syntax	Grammatical subject		Grammatical direct object

Passive voice

Reference	Referent 1	≠	Referent 2
Semantics	Logical direct object		Logical subject
Syntax	Grammatical subject		Adverbial

Middle voice

Reference	Referent 1	=	Referent 2
Semantics	Logical subject		Logical direct object
Syntax	Grammatical subject		Grammatical direct object

Figure 25.1. Correlations between voice and verb valency.

Reference	Referent 1	≠	Referent 2	≠	Referent 3
Semantics	Causer		Logical direct object		Logical subject
Syntax	Grammatical subject		Grammatical direct object		Grammatical dative object

Figure 25.2. Verb valency in the causative voice.

25.2 The passive voice

In general, there are three (frequently overlapping) reasons why speakers/ writers may prefer a passive construction over an active sentence.

One important reason for preferring a passive construction is that the grammatical subject is in an important sense the point of departure for the message conveyed by a clause or sentence. The passive voice will therefore often be chosen if the (part of the) text that a given clause belongs to is principally about the logical direct object, rather than about the logical subject. Thus, in a text about the baby, where Alain plays only a minor role, (2) above will tend to be preferred over (1).

Similarly, (5) below will often be preferred over (6), even though both pairs of sentences describe the same situation in the world, because the logical direct object, Olof Palme, is identified explicitly, and will already be known to many hearers, whereas his killer is still unknown, and therefore a less suitable point of departure for the message:

(5) Olof Palme, Premier Ministre de Suède, fut assassiné en février 1986 (par un inconnu).

(6) Un inconnu assassina Olof Palme, Premier Ministre de Suède, en février 1986.

The other major reason for preferring the passive over the active voice is that, as we saw in (2) and (5) above, passive constructions allow speakers to forgo mention of the logical subject due to the grammatical optionality of the *par*-adverbial. There are various kinds of context where that may be deemed desirable, for instance for politeness reasons or because, as in the case of (5), the speaker/writer simply does not know what entity or individual is responsible for a particular action.

Finally, in grammatical subject position, French prefers noun phrases that are both definite and animate. Therefore, there is a tendency for the passive voice to be chosen if the logical subject is indefinite (as in (5)–(6) above) and/or inanimate (as in (7)–(8) below), whereas the logical direct object is definite and/or animate:

(7) Madame Dupont$_{LogDirObj[Definite/Animate]}$ a été écrasée par un bus.$_{LogSubj[Indefinite/Inanimate]}$

(8) Un bus a écrasé Madame Dupont.

25.2.1 The canonical passive in French

The 'canonical' French passive takes the form of a construction with the auxiliary *être* followed by a main verb in the past participle. The tense of a canonical passive clause is identical to the tense of the auxiliary, as shown in (9)–(11) below:

(9)   Les prisonniers <u>sont</u> fusillés. (*présent*) = 'The prisoners are shot.'

(10) Les prisonniers <u>ont été</u> fusillés. (*passé composé*) = 'The prisoners have been/ were shot.'

(11) Les prisonniers <u>seront</u> fusillés. (*futur*) = 'The prisoners will be shot.'

Note that in contrast to English, which is cross-linguistically unusual in this respect, only the logical direct object can become the grammatical subject of a canonical French passive, as in (16) below. The logical dative object can never be promoted to grammatical subject in this construction. Thus, while (14) below is possible in English, its direct translation into French, seen in (17), is ungrammatical:

(12) Samantha gave Walter this book.

(13) This book was given to Walter by Samantha.

(14) Walter was given this book by Samantha.

(15) [Samantha]$_{Subj/LogSubj}$ a offert [ce livre]$_{DirObj/LogDirObj}$ [à Walter.]$_{DatObj/LogDatObj}$

(16) [Ce livre]$_{Subj/LogDirObj}$ a été offert [à Walter]$_{DatObj/LogDatObj}$ [par Samantha.]$_{Adv'al/LogSubj}$.

(17) *[Walter]$_{Subj/LogDatObj}$ a été offert [ce livre]$_{DirObj/LogDirObj}$ [par Samantha.]$_{Adv'al/LogSubj}$

So if French speakers want to make the logical dative object the grammatical subject of a clause, they have to resort to **reflexive causative constructions** with *se faire/se voir* + infinitive, as in (18)–(19) below. These constructions are treated in section 25.4.2:

(18) Walter s'est <u>fait offrir</u> ce livre par Samantha.

(19) Walter s'est <u>vu offrir</u> ce livre par Samantha.

In addition to not allowing logical dative objects as grammatical subjects, the *être* + past participle construction is, in fact, not particularly frequently used, as its meaning is often ambiguous.

25.2.1.1 Possible interpretations of *être* + past participle

Depending on the context, the *être* + past participle construction may have three different interpretations:

(i) Passive voice

In this case, the situation described by the clause is interpreted as **dynamic** in nature, as an event or on-going activity. This is exemplified in (2), (5), (7), (9)–(11), and (16) above.

(ii) *Être* + subject attribute

On this type of interpretation, the situation described by the clause is **static** in nature. This is exemplified in (20) below:

(20)   A: La réunion dure encore ?
       B: Non, elle est terminée depuis une heure. ('No, it has been over for an hour.')

(iii) Compound tense

If the past participle represents one of the 17 plus intransitive verbs that take *être* as their auxiliary in compound tenses (see section 8.2.4), the clause is in the active voice. In most cases, the situation it describes will moreover be interpreted as dynamic in nature. This is exemplified in (21) below:

(21)   Marie est venue. ('Marie has come/came.')

Unlike what we saw to be true of the canonical passive, the tense of the clause as a whole is not identical to the tense of the auxiliary in this construction. Thus, the tense of (21) is the *passé composé*, not the *présent*.

In a very small number of cases, such as that in (22) below, the construction is in principle three-ways ambiguous. Depending on context, (22) could thus be translated by, for instance, 'It [e.g. the suitcase] is being carried up', 'She is upset', or 'She has gone upstairs':

(22)   Elle est montée.

In the first case, *monter* is being used transitively, in a passive clause in the *présent*. In the second case, *montée* is used in a figurative sense, as the subject attribute of an active clause, also in the *présent*. Finally, in the third interpretation, *est montée* is again used in an active clause, in the *passé composé*.

In most cases, however, the potential ambiguity will be between only two possible intrepretations. In isolation, (23) below is thus ambiguous between interpretations (i) and (ii), while (26) is ambiguous between interpretations (ii) and (iii). In both cases, the construction can be disambiguated by adding further elements to the sentence, as shown in (24)–(25) and (27)–(28):

(23)   L'exposition sera ouverte.

(24)   L'exposition sera ouverte *par la reine elle-même*. (= passive voice)

(25)   L'exposition sera ouverte *jusqu'au mois d'août*. (= *être* + subject attribute)

(26)   Elle est sortie.

(27)   Elle est *toujours* sortie quand je passe la voir. (= *être* + subject attribute)

(28)   Elle est sortie *il y a dix minutes*. (= *passé composé*)

The addition of an agentive *par*-adverbial, as in (24), will always result in a passive interpretation, while a punctual time adverbial like that in (28) will often suggest a compound tense. Durative adverbials like those in (25) and (27), on the other hand, will favour an interpretation of the past participle as a subject attribute.

Moreover, the ambiguity between (i) and (ii) is of importance only for telic situations (cf. section 7.2), such as that in (23) above. If the situation is atelic, like that in (29) below, there is essentially no semantic difference between the two interpretations:

(29)   La directrice est respectée.

25.2.1.2 Expressing the logical subject in a passive construction

The normal way to express the logical subject in a passive construction is by using a prepositional phrase headed by *par*, as in (30) below:

(30)   L'équipe anglaise a été battue par les Danois.

In some cases, the preposition used is *de*, however. This is the case with verbs of the types in (a)–(c) below:

(a) Verbs of **accompaniment**, as in (31):

(31)   La ministre était suivie <u>de son secrétaire</u>.

(b) Verbs of **emotion**, as in (32):

(32)   Le nouveau maire n'est guère aimé <u>de ses alliés politiques</u>.

(c) Verbs of perception and cognition, as in (33):

(33)   Son malheur fut ignoré même <u>de ses proches</u>.

The use of *par* remains possible with these types of verb, however, mainly if the logical subject is perceived as particularly active, or if the complement of the preposition is a relatively heavy phrase, like that in (34) below:

(34)   Elle risquait d'être détestée <u>par ceux qu'elle avait aidés</u>.

Only *de* can be used if the complement of the preposition is a noun with a zero determiner, as shown in (35):

(35)   Il fut accablé <u>de/*par honte</u>.

25.2.2 Alternatives to the canonical passive

Because of the ambiguity of the *être* + past participle construction, French has a variety of alternative constructions available to express passive meaning.

'Regular' reflexive constructions, discussed in section 25.3 below are one alternative, and reflexive causatives, which are treated in section 25.4.2, are another.

However, a very common alternative is to use an active construction with the generic clitic *on* as the subject. While this construction does not promote the logical direct object to subject status the way the canonical passive does, it is passive-like in leaving the logical subject unidentified. This explains why French active sentences with the generic subject *on*, such as (36), are often translation equivalents of passive sentences in English (cf. (37)):

(36)   <u>On</u> m'a volé mon porte-monnaie !

(37)   My wallet has been stolen!

Further details on the generic clitic *on* can be found in section 15.2.3.

25.3 The middle voice and the reflexive passive

The French reflexive construction has several different interpretations (discussed further in section 15.4.1), of which two are relevant to the issue of voice.

25.3.1 The standard reflexive construction

As we saw in section 25.1 above, the grammatical subject of a clause in the middle voice directs an action or activity at itself as the grammatical direct object. In other words, the same referent simultaneously plays two roles in the clause. The standard reflexive construction in French (cf. section 15.4.1.1) thus expresses middle voice. This is exemplified in (38), where the reflexive pronoun *se* refers to Hugues:

(38)   Hugues se regarde dans la glace.

25.3.2 The reflexive passive

It is, however, quite common for reflexive constructions in French to get a passive interpretation, as exemplified in (39) below:

(39)   [La lettre x]$_{Subj/LogDirObj}$ se prononce rarement à la fin des mots français.

(39) is not meant to suggest that the letter x pronounces itself, but rather that French speakers rarely pronounce it when it occurs word-finally. The grammatical subject of (39), *la lettre x*, is thus a logical direct object, just like the grammatical subject of a canonical passive construction.

While this is not an absolute rule, the reflexive passive is typically used if the logical direct object is inanimate, and in contexts where the canonical passive construction might be interpreted statically, as *être* + subject attribute (cf. section 25.2.1.1 above). The logical subject is very rarely expressed.

Two different interpretations of the reflexive passive are found:

(i) A more common **generic interpretation**, where the construction expresses a more or less general rule, as exemplified in (39) above.

On this interpretation, the reflexive passive often has an **additional modal nuance** of possibility or necessity. The tense of the verb is either the *présent* or the *imparfait*, and the logical subject is typically an implicit generic *on*. Thus, (40) below expresses a general property of the door in question, namely that is was not possible to open it. In contrast, the canonical passive in (41) makes a statement about a particular occasion where the door had remained unopened, but does not suggest any impossibility of opening it:

(**40**)   Cette porte ne s'ouvrait pas. ('This door couldn't be opened./This door wouldn't open.')

(**41**)   Cette porte n'avait pas été ouverte. ('This door hadn't been opened.')

(ii) A less common **specific interpretation**, where the construction describes a one-off event.

In this case, the verb may be in any tense, and the implicit logical subject may be a single individual, as in (42) below, where we will usually understand that a particular person opened the door, even if the precise identity of that person is unimportant in the context.

(**42**)   A cinq heures, la porte s'ouvrit.

25.4 The causative voice

As already mentioned in section 25.1, the French causative *faire* + infinitive construction arguably constitutes a fourth type of voice, as these constructions involve an increase in the valency of the verb.

Thus, for instance, the verb *venir* in the regular active voice is intransitive and monovalent,[3] taking only a subject, as illustrated in (43) below. As (44) shows, no further valency elements can be added:

(**43**)   Jean <u>vient</u>.

(**44**)   *Jean <u>vient</u> Jacques.

In the causative construction, however, *venir* becomes transitive, taking a subject and a direct object, as shown in (45). Both these elements must be present, or the clause will become ungrammatical, as seen in (46). Notice

---

[3] For the notion of intransitive and monovalent verbs, see section 1.2.

that *Jean*, who is both the grammatical and logical subject of the monovalent *venir* in (43), becomes the grammatical direct object in the causative construction in (45). The new valency element, the logical causer *Jacques*, on the other hand, becomes the grammatical subject:

(45)   Jacques <u>fait venir</u> Jean.

(46)   *Jacques <u>fait venir</u>.

25.4.1   The grammatical realization of the logical subject in the causative voice

In (45) above, the logical subject of the main verb *venir* is expressed as a grammatical direct object in the causative voice. However, as we saw in connection with (4) in section 25.1 above, that is not always the case.

If the causative construction has only one complement, that complement is always realized as a grammatical direct object, irrespective of its role at the logical level. Consider a verb like *chanter*, which in the regular active voice can be used both intransitively and transitively, as in (47)–(48) below:

(47)   [Les enfants]$_{Subj}$ chantent.

(48)   [Les enfants]$_{Subj}$ chantent [une chanson.]$_{DirObj}$

In the causative voice, intransitive *chanter* behaves like *venir*, i.e. the logical subject becomes the grammatical direct object, as in (49) below. As shown in (50), *les enfants* can therefore be pronominalized as a direct object pronoun in this case:

(49)   [Ludivine]$_{Subj/Causer}$ fait chanter [les enfants.]$_{DirObj/LogSubj}$ ('Ludivine makes the children sing.' → Les enfants chantent.)

(50)   Ludivine <u>les</u> fait chanter.

Transitive *chanter*, however, may be used causatively without any explicit mention of the logical subject, in which case the logical direct object becomes the grammatical direct object, as in (51):

(51)   [Ludivine]$_{Subj/Causer}$ fait chanter [la chanson.]$_{DirObj/LogDirObj}$ ('Ludivine has the song sung.' → Quelqu'un chante la chanson.)

(52)   Ludivine <u>la</u> fait chanter.

If the causative construction has two complements, however, the logical direct object of the main verb will always become the grammatical direct object in the causative, while the logical subject will become a grammatical dative object, as shown in (4) above and (53)–(54) below:

(53) [Ludivine]$_{Subj/Causer}$ fait chanter [la chanson]$_{DirObj/LogDirObj}$ [aux enfants]$_{Da-tObj/LogSubj}$ ('Ludivine makes the children sing the song.' → Les enfants chantent la chanson.)

(54) Ludivine la leur fait chanter.

25.4.1.1 *Laisser* + infinitive and verbs of perception + infinitive

A formally similar construction can be found with the verb *laisser* (also known as the 'permissive' construction) and, more rarely, the verbs of perception *voir* and *entendre*, when they are followed by an infinitive, as shown in (55)–(58) below:

(55) Ludivine laisse chanter la chanson aux enfants.

(56) Ludivine la leur laisse chanter.

(57) Ludivine entend chanter la chanson aux enfants.

(58) Ludivine la leur entend chanter.

With these verbs, the construction type seen in (59)–(62) below, involving a direct object noun phrase and an infinitival clause as an object attribute or free indirect attribute, is more common, however:

(59) Ludivine laisse [les enfants]$_{DirObj/NP}$ [chanter la chanson.]$_{ObjAttr/InfCl}$

(60) Ludivine les laisse la chanter.

(61) Ludivine entend [les enfants]$_{DirObj/NP}$ [chanter la chanson.]$_{FIA/InfCl}$

(62) Ludivine les entend la chanter.

25.4.2 Reflexive causatives with passive meaning

In addition to the basic causative with *faire* + infinitive, French also has a reflexive causative construction using either *faire* or *voir* as the auxiliary, as shown in (63)–(64) below:

(63) Je me suis fait renverser par un camion. ('I was run over by a truck.')

(64)   Les réfugiés politiques <u>se sont vu refuser</u> l'accès au meeting. ('The political refugees were refused access to the rally.')

As in both these examples, the grammatical subject of a reflexive causative must be animate, and as shown by the translations the construction normally receives a passive interpretation.

With main verbs which are directly transitive in the active voice, like *renverser* in (63) above (cf. *X renverse Y*), use of the reflexive causative tends to suggest that the event or activity described is unpleasant for the subject. These uses are similar to the English *get*-passive, cf. (65):

(65)   I <u>got</u> run over by a truck.

With main verbs that take a dative object in the active voice, however, such as *refuser* in (64) (cf. *X refuse Y à Z*), the reflexive causative is the only means of promoting a logical dative object to grammatical subject position in a clause with passive meaning. As we saw in connection with (12)–(17) in section 25.2.1 above, the French canonical passive construction allows only the logical direct object to be promoted to subject. Therefore, when a logical dative object is the grammatical subject of a reflexive causative, the described event may well be one which would normally be conceived of as very pleasant for the subject, such as that in (66) below, whose active counterpart is given in (67):

(66)   Lola <u>s'est fait décerner</u> le prix Médicis pour son dernier roman. ('Lola was awarded the Medicis prize for her latest novel.')

(67)   On a décerné le prix Médicis *à Lola* pour son dernier roman.

26

Dislocation, (pseudo-)clefts, and presentative constructions

Learning objectives

- To understand the notion of managing information flow in discourse, and the related notion of utterance topic.
- To understand the grammatical structure of clauses featuring left- and right-dislocation, of cleft and pseudo-cleft sentences, and of presentatives, and how these differ from the canonical clause-/sentence-structure.
- To understand the types of contexts and registers where non-canonical clause-/sentence-structures may be preferred, and why they may be preferred.

26.1 Information flow and 'canonical' clause/sentence structure

In written standard French, the normal—or 'canonical'—order of major constituents in declarative clauses is **subject—predicator—complement(s)**,

The Structure of Modern Standard French. First edition. Maj-Britt Mosegaard Hansen.
© Maj-Britt Mosegaard Hansen 2016. First Published 2016 by Oxford University Press

and both the subject and the complement(s) regularly take the form of full
noun phrases or prepositional phrases, as in (1)–(2) below:

(1)   [Le petit garçon blond]$_{Subj/NP}$ [embrasse]$_{Pred/FinV}$ [la grande fille brune.]$_{DirObj/NP}$

(2)   [La grande fille brune]$_{Subj/NP}$ [pense]$_{Pred/FinV}$ [au petit garçon blond.] $_{PrepObj/PP}$

However, particularly (but not exclusively) in less formal (especially
spoken) registers, alternative, non-canonical, ways of structuring clauses
and sentences are widely used for purposes of managing the flow of information in the discourse.

A typical utterance will contain some information that is assumed to be
already known to the hearer/reader—usually because it has been mentioned
in the previous discourse—as well as some further information that has not
been previously mentioned, and which therefore is assumed to be new to the
hearer/reader.

At the same time, a typical utterance can be said to be 'about' a particular
referent. Out of context, (1) above intuitively appears to be principally
about the little blond boy and what he did. While the tall dark-haired girl
is involved in what the boy did, the utterance does not seem to be about her
in quite the same way. Thus, (1) is a more natural answer to the question
in (3) below than to the alternative question in (4):

(3)   Que fait le petit garçon blond ?

(4)   Qu'arrive-t-il à la grande fille brune ?

The referent that an utterance is 'about' in this sense is called the **topic** of
that utterance. In French, the topic of an utterance (a) is typically already
known to the hearer, and (b) occurs at the beginning of the utterance.

As seen in (1)–(2) above, the canonical sentence structure puts the subject
at the beginning of a declarative sentence. That implies that ideally, subjects
will also be utterance topics. Given the correlation between topics and
known information, topics should preferably be grammatically definite.
Grammatically indefinite subjects therefore tend to be dispreferred in
French, particularly in more colloquial spoken registers.

As discussed in chapter 25 above, voice alternations represent a way in
which the canonical clause structure can be manipulated so as to comply
with the communicative drive to have more topical referents appear before
less topical ones in the utterance. However, French also has a range of non-
canonical sentence structures which can achieve similar aims. Below, four

such constructions, viz. dislocation, cleft and pseudo-cleft sentences, and presentatives, will be discussed in turn.

26.2 Left- and right-dislocation

In dislocation constructions, which are very widely used in informal spoken French in particular, a valency element[1] is moved from its canonical position inside the clause and is placed either at the beginning or at the end of the clause. This 'dislocated' constituent is represented inside the clause by a clitic pronoun (either a personal clitic or a pronominal adverb)[2] or by the neutral pronoun *cela/ça*. Thus, if we take a canonical simple sentence like (5) below as our point of departure, (6)–(11) represent the possible dislocation patterns. If the dislocated element is placed at the beginning of the clause, we speak of left-dislocation (cf. (6)–(8)); if it moves to the end of the clause, it is called right-dislocation (cf. (9)–(11)).

(5) Benoît a donné ces fleurs à sa grand-mère.

(6) Benoît, *il* a donné ces fleurs à sa grand-mère.

(7) Ces fleurs, Benoît *les* a données à sa grand-mère.

(8) Sa grand-mère, Benoît *lui* a donné ces fleurs.

(9) *Il* a donné ces fleurs à sa grand-mère, Benoît.

(10) Benoît *les* a données à sa grand-mère, ces fleurs.

(11) Benoît *lui* a donné ces fleurs, à sa grand-mère.

In writing, the dislocated element is separated from the rest of the clause by a comma, as the above examples show. In speech, right-dislocated constituents will be separated from the preceding clause by an intonation break. Left-dislocated elements may, but need not, be separated from the clause that follows by such an intonation break.

If the dislocated constituent is a dative object, a prepositional object, or a locative object, it will normally appear without a preposition in left-dislocation, but will retain the preposition in right-dislocation, as shown in (8) and (11) above.

---

[1] For the notion of valency, see section 1.2.1.1.
[2] For the notion of clitics, see section 14.2.

Dislocation is possible in both independent clauses like those in (6)–(11), and in subordinate clauses like those in (12)–(13) below. As (12) shows, left-dislocated constituents follow conjunctions (incl. coordinating conjunctions):

(12) *Tant que* Benoît, il (n')aura pas donné ces fleurs à sa grand-mère, la vieille dame continuera à lui faire la moue.

(13) A: Où sont les fleurs que tu avais achetées ?
B: Il faudra que j'en achète d'autres, *parce que* Benoît les a données à sa grand-mère, ces fleurs.

Left-dislocation allows the speaker to signal which constituent is the topic of the utterance. Thus, if we look again at (6)–(8) above, (6) is likely to be preferred if the point of the utterance is mainly to inform the hearer about what Benoît has been up to. If, on the other hand, the speaker wishes to make a point about the flowers, then (7) will be preferred. Finally, if it is Benoît's grandmother who is being discussed, (8) is more likely to be uttered.

Where the topic is new to the discourse, left-dislocation also allows the speaker to introduce it as a separate unit before going on to say something about it. Thus, it frequently serves to reorient the conversation to a greater or lesser extent, as in the authentic conversational excerpt in (14) below, where the global topic of the passage is subjects studied in high school, but where the more specific topics of the individual utterances move from English (prior to the excerpt shown here) to philosophy, and from there to Latin:

(14) [The interlocutors are discussing their high school days. B has just mentioned that she did poorly in English.]
A: Non, la philo aussi, *c'*était . . .
B: La philo, *c'*était bon.
A: C'était bon, hein !
C: C'était . . .
B: Ma meilleure note !
C: C'était plutôt le grand sujet. J'prenais pas . . .
A: Le latin, *ça* a pas été terrible, hein !
C: T'as eu du latin, toi ?

Dislocation may be used to explicitly contrast the topics of two different utterances, as in (15) below:

(15) Toi, *tu* peux y aller. Moi, *je* n'ai pas envie.

Right-dislocation similarly marks the topic constituent. It is typically used when the speaker is assuming that the hearer is already aware of the entity that is being talked about, but wants to avoid ambiguity, as in (16) below. If a right-dislocated constituent has not been spoken of previously, it will usually be saliently present in the physical environment that speaker and hearer share, as in (16). New topics that are not present in the environment are not normally introduced using this construction.

(16)   [Looking at a painting in a gallery:] *Elle* est vraiment bien, <u>cette toile</u>, hein !

It is possible (although in practice not very frequent) to dislocate more than one clause constituent at a time, the maximum being three, as seen in (17) below. In such cases, the element placed first will typically be a non-clitic personal pronoun referring to a topical entity, the second dislocated element will refer to something that can be identified via that topical entity, while the third dislocated element will refer to something that can be identified via the immediately preceding one, as shown in (17):

(17)   <u>Moi</u>, <u>mon frère</u>, <u>sa voiture</u>, *il* (ne) veut plus *me la* prêter depuis que j'ai eu mon accident.

26.3 Cleft and pseudo-cleft sentences

Cleft and pseudo-cleft sentences consist of two (or more) clauses, which together describe a single situation. The notion of a (pseudo-)cleft sentence is best understood if we assume that underlying such a sentence, there is a simpler sentence describing the situation in question, and that that simpler sentence has been split down the middle, as it were, and its constituents distributed over at least two new clauses.

Thus, the cleft sentence in (18) below consists in two clauses, each containing a finite verb (underlined). However, the situation it described is objectively speaking the same as the one described by the simple sentence in (19). Similarly, the pseudo-cleft sentence in (20) consists of two clauses which together describe the same situation as the simple sentence in (21):

(18)   C'<u>est</u> la robe bleue que je <u>préfère</u>.

(19)   Je <u>préfère</u> la robe bleue.

(20)   Ce qu'il <u>veut</u>, c'<u>est</u> ma peau !

(21)   Il <u>veut</u> ma peau !

26.3.1 Cleft sentences

Cleft sentences have the structure seen in (22) below:

(22)   *Ce* + finite 3.p. form of *être* + X + relative pronoun *qui/que* + Y

X can represent any constituent of the underlying simpler sentence, except the predicator. Y represents the remainder of the underlying sentence. Thus, in (18) above, the noun phrase *la robe bleue* corresponds to X, and it represents the direct object of the underlying simpler sentence in (19). (19) may also, however, underlie the cleft sentence in (23) below, where X is the non-clitic personal pronoun[3] *moi*, which represents the subject of the underlying sentence:

(23)   C'est <u>moi</u> qui préfère la robe bleue.

The form of *être* that follows *ce* is always third person. In more formal registers, it may be singular or plural, depending on the number marking on X: in (18) above *être* is in the singular because *la robe bleue* is a singular noun phrase; in (24) below, on the other hand, *être* is plural because *les robes bleues* is plural. However, if X is either of the pronouns *nous* or *vous*, *c'est* is always used, as shown in (25):

(24)   Ce <u>sont</u> *les robes bleues* que je préfère.

(25)   C'<u>est</u> *vous* qui préférez la robe bleue.

In more colloquial registers, *c'est* tends to be used irrespectively of the number marking on X, as in (26) below:

(26)   C'<u>est</u> *les robes bleues* que je préfère.

When X represents the subject of the underlying simpler sentence, as in (23) and (25) above or (27) below, the form of the predicator in the relative clause agrees with X in both person and number:

---

[3] For the distinction between clitic and non-clitic personal pronouns, see sections 15.2–15.3.

(27) Ce sont *eux* qui pré<u>fèrent</u> la robe bleue.

The tense of the relative clause is variable. In more formal registers, *être* must be in the same tense as the finite element of the predicator in the relative clause, cf. (28)–(29) below:

(28) C'é<u>tait</u> Luc qu'elle *avait épousé.*

(29) Ce <u>fut</u> Mathilde qui *entra.*

In more colloquial registers, invariable *c'est* is typically used, as in (30):

(30) C'<u>est</u> Luc qu'elle avait épousé.

While cleft sentences are found in English as well, they are considerably more frequently used in French. One reason for using a cleft sentence is that it allows speakers to contrastively highlight the constituent in X. Thus, one way in which the meaning of a cleft sentence like that in (31) below differs from the corresponding simple sentence in (32) is that (31) may serve to mark the fact that someone phoned Marie as information that is already taken for granted by both speaker and hearer. What is at issue is then merely the identity of the caller. In such contexts, the X element of the cleft sentence is often assumed to be drawn from a restricted pool of candidates; in (31), the pool of potential callers might, for instance, comprise Jean, François, and Jacques in addition to Pierre. The simple sentence in (32), on the other hand, does not mark any part of it as taken for granted, nor does it suggest that there is a limited number of people who could have phoned Marie:

(31) C'est Pierre qui a téléphoné à Marie.

(32) Pierre a téléphoné à Marie.

Clefts are also found in English, but in spoken English a contrastive reading is often achieved by stress placement instead, as in (33) below. However, as French does not have similarly mobile stress, that language tends to use clefts.

(33) PETER phoned Mary.

However, while English clefts typically have the contrastive meaning explained above, that is not necessarily true of French clefts, which often convey all new information, with no implied contrast between the X element and any other entity. In such cases, the structure is typically used to avoid putting a referent that is new to the discourse in subject position. Thus, in the scenario in (34) below, Grégoire's reply is more likely to take the form in

(b) than that in (a), because his wife is at that point completely new to the discourse:

(34) [Grégoire and his colleague Yannick pass each other in the hallway and exchange greetings.]
Yannick: Il est beau, ton costume !
Grégoire: (a) Merci. Ma femme me l'a acheté.
          (b) Merci. C'est ma femme qui me l'a acheté.

26.3.2 Pseudo-cleft sentences

Pseudo-cleft sentences take the form in (35) below. Unlike clefts, the Y component of a pseudo-cleft can take different forms, i.e. a noun phrase as in (36), a subordinate clause, as in (37), or an infinitival clause, as shown in (38):

(35) Free relative pronoun + X + *c'est/ce sont* + Y.

(36) Ce dont je rêve, c'est (d')un voyage dans l'Antarctique.

(37) Ce qui m'embête, c'est que Hugo soit toujours en retard.

(38) Ce qu'ils veulent, c'est de voir leur fille heureuse.

In a pseudo-cleft, the Y element is the focus of new information, and the X element is somehow implied by the previous discourse (although not necessarily taken for granted). In the context, Y is understood to exhaustively specify X: thus, in (36), for instance, the assumption is that the only contextually relevant thing that the speaker is dreaming of is a voyage to Antarctica.

Pseudo-clefts are often used to point out things or facts that are considered noteworthy (cf. (39) below), to provide explanations (cf. (40)) or to correct erroneous assumptions (cf. (41)).

(39) Les comédiens eux-mêmes ont proposé des facettes différentes du personnage. Mais ce qui est frappant, c'est qu'au-delà du prince de Danemark, les autres protagonistes ont conduit à de nombreuses œuvres.
F. Foreaux, *Dictionnaire de culture générale* (Pearson, 2010), 180

(40) Par ailleurs, plusieurs utiliseront le terme de « barbarie », alors que d'autres en souligneront le caractère problématique. Pour ma part, j'en revendique l'utilisation.
Car ce qui m'inquiète le plus avec la barbarie qui a frappé Charlie Hebdo, c'est que le risque est grand, voire assuré, qu'elle soit suivie par la barbarie qui, elle, prend le visage du défenseur de la République pour cracher sa haine.

L. Moquin-Beaudry, 'Charlie-Hebdo: au-delà de l'attaque, le vrai danger', *ricochet* (7 January 2015), https://ricochet.media/fr/282/charlie-hebdo-au-dela-de-lattaque-le-vrai-danger.

(41)   Je ne veux pas qu'on en discute, je ne veux pas qu'on se dispute.
Je ne veux pas que tu m'expliques, je ne veux plus de polémique.
Tout ce que je veux c'est que tu partes.
Été 67, 'Tout ce que je veux', paroles N. Michaux, in *Été 67* (Wagram, 2007)

26.4 Presentative constructions

Presentative constructions, unlike (pseudo-)clefts, are almost exclusively used in speech. They are formally rather similar to clefts, but they never have contrastive meaning. Instead, they allow speakers to convey information about situations all aspects of which are new to the discourse. As mentioned in section 26.1, new referents in subject position are rather strongly dispreferred in French, particularly in the spoken language. If the other constituents of a given clause are also new to the discourse, more colloquial registers of spoken French will prefer to use a presentative construction.

Most commonly, presentatives take one of the forms in (42)–(43) below, exemplified in (44)–(45):

(42)   *(Il) y a* + X + relative pronoun *qui/que* + Y

(43)   Personal subject clitic + finite form of *avoir* + X + relative pronoun *qui/que* + Y

(44)   (Il) y a ma voiture qui est en panne.

(45)   J'ai ma voiture qui est en panne.

In the structure in (43), the first person singular subject clitic *je* is by far the most common item used, as illustrated in (45), but other clitics are possible, as seen in (46) below:

(46)   Toi, tu avais ta mère qui était malade, non ?

In this structure, moreover, the verb *avoir* is often completely bleached of any meaning relating to possession, and simply indicates the existence of the X element, just as is the case with *il y a*. It is thus perfectly possible to utter the sentence in (47) below without any sense of contradiction (indeed, the example is authentic):

(47) J'ai encore un formulaire que j'ai pas.
F. Gadet, *Le français populaire* (PUF, 1992), 77.

An example of an appropriate type of context for the presentatives in (44)–(45) to be uttered would be one where the speaker was arriving late for an appointment and the hearer was not expected to know what means of transportation the speaker had used to get there. In such a context, the simple sentence in (48) below would tend not to be used in colloquial speech because it suggests, on the one hand, that the hearer is already aware that the speaker has a car, and on the other hand, that that car is already established as a topic of discourse. The advantage of using a presentative structure in this type of context is that it introduces the car as a new referent in the first clause, and only then proceeds to say something more about it in the second clause.

(48) Ma voiture est en panne.

Appendix A
Overview of grammatical functions

Sentence and clause-level grammatical functions

Name	Example(s)	Introduced
Predicator	Jeanne <u>mange</u> ; Jeanne <u>a peur</u> des chiens	section 1.2.1
Subject	<u>Jeanne</u> mange ; <u>Elle</u> mange ; <u>Ce que Jeanne mange</u> est délicieux	section 1.2.2
Anticipatory subject	<u>Il</u> est possible que Max vienne	section 3.1.2
Postponed subject	Il est possible <u>que Max vienne</u>	section 3.1.2
Subject attribute	Jeanne est <u>belle</u>	section 1.2.3.1
Direct object	Max a acheté <u>un chien</u> ; Max <u>l'</u>a acheté ; Jeanne sait <u>que Max a acheté un chien</u> ; Jeanne <u>le</u> sait	section 1.2.3.2
Object attribute	Max a appelé son chien <u>Médor</u>	section 1.2.3.8
Dative object	Max montre son chien <u>à Jeanne</u> ; Max <u>lui</u> montre son chien	section 1.2.3.5
Prepositional object	Jeanne a peur <u>de Médor</u> ; Jeanne <u>en</u> a peur ; Max s'attendait <u>à cela</u> ; Max s'<u>y</u> attendait ; Max s'attendait <u>à ce que Jeanne ait peur de Médor</u>	section 1.2.3.4
Locative object	Jeanne habite <u>à Marseille</u> ; Jeanne <u>y</u> habite	section 1.2.3.7
Measure complement	Marie pèse <u>59 kilos</u>.	section 1.2.3.3
Free indirect attribute	<u>Très agressif</u>, Médor fait peur à Jeanne	section 3.2.4.1
Adverbial	Jeanne évite Max <u>à cause de son chien</u> ; Jeanne évite Max <u>parce qu'il a un chien agressif</u>	section 1.2.4
Subordinator	Jeanne évite Max <u>parce</u> qu'il a un chien agressif ; Max pense <u>que</u> Jeanne est bête	section 3.2.1.1
Coordinator	Jeanne évite Max <u>et</u> cela lui est égal	section 3.2.1.1

Phrase-level grammatical functions

Name	Example(s)	Introduced
Head	un <u>garçon</u> blond ; a <u>perdu</u> ; très <u>content</u>; <u>sans</u> doute	section 2.3
Premodifier	une <u>petite</u> fille ; <u>très</u> content	section 2.3
Postmodifier	un garçon <u>blond</u> ; une fille <u>que je connais</u> ; fier <u>de son fils</u> ; aussi vite <u>que possible</u>	section 2.3
Appositional postmodifier	Mon frère, <u>qui—d'ailleurs—est architecte</u>, ...	section 3.2.4.2
Determiner	<u>mon</u> frère ; <u>ces</u> enfants	section 2.3.2
Complement of preposition	sans <u>doute</u> ; pour <u>Pierre</u> ; à <u>ce que je sache</u>	section 2.4.1
Auxiliary	<u>a</u> perdu ; <u>être</u> parti ; <u>va</u> partir ; <u>fait</u> partir	section 2.3.1
Coordinator	une femme pauvre, <u>mais</u> intelligente	section 2.5

Appendix B
Word classes in French

Verbs				être, lire, écouter, concevoir, …
Nominals	Nouns			garçon, chaise, lune, haine,…
	Proper nouns			Jeanne, Sarkozy, Paris, l'EDF,…
	Pronouns	Personal pronouns	Clitic/Bound/Unstressed	je, on, la, leur,…
			Non-clitic/Stressed	moi, toi, eux, …
		Reflexive pronouns	Clitic/Bound/Unstressed	se
			Non-clitic/Stressed	soi
		Pronominal adverbs		en, y
		Possessive pronouns		le mien, la nôtre, les leurs,…
		Demonstrative pronouns		celui, celle, ceux, celles
		Neutral pronouns		ce, il, cela, ceci
		Relative pronouns		qui, que, dont, …
		Interrogative pronouns		qui (est-ce qui/que), quoi, lequel, …
		Indefinites		autre, chaque, quelque chose, tel,…
	Adjectives			beau, jaune, ivre, africain, …
	Articles	Indefinite articles		un, une
		Definite articles		le, la, les
		Partitive articles		du, de la, des
		Possessive articles		mon, sa, nos,…
		Demonstrative articles		ce, cet, cette, ces
		Interrogative articles		quel, quelle, quels, quelles
	Numerals	Cardinal numerals		un, deux, trois, …
		Ordinal numerals		premier, deuxième, troisième,…
Particles	Adverbs			hier, d'abord, où, vite, …
	Prepositions			à, dans, en raison de, par rapport à, …
	Conjunctions			et, mais, que, si, …
	Infinitive markers			à, de
	Interjections			oui, non, aïe, hélas,…

Appendix C
Subordinate clause types in French

	Type	Syntactic function(s)	Subordinators
Nominal clauses	Complement clause	Subject, postponed subject, direct object, subject attribute, complement of preposition	*que, ce que, le fait que, l'idée que*
	Indirect interrogative	Direct object, complement of preposition	*si*, interrogative pronouns, adverbs, and articles
	Free relative clause	Subject, subject attribute, direct object, complement of preposition	*ce* + relative pronoun (= free relative pronouns)
Adjectival clauses	Restrictive relative clause	Postmodifier	Relative pronouns and adverbs
	Non-restrictive relative clause	Appositional postmodifier	Relative pronouns and adverbs
	Predicative relative clause	Free indirect attribute, object attribute	*qui*
Adverbial clauses	Temporal clause	Adverbial (or—in some cases— postmodifier)	*quand, lorsque, dès que, après que, comme pendant que, alors que…*
	Causal clause		*comme, puisque, parce que, non que, …*
	Conditional clause		*si, à moins que, pourvu que, à condition que…*
	Concessive clause		*quoique, bien que, encore que, même si, quand (bien) même, …*
	Purpose clause		*pour que, afin que*
	Result clause		*que, si bien que, de sorte que, …*
	Comparison clause		*que, comme, comme si, de même que, ainsi que*
	Modal clause		*sans que, que*

Appendix D
Examples of sentence analyses to word level (function/form)

La	jeune	fille	française	va	aller	en	Colombie	demain
Subject/NounPhrase				Predicator/CompoundVerb		Locative Object/Prepositional Phrase		
Determiner/Definite Article	Premodifier/Adjective	Head/Noun	Postmodifier/Adjective	Auxiliary/Finite Verb	Main Verb/Infinitive	Head/Preposition	Complement/Proper Noun	Adverbial/Adverb

Cela	m'	étonne	que	ton	frère	ait	pu	faire	une	telle	chose
			Postponed Subject/Complement Clause								
				Subject/NP		Predicator/CompoundVerb		Direct Object/Infinitival Phrase			
									Direct Object/Noun Phrase		
Anticipatory Subject/Neutral Pronoun	Direct Object/Personal Pronoun	Predicator/Finite Verb	Subordinator/Subordinating Conjunction	Determiner/Possessive Article	Head/Noun	Auxiliary/Finite Verb	MainVerb/Past Participle	Head/Infinitive	Determiner/Indefinite Article	Premodifier/Indefinite Pronoun	Head/Noun

Je	ne	vois	pas	ce que	cet	homme	veut	dire
				Direct Object/Interrogative Clause				
					Subject/Noun Phrase			
				Direct Object/Interrogative Pronoun				
Subject/Personal Pronoun	Adverbial/Adverb	Predicator/Finite Verb	Adverbial/Adverb		Determiner/Demonstrative Article	Head/Noun	Predicator/Finite Verb	Direct Object/Infinitive

Appendix E
Overview of the French tenses

	Primary tenses (R and E are simultaneous)			Secondary tenses (R and E are not simultaneous)					
Generally	Present	Past	Future	Present perfect	Past perfect	"Post-present"	Future perfect	Future in the past	Future perfect in the past
French	*Présent*	*Imparfait; Passé simple; Passé composé; viens de* + inf.	*Futur simple*	*Passé composé; vient de* + inf.	*Plus-que-parfait; Passé antérieur; Passé surcomposé; venais de* + inf.	*Futur composé*	*Futur antérieur*	*Conditionnel; allais* + inf.; *devais* + inf.	*Conditionnel passé*
English	Simple present; present progressive	Simple past; Past progressive	N/A (closest equivalent: *will* + inf.)	Present perfect (progressive)	Past perfect (progressive)	*is going to* + inf.	N/A (closest equivalent: *will* + compound inf.)	N/A (closest equivalent *would/was going to* + inf.)	N/A (closest equivalent: *would* + compound inf.)

Further reading

Readers wanting to know more about aspects of French grammar which have not been treated exhaustively in this book, and/or who seek to supplement the perspective taken here with alternative ones, may wish to consult one or more of the works listed below. As there is a vast literature, both descriptive and theoretical, on Modern French grammar, the list is necessarily selective.

It is worth noting that there is no single approach to French grammar that is universally agreed upon, nor is there a single set of grammatical terms that are used by all scholars. In many cases, the terminology used and the modes of presentation of specific rules of grammar found in the works listed below will therefore differ to a greater or lesser extent from those adopted in the present work.

The following are some standard grammars of French written for native speakers of English:

Hawkins, Roger and Richard Towell, *French Grammar and Usage* (4th edn, London: Hodder Education, 2014).

Offord, Malcolm, *A Student Grammar of French* (Cambridge: Cambridge University Press, 2006).

Price, Glanville, *A Comprehensive Grammar of French* (6th edn, Oxford: Blackwell, 2008).

The following are some standard reference grammars of French written with native and non-native speakers in mind:

Grevisse, Maurice and André Goosse, *Le bon usage* (15th edn, Bruxelles: De Boeck/Duculot, 2011).

Riegel, Martin, Jean-Christophe Pellat, and René Rioul, *Grammaire méthodique du français* (3rd edn, Paris: Presses universitaires de France, 2008).

Togeby, Knud, *Grammaire française*, eds Magnus Berg, Ghani Merad, and Ebbe Spang-Hanssen, vols I–V (Copenhagen: Akademisk Forlag, 1982–85).

The following are theoretically oriented grammars of French:

Jones, Michael Allan, *Foundations of French Syntax* (Cambridge: Cambridge University Press, 1996).

Rowlett, Paul. *The Syntax of French* (Cambridge: Cambridge University Press, 2007).

Wilmet, Marc, *Grammaire critique du français* (3rd edn, Bruxelles: Duculot, 2003).

The following books are all-round introductions to the history of the French language and its contemporary grammar and sound structure:

Battye, Adrian and Marie-Anne Hintze, *The French Language Today* (London: Routledge, 1992).

Fagyal, Zsuzsanna, Douglas Kibbee and Fred Jenkins, *French: A Linguistic Intro-duction* (Cambridge: Cambridge University Press, 2006).

The following works deal specifically with colloquial spoken French:

Ball, Rodney, *Colloquial French Grammar* (Oxford: Blackwell, 2000).
Gadet, Françoise, *Le français ordinaire* (Paris: Armand Colin, 1989).

In addition, the author wishes to acknowledge her debt to the long-standing Danish tradition of research into French grammar. In particular, the following works have been a source of inspiration for the approach taken in this book:

Herslund, Michael, Hanne Korzen, Henning Nølke, and Finn Sørensen, *Det franske sprog*, vols I–VIII (Copenhagen: Copenhagen Business School, 1997–2004).
Pedersen, John, Ebbe Spang-Hanssen, and Carl Vikner, *Fransk grammatik* (Copen-hagen: Akademisk Forlag, 1980).
Rasmussen, Jens and Lilian Stage, *Moderne fransk grammatik* (Copenhagen: Schønberg, 1993).
Togeby, Knud, *Fransk grammatik* (Copenhagen: Gyldendal, 1965).

Index